BLOOD
AND THE
BADGE

BLOOD
AND THE
BADGE

THE MAFIA, TWO KILLER COPS,
AND A SCANDAL
THAT SHOCKED THE NATION

MICHAEL CANNELL

MINOTAUR
BOOKS
NEW YORK

First published in the United States by Minotaur Books,
an imprint of St. Martin's Publishing Group

www.minotaurbooks.com

Designed by Steven Seighman

Endpapers: Marianne Barcellona/Getty Images

The Library of Congress Cataloging-in-Publication Data is available upon request.

ISBN 978-1-250-81778-5 (hardcover)
ISBN 978-1-250-81779-2 (ebook)

Frst Edition: 2025

10 9 8 7 6 5 4 3 2 1

In Memory of Peter and Ann Cannell

CONTENTS

AUTHOR'S NOTE ix

PROLOGUE 1

PART I

1. A HOMECOMING 5

2. THE SIDEKICK 22

3. THE GAMBINO FILE 26

4. FRAMED 40

5. A SILENT PARTNER 47

6. RICO RISING 61

7. THE BOTCHED HIT 71

8. A TIME OF DISORDER 88

9. GASPIPE IN EXILE 128

10. OPERATION GANGPLANK 145

11. DESERT RETIREMENT 165

12. GRABBING GASPIPE 170

13. A FENCE IN HIDING 183

14. A MAN WITHOUT A COUNTRY 188

15. THE LAST TRUE BELIEVER 193

PART II

16. A CASE REVIVED   203

17. THE RELUCTANT WITNESS   228

18. THE UNDERCOVER ACCOUNTANT   237

19. A CASE DIVIDED   247

20. CUFFED AT PIERO'S   251

21. JUDGE WEINSTEIN'S COURTROOM   263

22. JUSTICE FORESTALLED   297

23. JUSTICE FULFILLED   310

EPILOGUE   315

AFTERWORD   319

ACKNOWLEDGMENTS   323

NOTES   325

INDEX   347

AUTHOR'S NOTE

I'M NOT THE FIRST TO WRITE ABOUT LOUIE EPPOLITO and Stephen Caracappa, the NYPD detectives who secretly worked for the Lucchese crime family in return for cash and a perverse form of prestige. I am, however, the first to recount their long, entwined story in something like its totality. Those who preceded me, including two government investigators and a tabloid reporter, published books based on their involvement at the time, years before events reached their conclusion. I've tried to convey a complete story, in all its lurid twists and complexity. Much of what I've written here has gone unreported until now.

Stories have a way of clarifying over time. Nineteen years have elapsed since the disgraced detectives entered their prison cells. Only now are federal agents, detectives and prosecutors, and their mob counterparts willing to talk about what may qualify as the NYPD's darkest chapter. These sources are, in most cases, deep into retirement and inclined at last to let go of old secrets—to share for posterity. The reader is, I hope, the beneficiary.

This is a work of nonfiction: nothing in these pages is invented. For the most part, I've built this account on trial transcripts, court documents, newspaper reporting, books, and, most significant, author interviews. I spoke to some fifty-five people from all quarters of the story, in some cases many times over. I've attributed every quote to a source, cited in the notes. The members of the Eppolito and Caracappa families did not consent to interviews, except for Lou Eppolito, Jr., who graciously told the story of a half-estranged son. Stephen Caracappa's wife, Monica, and I exchanged emails, but did not conduct a formal discussion. I agreed to change the names of three sources, plus a fourth I never interviewed, to protect their identities.

The sunlights differ, but there is only one darkness.

—Ursula K. Le Guin

PROLOGUE

IN THE EARLY EVENING OF NOVEMBER 6, 1990, forty-eight-year-old Eddie Lino drove his black Mercedes east through a clog of rush-hour traffic on the Belt Parkway, along the rounded southern belly of Brooklyn. Lino was a short, hard-bitten capo, or captain, in the Gambino crime family. He led a crew that trafficked heroin and cocaine, skimmed money from unions, and fattened up on a full portfolio of other rackets. Five years earlier he aided his close friend John Gotti's rise to power by helping to ambush the Gambino boss, Paul Castellano, and his bodyguard, Tommy Bilotti, outside Sparks Steak House in Midtown Manhattan.

Lino had spent the afternoon conducting business at the Mother Cabrini Social Club, in the Gravesend neighborhood, where capos received petitioners seeking favors and pocketed unlawful profits delivered by foot soldiers. Lino, acting for the Gambinos, spoke to his Colombo family contacts that day above the din of card games and the clink of espresso cups. Then he headed home wearing a tan trench coat against the autumn chill.

By 6:50 P.M., an hour after sunset, Lino was driving the first dark miles of his hour-and-a-half trip home to Fort Salonga, a town on the north shore of Long Island. Like many mafiosi of his generation—the Soprano generation—he had left the old neighborhood for the suburbs. He, his wife, and their three children lived in a house set back from the road in a hilly, wooded section two miles from Long Island Sound.

As Lino neared Brighton Beach, a dark, unmarked sedan, a Crown Victoria, flashed police lights behind him. Lino endured wiretaps and surveillance as an occupational hazard, but the pull-over on the Belt Parkway had likely struck him as the result of a routine traffic infraction, an inconvenience and nothing more. Still, he kept the car in gear, just in case, after stopping on the grassy shoulder of a service road beside Abraham Lincoln High School. Lino lowered his window as two plain-clothes detectives wearing badges walked up for a word—one with a portly, walrus-like profile, the other as skinny as a crane.

What's that on the floor? one of the detectives asked. As Lino leaned over in his seat to see, the thin detective raised a revolver and shot him nine times in the head and back. Lino's lifeless foot slipped off the brake and the car rolled to the right, stopping hard against a fence enclosing a high school sports field. Lino lay slumped on the passenger seat, bleeding onto the leather upholstery. The detectives returned to their Crown Victoria and drove into darkened Brooklyn streets lined with bodegas and stoop sitters, corner delis, and split-level homes with tiny lawns watched over by statues of the blessed mother.

PART I

A HOMECOMING

ON AN EARLY OCTOBER DAY IN 1979, A THIRTY-ONE- year-old detective named Louie Eppolito and his wife, Fran, drove their blue Chrysler New Yorker from their home in the Long Island town of Holbrook to a Brooklyn funeral parlor to pay last respects to Louie's uncle, Jimmy Eppolito, who was known to his associates in the Gambino crime family as Jimmy the Clam.

Until his shooting death on the night of October 1, Jimmy the Clam had served as a capo, a man of status and authority who for two decades commanded a crew plying the dark trades of loan-sharking, bookmaking, and burglary.

Dignitaries from all five New York crime families, allies and adversaries alike, gathered at the wake to honor a well-liked Mafia veteran marked for death through no fault of his own. While the families variously collaborated and feuded, often with mortal consequences, they by custom convened at wakes and weddings for a few peaceable hours of small talk and ice-cold geniality. In the underworld, wakes were work events.

A parade of middle-aged men entered, wearing wide-lapel suits and broad ties. They had arranged their hair in Brylcreem pompadours, comb-overs, and shameless toupees. Let us assume the room smelled of Parliament cigarettes and Aqua Velva aftershave, the odor of underworld gatherings. Bodyguards, cronies, and hangers-on stood at a discreet remove while bosses shook hands, squeezed arms, crossed themselves, and bowed heads in doleful expressions of mourning. They spoke in low, gravel-throated tones in English and Italian. Jimmy the Clam was a good man, they said, a man of honor. *Che tragedia.* What a tragedy.

Louie Eppolito was hard to miss among his uncle's mourners. He was a big man with a weight lifter's physique gone to paunch. If he resembled anyone, it was Jackie Gleason. With a mustache and gut, he looked like a greaser dressed in a size-fifty suit for a casino night. One by one the mafiosi shook his hand. They kissed both cheeks in the Mafia manner, and asked after his daughters, Andrea and Deanna, and his son, Tony.

For Eppolito, the funeral was an uncomfortable homecoming of sorts. He was born into an established Mafia family, but he worked as a New York City detective. Police regulations prohibited him from fraternizing with criminals.

In a strict professional sense, Eppolito stood for these few hours behind enemy lines, though the surroundings were familiar. He had grown up among these men. A handful had visited his childhood home in East Flatbush, a Brooklyn neighborhood then known as Pigtown, where they conferred with Eppolito's father, Ralph, known as Fat the Gangster, who had teamed up with Jimmy the Clam and a third brother, Freddy, in the Gambino operations. Their associates knocked on their door at odd hours. They huddled in the living room and spoke in low tones.

Louie, meet some friends of mine, Fat the Gangster would say. Louie stood and shook hands. They nodded in approval. Kid has a lot of respect, they said. His father often left with the men. The family might not see him for days.

Young Louie learned respect the hard way. His father was a short, stout man with an abusive temperament. In Louie's recollection, his father hit for the mildest infraction. "I'd get smacked for looking the wrong way at my mother," Eppolito later wrote in a memoir. "I'd get smacked for using the wrong tone of voice with my sister. I'd get smacked for being more than thirty seconds late for dinner." Ralph hit his son with fists or whatever was handy—a two-by-four, a ketchup bottle, and, on one occasion, an Italian baguette. It was tough love, but without much love.

Ralph delivered his smacks with lectures on the Neapolitan code of conduct: always shake hands, show respect to family and strangers alike. No matter what, avoid dishonoring the family with *una brutta figura,* a bad showing.

When Louie turned twelve, he joined his father on afternoon trips to a private room above the Grand Mark Tavern, in Bensonhurst, where his Gambino associates talked business over rounds of craps and a Sicilian card game called Ziginette. Louie carried drinks and swept up. He also played errand boy. Every day he delivered an envelope of cash to patrolmen who, by long-standing arrangement, parked across the street, in front of Za-Za's pool hall. Louie was careful not to hand the envelope directly to a cop, only to drop it onto an empty car seat.

Fat the Gangster hated the Irish-heavy police with an inordinate fury. "I guess my father despised them because they could be bought so cheap," Eppolito said.

One afternoon in March 1968, Louis, by then nineteen, returned home from his job as a telephone installer to find his maternal grandfather standing outside their apartment building. "You better head inside fast, Louie," the old man said. "Everybody's crying, and I think your father's dead."

Fat the Gangster had died of a heart attack. Days later, a cortege of eighteen black limousines carried gamblers and hit men, capos and consiglieri to a funeral mass at the Church of St. Blaise. FBI agents watched from a distance.

Within weeks of the funeral, Eppolito did what his father would have hated most: he enrolled in the police academy.

Eppolito passed his defection off as caprice. He applied without much thought, he said, after coaching his brother-in-law, Al Guarneri, as he jogged and jumped rope in preparation for the police academy fitness test. Eppolito lied about his family's ties to organized crime in the NYPD screening, though it may not have mattered. The academy had relaxed its background checks to replenish its ranks after the Vietnam-era draft drastically reduced the applicant pool. With race riots and anti-war protests flaring, the NYPD would hire practically any young man capable of lacing up shoes and walking the streets.

Eppolito claimed to have signed on impulsively, though it is hard to see his enrollment as anything but an act of rebellion against his abusive father, a defiant slap back that he dared not deliver until his father had passed. His friends and family could scarcely believe his change of allegiance. "They all told me I'm crazy," he said. "What do you want to do that for?"

Even in the academy Eppolito could not escape his father. During a lecture, a police instructor showed recruits a hierarchical chart of organized crime figures—soldiers, capos, consiglieri, and bosses—illustrated with mug shots and grainy surveillance photos. "Hey, Louie," a classmate said, "there's a guy with your last name." The jowly man in the mug shot was his father.

As a rookie patrolman assigned to South Brooklyn, Harlem, and Bedford-Stuyvesant, Eppolito found that the bully tactics he had learned from his father worked just as effectively in a blue uniform. He ignored police procedures, instead imposing what he called street justice. "We broke their hands. We broke their arms. We broke their legs," he said of an off-duty raid that sent thirty-seven homeless drug addicts to the hospital. "And I didn't give a fuck, and I still don't. . . . When you live on the street, you abide by the law of the street."

Eppolito's aggressive methods led to notable arrest numbers in the city's roughest neighborhoods—enough arrests to earn commendations and a smattering of headlines. Though he may have benefited from tips passed to him by underworld acquaintances.

Eppolito advanced his reputation by portraying himself to crime reporters as a protector of women and children. His brag worked. The *New York Daily News* recounted how he dressed up as an elderly matron—complete with rouged cheeks and an old dress—to catch muggers in the act; how he ran down five robbers on foot after their getaway car rammed his police cruiser; how he intercepted a burglar fleeing the Kings Lafayette Bank with $1,500 in cash; how he caught a pickpocket while working undercover as a coffee shop waiter. Eppolito had, the newspaper wrote, "a reputation for quick thinking and possessing 'street smarts' vital to his team."

Eppolito told reporters that he had broken the rookie arrest record. He later asserted, without evidence, that he was the eleventh most decorated police officer in the city's history. Exaggerated or not, his claims made their way into type. I'm the son of a Gambino crime soldier, he liked to say, but look what I've made of myself.

After a brief marriage that produced a son, Lou Jr., Eppolito met Frances Todisco, the daughter of a Bronx elevator operator. Coincidentally, he spotted her stepping from an elevator at a resort hotel in Puerto Rico. At their wedding, in 1973, Eppolito asked the band to play the theme from *The Godfather*. Together they had two daughters and a son.

Meanwhile, Eppolito waited impatiently for promotion to detective. He avoided working in narcotics, a prestigious post in the drug-heavy 1970s, for fear he would cross paths with his relations. The decision no doubt hurt his prospects. For three straight years he planned a party, only to cancel it when his name did not appear on the promotion list. "I wasn't ignorant of the fact that there were people in the department who remembered my roots, where I came from," he later wrote in a memoir. "Still, I was naïve enough to figure I could overcome my father, my uncles, my family."

Finally, in 1977, Eppolito advanced. He was promoted to detective and assigned to the Brooklyn Armed Robbery Squad. "In my mind I was being promoted three years too late," he said. "And I never forgot the snub."

Detective Eppolito was the loudest, crudest voice in the squad room. "He was always telling crazy stories,"said Detective Phil Grimaldi, who worked in a neighboring precinct. "He had a bunch of chains and rings, and he looked like an organized crime character from central casting."

By Eppolito's own admission, his partner once had to stop him from flogging a suspect to death. "The public will never understand the mentality of a cop—a good cop, anyway," Eppolito said. "In a way, it's very similar to the mentality of organized crime. You do what you have to do and don't think twice about consequences." Like any vigilante, he believed the righteous cause justified the brutality.

He earned both accolades—and distrust. It did not go unnoticed that Eppolito dressed like a cartoon mobster, with his pompadour, heavy gold necklaces, and a snake-head ring shining on his pinkie finger. "He was a tall guy, muscular, but he got overweight, [was] a sloppy dresser, never tightened his tie, wore a big .44 caliber revolver under his arm, and strong-armed people," said Detective Frank Pergola. "He put words in witnesses' mouths and put innocent people in jail."

Eppolito bragged that he routinely returned to the homes of domestic violence cases, after arresting the husband, to have sex with the abused wives, who were, by his description, eager for revenge. "He was sort of bragging about it," said Grimaldi. "Nobody knew if it was true or not."

On at least one occasion he interceded on behalf of a car thief, or tried to. When a young street thug brought six cars to a South Brooklyn used car dealership for resale, he mentioned, in passing, that a couple were "tag jobs," stolen cars with bogus VINs. The dealer recoiled; he would not touch them. The thief told him to relax. The dealer asked him to move the cars off the lot immediately.

When the dealer arrived at the lot the next morning, he found an unmarked police car parked out front. Eppolito got out and asked if they could speak. Listen, Eppolito said, the kid who brought the tag jobs is a good kid. Don't worry about him. I'll take care of the auto squad. You've got nothing to worry about.

Absolutely not, the dealer said, I won't do business with him. The dealer suffered no repercussions for his rebuff, but the lesson was clear. "It was known in the neighborhood that Eppolito was for sale," said Grimaldi. "If you had a problem, he could fix it."

While investigating a murder when he worked at the Sixty-Second Precinct, Detective Frank Pergola mentioned to Eppolito that one of the Romanian gypsies committing petty crime on Bath Avenue was harassing his daughter.

"Oh?" Eppolito asked. "What does he look like?"

"So I told him," Pergola said. "I figured he was going to rough the guy up. The next time I go to the Sixty-Second Precinct he said, 'Don't worry about that kid anymore.' I say, why? He says, 'He's not around.' I said, 'What the hell did you do?' He says, 'I threw him in the trunk of a car and I took him to Greenwood Cemetery and I threw him down a hill and told him to walk home. So he ain't never going to bother you again.' That's a true story. That's the way Louie was."

Eppolito later admitted that if a victim of his vigilante measures filed a grievance with the police department's Civilian Complaint Review Board for excessive force or abuse of authority, he simply lied his way clear.

By joining the police department Eppolito had, in theory, broken faith with the family business: he had switched teams. The rules of police conduct required that he distance himself from his family and its deep-seated ties with La Cosa Nostra.

Eppolito had made a nominal effort to resist the gravitational pull of acquaintances and family. In reality, he never truly separated himself. He later admitted to inviting mob pals into his squad car to talk. "I figured who was it going to hurt to stop and commiserate with an old Mustache Pete about his lumbago?" he said.

One night, after Eppolito dined with Fran in Brooklyn, an influential old Genovese capo named Toddo Marino, one of his father's closest friends, unexpectedly paid the couple's bill, then crossed the dining room to say hello. Eppolito kissed Marino on both cheeks. He did so unaware that the FBI was watching Marino. Eppolito was, by his account, summoned to the FBI office, on Third Avenue, to explain how he came to be on kissing terms with a Mafia capo.

Eppolito was named for his grandfather Luigi, a skilled watchmaker and a friend of 1930s mob boss Lucky Luciano. After his grandfather died at age ninety-one, in 1978, Eppolito saw his uncle Jimmy the Clam for the first time in six years. He was, as Eppolito remembered him, a gentlemanly capo who, unlike Eppolito's father, rarely raised his voice or spoke coarsely.

"Suddenly this warm feeling kind of washed over me," Eppolito later wrote. "He looked more like my father than I remembered. They could have been twins. I walked straight over to him, hugged him, kissed him. I almost cried."

In return, Jimmy teased his nephew, the big-shot detective, for ignoring his relations. In violation of police regulations, Eppolito agreed to drive Fran and the children to visit Jimmy the Clam and his wife, Aunt Dolly, at their large white home tucked behind a black wrought-iron gate a block from the waterfront in Bay Ridge, Brooklyn. After their visit, when Eppolito and Fran said goodbye, Jimmy the Clam handed his nephew an envelope. Fran opened it on the drive home: it contained $3,000 in cash and a note: "Take the kids on vacation."

"I almost drove off the highway," Eppolito said.

Accepting cash from a capo was a code-red police infraction, but Eppolito could not return the envelope without causing insult, or so he said. He kept the money, and began paying regular visits to talk with his uncle over cups of strong Italian coffee. He did so knowing that Jimmy the Clam, like Toddo Marino, might be under police surveillance. If so, Eppolito would be photographed or recorded in his company. Jimmy the Clam never asked about Eppolito's investigative work, Eppolito said, and Eppolito never asked about his uncle's rackets.

Eppolito was unaware that Jimmy the Clam's considerable influence was waning. As long as seventy-six-year-old Carlo Gambino presided over family operations, Jimmy the Clam had nothing to fear. Gambino was a courtly gray-haired patriarch and for many years the most powerful mobster in America. He was said to be the prototype for Don Corleone in *The Godfather*. Like the fictional don, Gambino suffered heart failure. He spent the night of October 14, 1976, at his yellow-brick waterfront home in Massapequa, New York, watching the New York Yankees beat the Kansas City Royals with a ninth-inning home run to claim the American League Pennant. Hours later he died of a heart attack, one of the few Mafia family bosses to die of natural causes. His throne passed to his cousin, Paul "Big Paulie" Castellano, whose business card identified him as a meat salesman. His profile was so low that law enforcement agencies knew little about him. He lived in a gaudy

Federal-style home, known as the White House, with his wife, Nina, a pack of guard dogs, and their live-in Colombian maid, Gloria, with whom he had a well-known long-term affair. His home stood on the highest elevation in New York City: 410 feet above sea level. The Dutch settlers called it Todt Heuvel, or Death Hill.

With his patron and protector gone, Jimmy the Clam had cause to worry. Castellano, the new boss, was related by marriage to Nino Gaggi, a capo with designs on Jimmy the Clam's territory. Jimmy the Clam had anticipated the coming conflict. In desperation, he asked for a meeting, or "sit-down," with the newly enthroned Castellano to complain that one of Gaggi's men had cheated his son out of $7,000 in a cocaine deal. He also claimed Gaggi was a government informant. He asked for Castellano's blessing to kill Gaggi.

Castellano prevaricated. Afterward, he privately warned Gaggi to beware of Jimmy the Clam. By doing so, Castellano tacitly gave Gaggi permission to strike back. Word inevitably got back to Jimmy the Clam through the Mafia's whisper channels: his execution was now inevitable. The only question was when and where.

Gaggi's opportunity came after Jimmy the Clam's son, a Gambino soldier known by his childhood nickname, "Jim-Jim," teamed up with a three-hundred-pound con man named John Ellsworth. With heavy girth and mutton chops, Ellsworth looked like a late-stage Elvis Presley. His twenty-one-year criminal career included more than a dozen charges of passing bad checks, forgery, and grand larceny.

Ellsworth could fast-talk his way into almost anything. In 1969, he stowed away on the Rolling Stones' US tour by posing as a Chrysler agent providing transportation. He then contacted Chrysler, claiming to work for the band. By this trickery Ellsworth came up with free tour buses. He stayed on, city after city. Nobody in the band's entourage balked when he signed arena leases and arranged security. Nor did he arouse suspicion by speaking for the Rolling Stones after Hells Angels killed four audience members at an Altamont Speedway concert, even though managers and musicians could not recall where he came from or who had hired him.

In the mid-1970s, Ellsworth and Jim-Jim formed a bogus charity to purportedly raise money for the International Year of the Child, a United Nations initiative to address starvation and other deprivations. They won endorsements from Senator Edward Kennedy and Hollywood actress Jane Russell, among others.

In reality, the charity was a scam. They solicited donations from labor leaders who would not deny a charity linked to the underworld, and then skimmed the proceeds. They also used the charity to launder income from loan-sharking and drug sales. Meanwhile, Ellsworth and Jim-Jim cruised New York in a chauffeured light blue limousine, stopping at Studio 54 and other night spots.

In December 1977, the two con men cadged invitations to the annual White House Christmas party for the children of Washington's diplomatic corps. While the kids drank pink punch and ate cookies in the state dining room, Ellsworth and Jim-Jim posed for photos with First Lady Rosalynn Carter by a holly-draped mantelpiece. They told her about their Santa-like plan to distribute gifts to underprivileged kids around the globe.

Seven months later, the ABC news program *20/20* reported that Jimmy the Clam's son had conned the first lady, and that he stole as much as $5 million earmarked for malnourished children. The Associated Press followed with an article published in dozens of newspapers.

The high swindle, and its attendant notoriety, sat poorly with Paul Castellano, the new Gambino boss. Mob rules required that crimes be efficient and discreet to avoid unwanted scrutiny. Now that Jim-Jim had embarrassed the first lady—and earned national headlines—the Gambinos braced for heightened scrutiny. The foolhardy young Jim-Jim had become a liability.

The grievance against Jim-Jim, and by extension his father, sealed their fate. "Just what the hell is happening with Jim-Jim?" Eppolito asked during one of his periodic visits. Jimmy the Clam shook his head. "It's going to be very bad for us." He knew that when they came for Jim-Jim, they would come for him as well. It was only a matter of time.

With Castellano's blessing, Nino Gaggi assigned the job to his associate, Roy DeMeo, a short, potbellied Gambino soldier fifteen years his junior. DeMeo grew up in the working-class Flatlands neighborhood of Brooklyn, where he started as a teenage loan shark. He had long since moved his family to Massapequa, a Long Island suburb populated by brokers and construction executives, where he led a conventional life of poolside barbecues and afternoon fishing trips on South Oyster Bay.

By outward appearance, DeMeo could be any suburban dad working the backyard grill. His gut hung over his belt like a sack of potatoes.

In reality, DeMeo headed a crew of young thugs who specialized in stealing luxury cars. With machinelike efficiency, they changed the VINs on hundreds of cars and exported them to wealthy buyers in Kuwait and other Middle Eastern countries.

DeMeo also owned a dilapidated corner bar, the Gemini Lounge, on Flatlands Avenue in the Flatbush section of Brooklyn, that doubled as a clubhouse where his young crew drank and played cards. It was also the location of at least seventy-five murders committed with fetishistic precision and planning. Every crime family includes at least one soldier who takes genuine pleasure in killing. For the Gambinos, that man was DeMeo. The murders were so savage, and so numerous, that Castellano urged Gaggi to restrain DeMeo. But Gaggi was reluctant to intercede. DeMeo's operations were too profitable to suppress.

DeMeo's killing technique came to be called the Gemini Method. After accepting a murder assignment, he invited his target to the Gemini Lounge for a friendly meeting on some trumped-up subject. With a Pabst Blue Ribbon or a Four Roses bourbon in hand, the prey unwittingly found himself lured into a back apartment rented to Joey Guglielmo, a tall, gray-complexioned Gambino hit man and DeMeo cousin nicknamed "Dracula." Guglielmo furnished the apartment with little more than a single mattress, but DeMeo equipped it like a slaughterhouse, complete with knives, ice picks, and saws.

The murders followed the same well-rehearsed course of action: the unsuspecting target walked the length of a hall where a crew member ambushed him and shot him in the head. DeMeo preferred a tidy murder, so the Gemini men immediately wrapped the victim's head in a turban of towels to stanch the blood while another stabbed him in the heart to stop blood from pulsing from the wound. To avoid staining their clothes, the crew stripped to their underwear.

The half-naked men then disrobed the body and dragged it to a shower where they disemboweled it and hung it upside down to bleed dry, as a hunter would bleed a deer carcass. They often ate dinner with bloodstained hands while the naked body drained in the next room. The *New York Daily News* later called their procedure "a collective derangement."

After dinner the Gemini crew laid their victims out on a thick plastic swimming pool liner unfurled across Dracula's living room floor. DeMeo had once worked as a butcher's assistant. He and his men used butchering techniques to sever sinew, joint, and muscle as they neatly dismembered the body into six parts. They methodically sheared off arms, legs, and heads, as a taxidermist would, and placed them in cardboard boxes lined with plastic bags that they discarded among the refuse heaps in the Fountain Avenue dump, a wasteland between the Belt Parkway and Jamaica Bay. DeMeo repeated a saying with impish pleasure: "No body, no crime."

Jim-Jim's imprudent breach of Mafia etiquette had earned him, and his father, a trip to the Gemini Lounge. The evening began, as mob assassinations often do, with the arrival of a trusted friend. On the night of October 2, 1979, a fifty-eight-year-old Gambino associate named Peter Piacenti came by the house to pick up Jimmy the Clam and Jim-Jim. Friends called Piacenti "Petey 17" because he once owned a Brooklyn nightclub with a 1717 street address. Jimmy the Clam had sponsored him as a Gambino associate. The two men had a long, warm relationship.

This evening Piacenti posed as an intermediary. He convinced Jimmy the Clam and Jim-Jim to meet with Nino Gaggi to resolve their dispute. Piacenti presented the meeting as no more than a sit-down to clear the air between feuding branches of the family tree. Jimmy the Clam must have suspected the worst, but he had no choice. So the three men—father, son, and friend—drove to a deserted playground behind a white-brick school, Grady High, in Brighton Beach, near Coney Island, where they met Gaggi and DeMeo.

By 9:40 P.M. all five were squeezed into a 1978 Thunderbird driving on a service road beside the Shore Parkway, probably headed to the Gemini Lounge. Jim-Jim drove with Gaggi beside him. Piacenti sat in back between Jimmy the Clam and DeMeo.

Jimmy the Clam knew how trips like this ended. He abruptly told his son to pull over, saying he had to urinate. When the car stopped, Gaggi and DeMeo both pulled guns before Jimmy the Clam could get out. Within seconds Gaggi shot Jim-Jim four times. DeMeo leaned forward, reached across Piacenti, and fired three times into Jimmy the Clam's head. Father and son died instantly.

Shooting two men in a car parked on a Brighton Beach street was exactly the kind of haphazard killing the Mafia avoided. The three killers could only disperse and hope for the best. DeMeo dropped his gun in a sewer and walked west alone toward Sheepshead Bay. Gaggi and Piacenti walked south, toward the beach.

Bad luck: a blond, baby-faced twenty-year-old from Bensonhurst named Patrick Penny and a girlfriend drove by at the exact moment that a stray bullet fired from within the Thunderbird shattered its windshield. The couple followed Piacenti and Gaggi from a distance. They hailed a cab dropping a passenger a quarter mile from the crime scene. They asked the driver, a man named Paul Roder, to radio the police.

As it happened, Roder had no need to call. He was an off-duty Housing Authority police sergeant. Penny told him that two shooters were walking toward Coney Island Avenue. Roder intercepted them. He pulled his cab up to block their way, opened the driver-side door, and ducked behind it as a shield with his service revolver in hand. He identified himself and called for them to stop. Gaggi pulled out a .38-caliber revolver and fired. Roder fired back, striking Gaggi in the chest. A second shot hit Piacenti in the leg, severing an artery. An ambulance took both men to Coney Island Hospital, where they refused to answer police questions.

Five months later Penny testified against Gaggi and Piacenti, though he lost a measure of credibility by admitting to more than a hundred burglaries and car thefts—a prodigious record for a twenty-year-old. The jury acquitted both men of murder charges after the mob bribed a juror. They were, however, found guilty of lesser charges.

The Brooklyn District Attorney's Office sent Penny into protective custody in Florida, but he refused to stay longer than two months. By May 13, 1980, he was drinking with friends at Ryan's, a dive bar in Sheepshead Bay, as Roy DeMeo and an accomplice waited outside. At 2 A.M. Penny put ten dollars on the bar to pay for drinks. He told his friends that he was going to fetch something from his Jeep. He was shot to death moments later.

In the early morning hours of October 2, 1979, Eppolito was at his precinct house preparing for the most prestigious assignment of his ten-year police career. At 9:15 A.M. Pope John Paul II would land at LaGuardia Airport. Eppolito's exemplary arrest record had earned him a place among the NYPD honor guard escorting the pope as he traveled to the United Nations, an Upper East Side lunch, St. Patrick's Cathedral on Fifth Avenue, St. Charles Borromeo Church in Harlem, a Bronx high school, and, finally, a mass at Yankee Stadium. Eppolito grew up among criminals, but he was still a Catholic. "I was somewhat overwhelmed knowing that I would be able to see [the pope]," he said, "even if it just meant trotting alongside his armored car."

Eppolito's wife, Fran, phoned the precinct house at 5 A.M. Minutes earlier she had received a frantic call from his aunt Dolly. Detectives had woken her with shattering news: patrolmen had found her husband, Jimmy the Clam, and son, Jim-Jim, shot to death in a Thunderbird parked out by the Shore Parkway. Father and son had not returned home, but Aunt Dolly distrusted the detectives. She wanted Eppolito to find out what happened.

"I knew in Louie's mind he had finally found a father figure again," Fran said, referring to his uncle Jimmy. "And when that call came in from Aunt Dolly, I was heartbroken for him. . . . After all those years of hating his father, hating what this family stood for, for this to happen just as they had gotten close . . ."

Detective Joe Piraino was typing up a report on the shooting when Eppolito walked into the Sixty-Second Precinct. "Eppolito was wailing," Piraino said. "'They took everybody from me, they took everybody from me.' I was stunned because the victim was a relative of Eppolito's and it would be considered a conflict of interest. He didn't belong there."

On a normal news day, a Mafia double murder would earn front-page headlines, but Gaggi and DeMeo, by accident or design, chose to kill Jimmy the Clam and Jim-Jim when the pope's visit dominated the news. The *New York Post* published a short item on page fifteen. The *New York Daily News* ignored the murders entirely.

Eppolito had time to identify the bodies before joining the pope's honor guard at LaGuardia Airport. In the cold of the examination room, he stood beside the two dead men covered in sheets. Tags affixed to their toes identified them as "James Eppolito, Jr." and "James Eppolito." He pulled back Jim-Jim's sheet first. "It was nothing I hadn't seen before in twelve years on the job," he said. "But all that blood, and Jim-Jim's brain blasted away."

His uncle was next. "Uncle Jimmy's face was just absolutely destroyed. His jaw and bottom lip were totally gone, torn off, giving him this long, buck-toothed look. . . . I cleaned him as best I could, combing his hair and washing the blood off his face. But water kept pouring out of his eyes, like he was crying."

That night, after the pope stood on the Yankee Stadium infield with his right hand raised in blessing to eighty thousand worshippers, Eppolito returned to his Brooklyn station house and sat on a bench. It had been a long day, weighted with tragedy and transcendence. According to Eppolito, two agents from the FBI's Organized Crime Division visited him at home that night. He took it as an insult, as if he might have been involved in his uncle's death.

"From that moment, I knew I could never truly be trusted by the Police Department," Eppolito later said. "I had family members who were also Family members. Yet, at least the mob guys I knew treated me with respect." He felt as if he no longer belonged among the police, as if "the badge I wore was somehow a mistake."

Eppolito had repudiated his family after his father died. Now, twelve years later, his uncle's death returned him to the fold. At the wake, among the cigar smoke and aftershave, he felt the pull of old allegiances. When Eppolito had shaken all the hands and exchanged the obligatory greetings, he and Fran made their way to the door. Eppolito stopped for a parting word with his cousin, Frank Santora, a big-shouldered mob subordinate with thick hands, a perpetual tan, and an abundance of satiny black hair swept back in a well-oiled wave. He was smooth, but tough. At the time, Eppolito had no way of knowing that his cousin would enable his darkest impulses and set his life on a new course.

Over the following weeks Fran noticed her husband's mannerisms change.

Eppolito underwent a conversion of sorts the night of the wake, as if Jimmy the Clam had posthumously beckoned him back to the world he had left behind—the world of his father, Fat the Gangster, and his grandfather Luigi. He had never seemed particularly Italian, but began to drink double espressos and say *salute* or *grazie* as he raised a glass of chianti. He gestured with his hands in the animated manner of a *paisan* bickering over politics. His musical taste had always favored doo-wop. Now he took Fran to hear nightclub singers perform the Italian classics "Malafemmena" and "Scapricciatiello." For the first time, he appeared to take pride in the world of his ancestry.

As Eppolito's family life changed, so too did his work life. In the mid-1970s, New York's fiscal crisis decimated the NYPD's budget. The downturn shrank the force by more than five thousand. For four years the department hired no recruits. The police academy sat empty. Meanwhile, the streets deteriorated. Crime reached historic levels. Women carried Mace in their purses. Garish swaths of graffiti covered subway cars. Dog walkers heard gunshots in parks. Prostitutes and junkies expired on the street.

In May 1980, eight months after Jimmy the Clam died, the fiscal shortfall forced the department to consolidate. Amid the shakeup, Eppolito was asked to submit the names of three precincts he would welcome for reassignment. He had worked twelve years on the crime-heavy streets and housing projects of Harlem and Bedford-Stuyvesant. He now went to the Sixty-Second Precinct, located on Bath Avenue in Bensonhurst, where the streets smelled of Old World delicacies. On Eighteenth Avenue, specialty pasta stores peddled homemade cavatelli. Wheels of Parmigiano cheese as big as tractor tires hung in *salumeria* windows beside strings of dried sausage. Bakers carrying trays of biscotti and pignoli cookies greeted customers in bursts of Italian. Pizzerias baked square pies in wood-burning ovens in the Sicilian manner. Sinatra sang from car radios. Stone-faced Mafia associates cruised in Cutlass Supremes with St. Christopher medals on dashboards and baseball bats stowed in their trunks.

In food shops and sidewalks, men greeted Eppolito by name and shook his hand. *Hey, hayadooin?* To the *goombahs* he was more than a detective: he was Fat the Gangster's son. They waved him in for a free espresso or beer and addressed him in the South Brooklyn manner, full of sarcasm and slang punctuated by slicing hand gestures.

More often than not, Eppolito accepted their offers. He knew they might be under police surveillance, but no longer cared. For better or worse, these were his people. "I felt like I was home," he said.

2

THE SIDEKICK

EPPOLITO COULD NOT HAVE BEEN EASY TO WORK with. In taverns and squad rooms, he was loud and bad mannered. When Stephen Caracappa first paired with Eppolito in the Brooklyn Robbery Squad, he complained privately to their supervisor, Sergeant Emilio Ponzi, that he needed a new partner. He said he could not work with Eppolito. The request could not have surprised Ponzi. The quiet, efficient Caracappa seemed an obvious mismatch with the brash Eppolito. Ponzi advised Caracappa to give their partnership a month. Come back, he said, if the pairing still seemed unworkable.

Caracappa never came back; he never again mentioned his misgivings. Whatever reconciliation—or collusion—he found with Eppolito went unrecorded. The two detectives overcame their differences and discovered a mutual willingness, an eagerness, to collaborate on what might qualify as the worst chapter of corruption in NYPD history. How they broached the subject of illicit side hustles in private conversation, how they entered into their strategems, will likely never be uncovered. They would be allied, as partners and friends, for the next twenty-six years.

"The first time I went out with [Eppolito] we sort of bonded," Caracappa later said. "We just had a lot of laughs. We became friends. The guy had balls, and I like balls on a guy. And he didn't mind me because I could sit in a car for six hours and not say a word."

Like many enduring partnerships, Eppolito and Caracappa were polar opposites. Eppolito was stout, loud, and excitable; Caracappa was rail thin—fellow detectives nicknamed him "The Stick"—and reserved to the point of silence. He was so quiet as to disappear into the background. Eppolito wore disheveled discount suits and a perpetually loosened tie. Caracappa came to work impeccably turned out in dark Italian suits. "They looked like Mutt and Jeff," said Detective Frank Pergola, "or the Odd Couple."

While Eppolito joined other detectives for rounds of beer and shots after their shifts, Caracappa slipped quietly home to read history books. He rarely drank and ate a mostly vegetarian diet long before such restrictions were commonplace. There was about him a sense of stealth and silent intelligence. He had the somber look of an undertaker. His middle-management mustache followed the corners of his mouth downward in a glower.

Caracappa grew up in a working-class Italian section of Staten Island, directly across the street from Tommy Bilotti, who would become underboss, or second-in-command, of the Gambino crime family. "He took a liking to me," Caracappa said. "He never beat the shit out of me."

Caracappa's family was poor—needful enough, at any rate, that he found it necessary to drop out of New Dorp High School at age sixteen to join his father on New Jersey construction sites. He tried to support his family with thievery as well. In 1960, a grand jury indicted him and a friend on a felony grand larceny charge after a botched attempt to load stolen insulation and wallboard into a rented truck in the middle of the night. As an eighteen-year-old, he got off with probation, no jail time, on the condition that he plead guilty to misdemeanor charges. Six years later he went to Vietnam, where his cunning and toughness, and skill as an army marksman, earned him a promotion to sergeant.

After his discharge, in April 1969, Caracappa joined the NYPD. The police academy accepted him despite his felony arrest. As the military draft ramped up, the police department had no choice but to take any able-bodied applicant, even those with dark spots in their personal histories.

Like Eppolito, Caracappa found it hard to distance himself from underworld acquaintances, as department policy required. He stayed in touch with Tommy Bilotti over the years. "He never asked me for anything," Caracappa said, "but he also knew that if he needed a favor, if I could do it, I would."

Whatever their differences, Eppolito and Caracappa grew up with the same outer-borough sensibilities. They shared a distaste for long hair and street protests. They listened to Frank Sinatra, not Jimi Hendrix. For young men of their background, 1969 was not the dawning of the Age of Aquarius. They belonged to a different America, one in which sons of blue-collar families stood up for law and order. Though whose law and what order might be in question.

In the course of their duties on the Brooklyn Robbery Squad, Eppolito and Caracappa somehow discovered a mutual inclination to supplement their day jobs with a second career in off-duty crime. Of the two, the cool, controlled Caracappa might have seemed by outward appearance the less likely to stray. In reality, he was by all accounts the more driven of the two.

In 1978, a year before Caracappa partnered with Eppolito, he was working undercover in narcotics as a buyer named Frankie Black. On January 24, he went to an apartment in the Bronx where a drug dealer named Richard Warme offered to sell him two kilos of cocaine. The next day he gave Caracappa a sample. Warme said he could sell him heroin as well, but he could not provide either drug yet because of a supply problem.

On March 2, Caracappa met Warme at a furniture store owned by Warme's mother-in-law. There, among loungers and living room sets, Caracappa paid Warme an advance of $1,200 toward the purchase of at least three ounces of cocaine. Twelve days later, Warme told Caracappa over lunch at the Crosstown Diner on Bruckner Boulevard that he could sell him seven ounces of heroin for $11,000. The heroin never arrived, but Warme delivered the equivalent value in cocaine. Officers arrested Warme and his wife, Diane Frisco, on March 31.

Caracappa had conducted creditable undercover work, but he did not leave it there. According to the *New York Post*, Caracappa went to Warme's apartment at a bleak intersection of Throgs Neck Boulevard, on the Bronx side of the Throgs Neck Bridge, to see Diane, who had been released on bail. Her husband was in jail awaiting trial. "You know I can help your husband when it comes time for a trial," she later recalled him saying. "Remember I'm holding all the aces."

According to the *New York Post,* Caracappa drove Frisco to the Town & Country Motel, just off the highway, and booked a first-floor room. "He put me on the bed and took my pants off," Frisco told a reporter. "I was frozen—crying and frozen." With his clothes off Caracappa looked, she said, "like a skinny gorilla."

Afterward, Caracappa warned Frisco that "if you say anything, no one's going to believe you." He was right. For the next twenty-eight years Caracappa and his friend Eppolito would rely on their police prerogatives to shield them from suspicions and accusations.

3

THE GAMBINO FILE

AT 6 A.M. ON MARCH 16, 1984, A TEAM OF FEDERAL agents and state troopers raided a Cherry Hill, New Jersey, home, arresting forty-one-year-old Rosario Gambino, a cousin of the late Mafia boss Carlo Gambino.

Rosario belonged to a Sicilian wing of the Gambino operation. He was a short, lean-faced man with a passing resemblance to the actor Adrien Brody. After illegally resettling in New Jersey from Italy in 1962, Gambino helped run one of the family's legitimate businesses, a chain called Father and Son Pizza. Gambino's main occupation, however, was smuggling a pure variety of heroin from Iran and Afghanistan, via Sicily, concealed in furniture and olive oil tins, with help from his brother-in-law and three cousins. They conducted business from Caffe Italia, a traditional café serving espresso in small white demitasse cups on the Eighteenth Avenue strip in Bensonhurst, an eight-minute drive from Eppolito's precinct house.

The FBI watched Gambino for six months. They deciphered the code words he used in wiretapped dealmaking—"pizza" for heroin and "wine" for cocaine. On January 18, 1984, Gambino's associates sold more than two pounds of heroin with a street value of $1.7 million to an undercover FBI agent at an Atlantic City casino hotel, then negotiated a standing order for twenty-two pounds of heroin a month. At one point the Gambino crew made the agent discuss the deal in a hotel swimming pool to assure that he wore no wire.

Seven months after his arrest, Gambino, his brother-in-law Erasmo, nephew Antonio, and a fourth man were convicted in Federal District Court in Newark of distributing wholesale quantities of heroin and cocaine. Days later, an officer in the Sixty-Second Precinct in Brooklyn notified Eppolito that the Internal Affairs Division, the police who police the police, expected him for a November 1 interview, known internally as a General Order 15, or GO 15, an inquiry normally triggered by suspicions of misconduct or corruption. The accused officer has no choice but to answer questions, under oath, posed by an Internal Affairs investigator. Refusal is grounds for dismissal.

As a matter of routine, Eppolito called Stephen Gardell, a detective in an adjacent South Brooklyn precinct who served as a delegate for the detectives' union. The two had known each other for at least seven years and worked together on a handful of homicides. "They'd shoot them in his district," Gardell said, "and dump them in mine."

Gardell told Eppolito that he was unaware of any complaint against him, but the GO 15 could arise from a number of issues. Eppolito was notoriously reckless. He might have slammed a suspect's head against a car window or ordered drinks in an off-limits mobster bar. "Of course, it didn't help that his old man was Fat the Gangster," Gardell said, "and his uncle was Jimmy the Clam." Internal Affairs officers usually alerted Gardell to the nature of the offense, but in this case they refused to disclose the charges: a bad sign.

On the morning of November 1, Gardell met Eppolito at a Brooklyn Heights coffee shop along with Howard Cerny, a lawyer retained by the detectives' union. Like Gardell, Cerny had tried, and failed, to use his connections to learn the nature of the inquiry.

After breakfast the three men walked to 72 Poplar Street, a decommissioned precinct house a block from the downslope of the Brooklyn Bridge on the ragged edge of Brooklyn Heights. A crime lab and police academy had occupied the building before Internal Affairs. By 1984 the rooms had a neglected institutional look. The gloom matched the division's mission. "Only simple fear will deter some people," said John Guido, chief of Internal Affairs and the most resented man in the police department. "We do create fear."

Guido had Winston Churchill jowls. Like Churchill, he was rarely seen without a well-moistened cigar. He was brought in to break the code of silence surrounding the entrenched, and widely publicized, corruption of the 1970s.

Eppolito and his advisers expected a sergeant to preside over the GO 15. Their concern intensified when Deputy Inspector Robert McCormack met them, accompanied by a sergeant and a lieutenant. "They'd hauled out the big guns," Eppolito said, "and I felt like there was a target painted on my face."

The two sides, accused and accusers, sat across a long table as the sergeant read preliminaries into the record. Then the questions began: What organized crime cases had Eppolito worked on? How did he feel about investigating the mob? Did he socialize with mob figures?

McCormack then homed in on a specific episode. He placed the thirty-six-page police file on Rosario Gambino down on the table and asked why Eppolito had removed it from the Intelligence Division headquarters, on Hudson Street in lower Manhattan.

Eppolito had a ready explanation, however dubious. In July 1983, he said, a low-level racketeer and neighborhood menace named Albert Veriale was shot to death at a busy Bensonhurst intersection. As was usually the case in mob neighborhoods, passersby saw nothing and said nothing. The one witness willing to cooperate, Eppolito said, was a teenage boy, a tourist, who said he might recognize the shooter.

According to Eppolito, Jimmy Shea, the homicide detective leading the Veriale investigation, asked Eppolito to escort the boy to the Intelligence Division on the long-shot chance that he could spot the shooter among the mobster mug shots compiled in albums. Eppolito made a logical escort, he said, because he was a veteran detective acquainted with South Brooklyn mobsters.

While the young witness paged through the albums, examining front and side mug shots of Bianchis and Mancinis, Rossis and Regios, Eppolito, by his account, wandered the maze of old rooms inside the Intelligence Division. His eyes happened to fall on the slender, dark-complexioned face of Rosario Gambino printed on a wanted flyer pegged to a bulletin board.

Eppolito said he asked an organized crime detective named Bill Sweeney why the Intelligence Division had bothered to print wanted posters for Gambino. According to Eppolito, Sweeney told him that the FBI had sought Gambino on drug charges, but agents had abandoned the case when Gambino returned to Sicily.

Eppolito said he told Sweeney that the agents were laughably misinformed. Gambino had never left. On any day they could find him seated at a window table at Caffe Italia in Bensonhurst. In Eppolito's recollection, Sweeney then handed him Gambino's file—a compilation of surveillance photos, criminal records, and an elaborate Gambino family tree—to carry back to the Sixty-Second Precinct since he was its unofficial organized crime expert. Eppolito at first demurred. He said that he felt no need for the file, but agreed to take it. He signed the file out of the Intelligence Division, he said, and stuffed it in an unlocked filing cabinet in the station house's haphazard organized crime archive.

From across the table McCormack now produced a sign-in log showing that Eppolito had not walked out with the file in July, as he claimed, but five months later, on December 13. Why did he go on *that* day, McCormack asked, and on whose order? Had he simply gone of his own volition to steal the file?

Flustered and defensive, Eppolito amended his account. He had forgotten, he said, that he returned to Hudson Street a second time, in December, at the suggestion of an assistant district attorney to see if the rows of filing cabinets contained a file on Herman Penny, a convicted murderer who, in a letter mailed from prison, had threatened to kill himself along with his estranged wife, Margaret, after his release. (By coincidence, Penny was, from an earlier marriage, the father of Patrick Penny, the twenty-year-old who reported the shooting of Eppolito's uncle Jimmy the Clam and cousin Jim-Jim.)

Eppolito told McCormack that he did not find a Herman Penny file on his second trip to the Intelligence Division. But on his way out, he said, he saw Detective Sweeney, who asked if the FBI had contacted him about Gambino's whereabouts. It was at that point, Eppolito said, that Sweeney gave him the Gambino file.

McCormack confirmed, and reconfirmed, that Eppolito stored the Rosario Gambino file and had not touched it, except to add a *New York Daily News* article about Gambino's arrest.

> **McCormack:** I just want to get this clear . . . You got it from Intelligence, apparently it was their file. You brought it back to the Six Two. . . .
> **Eppolito:** Made a folder.
> **McCormack:** Made a folder, put the . . . material in the folder.
> **Eppolito:** Yes.
> **McCormack:** Put it in a filing cabinet . . . and never touched it again until last Tuesday when you added [the newspaper article about Gambino's arrest]. Did you ever make any copies of that folder?
> **Eppolito:** None whatsoever.

Eppolito must have known that McCormack would not quiz him for more than an hour merely to accuse him of removing an intelligence file without proper permission. A far more serious allegation must be coming. Sure enough, McCormack eventually dropped his coy questions and made known the explosive grounds for the investigation:

> **McCormack:** Alright, Detective . . . how do you explain the fact that on March 16, 1984, copies of exactly what you have there in front of you were recovered by the Federal Bureau of Investigation and the US attorney while executing a search warrant at Rosario Gambino's residence in Cherry Hill, New Jersey? [. . .] Can you, in your experience as a detective, think of any reason how it might have gotten there?

Internal Affairs was alleging that Eppolito was a double agent, a decorated detective feeding thirty-six pages of confidential Intelligence Division reports to a ranking member of the Gambino crime family.

Gardell bristled at the pleasure McCormack took in his disclosure.

"He says it like we're all supposed to fall down with heart attacks," he later said.

Eppolito offered no explanation. McCormack picked up where he left off, with an even more damaging finding.

> McCORMACK: Okay, did you make copies of that material?
> EPPOLITO: Not once.
> McCORMACK: Not once? No, you didn't make a copy?
> EPPOLITO: No, I did not make copies of the material.
> McCORMACK: Would it interest you to know that the copies that were found in Gambino's house were run off, according to laboratory analysis, from the precinct copy machine in the Sixty-Second Precinct? You have no explanation for that at all?

As if that weren't damning enough, McCormack now disclosed a third bit of evidence, a final blow:

> McCORMACK: Detective, I have one more question. . . . The laboratory analysis of the [files] found in Gambino's house—copies of the information that was from the sixty-second police detective unit—also have your fingerprints on it. Can you tell me how those fingerprints got there? Do you have any idea at all?

Eppolito's lawyer, Howard Cerny, called for a recess. In a hallway huddle Eppolito claimed to know nothing about photocopies. They returned to the hearing ready to fire back. Cerny asked if Eppolito's fingerprints appeared directly on the copies passed to Gambino, or if the photocopier had simply reproduced fingerprints on the original pages. If the latter, then Eppolito may never have handled the copied pages passed to Gambino. Cerny made clear that his client would not respond to any more questions until they got an answer.

McCormack reminded Cerny that Internal Affairs officers are not obligated to answer questions, and that he had the authority to suspend Eppolito on the spot if he refused to respond. (Had McCormack answered Cerny, he might have explained that photocopiers do not pick up fingerprints. If the photocopies found at Gambino's home bore Eppolito's prints, then he had surely handled them. According to Inspector John Walsh, their presence on the copies was "overwhelming" evidence of guilt.)

Eppolito now spoke back to McCormack as he might speak to a barroom belligerent. "Let me tell you something," he said. "I never gave nobody no papers on Rosario Gambino. You tell me that the FBI has had this file for six months. What the hell have they been doing with it all that time?" Eppolito's voice conveyed such rage that Gardell glanced over to see if Eppolito was carrying his revolver.

For six months, McCormack said, FBI agents had surveilled him as he traveled about Bensonhurst performing his duties. They were watching, too, when he stopped at pork shops and cafés to shake hands and talk to Gambino capos. Internal Affairs had subpoenaed seven months of phone records for his Long Island home.

With that, the hearing ended.

For the next three weeks Gardell heard encouraging reports from sources within Internal Affairs. Yes, Eppolito had bungled the dates of his two trips to the Intelligence Division; yes, his fingerprints showed up on photocopies passed to Gambino. But Internal Affairs had no further proof.

Behind the scenes, however, gathering evidence cast doubt on Eppolito's explanations. Four days after his GO 15, Eppolito's acquaintance at the Intelligence Division, Detective Bill Sweeney, was summoned to Internal Affairs, where he denied pressing the Gambino file on Eppolito. On the contrary, he said, Eppolito specifically asked if he could take the documents to store in the Sixty-Second Precinct. A precinct supervisor in the Sixty-Second Precinct told investigators that he distrusted Eppolito; he would never have sent Eppolito to the Intelligence Division, he said.

Almost three weeks later, Stephen Caracappa woke Eppolito and Fran with a 7 A.M. phone call. It was Saturday, Eppolito's morning to sleep in. He and Fran had stayed up late watching television.

Have you seen the *Daily News*? Caracappa asked. Eppolito had not.

He went downstairs and pulled the newspaper from his mailbox. A double-decker headline ran across the top half of the front page: "Mob Big Got Data from Cop."

"At that time I lost my stomach," Eppolito later said.

Murray Weiss, the police bureau chief for the *New York Daily News,* got the scoop: a veteran Brooklyn detective had "passed confidential Police Department intelligence reports to a member of the Sicilian mafia" while under federal investigation. The detective, Weiss added, was expected to be brought up on Internal Affairs charges and suspended. He might also face separate criminal charges.

"I knew that my life as I had known it was over," Eppolito later wrote in his memoir. "I couldn't help but think that no matter what I did for the rest of my life, I'd be classified as a member of Organized Crime."

Eppolito had made a point of telling police acquaintances a dubious story about a recent run-in with Rosario Gambino—how Gambino had emerged from Caffe Italia while Eppolito and a partner happened to be driving down Eighteenth Avenue in a police cruiser; how Gambino grabbed his crotch and shook it at Eppolito; how Eppolito told his partner to "stop the fucking car"; how he walked across the street and wrapped his hands around Gambino's neck and lifted him off the ground.

Now it looked as if Eppolito might have fabricated the confrontation to immunize himself against suspicions of friendly dealmaking with Gambino. In his *Daily News* article, Weiss reported that in reality Eppolito and Gambino were close friends. They were often seen together at a Coney Island café.

Eppolito returned for his Monday overnight shift in the Sixty-Second Precinct. At 9 A.M. on Tuesday, a precinct sergeant called him at home to say that he had been charged with absence without leave, appropriation of police records, and divulging confidential police intelligence. He was suspended without pay and could face dismissal.

Eppolito drove in and relinquished his gun and badge to a sergeant at Internal Affairs headquarters on Poplar Street. Then he drove home. Fran had spent the morning taking her mother to a doctor's appointment.

"I figured by the time I got back he'd probably just be getting up," she said. "So I was a little surprised when I walked through the front door . . . to find him sitting at the kitchen table in his suit and tie."

Internal Affairs set a date for the department trial, then postponed it, and postponed it again. And again, until settling on April 4, 1985. Eppolito spent the homebound weeks leading up to Christmas, and the three following months, worrying over how to support his family without a paycheck.

Police friends dropped by with envelopes of cash. Fran's brother chipped in. Caracappa stopped for coffee almost daily. Gardell found Eppolito a job as a Toys"R"Us security guard paying $10 an hour, but he declined. His cousin Frank Santora tried to help by arranging mob-connected jobs in garbage and construction. Eppolito turned them down, or so he claimed, with a reminder that accepting a dirty job might reflect badly on a detective awaiting trial for colluding with organized crime.

Eppolito later said that mob contacts had tried to contribute, but he refused. "I never asked them for a favor," he said. "When I was down and out, they tried to send money to my house for me. I wouldn't accept it. I said no. If I accept money from you guys, I'm fucked."

In January, three detectives from the Sixty-Second Precinct rented a Bay Ridge banquet hall and sold ten-dollar tickets for the Louis Eppolito Defense Fund. A Queens cop performed with his doo-wop group, the Capris. They sold more than five hundred tickets. "When the take came in I had to laugh," Eppolito said. "Financially, it seemed like I was better off suspended."

When Eppolito walked into the small trial room on the fourth floor of One Police Plaza, the severe brown-brick police headquarters on the edge of Chinatown known as the Puzzle Palace, he entered what resembled a conventional wood-paneled courtroom with a spectator gallery, witness stand, and judge's bench. The room did not, however, contain a jury box. In police trials, the judge alone determines the verdict, though the police commissioner has the final say. No defendant can plead the

Fifth. Nor can they appeal a ruling. Officers can only be fired, nothing more. Though criminal charges can follow.

Eppolito may have hurt his cause with his wise-guy demeanor. "Once in a while police officers came into the trial room that were living a life of fiction, the result of Hollywood and the public glamorizing the police," said Deputy Commissioner of Trials Hugh Mo, who would act as judge. "Eppolito fit that mode. He looked like a hoodlum wannabe. He was almost bulging out of his clothes. He stood up and tried to ingratiate himself with me. His body language and manner were obsequious."

At a conference held at Mo's bench, both sides agreed to try the case "on stipulation," meaning Mo would rely entirely on evidence gathered before the trial and agreed upon by both sides. Mo would hear no live testimony. No questions. No answers. No cross-examination.

Internal Affairs rarely operated on stipulation. Of the three hundred cases Mo adjudicated over the course of his career, only a few were tried that way. Nobody involved would later recall who made the decision or how it was made, but the terms would omit some critical evidence. "I was astonished to see what information was not given to the trial court," Deputy Commissioner of Internal Affairs William Flack said years later. "That startled me."

As a result, Mo would not hear the most incriminating findings. "As the hearing unfolded it became more and more apparent that the evidence against this guy was insufficient," Mo said. "There appeared to be something missing, a gap. . . . So I'm thinking, unless they span this gap, Lou Eppolito is not guilty."

Forty-one items of evidence were read into the record. At 3:20 P.M. Cerny gave a short, straightforward summation of the defense in which he misstated several facts. He said that Eppolito had "rightfully received" the file from Sweeney (Sweeney testified that Eppolito had requested it) and that Internal Affairs had presented no evidence indicating that Eppolito gave the file to Gambino (though fingerprint analysis proved that Eppolito had handled the copies Gambino received). Cerny's counterpart, Sergeant

William Medican, failed to set the record straight: he offered no summation in his role as prosecutor.

Immediately afterward, Mo dismissed the case. Turning to Eppolito, he said that the evidence gathered by Internal Affairs had "failed to substantiate those charges that have been lodged against you."

The case would not be officially dismissed until Mo submitted a full written opinion, but Mo essentially ended it less than three hours after the trial began. Eppolito rose and hugged Gardell. In a short speech addressed to Mo, he portrayed himself as the victim of prejudice, a spiel he would exploit for years to come. "I have read newspaper articles that I am a friend of [Rosario Gambino's] and that I have been seen in cafes [with him]. . . . I told them I was willing to let them shoot sodium pentothal into me and give me a truth serum. I was willing to go through that. I am of Italian extraction but I am American and I don't understand how to speak Italian. I don't know or understand any of that. . . . I have dedicated myself, my time, and my life to this job. . . . I would never embarrass myself or the police department with something like that."

In closing, Mo noted that "the court is very much impressed with the presence" of Detective Stephen Gardell of the Detective Endowment Association, as if the union's support ensured Eppolito's innocence. (Sixteen years later, in June 2000, FBI agents came to Gardell's home, guns drawn. They led him away in handcuffs in front of his mother. The following year he pleaded guilty to leaking information to Mafia members.)

In his written ruling, Mo said that the court "cannot speculate as to how those documents came into Gambino's possession. The mere fact that [Eppolito] was reportedly the last known person who had possession of those documents is certainly legally insufficient to support the charge that he passed them to Gambino or some third party."

Five days later, on April 10, 1985, Mo forwarded his recommendation, along with a transcript of Eppolito's GO 15 hearing, down the hall to Police Commissioner Ben Ward for his approval. Ward was an attorney with ample experience handling disciplinary matters. He had the authority to overturn Mo's decision or ask for further investigation, as he often did. For whatever reason, he accepted Mo's ruling in its entirety within a day without question or comment.

It did not go unnoticed when Mo told Murray Weiss of the *New York Daily News* that there "was no evidence before me other than that Detective Eppolito epitomizes the finest in the department and is the unfortunate victim of circumstances."

Chief of Detectives Richard Nicastro disagreed. He refused to accept Eppolito back into the detective ranks until Commissioner Ward ordered him to do so.

Police headquarters may have exonerated Eppolito, but many of his fellow detectives working in mob-heavy South Brooklyn did not. As one said, "Something isn't right there." The prevailing suspicion, spoken or not, was that the underworld ran in Eppolito's bloodlines, and nothing could change that.

A few days after his acquittal, Eppolito went to Brooklyn to retrieve his gun and shield. He was inexplicably invited to select his new workplace. He chose the detective squad in the Sixty-Third Precinct, exactly the kind of South Brooklyn neighborhood where he could continue to consort with organized crime figures doing business in cafés and social clubs. The police department reimbursed him $11,000 in back pay and benefits lost during his suspension. He returned to the streets with his .38 in a shoulder holster.

Eppolito resumed the daily routine—writing up search warrants, questioning suspects, calling crime scene units to locations of bedlam and violence. He later petitioned for, and received, a promotion to detective second grade long before he would normally qualify. He argued that the department owed him for the humiliation he had endured during the Gambino investigation. His letter to Commissioner Ward distorted the hearing transcript and claimed, erroneously, that a highranking Internal Affairs officer concluded that there had been "no case" against him.

At the promotion ceremony, Eppolito crossed the stage and saluted Commissioner Ward, then saluted Hugh Mo, who attended in his capacity as a deputy commissioner. "As if I had anything to do with it,"

Mo said. Stranger still, Eppolito and his wife, Fran, barged into Mo's office after the ceremony with a police photographer. "He came in and acted like I was his godfather," Mo said. "He said, 'I want to thank you. You're the man.' He hugged me and his wife hugged me while his photographer took pictures."

Thirty-eight years later Mo would say that Eppolito "weaseled his way through the police department and he knew how to play the bureaucracy. Some rogue cops know how to play the system. They know how to manipulate and bring credit to themselves. He was streetwise, a con artist in his own way."

What twist of politics, corruption, or ineptitude had caused Commissioner Ward and his cabinet to acquit a detective caught leaking secrets to organized crime? Why did they try him on stipulation, send him to his preferred precinct, square in the Mafia homeland, and, finally, promote him out of turn? Was Ward simply trying to muffle further scandal after years of well-publicized police corruption? Was he trying to shelter a detective who had brought the NYPD a smattering of good press? Or had the commissioner been influenced by outside forces?

"Who knows?" said Mike Vecchione, who investigated hundreds of disciplinary matters as director of the department advocate's office. "The police department is like the Vatican. There's intrigue behind every door."

Sixteen years earlier Eppolito broke from his extended family, from its abuse and dark entanglements, and found a fraternity in the police department. But now the gravitational fields had reversed. He had found his way back to his family after the embrace of Jimmy the Clam's wake and the indignities of his Internal Affairs trial. In his mind, the NYPD had betrayed him, and now he would betray it back. His father, Fat the Gangster, had hated the police. That lesson stayed with Eppolito, even if he did not always know it.

In 1986, a documentary filmmaker named Maxi Cohen placed a classified ad in the *Village Voice*:

THE GAMBINO FILE   **39**

Angry????
WHAT MAKES YOU ANGRY?
I'M MAKING A FILM ABOUT ANGER.
PLEASE CALL 976–5757

Of the hundreds who responded, seven made the final cut—including a four-time murderer, a rape victim, a bickering couple, and, last, Louie Eppolito, who appeared on-screen with a mustache, pompadour, and an elaborate snake necklace. He claimed to have earned seventeen commendations for bravery and sixteen medals for valor, a preposterous boast. "I've been in seven gun battles in the streets of New York," he said. "I stood alone when the Black Liberation Army [was] killing cops . . . they fired forty-three shots at me, I had no fear. . . . I've gone into burning buildings, I had no fear."

But, he added, when he saw the front-page *New York Daily News* headline accusing him, "I lost my guts . . . this is my whole career shot down the tubes. . . . I'm angry enough right now that if I saw something happen in the street, there's a possibility I wouldn't do a thing about it. . . . I loved what I was doing. Now I wouldn't do shit."

4

FRAMED

BARRY GIBBS WAS A FAMILIAR FIGURE AROUND THE
Manhattan enclave of Sutton Place, a mailman who delivered packages
among the dignified co-op buildings staffed by uniformed doormen. A
stout, scruffy navy veteran of middle age, he greeted residents by name
in a husky Brooklyn accent and, parenthetically, offered them a bit of
offbeat humor. "I had great rapport with the people there," he said.
"They all loved me." He married a former Miss Canada, a woman he
met on his postal route. They had a son. After their divorce, he fell into
a dissolute life of clubs, drink, and drugs.

Gibbs was at a low ebb in early 1986. Con Edison cut his power when
he fell into arrears, leaving him to smoke crack alone in the dark. The
post office suspended him after he missed shifts. He tried to redeem
himself by enrolling in rehab. In the meantime, he worked at a deli
around the corner from his apartment, making BLTs and egg sandwiches. Gibbs stood out as a shabby white man of dubious habits living
in a mostly Black housing project in East Flatbush. He was noticed by
the police, including Eppolito, who worked in the local precinct.

On the afternoon of November 4, 1986, Peter Mitchell, a twenty-nine-
year-old former marine, went for an early afternoon jog on a bike path
along the Belt Parkway. He ran west for a mile or so, with the parkway to
his right and the weedy downslope to Jamaica Bay to the left. Along the

way he passed a gray two-door Oldsmobile Cutlass pulled awkwardly to the roadside. The driver was a white man with a "big nose, baggy face . . . like a prune," Mitchell later said. His salt-and-pepper hair was "combed down on the sides and frilly on top." He had the shadowy beginnings of a mustache. Beside him, in the passenger seat, sat a Black woman wearing a frowsy brown fur coat. "She was looking straight out at Jamaica Bay," Mitchell said, "like a dead stare."

Mitchell jogged another two miles to Floyd Bennett Field, a decommissioned airport, then retraced his route back toward his brother's apartment in Canarsie, where he was staying. When his knee began to ache he paused on a low bridge spanning an inlet. From there he spotted the same gray Cutlass he had seen forty-five minutes earlier. This time the Cutlass was pulling into a grassy area near a horseback riding school tucked among scraggly trees. He suspected the driver and his companion were looking for a private parking spot.

Mitchell watched from 150 feet as the man got out. He walked around to open the passenger door. He tugged on something. At first Mitchell thought he might be dumping garbage, then he saw the woman's calves and feet. Mitchell froze. "I was transfixed," he said. "I was shocked."

The man dragged the lifeless woman to a tree surrounded by high cattails and covered her in a quilt. He then took five Budweiser cans and scattered them around her. At that point the man looked over his right shoulder and spotted Mitchell. "He got up and ran around the car," Mitchell said. "He started it up and drove casually onto the expressway."

When the man was safely out of sight, Mitchell walked down and knelt beside the body. The woman's head protruded from the quilt, as if she were sleeping in a comfortable bed. Blood smeared her mouth. A deep abrasion from a rope or some other ligature encircled her neck like a necklace. The abrasion, Mitchell later said, stretched from "ear to ear."

Two years earlier, while stationed in California, Mitchell had pleaded guilty to a DUI. Police had found him driving erratically as he was returning from a club to his marine base. Months later he was convicted on a felony charge for trying to cash a stolen check for $300 at a drive-through bank. "The teller said, 'Wait here. I'm going to the vault,'" he said. "She never came back." He spent four months in jail, then was released on three years' parole. He had broken parole to stay with his brother for two weeks in Brooklyn.

Mitchell was a Black man with a criminal record. He was uncomfortably aware that an embroilment with the police, however innocent, could end badly for him. He could easily have jogged on to his brother's apartment, but he chose to stay. "I could have gone home," he later said, "but I wanted to do the right thing for the woman." So Mitchell entered the riding school and asked a manager to call 911. Two parks department police were already inspecting the body when Mitchell returned.

Detective Richard Canderozzi, Eppolito's colleague in the Sixty-Third Precinct, arrived and collected evidence, including jewelry removed from the victim and a short length of rope found beside her body. Canderozzi took Mitchell's statement. He described the man who had dumped the body as about five feet, six inches tall, fifty years old or so, with longish white hair flecked with gray. Canderozzi, who had worked in the Organized Crime Division, thought the description matched Steven Brigante, a neighborhood car thief with ties to the Mafia.

Eppolito arrived midafternoon and abruptly dismissed Canderozzi. He announced himself in charge. Mitchell pointed out the beer cans, which presumably contained fingerprints. Eppolito threw them away.

For the second time that afternoon Mitchell described the paunchy white-haired man, but Eppolito paid no attention. The detective, he said, "just ignored everything I said."

The woman's body was removed to the Kings County Mortuary, where a medical examiner found that she had died of strangulation with a cord or belt. Fingerprints identified her as a twenty-seven-year-old prostitute named Virginia Robertson, the mother of a young girl.

Mitchell later said that at about 6 P.M., just after dark, Eppolito drove him to an East Flatbush housing project. In Mitchell's recollection, they waited in the car until shabby, barrel-chested thirty-seven-year-old Barry Gibbs came out the front door. That's the guy, Eppolito said. No, Mitchell answered. The man who dumped the body was a shorter, thinner man with a faint mustache. He was considerably older, with whitish-gray hair.

Eppolito presumably knew Gibbs by neighborhood reputation. He may have targeted Gibbs for Robertson's murder in order to protect Brigante, an associate of the Lucchese crime family. Or he may have sought an easy way to boost his arrest count.

According to Mitchell, Eppolito then drove him to the precinct house and parked him in a cold interrogation room. He stood over Mitchell, saying that the man they saw, the lowlife Barry Gibbs, was a pervert and a pedophile. Eppolito asserted, with coercive force, that Gibbs was the suspect.

When Mitchell repeated that Gibbs was *not* the man he saw, Eppolito bore down. He told Mitchell about his commendations. He showed him pictures of his medals. The implication was clear: Who would take the word of a Black man with a criminal record over that of a decorated detective? Now Eppolito's threats turned explicit. I know where your mother lives, he told Mitchell. I know where your brother lives. What if the police found drugs in their homes? How would he like that? "He started talking like a mob guy," Mitchell said, "with the slang and 'ba-da-bing' this and 'ba-da-bing' that."

According to Mitchell, Eppolito told him, "You are going to do this, or else." By midnight, after almost six hours in the interrogation room, Mitchell agreed.

Eppolito contacted one of Gibbs's ex-girlfriends, a woman named Maryanne Carola, who had conducted a tempestuous on-again, off-again eight-year romance with Gibbs after meeting him in a Midtown bar. The gentle man she had first dated a decade earlier would have been incapable of violence, but now, under the sway of addiction, she wasn't sure what he might do. Eppolito convinced her to make a recorded phone call to Gibbs—Eppolito would listen in—in hopes that in the course of their unguarded conversation he might say something that could be used against him. She agreed.

Carola prompted Gibbs to unburden himself, to confide his feelings. He wept. He struggled with mood swings, he said, after quitting drugs.

He still loved her. On the second call Carola proposed lunch. She suggested they meet outside his apartment building. Gibbs showed up at the appointed time, but Carola did not. It was a setup. Eppolito and a partner made the arrest.

"I got thrown against a car and they tell me to empty out my pockets," Gibbs said. "I says what's this about? He throws me in the back of the car and he says I'm Detective Louis Eppolito."

They drove two blocks to the Sixty-Third Precinct. Upstairs in the squad room, Eppolito showed Gibbs a photo of Virginia Robertson's body. Eppolito had already determined that Gibbs had known Robertson; neighbors had seen them together. In panic or confusion, Gibbs lied: he denied knowing her. Eppolito smacked him on the back of the head. "He says, 'You know who that is,'" Gibbs said. "I said, 'I have no idea what you're talking about.' He smacked me again. I said, 'What are you doing?' He smacked me again."

Gibbs foolishly agreed to stand in a lineup without consulting a lawyer. "An innocent man has nothing to hide," he later said by way of explanation. "What do I need a lawyer for? I didn't do anything."

Gibbs did not consider that Eppolito might have bullied a witness into a wholesale lie. According to Mitchell, Eppolito showed him a Polaroid snapshot of Gibbs before the lineup assembled so that he would know whom to identify. At about 6 P.M. on November 14, Mitchell looked through one-way glass at six seated men, each holding a number. As instructed, Mitchell identified Gibbs as the man who dumped Virginia Robertson's body by the Belt Parkway, though he knew it was not the case.

Afterward an assistant district attorney named Tim Bakken asked Gibbs if he knew Robertson. Gibbs said no. Had he ever seen her? No. "But on the fourth or fifth question he stopped for a second or two," Bakken said, "then said they had smoked crack together and that at least once he had given her a ride home."

Fifteen months later, Mitchell testified against Gibbs, with Eppolito watching from the back of the courtroom. DNA testing was not yet conducted at New York crime scenes, and the fingerprints, hair samples, and other forensic evidence led to no clear conclusion. The jury relied instead on Mitchell's testimony—an account that Mitchell would later disavow.

Eppolito staged a brassy performance on the witness stand, though he became tetchy and evasive under cross-examination. He acknowledged that he did not consult with Detective Canderozzi about his initial findings, nor did he confer with the park police who had arrived first on the scene. He also failed to match footprints found around the body to shoes in Gibbs's apartment.

Gibbs naively assumed the jury would acquit him. When the verdict came in, Gibbs's lawyer put his hand on his shoulder. "He asked me if I heard what they said," Gibbs said. "I couldn't answer him. I was in shock." The jury had convicted Gibbs of murder in the second degree.

Gibbs was taken to Attica Correctional Facility in upstate New York. In his recollection, he arrived on a particularly dark night. "We walk through the entranceway," he said. "I get to the prison and they slam the doors. What a frightening feeling."

The judge sentenced Gibbs to a minimum of twenty years. After that a parole board would consider his case. But for Gibbs, release was unlikely. Parole boards rarely release inmates unless they express remorse. By maintaining his innocence, Gibbs disqualified himself.

In the meantime, Gibbs adjusted. He made friends. He attended Jewish services and walked the prison yard selling black market deli meat sandwiches he concealed in pockets sewn into his jacket.

Gibbs continued to press his case. He tried through persistent phone calls and letters to arrange for the DNA testing of hair samples and bits of skin found under Robertson's fingernails. On January 30, 1992, he wrote to Dr. Edward T. Blake, a prominent forensic scientist in California who, in turn, referred him to the Innocence Project, a nonprofit that advocates for the wrongfully convicted.

The Innocence Project accepted Gibbs's case in hopes that DNA tests could exonerate him. Vanessa Potkin, his attorney, obtained a police document listing all crime scene evidence. "New York is a particularly problematic jurisdiction for finding evidence," she said. "It's very complicated because the storage for evidence was archaic. They relied on carbon copy papers. If a paper was misfiled it's hard to find the evidence."

Potkin marshaled a team of law students to locate the missing documents. "They called police departments, they called property clerks, asking if anyone could find the evidence. We found nothing. . . . We filed motions in court to compel the evidence search. We got affidavits back saying they couldn't find any of it. There were fires and floods. There were a million excuses why the evidence didn't exist."

Gibbs called over and over, directing the young lawyers to evidence storage locations he had tracked down on his own. "He kept calling us," said Potkin. "He said, 'No, you're not looking at the right evidence voucher number. Search for this.' We followed through on every lead that he gave us."

The search continued for years, but eventually ran dry. The original police file had mysteriously disappeared or been destroyed, and much of the evidence could not be located. Potkin noted that Eppolito was the last person to have custody of several critical items, including the police file.

"Ultimately we just couldn't find the evidence in his case," Potkin said. "And if we can't find the evidence, we're in a very unfortunate position where we have to close the case." Gibbs was fifty-six when the Innocence Project reached its final impasse. At this point he had been imprisoned for eighteen years, almost a third of his life. He accepted that he would likely die in Attica.

5

A SILENT PARTNER

AMID THE ROUGHNESS AND DISORDER OF 1980S outer-borough New York, Detectives Louie Eppolito and Stephen Caracappa found ways to earn illicit profits by doing favors for friends. Operating under the cover of the law, they conducted all manner of dirty street-level deals and deceits. But the small-time stuff, like framing Barry Gibbs, was not enough for them. They aspired to criminal careers that would put them on par with Eppolito's father, Fat the Gangster, and his underworld cronies. To play at the next level, however, they would need a Mafia boss to act as their silent partner. Eppolito asked his cousin, Gambino associate Frankie Santora, to look out for potential patrons who could use a little help, who might pay two detectives for some moonlighting work. They would do anything, Eppolito said.

In midwinter 1965, a Brooklyn man named Burt Kaplan drove to Connecticut with a dead body folded in the trunk of his car. "I drove by myself and it made me very, very uncomfortable," he later said. "I trembled all the way up to Connecticut in the car by myself. I was scared to death."

Kaplan did not look like a man who would transport a corpse. He was a nebbish with a prominent bald dome and owlish, horn-rimmed glasses perched on a Mr. Potato Head nose. Even at age thirty-three he stooped like an old man.

Kaplan had no choice. A policeman turned loan shark named Wes Daley had asked him to deliver the body to a friend. All Kaplan had to do, Daley said, was drive the body to its grave site. The friend would do the rest. Kaplan could not refuse, given the sum of money he owed Daley. Profligate borrowers like Kaplan sometimes became indentured servants; they paid off their debts by running errands.

In the predawn hour Kaplan met Daley's friend. He had planned to dig a grave, but the hard winter ground refused the spade. Instead, they drove to a river. "He asked if I would go with him and throw the body in the water," Kaplan said, "and I did."

Delivering a body to Connecticut and consigning it to the dark river would be Kaplan's only firsthand brush with Mafia brutality. He was ill-equipped for such work. Instead, the borrower became a brainstormer and confidant. He came to play a prominent role in the elaborate eco-system of organized crime as an adjunct money mastermind capable of finding loopholes, dreaming up schemes for untapped revenue, and performing financial sleight of hand. He abetted any offbeat enterprise that could fetch a profit. Eppolito and Caracappa would, in time, become central to his success.

Burt Kaplan, the son of an appliance salesman, grew up above his family's liquor store in a three-story walk-up on Vanderbilt Avenue in the Prospect Heights section of Brooklyn. He was a promising student at Brooklyn Tech, one of the finest public high schools in America. After his bar mitzvah at age thirteen, his father took him to a racetrack, an outing that would derail his life. All through freshman year of high school he spent afternoons compulsively betting on trifectas and playing poker. If his friends lost a few dollars they returned mildly disappointed to algebra homework or basketball practice. Kaplan stayed on and lost more—and still more. The steeper his losses, the riskier his bets in long-shot bids to recoup his deficits. He had the incorrigible gambler's conviction that the next bet would right his ledger. It rarely did.

Kaplan's gambling addiction ruined his grades. He transferred for sophomore year to Manual Training High School, a humiliating demotion.

After graduation in 1952, he joined the US Navy, where he landed a prized Cold War post in Japan, decoding and analyzing Soviet transmissions. The National Security Agency recruited him, but he chose to return to Brooklyn. Money motivated him, not the wonky prestige of intelligence work.

He married Eleanor, a good girl from an upstanding Brooklyn family, and moved to a two-story brick house in Bensonhurst. He worked with his father installing rooftop television antennas and hulking Westinghouse air conditioners with plastic grilles. His house calls included a visit to the Grand Mark, the Gambino clubhouse on Grand Avenue, to install an air conditioner in the upstairs room where Eppolito's father, Fat the Gangster, and his uncle Jimmy the Clam played cards. He measured the window, hoisted the appliance in place, and sealed it. Then, with the appliance hissing to life, he seated himself in the cooling room for the first of many rounds of cards with the old men.

Kaplan did not look like somebody who would play cards with mafiosi. He seemed more like a salesman, which, in fact, is how he earned a living for most of his life, though that occupation, like everything Kaplan touched, inevitably turned to crime. While helping a friend shop for a leisure suit Kaplan found that he could buy racks of stolen clothes at a discount—"swag," in crime jargon—and resell them at fat markups. He began trading in clothes plundered from hijacked trucks and peddled illegal knockoffs of disco-era brands—Christian Dior shirts, Gloria Vanderbilt jeans, Sergio Valente tank tops—imported from Hong Kong. "We bought sweatshirts from China, had them made to the exact specification of Champion," he said, "and put their labels on it." He owned a warehouse full of contraband polyester bell-bottoms and silky patterned shirts. For the next two decades Kaplan would finance his gambling habit by fencing not just stolen clothes but hair dryers, wristwatches, and other goods.

As Kaplan's income grew, so too did his gambling. Paradoxically, the more he earned, the more debt he accrued with a dozen Mafia loan sharks who charged exorbitant interest, or vig, as mobsters call it. On his worst days he lost tens of thousands of dollars, then struggled to pay the 20 percent weekly vig. He perpetually scrambled to sell enough stolen leisure suits and halter tops to reduce the principal. The threat of broken knees, or worse, was never far from his mind, yet he gambled on. He acknowledged that he was, in his words, "a degenerate gambler," but he could not restrain the urge. By his own estimate, he lost roughly $3 million over the course of his life.

Kaplan's arrears grew so grievous that his father-in-law, a retired policeman, interceded. In those days, patrolmen were on more intimate terms with neighborhood mobsters. They grew up on the same blocks, attended the same schools, and drank in the same bars. Though technically forbidden from fraternizing with criminals, most police were not averse to finding accommodations.

And so Kaplan's father-in-law walked him over to an eighteen-hole public golf course laid out near the southernmost stretch of the Brooklyn-Queens Expressway. There, on Fourteenth Avenue, they entered the 19th Hole Bar, a dark one-story corner tavern. The 19th Hole was a neighborhood spot that doubled as a command post for the Lucchese crime family. Like any of the dozen or so Mafia clubhouses throughout the city, the 19th Hole was where capos received petitioners. Here favors were asked, deals were struck, debts were paid. On any day or night, a supplicant could conduct business among pomaded hustlers and hangers-on wearing the uniform of mafiosi at leisure: windbreakers, track suits, polyester-blend pants, and velour zipper jackets with medallions. They wore fedoras while playing cards and smoked cigars. Kaplan's father-in-law asked the Luccheses if, for now, he could pay off the principal without interest. They agreed.

In the following years Kaplan got to know the Lucchese leaders— the boss, Antonio "Tony Ducks" Corallo, the consigliere, Christopher "Christie Tick" Furnari, and, most of all, the soldier and later underboss Anthony "Gaspipe" Casso. As they grew to trust Kaplan and to appreciate his acumen and wide-ranging connections, he advanced from Lucchese borrower to partner, money launderer, instigator, and architect of dozens of schemes.

As a Jew, Kaplan could not formally join the Lucchese family. Ancestry had to be Italian, at least on the father's side. Still, an ambitious, money-minded associate like Casso eagerly looped Kaplan into his planning, regardless of Kaplan's background. Casso was accustomed to doing the talking. With Kaplan he mostly listened.

Kaplan's alliance with Casso helped support his family and pay his gambling debts. It also gave him neighborhood clout. "Nobody could touch him," a detective later said. "He could do anything he wanted."

However shrewd Kaplan's illicit schemes, they were not clever enough to keep him out of trouble. He was arrested three times in the 1960s, getting off each time with probation or acquittal. Kaplan tried to disguise his involvements from law enforcement by maintaining at least one degree of separation between himself and the street operatives. His connections nonetheless came to the attention of an FBI agent named Patrick Colgan, who tried repeatedly, and unsuccessfully, to turn Kaplan into an informant. They were on cordial terms, but Kaplan was rock-hard in his refusals.

"I would just stop and knock on his door and say hello," Colgan said. "He was always very polite, very professional, and I never knew him to lie, but he wouldn't tell me anything about the guys he was running with. He was very old school. He followed the Mafia rules more faithfully than most."

On June 1, 1972, Kaplan, now thirty-seven, was arrested for possession of 157 boxes of women's pants, worth $40,000, stolen at gunpoint from a tractor trailer at Canal Street and Sixth Avenue in the Soho neighborhood of Lower Manhattan. The FBI found the boxes in a warehouse Kaplan owned on Staten Island.

Kaplan's lawyer, Gerald Shargel, called Agent Colgan at home to say that Kaplan wished to see him. Colgan spent about thirty minutes with Kaplan at the Metropolitan Detention Center in Brooklyn, a jail used to hold those with pending court cases. "We laughed and had a few jokes," Colgan said. "He said, 'Pat, how do I get out of this mess?' I said there's only one way. You've got to testify against all the Mafia figures you're aware of. It's not going to be pretty, but you can go into the Witness Protection Program and I'll facilitate it with the U.S. Marshals. He said, 'Pat, I can't do that.'"

Judge Jack B. Weinstein, a US district judge, was known for compassionate sentencing; he took the families into consideration. Six years earlier he had granted Kaplan probation in a fraud case after he swore to mend his ways. Kaplan's wife, Eleanor, and their daughter, Deborah, begged Judge Weinstein to spare Kaplan again. He refused. This time he sentenced Kaplan to four years in the federal penitentiary in Lewisburg, Pennsylvania. Kaplan left behind the usual debts.

By all accounts, Deborah was unusually attached to her father—and he to her. His conviction and imprisonment motivated her to study law. On some subconscious level she knew she would attend St. John's University School of Law a decade later, a family friend said, "so she could get him out of jail."

Four years later, Kaplan was home, an ex-con still working the angles. Still hustling, still dealmaking. He profited handsomely from the garment trade, but his gambling debts drove him to chase after easy profits earned in the drug trade of 1970s New York. He set up an elaborate operation importing marijuana from Juárez, Mexico. Produce trucks, Winnebagos, and private cars smuggled bundles across the border to a restaurant Kaplan owned in El Paso. In his best year he sold as much as 13,000 pounds. While at law school, his daughter, Deborah, typed and managed paperwork in the Staten Island warehouse. She later claimed to have no knowledge of the illicit businesses—the constant churn of illegal goods—conducted around her. Kaplan made it a habit to protect those close to him, and himself, by separating the spheres of family and work. Nobody knew more than they had to.

Kaplan delegated the smuggling operation to Tommy Galpine, a younger man with a faint mustache and an appetite for petty crime. Kaplan had hired Galpine when he was an aimless sixteen-year-old who had been fired from an appliance warehouse. The two grew so close that Kaplan routinely introduced Galpine as "like a son to me."

Galpine attended family bar mitzvahs and birthdays. He took Kaplan's mother to the hospital, moved Deborah into her college dorm rooms at SUNY Albany, took their cars for servicing, and administered drops in Kaplan's left eye after retina surgery. "I'm a doer," Galpine said, "not a talker. I take care of things."

Galpine handled a wide range of chores—personal and illegal. "We made some quaalude moves," Galpine said. "We made some marijuana moves. We made some money."

In 1979, the DEA arrested Kaplan for setting up a lab to manufacture quaaludes, then a popular party drug. His chemist, a defector from a pharmaceutical company, agreed to testify against Kaplan to spare himself a harsh penalty. A jury convicted Kaplan. He served three years in Allenwood, a federal penitentiary 150 miles northwest of Philadelphia.

Day after day, month after month, Kaplan walked around the oval outdoor track on his arthritic legs. It was as if he were trying to walk, lap by lap, to his release. The inmates around him played bocce or handball or any of the half dozen sports offered in the recreation yard. But Kaplan may have been the least athletic of the thousand or so inmates. So he walked. The other inmates could see him out there, a smallish man, just five feet eight and 165 pounds, wearing gray sweat clothes purchased in the commissary.

When he wasn't walking, Kaplan was often gambling on televised sports. Instead of money, he bet the jailhouse currency—stamps, tins of sardines, and cartons of cigarettes.

Incarceration is meant to curb criminal behavior, but for men in the Mafia orbit, men like Kaplan, jail often serves as a relaxed retreat in which to bond and network with other offenders. Kaplan, for example, formed a friendship with Frankie Santora, a beefy Gambino associate and, as it would happen, Eppolito's cousin, the one who greeted him after their uncle's wake. Santora was serving time for plundering more than $11 million in stocks, bonds, and other assets from the estate of Frederick Lundy, the reclusive owner of Lundy's, an enormous and enormously popular Sheepshead Bay seafood restaurant with a red-tile roof and striped awnings.

Kaplan and Santora grew up in the same neighborhood. They had friends in common. In prison, they slept a few beds apart in Dormitory 6 and worked together in the boiler room. They looked out for each other, as prison friends do.

In Allenwood, Santora told Kaplan that his cousin, Louie Eppolito, and Louie's friend Stephen Caracappa might be willing to do "business on the side if the price was right." Eppolito worked as a detective, Santora said, but he was really one of them. "Frankie approached me and said that if I wanted, his cousin [could] get me information and could help me if I ever have a problem and could probably help me on ongoing investigations," Kaplan said.

Santora told Kaplan that Eppolito and Caracappa could do more than run license plate numbers or share sensitive information about who the police surveilled and which Mafia soldiers had turned informant. The detectives would do anything, Santora said. *Anything*. If Kaplan "had any serious problem," Santora said, "he, his cousin and his cousin's partner were capable of doing a murder." He posed the possibility, as if they'd done it all before.

Santora assured Kaplan "that they were good stand-up guys and that he would have no fear of . . . doing anything with them." In the language of organized crime, "a stand-up guy" refused to divulge information to law enforcement, even if his refusal resulted in jail time. A stand-up guy would never inform, never betray.

Kaplan initially declined Santora's offer, explaining that he "didn't want to do business with any cops" because it "possibly could come back and haunt [me] if one of them would later on in life become an informant." Though Kaplan acknowledged that he might hire them if he encountered a serious problem.

By 1985, both Kaplan and his jailhouse friend Frank Santora had served their federal sentences at Allenwood Penitentiary and resumed criminal lives in Brooklyn. Kaplan returned in time to see his daughter marry Harlan Silverstein, a fellow graduate of St. John's School of Law. They recited their vows at Temple Israel, in the Long Island town of Lawrence, followed by a reception at a nearby catering hall, where Kaplan's Allenwood friends and Lucchese associates—including Gaspipe Casso—and their wives occupied a center table with a towering floral arrangement.

Kaplan had spent his entire life segregating his straight life from the crooked. He had a foot in each world. For this one day, his family and friends mingled with the mobsters over canapés and champagne.

Deborah, the bride, was studying for the bar exam at the time of her wedding. She was unaware that her father had borrowed $150,000 from Casso to pay for the reception. Later Kaplan would claim that he invited his mob associates to line up potential law clients for his daughter. "At the time of my daughter's wedding, I didn't know what she would do down the road," he said. "I thought she might be a criminal-defense lawyer."

On Friday, August 2, 1985, a handsome thirty-five-year-old New York diamond dealer named Israel Greenwald stepped off a flight from London and into the arms of the FBI.

Greenwald grew up in Israel, the son of Holocaust survivors. He was returning to New York, to his wife and two daughters, after a work trip. In London he had cashed two treasury bills on behalf of a Diamond District acquaintance named Herman Tabak, who in turn was secretly working in partnership with Burt Kaplan. It was not unusual for Greenwald to transact business abroad, away from the scrutiny of US regulators. In this case there was an added reason for stealth: whether Greenwald knew it or not, the treasury bills were stolen. He was fencing property.

When Greenwald presented his passport at Kennedy Airport, customs agents pulled him out of the line for questioning. That night, or the next morning, he spoke briefly to Beverly Bartzer, an agent assigned to an FBI group investigating theft of government securities, counterfeit, and forged checks. A source in London had alerted the IRS that Greenwald had sold stolen treasury bills. The IRS, in turn, contacted the FBI. Greenwald claimed to be unaware that the bills were stolen.

When they spoke again, on Monday morning, August 5, Greenwald told Agent Bartzer that Tabak had visited his Rockaway Beach home that Saturday evening to reassure him that the stolen treasury bills were just a misunderstanding. Tabak had received the bills, he said, in lieu of cash payment in a real estate deal. He had no idea they were stolen, he said. Nonetheless, Tabak warned Greenwald not to discuss the matter with anyone, "or he would be sorry," Bartzer later said. "[Tabak] also told [Greenwald] that this was a mafia sort of thing and that Italians were involved with it."

Bartzer urged Greenwald to cooperate with the FBI. He could start, Bartzer said, by wearing a mini cassette recorder in his pocket when he met with Tabak later that day. He agreed. The device picked up snippets of conversation until Tabak patted Greenwald's coat and found the recorder. Or so Greenwald said. "I was not certain whether to believe him or not," Bartzer said.

Bartzer paused the investigation for three months. "We let the whole situation cool down," she said, "which we often do in law enforcement. We felt that we could perhaps ask [Greenwald] to talk to [Tabak] again."

With that in mind, Bartzer waited to shore up Greenwald's cooperation. Then, on February 5, 1986, she called Greenwald's attorney to arrange for him to make undercover recordings, this time with a more discreet device. Six days later Greenwald's attorney told Bartzer that he had disappeared.

Tabak had earlier warned Burt Kaplan, his coconspirator, that Greenwald might be informing on them. Kaplan understood what that would mean for him. He had walked out of Allenwood a year earlier. Another conviction would carry a lengthy sentence. Kaplan was not eager to return to the deadening routine of cellblock confinement, petty jailhouse tussles, and the years away from his wife and the daughter he adored.

Kaplan could not glean what Greenwald might have told Agent Bartzer, or what degree of cooperation he had agreed to. Whatever the case, Kaplan knew that he must find a way to prevent Greenwald from testifying in court. At some point in early 1986 Kaplan contacted Santora, his jailhouse confidant, to ask if his cousin, Detective Eppolito, was still available for extracurricular work.

On February 10, 1986, Israel Greenwald's daughter Yael, age seven, passed a fluish night coughing in an upstairs bedroom of the family's redbrick colonial in Far Rockaway, Queens. Her father stayed up with her, doing what he could to soothe his younger daughter. In the morning he dressed for work in a pinstripe suit and yarmulke, as he always did. As he left the house at 7:30 A.M., he stopped to play with Udi, the family's pet squirrel monkey. He told his wife, Leah, a part-time teacher, that he would return home by 6 P.M., when a prospective buyer would stop by to inspect a Cadillac they hoped to sell.

Greenwald hugged his older daughter, Michal, aged nine, at a school bus stop, then drove twenty miles to his office on West Forty-Seventh Street, in the heart of the Diamond District in Midtown. He called home at 10:30 A.M. to ask Rosalba, the housekeeper, if Yael felt better. The family never heard from him again.

Eppolito, Caracappa, and Santora caught Greenwald on his way home that afternoon. The detectives had pulled Greenwald's home address, car model, and plate number from the Department of Motor Vehicles. They lay in wait, then drove up behind him. They flashed police lights and pulled Greenwald over, telling him that he was a suspect in a hit-and-run. They had to take him into a precinct, they said, to stand in a lineup. As instructed, Greenwald got into the back seat. At some point over the next half hour or so Greenwald must have realized with rising alarm and panic that the two detectives, or whoever they were, had not detained him for a police lineup. And they were not driving him to a police precinct.

Peter Franzone was sitting in a booth at the entrance to his parking lot on Nostrand Avenue in Brooklyn, when Frank Santora showed up with three other men. Franzone was a conspicuously short man with a sixth-grade education. He was practically illiterate but had worked hard to overcome his disadvantage. He had quit a city job with seventeen years' worth of unused vacation time to start his own towing and car repair business. He owned his lot, complete with a body shop and a row of graffiti-covered one-car garages leased by the month.

Franzone grew friendly with Santora after repairing his white Cadillac. Santora told Franzone that he worked for a Long Island construction company, though Franzone could guess his real occupation. Santora paid for their occasional lunches from a fist-thick wad of cash. Towing operators typically found some accommodation with the mob. If Santora was a wise guy, then so be it. Franzone found it advisable not to ask.

Franzone's worst suspicions must have sprung to mind when Santora entered the lot with three other men. Franzone recognized one of them. He had met Santora's cousin Louie Eppolito at Santora's home. Without saying a word, Eppolito parked his car facing outward, as if prepared for a quick departure. He sat in the driver's seat watching the street while Santora entered a single-car garage with a gaunt man wearing a trench coat with its collar turned up (Franzone would later learn he was Stephen Caracappa) and a man wearing a yarmulke.

The three stayed in the garage for about twenty minutes. Only Santora and Caracappa emerged. Santora came to the shed that Franzone used as an office. He said he wanted to show Franzone something. He opened the garage door and told Franzone to go inside. "I turned the light on," Franzone later said, "and I saw a man slumped against the wall." Santora then took two shovels from the trunk of his Cadillac and told Franzone to start digging a grave in the dirt floor of the garage. "Frankie told me that I got to help bury the body," Franzone said, "because I'm an accessory with it, and if I didn't help him, if I go and tell anybody, that he would kill me and my effing family."

Franzone was nearly immobilized with fear. He knew that Santora had killed the man. More disturbing still, he had done so with the help of NYPD detectives.

Franzone dug for more than an hour. The hole was five feet deep by the time he finished. "I was afraid that [Santora] might make me dig it deep enough and leave me in there." They rolled Greenwald's body into the hole and doused it with jugs of lime to accelerate decomposition and hinder identification. They finished it with layers of wet cement.

"It was daylight when I went in," Franzone said, "and when I came out it was dark."

He walked home well past dinnertime. His wife was eight and a half months pregnant. She was asleep when he reached their apartment. He told her nothing. He never went to the police. He assumed that "no one would believe me if I said a cop was involved in this." If he said anything he felt sure that Eppolito "would lock me up and have somebody kill me in jail."

Franzone went to work each morning uncomfortably aware of the body lying five feet beneath the garage floor, and the dreadful knowledge of his role in the secret burial. When Franzone and his wife brought home a newborn, Santora stopped by to give them a black plastic bag filled with baby clothes. Neither man mentioned the murder. Franzone assumed Santora had stolen the clothes and threw them out.

In 1988, Franzone saw Eppolito's friend Stephen Caracappa at a sweet sixteen party thrown for Santora's daughter Tammy. He did not say hello. Franzone would not disclose his knowledge of the crime for another eighteen years, and only then under duress. "Whatever I knew," he said, "I wasn't going to tell nobody."

Later, when Santora confirmed that he and the detectives had carried out their assignment, Kaplan paid him $25,000 to divvy up with Eppolito and Caracappa. Of his own volition, Kaplan paid an extra $5,000, which Santora pocketed. He never told Eppolito and Caracappa about the bonus.

Israel Greenwald did not come home that evening. He was an unusually attentive family man. An unexplained absence was out of character. The next day his wife, Leah, contacted the 101st Precinct on the eastern end of the Rockaway Peninsula and filed a missing persons report. She also asked Herman Tabak what he knew about her husband's whereabouts. He denied any knowledge and refused to speak with the police or FBI, he said, for fear that he too might disappear.

Meanwhile, FBI agents searched Greenwald's neighborhood, looking for his blue Pontiac. They eventually found it abandoned at a long-term parking lot at Kennedy Airport. The FBI knew that Greenwald had a Liberian diplomatic passport, in addition to his United States passport. "We didn't know quite what to think," Agent Bartzer said. "We thought it may be possible that he left the country to avoid cooperating further."

Leah insisted on her husband's innocence. "He was a very good man," she said, "and just got stuck in the middle of something and didn't know any mafia people at all."

For the next nineteen years, Greenwald's family had no hint of his fate. Leah could not claim widow's benefits because she could not prove herself a widow. Nor could she collect life insurance without a body. The FBI told her they could provide no further help. They offered to send a copy of the case file, provided her husband could sign for it.

Leah kept the household afloat by working day and night jobs, selling health products and soliciting advertisements. Michal Greenwald watched from a window as men repossessed the family station wagon. She and her sister switched schools four times.

"As a child, I never felt normal," she later wrote. "I was unique in that I had no clear answer to what happened to my father. . . . I blamed it all on my mother, for who else was there to take the brunt of my anger and pain."

Leah affected a removed and unavailable manner, as if she resided apart from the girls in a suspended state of perpetual trauma. The daughters had lost not just their father but their mother as well. "They came home from school, and I wasn't there for them," Leah said years later. "I couldn't date and move on. I was psychologically damaged for a relationship. I buried myself in work and used the excuse that I had to survive and pay bills." Yael wrote that as a child she overheard other children whisper *nebach,* the Yiddish word for "an unfortunate case," when she walked by.

Leah and the girls moved between a series of apartments. By macabre coincidence, they happened to live for a stretch across Nostrand Avenue from the repair shop where the long-missing husband and father lay doubled over in his makeshift grave.

6

RICO RISING

THE ISRAEL GREENWALD MURDER WAS A TEST CASE,
proof of how useful Eppolito and Caracappa might be to Burt Kaplan
and, by extension, his contacts and collaborators within the Lucchese
crime family. The Lucchese crews fielded their own accomplished killers,
of course, but delegating murders to the detectives held certain advan-
tages, given how easily they could abduct their prey with badges out and
police lights flashing—not to mention their ready access to critical inside information about wiretaps, pending raids, and other investigative
details. Like any well-placed moles, they could change the game.

The FBI, as it turned out, was dusting off its own secret weapon. In
the years ahead, Kaplan and his Lucchese friend, Gaspipe Casso, would
come to rely on the detectives not just for convenience but for survival,
as law enforcement upped its game with a new genre of law designed to
extinguish the mob forever.

In the evenings, after long, frustrating days probing organized crime
at the FBI's New York field office, Jules Bonavolonta would often retire
with other agents to a dimly lit restaurant called Sun Luck, at Sixty-
Eighth Street and Third Avenue. They sat around the U-shaped bar, ties
loosened, drinking Smirnoff or Heinekens served by a bow-tied bar-
tender named Charlie.

Bonavolonta and his companions called themselves the Sun Luck Club.

Most had joined the FBI around 1970, after serving in Vietnam. Bonavolonta fought with the Green Berets. His friend, Agent Jim Kallstrom, completed two tours of frontline combat as a marine lieutenant. They returned embittered by military mismanagement—the infighting, the ill-considered plans imposed by higher-ups, the focus on short-term statistics at the expense of long-term gain. "That's why so many of us Vietnam vets signed on for organized crime," Kallstrom said. "The war against the mob was our second chance—a war we could fight until it was truly over."

Bonavolonta and his friends belonged to a new generation of war-hardened investigators trained at the bureau's Quantico campus to replace older agents who had probed the underworld without much success under the rigid strictures of FBI director J. Edgar Hoover, who stubbornly, and unaccountably, denied the Mafia's existence for many years. In fact, it did not take long for younger agents to see that the so-called war on organized crime was waged as ineffectually as Vietnam. Under Hoover, the FBI arrested only low-level loan sharks and muscle men. The mob replaced the underlings as quickly as the government seized them. The bosses went untouched.

"Here was the real problem with the Hoover system," Bonavolonta later wrote. "We were getting only the chumps, the mopes, the guys dealing the cards and rolling the dice." As a result, the five crime families remained entrenched. They worked their rackets with impunity, as if they owned New York. At Sun Luck, the young agents lamented over their drinks that they had ceded in Khe Sanh and Van Tuong. Now they were losing in the streets of Bensonhurst and Bay Ridge.

Their prospects would change. In August 1979, Bonavolonta and three other agents drove four hours north in a government-issue Chevrolet to attend a seminar at Cornell's law school. The four would spend the week sleeping in dorms and eating in the student cafeteria. The trip wasn't their idea. A supervisor insisted they go. "It was a week of spending time away from the family," said Agent Kossler. "I wasn't really seeing what benefit it was to me or to us. I went kicking and screaming, but as it turned out, it would change everything."

The next morning, the four agents took seats in an imposing lecture hall for three days of talks with G. Robert Blakey, a lawyer and professor who, as chief counsel for the Senate Subcommittee on Criminal Laws and Procedures and an acolyte of Robert Kennedy, helped shape the anticrime measures of the 1960s and early 1970s. Courtly, soft-spoken, and balding, he fit the Hollywood conception of a seasoned law professor.

Ten years earlier Blakey had written, and Congress enacted, the Racketeer Influenced and Corrupt Organizations Act, known as RICO. The law, in theory, allowed law enforcement to pursue entire criminal organizations, "conspiracies" as Blakey called them, rather than picking off individuals.

Under RICO, the Mafia soldier caught murdering or extorting could be treated as a piece in a pattern of criminal activity committed by the conspiracy. The entire membership would be liable for one man's actions. In this way, prosecutors could indict the big bosses, even if they didn't pull the trigger. "Instead of going after all the low-level guys at the gaming tables," Bonavolonta wrote, "you would try to connect up all the illegal gaming tables, then go after the organization running the show." The goal, Blakey told the agents, was to "zap the mob, not the mobsters."

When Blakey wrote the RICO statute, Attorney General John Mitchell called the bill "one of the most imaginative proposals to combat organized crime ever introduced in the Congress."

Maybe so, but nobody noticed. In its first eight years, RICO was invoked in just thirty-seven cases. US attorneys may have found its intricacies daunting. Maybe they doubted juries would understand it. They may not have grasped it themselves.

In any case, Blakey spent a decade promoting RICO with the zeal of a man who had found a magic bullet. Everywhere he went, including the FBI academy, the US Attorney's Office in Manhattan, and the Department of Justice in Washington, his audiences dismissed him as an academic lacking in street acumen. What could a professor teach them about fighting crime?

In 1979, Blakey changed his strategy. Rather than travel the country like a missionary, he invited law enforcement to seminars he conducted at Cornell. Maybe on his home ground, under the law school's Gothic spire, he would carry more weight. Maybe the Ivy League surroundings would confer credibility.

The FBI agents assumed they would endure days of dull legal training. Nothing prepared them for Blakey's evangelical energy. He began by dimming the lights and playing the 1931 movie *Little Caesar,* in which Edward G. Robinson plays a gangster based on Al Capone. (Blakey refused to say if the gangster's nickname, "Rico," inspired the statute's acronym.) "What about Big Boy?" Blakey said when the lights came back on, referring to Rico's boss. "Big Boy—nothing ever happens to him. He's still in charge. Oh, sure, they got Rico. What's the use of that?" Like the heads of New York's crime families, Big Boy continued to prosper while his soldiers took the fall.

Afterward, Blakey paced the classroom outlining the basics. He spoke of predicate acts and forfeitures as if they were the most urgent topics imaginable. He drew feverishly on the blackboard. "To me, it was an epiphany," Agent Kossler said. "Now I knew what to do. Blakey gave us a road map for conducting investigations that would go after entire organizations, not individuals."

During breaks the agents huddled around Blakey, peppering him with questions. The seminar was a revelation and affirmation of all their frustrations. "Get off the carousel," he told them.

RICO was exactly the kind of weapon they longed for during their nights of demoralized drinking at Sun Luck. The agents, accompanied by a handful of colleagues, drove back to Ithaca in January 1980 and checked into a Holiday Inn. They next day they asked Blakey a long series of questions in a rented conference room.

The following November, Jim Kallstrom sat at his desk in the FBI's New York office and wrote what he called "The Plan," a ten-page memo charting an aggressive strategy for investigating and prosecuting organized crime using the RICO statute as a centerpiece. The memo made its way up the chain to the desk of FBI director William Webster, who sent it back with his approval.

The RICO laws had gone unutilized for almost a decade. The young coterie of FBI agents led by Bonavolonta, Kallstrom, and other members of the Sun Luck Club would now try to use RICO to bust the highest levels of the mob—to kill the snake by severing its head. They were not yet aware that the Mafia had its own secret weapon.

The RICO laws alone would not vanquish the underworld. The FBI first needed to amass evidence of ongoing conspiracies. The investigation began with garbage trucks patrolling the subdivisions springing up forty miles east of New York City.

Like many veterans, Jerry Kubecka settled in the burgeoning Long Island suburbs after World War II. He moved to the quiet town of Greenlawn, where he supported his young family by driving a milk delivery route. In those days, most households had bottles of fresh milk brought to their back doors. Towns in the rural stretches of Long Island did not yet have municipal garbage pickup. Consequently, many of Jerry's four hundred or so customers asked if he could take their trash to the dump after dropping their milk bottles. He obliged until the health department objected to carrying garbage alongside milk. So he quit his job, bought a twenty-five-dollar fertilizer truck, and charged customers a dollar a week to remove their trash. His plan succeeded. He soon owned a small fleet of trucks.

One day in 1956, two men invited Jerry to join the Private Sanitation Industry Association, linked to the Lucchese family, for an annual fee of $5,000. In return, the group would fix prices and rig bids. The association, they added, would also help Jerry avoid unspecified "troubles." Jerry asked what sort of troubles. They wouldn't say. He told them to go to hell.

Days later his drivers could not start their trucks. A saboteur had poured honey in the gas tanks. After that, Jerry found shattered windshields and dumpsters dropped in the Nissequogue River. A driver quit after three men threatened to break his legs. The warnings and sabotage continued for years. Jerry received a call from a gas station pay phone: play by our rules, the caller said, or we'll rub you out. The bully tactics only hardened Jerry's resolve. He refused to fall in line.

When Jerry developed heart disease in 1979, his son Robert gave up a promising career in environmental science to take over the business.

Along with the garbage routes, Robert continued the long, stubborn holdout against the Lucchese family. He and his brother-in-law, Donald Barstow, managed to keep the business going outside the rules imposed by the mob, no matter the risk. With their longish hair and glasses, the two men looked like hippie high school science teachers, but they proved their firmness.

The campaign of harassment continued for years—with slashed tires and threatening late-night phone calls. Corrupt union representatives warned the firm's commercial customers to hire other carters or face picketing. On several occasions Robert noticed cars following him. He began sleeping in the office to safeguard the trucks.

In 1982, Robert read a newspaper article about the New York State Organized Task Force, a joint federal, state, and local investigation into organized crime. The task force, he learned, was focused on specific industries, including private sanitation. Robert called and offered to share his story.

A short time later Richard Tennien, a forty-eight-year-old retired Suffolk County detective now working as a task force investigator, came to Jerry Kubecka's home in Stony Brook, New York, to meet the Kubecka and Barstow families while Robert and Donald were at work. Donald Barstow's wife, Cathy, was just twenty-three. She put their five-month-old daughter in an upstairs crib while she made chocolate chip cookies and brewed a pot of tea. She then sat with her mother, Joy, and father, Jerry, in a pine-paneled sitting room. Tennien complimented Cathy on the cookies, then turned to the topic at hand. Though not trained for undercover work, Robert and Donald had already agreed to wear recording devices taped to their stomachs. Tennien acknowledged the danger, but assured the families that the task force would protect them. "I'm a professional," he said. "They'll be safe."

Over the following two years, Robert and Donald secretly recorded dozens of conversations in diners and offices as rival carters and union officials continued to threaten them. Most significant, Tennien learned from the tapes that the Lucchese boss, Anthony "Tony Ducks" Corallo, conducted much of his business from the back seat of a black Jaguar owned by his associate Sal Avellino, nicknamed "The Golfer" for his loud polo shirts and patterned polyester pants.

Corallo had earned his nickname by ducking arrests. He was a short, stocky man with a subdued air of menace. He started as a tile setter in the Italian section of Harlem before helping Jimmy Hoffa gain control of the Teamsters Union in New York. Now, at seventy-three, he was the boss.

Corallo lived a relatively private life, gardening and listening to opera in his sizable home in East Norwich, a few miles from the mansions that prominent families built on Long Island's north shore. On most mornings Avellino picked Corallo up and drove him on his rounds of meetings in Brooklyn, Queens, and Staten Island, weaving along back roads to avoid followers.

Robert and Donald's secret recordings captured fragmented discussions of the corrupt union's bully tactics—enough, at any rate, to persuade a judge to authorize Tennien to plant a miniature radio transmitter and microphone, a bug, in Avellino's Jaguar. Though it was not clear how he might manage to put the bug in place.

Tennien's team practiced on a Jaguar the DEA had seized from a drug dealer. Technicians planted the bug in various spots on the car, then drove the Connecticut roads to test the sound. They concluded that a bug wired behind the heater yielded the best reception.

If the chance arose to install the bug, they would likely have mere minutes. They whittled the installation time down with practice. Over and over, with a stopwatch ticking, they raced to unscrew the dashboard, wire the device to the car's electrical system, and reinstall the dashboard.

For months, Tennien and his team trailed Avellino's Jaguar, watching to see if he left it unattended. On the night of March 18, 1983, Tennien and two technicians followed Avellino to Huntington Town House, a catering hall, where he attended the annual black-tie dinner and dance for the private sanitation union. Fortunately for Tennien, Avellino arrived late. He was forced to park at a far end of the lot. Avellino went inside in his tuxedo, leaving two underlings to keep an eye on the Jaguar. A severe rainstorm swept across Long Island that night, with winds gusting from the east. Temperatures hovered just above freezing. Tennien watched from a van parked just outside the parking lot when the two guards, soaked and shivering, stepped inside to warm up.

Here was Tennien's opportunity, however risky. He and two agents jumped a fence and sprinted through the rain. As they had rehearsed, they opened the car door with a master key Jaguar had provided and dimmed the overhead lights. The two men huddled in front while Tennien sat in back with a walkie-talkie. He listened for word from lookouts watching for the guards. The men in front struggled to remove the wood-grained dashboard as the rain battered the windows. Tennien held the walkie-talkie to his ear, expecting the call to abandon the car. At last they put the dashboard back in place, concealing a three-inch-long bug capable of transmitting to receivers as far as half a mile away. As the men fled, Tennien mopped up telltale pools of water gathered on the car seats with a rag, then ran back across the parking lot and over the fence.

Around dinnertime on February 25, 1985, FBI agents fanned out across New York City to arrest the nine most prominent leaders of the New York underworld. The sweep included the heads of the five ruling crime families—Gambino, Bonanno, Genovese, Colombo, and Lucchese—along with four underbosses. The FBI timed the arrests for the evening so the nine Mafia leaders would be forced to spend the night in jail; no judge could arraign them until the next morning. (The Gambino underboss, seventy-year-old Aniello Dellacroce, was rushed to Beekman Downtown Hospital after complaining of chest pains. The Bonanno boss, Philip Rastelli, was already in jail.)

The next day Rudolph Giuliani, the US attorney for the Southern District of New York, unsealed a fifteen-count racketeering indictment charging the men with conspiring to commit murder, engage in loan-sharking, gambling, prostitution, and other felonies. He accused them of acting as an all-powerful "crime commission," a shadowy board of directors adjudicating disputes, divvying profits, and orchestrating illicit operations conducted by a collective 25,000 members and associates in the New York area.

At 11:30 A.M. the next day, Giuliani faced a hundred reporters, photographers, and cameramen gathered at a press conference in the federal office building across the street from the United States Courthouse at Foley Square. Television lights shone on Giuliani's ashen complexion. He had worked twenty-seven straight days—long days—leading up to the arrests. He spoke in rapid, lightly lisping phrases, his eyes in nervous motion.

Giuliani told interviewers, and there were many, that he had originally learned of the commission by reading *A Man of Honor,* a memoir written two years earlier by eighty-year-old mob boss Joe Bonanno. Giuliani recognized that Bonanno's description of the commission perfectly matched the "pattern of racketeering activities" that G. Robert Blakey had written into law in 1970.

"We had RICO for almost ten years before we knew what to do with it," FBI director William H. Webster said after the February arrests. This would be the first time the government used RICO to prosecute a major federal case.

Giuliani secured the indictments with roughly a thousand hours of wiretaps, including seventy-five critical hours recorded in the black Jaguar. As Avellino drove Tony "Ducks" Corallo back and forth between Long Island and Brooklyn, Corallo spoke of murder, extortion, and, most important, the workings of the five-man commission.

As a young man, Giuliani had intended to join the priesthood. He looked the part, with his pale, severe expression and monkish bangs. He joined the catechism club at Bishop Loughlin Memorial High School, in Brooklyn, and volunteered to give religious instruction to the underprivileged. His senior year, he visited seminaries with the intention of applying. He had a priest's solemnity but a politician's ambition. The latter prevailed.

As a prosecutor, he conducted himself with a muted intensity. Out of earshot, defense lawyers called him "Eliot Ness with an attitude." Giuliani must have known that busting mobsters was a proven path to political advancement.

At the press conference, Giuliani spoke deliberately, as lawyers do, but reporters inclined to notice such things could read subtle passion at play behind his sober pronouncements. Nobody hated the stain of the Mafia as ardently as an Italian son of Brooklyn, the grandson of immigrants. "It's about time law enforcement got as organized as organized crime," he said.

He was joined by seventeen law enforcement officials, including FBI Director Webster. Unlike many of those standing beside him, Giuliani used the term "Mafia." The Department of Justice had banned the designation since 1970, when Attorney General John Mitchell succumbed to pressure from Italian American groups. Francis Ford Coppola removed "Mafia" from the script for *The Godfather* for the same reason.

Giuliani, however, did not hesitate to say the word out loud. His approach was to attack the Mafia head-on. Nor was he shy about promoting the indictments as a breakthrough in the fifty-year push to bust the mob, a long, mostly ineffectual campaign dating back to Prohibition. "This is a great day for law enforcement," he told reporters. "This is a bad day for the Mafia."

Until now, the government could do no more than prosecute specific crimes committed by mob underlings. As Blakey had illustrated, the associate who pulled the trigger might go to Sing Sing while the boss who ordered the shooting returned unscathed to his home in Bensonhurst or Bath Beach. The higher-ups were immune, beyond reach. Bonavolonta and his circle of FBI friends did their part to make the bureau aware of RICO's benefits. But Giuliani was the first prosecutor to use the statute to strike at the top, not the bottom.

"Our aim is to try to destroy the Mafia and Cosa Nostra," he said on *Good Morning America*. "I think we now have a chance to do that." Blakey agreed, telling reporters, "It's the beginning of the end. The mob is in trouble."

Alan Feuer, a crime reporter for *The New York Times,* called the impending trial "a sort of Waterloo for the New York mob." The government had adapted and evolved. The Mafia had not.

7

THE BOTCHED HIT

AFTER GIULIANI INDICTED HIM, ALONG WITH THE
rest of the commission, Tony Ducks Corallo knew that his long, prosperous run had ended. No more opera, no more gardening.

He would surely land in federal prison, probably for life. In preparation, he convened his top men to form a succession plan: Who would run the Lucchese operations when he was gone?

The obvious choice might have been his underboss, Salvatore "Tom Mix" Santoro, or his consigliere, Christie Tick Furnari, but they too faced charges. Corallo had to reach down the depth chart for a successor.

At the meeting, held at Furnari's Staten Island home, Corallo hinted that he favored forty-three-year-old Gaspipe Casso, which may have surprised his inner circle. Corallo was among the last of the old-fashioned Mafia dons, one of the few who still spoke earnestly and with conviction of the Sicilian virtues of honor and respect. With his chauffeur-driven Jaguar and cardigan sweaters, he came across as a dignified patriarch. By contrast, Casso belonged to a new breed of flashy, freewheeling mobsters who flouted the old ways. He seemed an unlikely choice.

Casso had risen rapidly up the Lucchese ranks, thanks to his facility for audacious moneymaking schemes. He simply earned more—*way* more—than most other capos. Like any flush gangster, he profited from kickbacks and shakedowns but set himself apart by developing a knack for the intricacies of 1980s white-collar crime and other innovative schemes. In partnership with Burt Kaplan, the drug dealer and deviser of illegal stratagems, Casso ran drugs, established elaborate money-laundering methods, and worked with criminal circles in Europe and Africa. It was as if Casso had absorbed by osmosis the lessons of Ivan Boesky and Michael Milken's greed-is-good Wall Street and applied their trickery to the streets of South Brooklyn.

Casso brought to his business arrangements a disposition so violent that even seasoned mafiosi feared him. He was capable of monstrous cruelty, even to his own people. If Casso dreamed an associate had informed on the family, that was sometimes reason enough to order his killing.

Casso filled a power void, as strongmen do. "All of the families are in a state of disintegration," said Ronald Goldstock, director of the State Organized Crime Task Force, "and the instability allows people like Casso to become powerful figures almost overnight."

People who knew Casso by reputation were often surprised by how small he was in person, a sturdy five feet, seven inches, with the hard, muscular build common among Sicilian laborers. He was handsome in the manner of Martin Scorsese's leading men, with steady, dark eyes and the squinty smile of a serpent. He walked the streets of South Brooklyn like a general, with a menacing sneer.

Casso grew up hard among tough men on Union Street, near the Brooklyn docks, where he staved off boredom by shooting hawks midflight from tenement roofs with a .22-caliber rifle and brawled with a street gang known as the Tigers. He inherited his nickname, "Gaspipe," from his father, a longshoreman who kept union dissenters in line with the swing of an industrial pipe. Casso hated the nickname, and often said so, but he allowed friends to call him Gas.

Casso left school at age sixteen to work as a collector for the Lucchese consigliere Christie Tick Furnari, muscling up on welshers and shopkeepers slow to hand over protection money. He ensured by any means necessary that the good citizens of Bensonhurst and Canarsie kicked money up or kicked it back.

In the early 1970s, he committed his first murder on Furnari's orders, luring a small-time Brighton Beach cocaine dealer suspected of ratting to a basement social club on Fifteenth Avenue. Furnari and his entourage waited at an International House of Pancakes while Casso and the drug dealer played cards on a folding table. The game ended when Casso shot his opponent in the head with a .22-caliber handgun equipped with a silencer.

With a murder on his résumé, Casso now qualified to become an official member—a "made man"—in the Lucchese family. With Furnari acting as his sponsor, Casso was taken to a secret location for the induction ceremony. Twenty-two years later, he described the formalities to a congressional committee:

> They have a ceremony with the boss, the consiglieri, and the under-bosses present at the time, and the captain who brings you in. They prick your trigger finger and make it bleed, and then they put it on a little piece of paper. They set it on fire, and you burn it in your hand, and you repeat after them that you will never betray La Cosa Nostra, or you will burn like the paper is burning in your hand. And your life does not belong to you anymore. Your life belongs to them.

Casso's Mafia elders tended to disguise their wealth. Extravagance, they feared, attracted the notice of nosy investigators. In defiance, Casso flaunted his new riches. He wore $2,000 suits to Regine's, a Park Avenue disco, and the Rainbow Room, on the sixty-fifth floor of Rockefeller Plaza, where he paid $1,000 dinner bills, and double that for the evening's wine. On at least one occasion he mixed the wine with Coca-Cola to show that he could do whatever he wanted.

Along the South Brooklyn waterfront, powerboats were becoming a common mob accessory. Casso owned one, of course. Among other things, he used it to converse safely outside FBI surveillance as he cruised the inlets flowing into Jamaica Bay. The agents could not eavesdrop as Casso's twin outboards whined and the wind whipped his black hair.

Corallo and the other old Mafia chiefs frowned on drug trafficking, a dirty business in their minds, better left to Blacks and Puerto Ricans. Drugs invited unwanted complications: narcotics convictions fetched lengthy sentences, which, in turn, motivated offenders to inform on the families. Casso ignored the drug prohibition. In the go-go 1980s, the money hustle eclipsed the old ways. In the underworld, as on Wall Street, profit spoke loudest.

With the inflow of drug proceeds and a scheme to defraud the government of gasoline tax conducted with the Russian Mafia in Brighton Beach, among other stratagems, Casso demonstrated a gift for inventing new forms of revenue, plus a warlike instinct for guarding his interests. He thus had earned consideration as a candidate to replace Corallo as boss of the Luccheses. Casso, however, did not wish to inherit Corallo's throne, despite its stature.

The Lucchese family was smaller than the Gambino and Genovese organizations, but still mustered more than a hundred members, or made men, and nearly a thousand associates spread across the five boroughs and New Jersey. Its rackets reached into scores of industries, including hotels, restaurants, construction, textiles, and private garbage hauling. As boss, Casso would have to administer these operations, plus manage the headstrong egos and petty feuds among his soldiers and capos.

Casso would rather concentrate exclusively on accumulating wealth, on pursuing the big score. In the end, it was agreed that the top position would go instead to Vittorio "Vic" Amuso, a bandy-legged heroin trafficker with a jutting chin who for years had served as Casso's closest associate and criminal partner, despite an eleven-year age gap. And so the question of succession was settled: Amuso would replace Corallo as boss with his friend Casso serving as second-in-command and supervisor of the Lucchese finances.

Amuso might have been the boss, but Casso was the lodestar. "Gaspipe was the brains of the new regime from the start," said Assistant US Attorney Greg O'Connell. "He handled the finances and influenced all critical decisions."

A decade after his induction into the family, Casso assumed a leadership position. He had climbed the ranks without ever serving as a capo.

In fact, he had skipped ahead so fast, thanks to his moneymaking machine, that he lacked the respect and weight a more seasoned mob boss would command. He appeared to be out of his league, or so people thought. It was almost inevitable that someone would test his authority.

On December 16, 1985, the legal scholar G. Robert Blakey attended a New York University Law School dinner in his honor. Ten months earlier, Giuliani had used the RICO laws written and promoted by Blakey to indict the nine Mafia leaders in the Commission Case. Blakey's appearance amounted to a victory lap.

FBI agents, prosecutors, and other law enforcement figures stood holding drinks in plastic cups at the pre-dinner reception. A few minutes before 6 P.M., the room rang with the chirp of pagers. In unison, a few dozen men and women read their messages, then scrambled for pay phones or rushed to the exit. Twenty minutes earlier, Paul Castellano, boss of the Gambino family, was shot in the face and killed along with Thomas Bilotti, his aide-de-camp and bodyguard.

Castellano had gone free on $2 million bail during the Commission trial. Three long, grinding months had passed since the opening arguments. That morning, the judge granted a rare day off. Castellano spent part of the afternoon with his lawyer, James LaRossa. Afterward, he and Bilotti distributed Christmas gifts to the women in LaRossa's office, then headed to Sparks for an early dinner. Christmas lights shone in store windows and shoppers packed the sidewalks as Castellano's black Lincoln crawled through Midtown traffic. Bilotti drove with Castellano beside him. They switched on the overhead lights while stopped at Third Avenue, within sight of the restaurant.

John Gotti, a forty-five-year-old capo from Howard Beach, and an associate, Sammy "The Bull" Gravano, saw the overhead light blink on from a parked car a few feet away. Gravano picked up a walkie-talkie to alert four gunmen dressed in long light-colored trench coats and fur hats standing in pairs on either side of the Sparks awning. "They're coming through," Gravano said.

The Lincoln crossed Third Avenue and stopped at the restaurant door. Bilotti cut the engine and hurried from the driver's seat. As Castellano clambered from the passenger seat, the four gunmen stepped forward, revolvers drawn. "The shots rang out in the night air," Gravano recalled. "People were running, screaming, falling, scrambling to get away."

Castellano collapsed to the sidewalk on his left side, still clutching a black leather glove in his right hand. Blood trickled from his ears, nose, and mouth. Bilotti lay on his back in the middle of the sidewalk, splayed like a snow angel. The gunmen hustled east toward getaway cars waiting on Second Avenue.

Castellano was buried four days later, in a Staten Island cemetery. Cardinal John J. O'Connor refused to grant him a public funeral mass or burial in consecrated ground.

John Gotti, the architect of Castellano's assassination, headed a rough-edged upstart Gambino faction based in Ozone Park, an Italian American neighborhood beneath Kennedy Airport's landing path. His crew operated from the Bergin Hunt and Fish Club, a handful of bare rooms in a dumpy brick building with an incongruously small window. It had a fortified look designed to ward off casual visitors.

Gotti had sent substantial sums up the chain to Castellano, as Mafia protocol required. Castellano, in turn, rewarded Gotti by appointing him capo of the Bergin crew and buying him a Lincoln Town Car. Castellano's generosity did not stop Gotti from griping. He resented how Castellano used the Gambino family's union connections to expropriate easy millions for himself while street operatives like Gotti shouldered the work of hijacking trucks and collecting loan shark payments.

Unlike Castellano, Gotti mixed easily with the frontline street associates, feeding them enormous catered meals of spaghetti and sausage at the Hunt and Fish Club. He laid the groundwork for his coup by spreading half-serious rumors that Castellano was impotent, and hinted to the twenty-two family capos that he might make a better, more equitable family boss.

On Christmas Eve, FBI agents huddled in a surveillance van parked on Mulberry Street, in Little Italy, saw passersby kiss Gotti on both cheeks. They took the well-wishing as confirmation that Gotti had replaced Castellano as boss of the Gambinos, the largest mob family in the country.

Unlike Castellano, who discreetly conducted business from his home on Todt Hill, Gotti fashioned himself as a throwback boss in the flamboyant style of Lucky Luciano or Al Capone. Flanked by a praetorian guard of toughs, he rolled into Sign of the Dove, an Upper East Side restaurant, with the elegance of a python. He wore double-breasted suits, silk ties, and a diamond pinkie ring, occasionally making *tsk-tsk* gestures at detectives watching him from parked cars. He made himself a boldface name and the smirking face of underworld defiance.

Months before he died splayed on the sidewalk, Paul Castellano had received a warning from Gaspipe Casso, who claimed that a short, dog-faced Gambino associate, Angelo "Quack Quack" Ruggiero, was an informant. Casso may have told the truth, or he may simply have tried to dispatch Ruggiero after years of mounting animosity. "They hated each other," said Gravano. "It was impossible to get them to sit down together." In any case, Castellano dismissed Casso's contention: Ruggiero, he concluded, was loyal. But Castellano refused to grant Ruggiero permission to strike back at Casso for his slander.

Now, with Castellano gone and Gotti installed in his place, Ruggiero was free to retaliate against Casso. With his close friend Gotti's blessing, Ruggiero asked his trusted friend Michael "Mickey Boy" Paradiso to stage a counterstrike. Paradiso, in turn, delegated the job to an underling named Jimmy Hydell.

Jimmy was a light-haired twenty-six-year-old minor league Gambino associate, a junior bully boy with a ragtag crew and an eager gun, who lived with his parents and three siblings on a block of nearly identical two-story peak-roofed houses on Bangor Street in Staten Island. He might have been described as handsome, except for a constellation of acne scars.

Jimmy typified the wannabes loitering in the outer orbit of crime families hoping to prove themselves by taking on the grimmest assignments, no matter how dangerous or foolhardy. Assassinating Casso qualified as both.

To his sister Lizzie, Jimmy "was a sweetheart. He went out of his way to help people. To this day I run into people who say they loved him. But there was definitely something wrong with him. He was always in trouble, and he was obsessive about girls." So obsessive that his aunt urged Jimmy's mother, Betty, to seek medical help for what appeared to be a serious emotional disorder.

Jimmy treated his pretty longtime girlfriend, twenty-seven-year-old Annette DiBiasi, "like gold," Lizzie said. He did chores around the two-story brick house on Bay Seventh Street that she shared with her widowed mother, and he built a backyard shrine to the Virgin Mary in memory of DiBiasi's late father. "He gave her whatever she wanted," Lizzie said. "He put her on a pedestal."

The couple broke up and reunited, over and over. They got engaged and called it off. When DiBiasi's affection strayed, as it sometimes did, an unhinged form of jealousy overcame Jimmy. He watched her house, as a stalker might, and threatened the men she dated. "She liked to go out with a lot of guys," Lizzie Hydell said.

In April 1986, Jimmy accused Annette of having an affair with a married man. They argued. Hydell kidnapped her and kept her handcuffed in a Brooklyn apartment. She escaped and pressed charges. Annette described the abduction to a grand jury, but the jurors elected not to indict Jimmy. He was exonerated, but the prospect of his ex-girlfriend talking to the authorities spooked Jimmy.

Whatever Jimmy's jealousy or resentment toward Annette, a hardworking young Brooklyn woman with a swirl of big eighties hair and a widowed mother, he also had a practical reason to wish her gone: in his world, those who spoke to law enforcement earned what they got. She knew too much about his criminal history.

Jimmy called on his friend Bob Bering to help silence DiBiasi. The two had met some years earlier, while Hydell was held in a Brooklyn jail on a gun charge. Bering was a big, bearded, rough-edged former transit cop in his forties, nicknamed "the Bear." The two teamed up for a string of drug deals, hijackings, car thefts, and at least two murders. "Bob Bering moved to Staten Island and got an apartment down the block from where we lived," Lizzie Hydell said, "and that was when all hell broke loose."

At 9:30 A.M. on April 30, 1986—two days after she spoke to the grand jury—DiBiasi was walking the three hundred feet on Bay Seventh Street separating her home from her new secretarial job at a mortgage consultancy where she was training to process home loans. Before DiBiasi reached her office door, Bering and Hydell yanked her into a red Thunderbird with a white top. Hydell raped her, then shot her in the head five times with a .22. They wrapped her naked body in a tarp and dumped it in a shallow grave in a wooded area near a gloomy motel on the West Shore Expressway in Staten Island. They shoveled dirt on her and threw plywood over the grave to disguise its location. Problem solved. As Bering drove the car away, Hydell cut up DiBiasi's clothes and the contents of her wallet with a pair of scissors and tossed them out the window.

DiBiasi's family offered a $2,000 reward for information about her disappearance. Nothing helped. They would wait ten months to learn her fate. In the meantime, Hydell made himself available for assignments from the Gambino higher-ups, including the brazen job of assassinating Gaspipe Casso.

Five months later, on the balmy late-summer evening of September 14, 1986, Gaspipe Casso ate Sunday dinner with his wife, Lillian, and their teenagers, Jolene and Anthony Junior, at their one-story brick home on East Seventy-Second Street in the Bergen Beach section of Brooklyn.

Bergen Beach is one in a series of South Brooklyn neighborhoods strung along the Belt Parkway, a highway running along the scruffy shore of Jamaica Bay. Here, on the southern outskirts of New York City, the streets were lined with split-level homes fronted by tiny driveways and postage-stamp lawns, as if residents wished to squeeze suburban niceties onto their small lots. Together these districts—Bergen Beach, Mill Basin, Flatlands, Bensonhurst—formed an Italian American homeland of sorts, a bulwark against the surging populations of immigrants and newcomers. This was the fertile crescent of organized crime.

The family finished dinner around 6:45. Afterward, Casso stepped out between the two white columns fronting his home and drove his tan Lincoln Town Car a block north to the Golden Ox, a neighborhood restaurant in a strip mall situated on a triangular plot where Veterans Avenue intersects Avenue U at an oblique angle. He had arranged to meet an acquaintance about a scheme to cash stolen checks.

The Commission trial had started six days earlier in Federal District Court in Lower Manhattan. It was a season of anxiety and uncertainty for Casso, as it was for nearly everyone he knew. Mafiosi talked about the need to "watch your mirrors," a shorthand term for heightened street awareness. All five crime families tensed under the double threat of RICO laws and a growing number of informants hidden in their ranks.

Casso made it a habit to vary his routes with detours and looping turns in order to throw off anyone—police or mob—who might follow him. He ran red lights. He swerved across lanes.

As he made his way east along Veterans Avenue past St. Bernard Parish, he indeed watched his mirrors. He cruised slowly past the Golden Ox, scanning the street, then made a U-turn and parked. Casso walked to a Carvel ice cream store in the strip mall and bought a cone. He ate it in the Lincoln while he waited.

Casso's contact did not come: the meeting was a ploy, an ambush. Instead, a Plymouth Fury with tinted windows pulled up to the driver's side of Casso's Lincoln. Inside, Jimmy Hydell and two sidekicks, Bob Bering and Nicky Guido, prepared themselves. The barrel of a pump-action 12-gauge shotgun emerged from an open window. Lead shots pockmarked the Lincoln's flank like a naval broadside. The Lincoln's driver's-side window shattered and fell to the cement. Casso dropped the cone. He slumped down and reached for the handgun he kept under the driver's seat. With his head lowered, he slid to the passenger seat and pushed his way out. He crouched momentarily on the far side of the Lincoln, in the relative safety of its cover, then bolted, hunched over, for the Golden Ox.

Two shooters stood in the parking lot firing the shotgun and a 9-millimeter handgun. Bullets smashed the restaurant's glass door as Casso entered. Diners looked up from plates of veal and shrimp scampi to see Casso stumble in. He was bleeding from two shots lodged in his left shoulder. As he ran through the dining room, he grabbed a tablecloth and pressed it to his wound. In the back, by the kitchen, he limped down a flight of stairs to a basement where he hid inside a massive walk-in refrigerator used to store platters of food for catered events.

Casso sat on a barrel, bleeding and cold. He waited for someone to find him, either the shooters or police. When neither showed up, he clambered back upstairs, slipped out a back door, and walked to a pay phone on Avenue U to call his friend Vic Amuso. "Jesus H. Christ, what happened?" Amuso asked.

Amuso drove Casso two miles to Kings County Hospital, where he told doctors that robbers had shot him. He allowed nurses to clean and dress his wounds, but he stopped doctors from extracting the slugs. He did not want police to collect evidence. He wished to do the investigating. "He's not cooperating," a detective told reporters. "He's very evasive. He says he went out to buy ice cream." The hospital released Casso to Lillian's care. The next day a surgeon known for discretion—a mob doctor—removed the slugs with forceps.

Aside from physical pain, Casso suffered embarrassment. The attack was an affront to his new authority as underboss. In the following weeks, the hunted became the hunter. As Casso convalesced at home, he began gathering information about his assassins.

He turned for help to Burt Kaplan, his partner in the drug trade and half a dozen other illegal ventures, who, as it happened, now had useful ties to Eppolito and Caracappa. "I told Casso that my friend Frank's [Santora's] cousin worked in that precinct," Kaplan later said. "He was a good guy and could probably help us" find Casso's attackers.

At this point, Kaplan had not actually met Eppolito and Caracappa. He didn't even know their names. His friend Frank Santora would work directly with them while Kaplan and Casso stayed in the background. Kaplan preferred it this way. He would keep all parties anonymous, compartmentalize them, in case one or more later became informants.

At first Casso was reluctant to hire the detectives. If they had betrayed the NYPD, might they also betray him? Kaplan assured Casso that Santora's cousin and his friend "had done something for [Kaplan] and that [Casso] could trust them." The "something" was the abduction and murder of Israel Greenwald. So Casso agreed to hire them.

Kaplan forwarded the request to Santora, who relayed it to his cousin Eppolito and Eppolito's partner, Caracappa. A few weeks later, Kaplan received a manila envelope containing a police report listing the men police identified as the assassins, along with their home addresses. An off-duty policeman had witnessed their getaway and noted the make and model of their car, along with their license plate number. "I opened [the envelope] and looked inside," Kaplan said, "and there was a picture of Jimmy Hydell." He walked the envelope over to Casso, who was holding court that day at a Thirteenth Avenue social club.

The detectives refused payment for delivering the envelope. Santora said the confidential police information was "a gift from my cousin and his partner. This is just to show you the kind of things that they would do. . . . My cousin and his partner won't take any money for something where somebody close to us got hurt. We're not that kind of people."

Casso knew his would-be assassin, Jimmy Hydell, in passing, the way a general might notice a wayward lieutenant. A year earlier, Casso was in the 19th Hole Bar when the owner of a Chinese restaurant two doors down the block complained that Jimmy was shaking him down for protection payments, and that Jimmy's snarling dog, a Doberman pinscher named Cult, scared his customers.

The Lucchese men did not tolerate disruptions on their turf, particularly those caused by a flunky loosely linked to another crime family. A pugnacious Lucchese soldier named Angelo Defendis, a retired Golden Gloves champion, pulled Jimmy from the restaurant. He stood on the street berating Jimmy. Every time Defendis gestured at Jimmy,

Cult lunged. Casso came over and told Jimmy to subdue his dog, or else. Jimmy ignored him. Casso then retrieved a pistol from the 19th Hole. He attached a silencer and shot the dog twice in the head. He told Jimmy to put Cult in his trunk and leave.

Now, a year later, Casso, communicating through Kaplan and Santora, hired Eppolito and Caracappa to deliver Hydell to him. Casso "asked me to call my friends to see if they can arrest [Hydell] and turn him over," Kaplan said, "not to kill him, to kidnap him. He wanted him alive."

On the morning of October 18, 1986, Eppolito and Caracappa drove a stolen black Plymouth Fury, a classic cop car, to the Hydell house on Staten Island. As with Israel Greenwald, the detectives had retrieved the address from police records, along with the model and plate number of Jimmy's car.

Jimmy wasn't home that morning. He had left his car behind, a gray Lincoln, so that his younger brother, Frankie, could drive to his job at a bagel shop on Avenue M in Brooklyn. Minutes after Frankie departed in Jimmy's Lincoln, he returned home and told their mother, Betty, that two detectives had stopped him. "They tried to grab me," he told Betty. "They thought I was Jimmy."

It was not unusual for the police to come by the Hydell house looking for Jimmy since his girlfriend, Annette, had disappeared six months earlier. The police had yet to find her body. Jimmy, of course, was a prime suspect. "We just thought Jimmy did something," his sister Lizzie said, "and they're watching him again."

Frankie took his mother outside. They could see the detectives drive down Bridgetown Street, three houses away. The driver looked right at them. The car passed by twice more.

Betty told Frankie to drive around the block to see if the detectives followed. They did. Meanwhile, Betty drove her own car around the opposite way. She stopped as she approached the detectives coming toward her. "I pulled up right next to them," she said. "There were two men sitting in the front." One detective was overweight, with a necklace, the other reed thin, with a mustache.

Betty lowered her window. "I asked who they were," she later said. "The driver pulled out a badge. I said, 'You should let people know who you are and what you are doing.'" None of your business, the fat detective said. Police business, he added.

By coincidence, Frankie Hydell had spotted the two detectives crossing the Verrazzano-Narrows Bridge a short time later as he was driving to the bagel shop. He watched as their Fury took the first exit and headed to Bath Beach, the Brooklyn neighborhood where Frank's brother, Jimmy, would spend the day.

At about 2:30 that afternoon, Jimmy called home from a pay phone at Bay Eighth Street. He told his sister Linda that he would return for dinner. He mentioned that he had parked another car two blocks from the 19th Hole Bar. "Jimmy knew something was up because he put a change of clothes in the car," his sister Lizzie said. "He said, 'If you find the car and the clothes are still there you know I never made it back to the car.'"

Jimmy planned to sit down that day with Mickey Boy Paradiso, the Gambino capo who had hired him to shoot Casso. They were to meet at a hot dog stand near a softball field at the edge of Dyker Beach Park. Jimmy worried that Paradiso would kill him to prevent him from blabbing about the failed hit. For his own protection, Jimmy asked his friend Bob Bering to alert the Sixty-Second Precinct to his meeting with Paradiso. A discreet police presence might provide a measure of protection. In any case, Paradiso didn't show up. Eppolito and Caracappa intercepted him instead.

It is not known how Eppolito and Caracappa located Jimmy. Bering called Jimmy's position in to the Sixty-Second Precinct, as instructed. Precinct detectives may have relayed the tip to Eppolito's brother-in-law, Detective Al Guarneri, since he was investigating Annette DiBiasi's disappearance and would therefore have had interest in Jimmy. Guarneri was home that day but he may, in turn, have forwarded Jimmy's location to Eppolito.

In any case, Eppolito and Caracappa acted as if they were taking Jimmy into police custody. They flashed their badges, handcuffed him, and put him in the back seat. Jimmy probably thought they would question him about DiBiasi, which he may have welcomed as sanctuary from Mickey Boy Paradiso.

Whatever relief Jimmy felt did not last. As with Israel Greenwald eight months earlier, Jimmy must have come to a sickening awareness that he faced abduction, not arrest, when the detectives drove him to Peter Franzone's garage on Nostrand Avenue. Santora was waiting for them. The three men laid Jimmy on the ground, tied his feet and hands, taped his mouth, and muscled him into the trunk of Santora's car.

Eppolito and Caracappa had offered to kill Jimmy, but Casso saved the job for himself. He wanted to hear directly from Hydell who had ordered the assassination at the Golden Ox, and who besides Jimmy had participated.

Santora drove ahead with Hydell in the trunk while Eppolito and Caracappa followed a short distance behind. As detectives, they could intercede if Santora was stopped for any reason. Along the way, Santora could hear Jimmy yelling and kicking in the back. He parked and pummeled Jimmy into submission.

Kaplan and Casso were waiting when Santora pulled into a narrow parking lot behind a Toys"R"Us off the Belt Parkway, as arranged. Kaplan took the car keys from his friend Santora and handed them to Casso. Twenty-two days had passed since Jimmy took aim at Casso outside the Golden Ox.

Casso asked about the two men waiting beside their car at the far end of the parking lot—a fat guy with gold chains and a skinny guy in a dark suit. Eppolito and Caracappa stood about a hundred yards away, observing the transaction. Santora explained that the detectives had followed him in case he encountered a problem. Until now, Santora had acted as the sole intermediary. Casso and Kaplan had not yet met the detectives.

Casso drove the unmarked car with its bound and gagged cargo, through residential neighborhoods of dog walkers and leaf rakers, past bodegas and homebound schoolchildren. He pulled into a garage attached to a house on East Seventy-Third Street in Canarsie. The house belonged to Jimmy Gallo, an associate in the DeCavalcante crime family in New Jersey. He had loaned Casso the use of his house while he was away on vacation.

By Casso's account, he opened the trunk. Jimmy lay inside, bleeding and handcuffed behind his back. "The kid saw me and he knew it was over," Casso said. "That's the rules."

Casso removed him, largely by pulling him by his hair, and dragged him to a wood-lined windowless basement, where he had unfurled a plastic tarp. Casso proceeded slowly and deliberately as a man accustomed to casual cruelties. He cut Jimmy's clothes off with a knife, then pulled out a black .22 automatic fitted with a silencer. As a boy Casso had earned a reputation as a marksman, a skill honed by shooting birds from rooftops. He now took aim and shot Jimmy in the left kneecap, then his right. He proceeded the way a sadistic child might torture an insect. Working his way downward, he shot Jimmy in both shins, both feet. He shot into his shoulders, elbows, and wrists. "Maybe I shot him ten times, twelve times," he later said. "It could have been fifteen." He then took aim and shot Jimmy in the penis.

Casso reloaded and went to work on the soft tissue, firing into the biceps, thighs, and calves. Casso avoided shooting Jimmy in the head. "I was in somebody's house," he later said. "I didn't want to make a mess."

Casso chose this moment to go upstairs and leave Jimmy to suffer alone in the dark basement. When Casso returned, he asked Jimmy who had ordered the assassination. "I wanted to know why I was shot," Casso said, "and who . . . gave the orders to shoot me."

By now Jimmy had given up all resistance. He told Casso who ordered the ambush: Mickey Boy Paradiso, on the direction of Gambino leadership. Casso sent a reliable Lucchese associate to invite Gambino boss John Gotti to the basement to hear Jimmy confess their treachery. Gotti refused, but to avoid an all-out war he sent two trusted captains, Joseph "Joe Butch" Corrao and Jack "Good Looking" Giordano.

The Gambino emissaries came downstairs, where Jimmy lay bleeding. Jimmy repeated for the two capos what he'd told Casso: Gotti had sanctioned the hit on Casso. They, in turn, claimed Gotti had nothing to do with it and backed out of the basement spouting denials and disavowals.

By now Jimmy knew he would die. He begged Casso to dump his body out on Seventy-Third Street. Without a body his mother, Betty, would not be able to collect on his $500,000 life insurance policy. Casso refused. Hydell's body was never found.

Naturally, Betty worried when Jimmy did not come home for dinner that night, as promised. He was a mama's boy who reliably called home, even on the night of his short-lived engagement, when he spent the night in a motel with DiBiasi. "We thought maybe he was just laying low somewhere," his sister Lizzie said. "But he and my mother were so close that when he didn't call we knew there was problem."

By the next morning, Jimmy's family expected the worst. "He never did that before," Betty Hydell later said. "He always came home." Betty had the presence of mind to write down the license plate number of the car driven by the two detectives who had watched her house. She worked at a car insurance company, so she was able to enter the number into the Department of Motor Vehicles database. The plate number, she found, did not match the car. Could they have driven a stolen car? "I just assumed they were undercover cops," she said. But now she didn't know who they were. Betty called Jimmy's friends. Nobody had seen him. Nobody knew his whereabouts.

Betty suspected the two detectives, or whoever they were, of snatching her son, but they had otherwise performed a faultless abduction. They had delivered Jimmy to Casso efficiently and without incident. In the process, they had shown how valuable they might be as Casso fortified himself against the pressures of the oncoming RICO indictments and the resulting rush of Lucchese informants eager to switch their allegiance to the Department of Justice.

8

A TIME OF DISORDER

AT 12:20 P.M. ON NOVEMBER 19, 1986, IN A HUSHED courtroom in Federal District Court in Lower Manhattan, a thin forewoman in a red blouse stood to announce the jury's verdict in the Commission Case. It would take her twenty-eight minutes and a full cup of water to say the word "guilty" one hundred and fifty-one times as the court clerk read the charges.

After ten weeks of testimony and six days of deliberations, the jury convicted eight Mafia principals on all charges, including Tony Ducks Corallo, the Lucchese boss, and his deputies, Tom Mix Santoro and Christie Tick Furnari. (The roster of defendants was reduced by one after Gambino boss Paul Castellano died on the sidewalk outside Sparks Steak House.) The eight surviving defendants stood at the defense table and received the verdict without tic or tremor. Only the jury forewoman brushed away tears.

Marshals escorted the men to their temporary quarters on the ninth floor of the Metropolitan Correctional Center, a rust-colored federal lockup sandwiched between the Church of St. Andrew and police headquarters, where they opened a smuggled bottle of red wine. They raised their glasses in a traditional Sicilian toast. *Cent'anni!* May you live a hundred years. They laughed. They knew they would have to live longer than that to see their release.

They were right. Two months later, a judge sentenced the three top bosses and four underlings to a hundred years each, saying he intended to send a "statement to those out there who are undoubtedly thinking about taking the reins of power."

The conviction and sentencing shook the family structure that had sustained organized crime since Lucky Luciano installed the Commission in the 1930s. "This has been the Mafia's worst year," Rudy Giuliani said. "We keep making gains and they keep getting moved backward."

The family bosses had imposed order on the underworld. Without them the ancient regulations and decorum of La Cosa Nostra were in danger of fracturing and falling away. "This is the twilight of the mob," said G. Robert Blakey, author of the RICO laws. "I don't see how the mob can survive this set of prosecutions."

Forty-two years earlier, the mob boss Lepke Buchalter walked from death row to the electric chair in Sing Sing. He might have negotiated a deal to save his life, but he chose not to. He would rather die than break the code of silence. Buchalter's brand of ironbound loyalty was fraying under the crackdown of the 1980s. As federal prosecutors closed in, a growing list of mafiosi made a strategic decision to put self before "family": they cast aside the much-romanced creed of omertà and enrolled as government informants.

In most cases, defectors chose to cut deals after an aggressive campaign of electronic surveillance produced damning evidence against them. Wiseguys had always accepted modest prison stints as an occupational hazard, but the stringent new RICO sentencing guidelines could send them away for life.

If RICO was the stick, the Witness Protection Program was the carrot. In 1970, along with RICO, Congress created the program to guarantee cooperators a safe escape for themselves and their families—new names, new homes, new jobs. For the first time, mafiosi could flip with some assurance of survival.

When dominions fall, blood and chaos often follow. For the mob-heavy neighborhoods of South Brooklyn, the late 1980s became a time of disorder and realignment, friendships betrayed and allegiances broken.

The Lucchese family, in particular, became a house divided, an organization neatly split between informers and those informed on.

Into the disarray strode Gaspipe Casso, an opportunist conveniently armed with a secret asset: a pair of detectives willing to act as his ears inside law enforcement and do his bidding on the streets. He referred to the detectives as his crystal ball, in part because he didn't know their names. At this stage, only the intermediary Frank Santora knew their identities.

Within the police department, Eppolito was hard to miss. He commanded attention with his boasts and braying vulgarities. By contrast, Caracappa was almost mute. He was soft-spoken but effectual in his quiet authority. By the early 1980s, he had moved on to the Eighty-Fourth Precinct in downtown Brooklyn, where fellow detectives found him highly capable, but oddly solitary and awkwardly removed from station house camaraderie. "He was going through a nasty divorce," said Detective Chuck Siriano. "I started to become really concerned about him because he was living in his mother's basement. On our swing days, or days off, I was always calling him to see what he was doing. He'd say, 'I'm in the basement watching TV.' He was a good guy, but people thought of him as strange."

Siriano also found Caracappa to be fixated on underworld manners. He could mimic Mafia speech patterns with disturbing fluency. He put on a masterly undercover performance, for example, while impersonating a hit man discussing terms with a customer who wanted his wife killed. "We arranged for Steve to meet the husband on the street," Siriano said. "I was in a van videotaping the meeting. Steve was wired so I could hear him negotiating the terms. The guy said to Steve, 'Listen, she's got to disappear. I don't want her body found.' So Steve says, 'That's going to cost you extra.' So the guy says, 'Why is it going to cost me more? She's dead.' So Steve says, 'What do you think, I eat them? I've got to get rid of the bodies, so it will cost you more money.' Steve was *very* convincing. I was almost sure he was going to actually shoot the wife."

At the Eighty-Fourth Precinct, Caracappa worked closely with Sergeant Jack Hart, a chain-smoking, upstanding cop of the old persuasion. When Hart advanced to the Major Case Squad, Caracappa went with him. "Caracappa was very well-connected," said Detective Siriano, who also moved to the Major Case Squad. "He knew a lot of bosses and he played his role really well."

The Major Case Squad was an all-star detective team housed on the eleventh floor of One Police Plaza. A bank of detectives seated at standard-issue metal desks investigated the kinds of cases that made headlines—hijackings, commercial burglaries, bank robberies, and other high-profile crimes.

Caracappa distinguished himself as steady and ever competent. He was reliably the first to arrive, at about 7 A.M., dressed in an expensive-looking suit. Every morning he removed his suit jacket, brushed it, and hung it up neatly. He carefully rolled the sleeves of his white dress shirt exactly twice to prevent the cuffs from rubbing against the desk. "If I came in early, I'd always see Steve at his desk, the only one in the office, reading *The New York Times*," said Detective Joe Piraino. "When he saw me, he'd cock his head and say, 'What are you doing in so early?' It was like he was saying I'd interrupted him. I'd say, 'Steve, I work here.' [. . .] He acted like I was an outsider whom he didn't trust."

One day in the mid-1980s, a *New York Post* reporter called Chief of Detectives Robert Colangelo to ask about a mob murder. Colangelo knew nothing about the case, and was forced to say so. In the wake of that embarrassment, he formed a subset of the Major Case Squad, called the Organized Crime Homicide Unit, to spot patterns of mob activity and help precinct detectives investigate murders. They also liaised with the FBI, DEA, and other federal agencies. Every detective in the new unit was assigned a crime family. By choice or coincidence, Caracappa monitored the Lucchese family, the same family that secretly employed him.

Caracappa arrived at One Police Plaza before normal work hours to compile updates from the squad detectives into a single report that he sent upstairs to Chief Colangelo by 10 each morning. In this way he established himself as the conduit of all intelligence. Every fact and detail came through him, the self-appointed conservator of records and information.

"Even though he wasn't the boss, he kind of acted like one," said Detective Piraino. "He prided himself on being the point man. All the information would come to him."

In the late 1980s, the Major Case Squad shared a single neglected computer parked outside a captain's office. Almost nobody used it, aside from Detective Siriano, who filled time between murders by laboriously typing up a database of more than five hundred organized crime figures.

Caracappa didn't need a computer. He could easily run license plate numbers by consulting Department of Motor Vehicles records. He could also call downstairs to the Bureau of Criminal Investigation, on the ninth floor, and request arrest records, warrants, and aliases associated with any name. Caracappa did not hesitate to abuse his access. In June 1985, he ran the name of his fiancée, Monica Singleton, to see if she had withheld misdeeds from him. She had not. (He had met her after she called in a complaint. The call came to Detective Siriano but, mindful that his friend Caracappa was a lonely divorcé, he handed the case off to him. "She sounded cute," Siriano said. Caracappa went to her apartment and took down the details. He drove her to an appointment. He called her for months before she agreed to a date. They eventually married.)

More sensitive police intelligence, such as imminent raids, wiretap locations, surveillance photos, and the identities of confidential informants, crossed Caracappa's desk when he assembled daily reports for Chief Colangelo. He was therefore well positioned to respond when Casso wished to track down Nicky Guido, a Gambino associate with a mustache and a helmet of dark hair whom Eppolito and Caracappa had identified as an accomplice in the botched ambush outside the Golden Ox restaurant.

Guido knew that he and Jimmy Hydell had made a ruinous mistake by allowing Casso to run into the restaurant for safety that evening. "How could you let [Casso] live?" Bobby Farenga, a cocaine dealer, asked Guido after the failed assassination. "If you were going to shoot him, you should have made sure you were going to kill him. . . . If I need anybody killed it definitely would not be you that I would ask."

Guido explained that his gun jammed. By the time he cleared it, Casso had vanished into the Golden Ox. "Nicky," Farenga said, "I would have drove the car through the restaurant."

Guido was a big, savage-looking twenty-nine-year-old junior thief recruited as a strong arm, a heavy. He had no criminal record, and was therefore hard to track down. On November 11, 1986, Caracappa retrieved the scant details about Guido available to him through police resources. He then passed the information to Eppolito's cousin, Frank Santora, who forwarded it to the second intermediary, the drug dealer Burt Kaplan, who in turn gave it to Casso. Like many underworld arrangements, the method was roundabout and indecipherable to outsiders.

This would be their way of working for the next five years: with Santora and Kaplan acting as go-betweens, Caracappa and Eppolito could send Casso proprietary police information without meeting him in person. Kaplan segregated everyone for security. The arrangement also gave Kaplan a measure of control over Casso, a dangerous man known to turn on his own.

The supply chain of information Kaplan devised usually worked, but not in the case of Nicky Guido. What went wrong is not entirely clear.

According to Kaplan, Eppolito demanded an extra $4,000 for Guido's home address. Casso found the demand greedy, especially since he had paid the detectives a $5,000 bonus for kidnapping Jimmy Hydell. Casso later said that he rebuffed them and retrieved Guido's address from a contact within Brooklyn Union Gas, a utility company, though that proved not to be true.

Whatever the particulars, Casso obtained an address for a Nicky Guido, but it turned out to be the wrong Guido. The two Nickys could easily be confused: they were within three years in age and lived in adjacent Brooklyn neighborhoods.

By now Casso had assigned the job of assassinating Guido to George

"Georgie Neck" Zappola, a Lucchese associate who spent his days watching sports in Brooklyn bars and sitting for massages and pedicures at Bruno's Hair Salon in Bensonhurst. (Ten years later, Zappola would cause a stir by bribing a guard with $1,000 in clothing-store credit to help smuggle vials of his sperm out of the Metropolitan Detention Center in Brooklyn, in hopes of impregnating his girlfriend.) Zappolo in turn recruited Frank "Big Frank" Lastorino, a Lucchese hit man, and Joseph Testa, part of the crew Roy DeMeo employed to kill and dismember bodies at the Gemini Lounge.

Nicky Guido, an innocent and unsuspecting twenty-six-year-old now erroneously marked for death, spent Christmas Day at his parents' three-story brick row house in Windsor Terrace. He was by all accounts a likable young man. He dated neighborhood girls, bowled with friends, and played on a softball team. He worked a decent job installing phone lines, but had recently applied to the fire department. He was, his brother Mike said, "a beautiful, hardworking kid. A dream of a brother and son."

Guido's mother, Pauline, had served her customary Christmas manicotti that day to a family gathering, as she always did. Afterward, while Pauline washed dishes, Guido stepped outside to show his uncle Tony his car, a bright red Nissan Maxima he had bought two months earlier. He wore a white baseball jacket, a gift from a friend. He and his uncle sat side by side admiring the dashboard controls when two men in leather jackets and knit caps got out of a Cadillac and walked up Seventeenth Street. They drew guns and fired twice, through the windshield and a side window. Guido threw himself across his uncle to protect him. Moments later, the uncle dislodged himself and ran inside, wailing that two men had shot Nicky.

Pauline dashed out to find blood splattered on her son's white jacket. His left leg dangled from the open car door with the toe of his white sneaker barely touching the asphalt. "He was sitting at the wheel," she said. "I went to touch his hand, and he must have just died. His fingertips were cold."

Guido was buried inside the gates of Green-Wood Cemetery, three blocks from where he died. "We never had another real Christmas," said Mike Guido. "We've gone through the motions, but it's never been the same." Instead, Pauline went to Green-Wood Cemetery at Christmas to visit her son's grave.

"They tell me that there is no word in the English language to describe a parent who loses a child," she wrote to Mayor Michael Bloomberg in 2006, twenty years after the shooting. "If you lose your parents, you are an orphan but there is no word for what I became when I lost my son."

The family accepted the death as a tragic case of mistaken identity, but some neighbors did not. The talk at Farrell's Bar and the American Legion Post clung to suspicions. "There was always gossip that we were involved in organized crime, or Nicky specifically, and that kind of tainted the family," said Nicky's uncle, Joe Carbonaro, a Staten Island detective.

Nicky's father never recovered from the heartbreak. "My father stopped eating, stopped caring," said Mike Guido. "He died the same day as my brother. It just took him three years to stop breathing." Gabe Guido was buried in Green-Wood Cemetery beside his son.

Guido's mother kept Nicky's room just as he had left it on Christmas Day. For the rest of her life, she would blame herself for naming him after his maternal grandfather, in the Italian tradition. "She used to say, 'Had I not given him that name, he'd still be alive,'" according to her niece Louise Carbonaro.

Casso shrugged when asked about the death of a guiltless man. "Hey, it's a mistake," he told an interviewer some years later. "No big deal."

Casso did not let the botched Guido assassination slow his campaign of revenge. It was clear by now that he intended to systematically execute all those who had fired on him in the Golden Ox parking lot. The list included Bob Bering, Jimmy Hydell's friend and criminal partner. He should not have been hard to find. The envelope that Eppolito and Caracappa gave Kaplan, and that Kaplan forwarded to Casso, contained Bering's name, photograph, and home address.

Casso drove to Bering's apartment in a dreary Band-Aid-colored housing complex on Daffodil Lane, in Staten Island, but Bering never showed up. Bering's biography does not suggest a shrewd man, but he was street smart enough to not be found.

Casso wasn't the only one trying to find Bering. An informant told Larry Holland, an NYPD detective working as an investigator in the Brooklyn DA's office, and FBI agents Marvin Tolly and Neil Moran, who collaborated on mob investigations, that Casso was looking for Bering with the intention to kill him. Bering would be a prime candidate to flip, if they could find him before Casso.

The trio of investigators learned that Bering and Jimmy Hydell had quickly repainted the Thunderbird used to pick up Annette DiBiasi on the morning of her death. Holland, Tolly, and Moran guessed that the killers would have hired Earl Scheib, a chain of auto shops specializing in low-cost overnight work. They judged its franchise on Neptune Avenue, in Coney Island, a likely choice. When they asked to see the accounts of recent work, the manager said he had, by coincidence, just thrown them in a dumpster. The three men tipped the dumpster over and combed through the mounds of paperwork. Eventually, after narrowing the pile of records down by date, they plucked a receipt signed by Bering. It showed that he had dropped off a red-and-white Thunderbird, the exact model and color of the car used to abduct DiBiasi. On April 30, 1986, Bering picked the car up, now painted black. The receipt clearly implicated Bering. "It was like hitting the lotto," Tolly said.

An informant gave the investigators a phone number for Bering in his hiding spot. He was laying low at a friend's home on Long Island when he heard a nightly news report about Nicky Guido's murder. He assumed that Casso had killed his friend, the minor league mobster Nicky Guido, just as he had killed Jimmy Hydell. Bering had no way of knowing that the shooters had instead killed an innocent namesake.

The investigators called Bering and he agreed to meet them at a Long Island diner. "We told Bering, 'Listen, we got you,'" Holland said. "'You might as well come on board because Jimmy [Hydell] is missing and probably dead somewhere. They killed the wrong Nicky Guido. And guess who's next?' Bering says, 'If you had me, you would have taken me already.' I take the Earl Scheib receipt out of my pocket. I unfold it in front of him. He puts an unlit cigar in his mouth, pointed up. When it dawned on him what we had, the cigar went down, like in a cartoon."

After seeing the receipt—proof of his involvement in the DiBiasi murder—Bering at once agreed to cooperate. Better to flip, he figured, than face Casso's gunmen on the street. Within hours, the investigators checked Bering into a hotel by Kennedy Airport, where detectives guarded him twenty-four hours a day while he watched sports on television. The detectives stayed by his side when he went downstairs for the hotel buffet or ventured out for a movie. (Bering told the detectives that he found horror movies too scary.)

Meanwhile, Bering told investigators everything, including how he and Jimmy Hydell had murdered Annette DiBiasi. He led police to a wooded area behind a motel in a sparsely populated stretch of Staten Island. There, in a shallow grave covered by a sheet of plywood, police found DiBiasi's decomposed body.

Meanwhile, the surviving Nicky Guido had gone into hiding for the same reason as Bering: to escape Casso's revenge. "Gaspipe will put me on a table, cut my heart out, and show it to me," he told associates.

As with Bering, the three investigators set out to find Guido before Casso did. Department of Motor Vehicles records showed that Guido had received a speeding ticket less than two years earlier as he drove his mother's car, which was registered to a house in Fort Myers, Florida.

Holland flew down and spent two days watching the house with help from local FBI agents. He did so on a hunch: if Guido was hiding from Casso, he might do so in his mother's house. "Sure enough, he shows up," Holland said. "Now I know Guido's there. So I say, 'What am I going to do now?'"

Holland arranged to fly Bering to Fort Myers. His cooperation deal obliged him to visit Guido posing as an old friend and fellow fugitive while wearing a wire. Bernice Luhrs, a detective investigator in the Brooklyn DA's office, posed as Bering's girlfriend, though Holland worried that Guido might find the pairing suspicious. Luhrs, Holland said, "was too angelic" to pass as Bering's girlfriend.

When they knocked on the door, Guido "looked like he'd seen a ghost," Luhrs said. Bering and Luhrs said they were in Fort Myers to visit her ailing mother, and thought they'd stop by. Bering asked Luhrs to wait outside while he went in to speak with Guido.

"It wasn't a home run," Holland said of the recorded conversation, "but it was a double." Guido unwittingly said enough to incriminate himself, but he would not be charged until a year later, when the FBI arrested him in a sweep of drug dealers back in Brooklyn.

In the following weeks Casso took the audacious step of hiring Eppolito and Caracappa, and Eppolito's cousin, Frank Santora, to kill Sammy Gravano, underboss of the Gambinos, the family that had ordered his ambush outside the Golden Ox. Communicating through Kaplan, as always, Casso agreed to pay for the murder, but only if they succeeded.

The two detectives, accompanied by Santora, trailed Gravano to his house and the office of his legitimate business, a construction company on Stillwell Avenue in Gravesend. They found that Gravano was rarely alone. "They followed Gravano *to* his house and *from* his house on a lot of occasions," said Burt Kaplan. "They told me he was always dropped off by people or picked up by people in other cars."

They also watched Gravano—sat on him, to use the Mafia term—from a car parked outside Tali's, the bar he owned on Eighteenth Avenue in Bensonhurst, until a third detective showed up by chance. The detective "came up to them in a car and started a conversation with them, asking, 'How you doing, what are you doing here?'" Kaplan said. "They said they were just there to meet somebody. They didn't think they should go to that spot anymore. . . . They didn't have a chance to fulfill the contract." Gravano survived, but barely.

At 4:22 P.M. on September 3, 1987, Eppolito's cousin Frank Santora was walking down Bath Avenue in Bensonhurst, a quiet stretch of shops and well-kept homes, when a man walked up behind him and unholstered a .38 revolver. Santora was not the target. The shooter aimed instead at Santora's friend, thirty-one-year-old Carmine Varriale, a member of the Lucchese family. Varriale fell dead on the doorstep of the Bath Avenue Dry Cleaning and Tailor Shop. Meanwhile, Santora took two stray bullets in the torso. He dribbled a trail of blood as he stumbled to the doorway of a delicatessen, G & T Salumeria, but did not enter. Instead, he teetered and fell to the ground in a wide alley between the delicatessen and the dry cleaner. He was pronounced dead thirty minutes later at Victory Memorial Hospital.

The gunman dove into the passenger-side window of a getaway car, a dark blue Chevy Malibu. It headed southwest, toward the Verrazzano-Narrows Bridge. A witness wrote down the plate number. Police matched the number to a car stolen that morning in Borough Park.

When Eppolito learned of his cousin's death, he stood weeping unashamedly in a station house as Caracappa consoled him. For Eppolito, the loss was personal, but also financial. The extracurricular work he and Caracappa performed for the Lucchese family depended entirely on Frank Santora. It was Santora who originally pitched the possibility of hiring the detectives to his jailhouse friend Burt Kaplan. And it was Santora who put the proposal into action, starting with the murder of Israel Greenwald and the abduction of Jimmy Hydell.

In fact, Casso and Kaplan did not even know the detectives' names. They had seen Eppolito and Caracappa only twice—once from a distance, standing at the far end of the Toys"R"Us parking lot after they delivered Jimmy Hydell in the trunk of a car, and a second time at the Vegas Diner in Bensonhurst. "They were sitting in the first booth eating together," Kaplan said. "We didn't speak, but they nodded at me."

The arrangement seemed destined to unravel without Santora to play go-between, until, several weeks after Santora's death, his widow walked into the store where Kaplan sold knockoff clothes. She invited him to her home, six blocks from Kaplan's, in Bensonhurst. Kaplan arrived to find Eppolito seated in the dining room. The widow left them to talk.

"Louie says, 'I'm pretty sure you know who I am,'" Kaplan recalled. "I said, 'Yes, I know who you are . . . you're Frankie's cousin.' . . . [Eppolito] asked me if I had a desire to continue the business that we were doing together."

Eppolito made a straightforward proposal: Casso would pay the detectives a $4,000-a-month retainer, using Kaplan as the sole intermediary. In return, Eppolito said, he and Caracappa would "give you everything that we get on every family, any bit of information we get about informants, about ongoing investigations, wiretaps, and imminent arrests." Murder contracts would cost extra.

After leaving the house, Kaplan noticed a thin man with a mustache in the passenger seat of a parked car watching the house. Kaplan remembered him from the Toys"R"Us parking lot and the Vegas Diner. "I didn't know his name," Kaplan said, "but I recognized him as Louie's partner."

Kaplan discussed the proposal with Casso. "He said what do you think?" Kaplan said. "I said, well, so far they've been real good to you. He says, yes, I agree with that. Let's do it."

Casso accepted the terms on the condition that Eppolito and Caracappa work exclusively for him, that they not pass any information to other crime families. Casso would dole the findings out to the Gambinos, Bonannos, Genoveses, and Colombos as a favor, and claim a favor due him in return.

For the next eight years, Kaplan met Eppolito in discreet locations—a rest stop near exit 52 on the Long Island Expressway, Perkins Pancake House on Staten Island, and the apartment that Eppolito's mistress,

Cabrini Cama, shared with her teenage son in Bensonhurst. They also met at Kaplan's house after 10 P.M. Eppolito watched from a parked car until Kaplan turned off the porch light, then tapped on a front window. They also talked while walking among the headstones in a Staten Island cemetery near the home of Caracappa's mother. "I would come down the block, beep my horn," Kaplan said. "Stephen would get in his car, make a U-turn, and we would go to the cemetery."

Kaplan, the former navy cryptologist, enveloped their communication in secrecy. From the beginning, he said, "one of the goals of the relationship [was] to conceal the relationship." Kaplan never talked to the detectives on his home phone, only pay phones. When Kaplan called their houses, he left a message asking them to call Marco, his code name. He kept the various players safely confined in their secret roles.

At some point, in late 1988 or early 1989, Kaplan and Eppolito fell out after Eppolito came to Kaplan's house and demanded a raise. Eppolito also wanted to meet Casso, to work with him more directly, but Kaplan refused on both counts. Voices were raised. Kaplan showed Eppolito the door and asked him not to come back.

About a month later, Caracappa brought a box of cookies to Kaplan's house as a peace offering. He suggested they resume their arrangement, with Caracappa acting as Kaplan's main contact. Kaplan agreed. The two men met more than once at Caracappa's apartment on East Twenty-Second Street, near Union Square in Manhattan, until Eppolito smoothed things over with Kaplan.

In return for his $4,000 monthly payments, Casso received a catalog of privileged information drawn from organized crime investigations, including alerts about Mafia capos and associates secretly cooperating with law enforcement. For the next seven years, Casso outpaced investigators by systematically eliminating the double-crossers.

A former boxer and safecracker operating on the fringes of the Lucchese family named John "Otto" Heidel was among the first to go.

Heidel was a member of the Bypass Gang, a virtuosic team of safecrackers, alarm experts, and cat burglars whose ingenuity and daring could be torn from the script of *Ocean's Eleven*. They entered banks, jewelry stores, and luxury retailers in successive teams, each departing before the next arrived in order to ensure anonymity.

In the Bypass Gang, as in any complicated choreography, participants played carefully specified roles. One team deactivated, or bypassed, the alarm so that it appeared still active. A second team cut a hole in the roof with a pickax. A third lowered themselves inside to open the vault and safe-deposit boxes with precision drilling. A fourth watched for police. On the biggest heists, Casso waited outside to make sure the Lucchese family got its share. Throughout the 1970s and 1980s, the Bypass Gang stole as much as $100 million from the European American Bank, the First Nationwide Savings Bank, Jewelers of Bond Street, and Bradlees Department Store, among others.

Heidel's fluency with electronics and radios contributed to their success. He gauged the safety of burglaries by monitoring police scanners and communicated with gang members inside and outside the building.

In the mid-1970s, FBI agents arrested a group of men, including Heidel, at a warehouse stocked with thousands of pounds of stolen industrial copper sheets unloaded from a hijacked truck. In keeping with procedure, agents took the thieves to the FBI field office on East Sixty-Ninth Street in Manhattan for fingerprinting. Agents processed the men separately so that they could ask in private if the suspects would consider enrolling as criminal informants—defined as sources who share inside information on criminal acts without an obligation to testify—in return for reduced sentences and cash payments doled out, one by one, for every secret divulged. Heidel immediately agreed. He told agents that he worried that his pretty wife, a Marilyn Monroe lookalike, might stray during his incarceration.

Heidel fed details of the Bypass Gang's plans to Agent Patrick Colgan of the FBI in return for pay. In keeping with FBI procedure, nobody but Colgan knew that Heidel was cooperating, not even Colgan's supervisors. Heidel went by a code name: Mr. Greenberg.

For years Heidel and Colgan talked by phone or met in Heidel's van parked at Marine Park, a sprawling recreational area on Jamaica Bay. "I was in regular contact with him," Colgan said, "and he with me." In total, the FBI would pay Heidel more than $100,000.

Over the long Thanksgiving weekend in 1986, the Bypass Gang cut a hole through the roof of a Bulova Watch warehouse in Queens, severing an alarm connected to a precinct just blocks away, and loaded more than $250,000 worth of wristwatches onto a truck. They skipped the $4,000 models, choosing instead the cheaper versions that would be easier to sell on the street. The Bypass Gang assigned Heidel the job of delivering the truckload of Bulovas to the Staten Island warehouse where Burt Kaplan stored stolen goods before selling them.

Something in Heidel's manner aroused Kaplan's suspicion that day. He asked his helper, Tommy Galpine, to wipe the watches for fingerprints and move them to another storehouse. Kaplan's misgivings proved prescient. "The next day, law enforcement went to [the warehouse] and were looking for the Bulova watches," Kaplan said, "but they weren't there."

On February 14, 1987, Heidel told Agent Colgan that his close friend Gaspipe Casso had casually mentioned that a detective in the Sixty-Third Precinct was feeding him inside police information about organized crime investigations. Casso said that he did not know the detective's name because they communicated through an intermediary. But he knew the detective could access information from other agencies, including the FBI and DEA. News of a mole lurking within the NYPD understandably alarmed Heidel. If the corrupt detective, in the course of his duties, learned that Heidel was a criminal informant, he would surely alert Casso. Heidel knew what would follow.

Colgan reported the existence of a corrupt detective within the Sixty-Third Precinct in an internal FBI memo, but as far as he knew, nobody followed up.

In the early months of 1987, Heidel began giving Colgan details of a Bypass Gang scheme to burgle the Atlantic Liberty Bank in the Midwood section of Brooklyn. Their plan was to break into the vault over the Martin Luther King, Jr. weekend. They often chose holiday week-ends so they had three leisurely days to gain entrance and clean out the vaults and safe-deposit boxes. "They arrived with enough food for days," Colgan said. "It was like a weekend outing."

As the break-in plans shaped up, Colgan began to suspect that Heidel might break his pledge to refrain from illegal operations. "He brought me information [about the break-in] piecemeal over six or seven months," Colgan said. "How did he know all of this information if he wasn't a part of it? He insisted that he wasn't, that he was social-izing with these people and hearing their plans. . . . I never completely trusted him, even though he was an informant. I always sensed that he was holding back."

Colgan was right. A second informant, an alarm company employee named Frank Spatafora, who disabled bank alarms from company head-quarters on behalf of the Bypass Gang, confirmed that Heidel had partic-ipated in the Liberty Bank break-in. And that wasn't the only one. Seven months later, Heidel was arrested while breaking into the Harkels Jewelry Manufacturing Company.

Heidel's arrest disqualified him from any further work with Col-gan. "By FBI policy, he absolutely had to be closed as a criminal infor-mant," Colgan said. Heidel now reverted from a confidential witness to a cooperating witness for a bank robbery task force run jointly by the FBI and NYPD. As such, Heidel's faithlessness would no longer be secret. Instead, he would be obliged to testify in court against his friends in the Bypass Gang, and his status as an informant would not be cloaked in FBI secrecy. His role as a cooperating witness would be evident to anyone, including Caracappa, with access to the task force records.

One day that summer, Kaplan was eating lunch at El Caribe, a Mill Basin beach club and catering hall where members of the five families played cards and sunned themselves by the pool. (The club was owned in part by Michael Cohen, Donald Trump's former lawyer.) Kaplan was joined at the lunch stand by Tommy Pitera, a Bonanno assassin with the bulldog face of an old-time movie gangster. He had earned the nickname "Tommy Karate" after studying martial arts in Japan. For a time, he wore his hair in a brush cut in imitation of Bruce Lee.

Heidel sauntered over after a match played in one of El Caribe's two racquetball courts. Pitera received him with distaste. "Personally," he told Heidel, "I think you're a stool pigeon." Heidel reacted with an ardent display of shock and denial. Pitera did not back down.

Kaplan reported the confrontation to Casso. "I told him exactly what happened, the exchanges between the two of them," Kaplan said, "and I said . . . I know you're close to this Otto Heidel, and [Casso] says yes, 'We've been friends and doing things together for years. We never had no problems with him.' I said, 'To me it didn't look right.'"

Casso asked Kaplan to consult their crystal ball. Eppolito and Caracappa confirmed that Heidel was, in fact, an informant. At about that time, Heidel told his daughter, Tina, that he "was in trouble," that "two crooked cops" had tried to intimidate him, and that "he knew he was being followed." He was, he said, "genuinely afraid for his life."

On the afternoon of October 8, 1987, Heidel was playing handball in Marine Park with friends. He was wearing a white tank top over a dark long-sleeve jersey. After 4 P.M. he returned to his car, a blue Pontiac parked on Avenue U. He found the Pontiac's right rear tire flat, and he set about replacing it. A flat tire was a common ruse used by Mafia assassins. Heidel may have suspected as much. He laid his .25-caliber pistol within reach and stretched out on the pavement to muscle off the flat tire.

While Heidel lay prostrate, two men pulled up in a light blue Oldsmobile. Heidel took six close-range shots in the chest, back, and buttocks. Abandoning his gun, he limped around the corner and dodged cars as he ran up East Thirty-Fifth Street, a shaded stretch lined with stoop-fronted two-story homes. The Oldsmobile followed, driving upstream on a one-way street. It caught up to Heidel hiding behind a parked car halfway up the block. A passenger in a hooded sweatshirt got out of the Oldsmobile and cornered him. He fired three more close-range shots. That was the end of it. Heidel lay dead in the street like a man asleep in his own bed.

Policeman Phillip Salmon was driving a patrol car with his partner when the dispatcher alerted them. They secured the crime scene, called an ambulance, and took down a description of the shooter from witnesses. Salmon was surprised to find that he recognized the victim. They worked out in the same gym. Salmon knew him only as an ex-con named Otto. "No matter what time of day I went to the gym, he was there," Salmon said. "It was pretty obvious he didn't have a 9-to-5 job."

Meanwhile, a detective from the Sixty-Third Precinct hustled to Heidel's Bergen Beach apartment—his residence since divorcing the Marilyn Monroe look-alike—to collect whatever evidence of his government cooperation might be lying around before the Mafia could find it. The detective retrieved microcassette tapes hidden in a bathroom, which he put in the thick plastic bag police used to collect crime scene evidence. These items would normally be "vouchered"—cataloged, labeled, and logged in. But the detective wanted to listen to the tapes as part of the murder investigation, so he stored them temporarily in a supervisor's office adjacent to the Sixty-Third Precinct's squad room, just a few feet from Eppolito's desk.

Eppolito must have found them. Kaplan later said that Eppolito delivered a casette to him as confirmation of Heidel's duplicity. "This will prove that I was right," Kaplan recalled Eppolito saying, "that the guy was cooperating, and that he was taping people."

In the open room occupied by the Organized Crime Homicide Unit, Caracappa's desk faced the desk of his friend Detective Chuck Siriano. The two had worked together for years, dating back to their time in the Eighty-Fourth Precinct. Unlike Caracappa, who rarely left the office, Siriano considered himself a street detective. The truth, he said, is in the neighborhoods. He disliked the idle hours wasted inside One Police Plaza waiting for the next mob murder to set them in motion. "I would sit around in a three-piece suit bored to death listening to guys talk to their girlfriends on the phone," he said. "There was nothing to do."

Siriano eventually received permission to embed himself in the mob-heavy neighborhoods of South Brooklyn, provided he regularly check in by phone. "I worked alone. I never wore a suit," he said. "I wore dungarees and gold chains. When I walked around, I fit right in."

One evening in 1988, Siriano was headed home when Frank Russo, a detective in Brooklyn's Seventy-Second Precinct, contacted him to say that he had arrested a career criminal, a man in his fifties, who was breaking into a woman's apartment to steal a diamond ring. He had picked her lock. The burglar had mob ties, Russo said. Did Siriano want to talk to him? "I had friends all over the city," Siriano said. "They all knew that my specialty was talking to gangsters."

The intruder already had a lengthy criminal record. Now he faced a first-degree burglary charge. "So he knew he was going away for a long, long time," Siriano said. "He indicated that he wished to cooperate. So I said, well, I'll listen to anything." Siriano registered him as a confidential informant with the code name Chicky.

Chicky told Siriano that he was a member of the Bypass Gang. His role was to fabricate keys for interior doors by twisting a blank key in a keyhole until scratches revealed the outline of a workable key.

Chicky never learned the identity of his Bypass Gang partners due to the group's compartmentalization of duties, with one exception: he happened to meet a safecracker named Dominick in a Bensonhurst diner.

Siriano consulted the Department of Consumer Affairs, which licensed locksmiths. He collected the applicant files, including photographs, of the half dozen Brooklyn locksmiths named Dominick. He spread their photos out on a table. Chicky identified the locksmith he met in the diner as twenty-six-year-old Dominick Costa, a strikingly handsome former Marine Corps sniper.

Costa was a licensed locksmith and safe technician who doubled as a safecracker—among the best, by his own estimate. He had cracked roughly three hundred safes using a special technique: he penetrated vaults with a diamond drill, then snaked an optical scope inside to examine the levers, bolts, and other mechanics. "I never met a safe I couldn't crack," he said.

Costa led a tenuous double life—daytime locksmith, nighttime safecracker. In his capacity as a legitimate locksmith, he was occasionally hired to repair the safe he had cracked the night before.

Siriano and two detectives followed Costa for more than six months, trying without success to collect enough evidence for an arrest. In the end, they simply seized him off the street two blocks east of Times Square, where Costa taught a locksmithing class, and took him into custody in Nassau County, part of Long Island, where his detainment could more easily be kept secret. Costa was a technician, not a hardened criminal. Siriano easily persuaded him to become a confidential informant and to wear a wire rather than face jail time. "He was working under the impression that if he didn't cooperate, that we were going to arrest him," Siriano said. "But the truth, is we had nothing."

In October 1988, Costa told Siriano that over Thanksgiving weekend the Bypass Gang planned to burgle a Queens facility where Chase Bank stored cash drawn from local branches. Costa had agreed to help break into the five safes.

"We decided to let the burglary go down and catch them in the act," Siriano said. "That would be the best way to take this crew down. We made plans to set up all sorts of surveillance equipment." Motion detectors would alert detectives when the gang entered. Video monitors would capture them in the act of cracking the safes. "We would probably let them violate one safe," Siriano said, "before we went down and took them."

As the Bypass Gang finalized its plans, Eppolito and Caracappa sent word to Casso that Costa, his most gifted locksmith, was cooperating with law enforcement. They also forwarded Costa's address, just off the Bay Ridge Parkway, and a description of his car: a white Pontiac sedan with the plate number RGG 961.

On the night of October 12, five weeks before the planned break-in, Siriano received a beeper message from Al Guarneri, Eppolito's brother-in-law and a detective in the Sixty-Second Precinct. "Al asked if I knew a guy named Dominick Costa. I said, why do you want to know? Al said because he just got his brains blown out on Seventy-

Fifth Street and Nineteenth Avenue. I ran over. I saw brain matter all over the car."

Costa was backing into his garage just after midnight when two men, their faces obscured by hooded sweatshirts, fired through the car window. They hit Costa twice in the head and once in the shoulder. His wife stood by screaming his name.

Doctors at Kings County Hospital resuscitated Costa. He survived, in spite of the close-range salvo. "They broke my skull in half," he later said, "but I'm still alive."

Costa's shooting led Siriano to conclude that a detective in their ranks—likely one of the men seated beside him in the Organized Crime Homicide Unit—was doing the unthinkable: he was leaking the identity of informants to the Mafia. "When Dominick got shot," Siriano said, "I decided that there was something wrong someplace."

A week later, the decomposed body of another informant, a twenty-eight-year-old low-level street thug named Victor Filocamo, was found facedown in the unlocked trunk of his white BMW convertible parked in Bay Ridge. "His body was like soup in the back of the car," said Siriano, who had been trying to contact Filocamo for days.

"That was it for me," Siriano said. "I knew there was a leak someplace."

Siriano's immediate concern was for the safety of Chicky, his surviving informant. "When you get somebody to cooperate, you're responsible for their life," he said. "It's a very dangerous position for them."

Siriano withdrew $2,000 of his own money and gave it to Chicky. "I said there's a leak someplace," Siriano said. "You've got to get out of town. I won't be responsible for your life if you stay. Go someplace and beep me when you get there. He was a thief but otherwise a decent human being. He never did anything violent in his life." Chicky drove to Florida with his wife and daughter.

Meanwhile, Siriano and Al Guarneri guarded the hospital room where Costa lay unconscious. "One night I was sitting there with Al reading magazines," Siriano said. "The nurse said your guy is waking up in there. So Al and I go in. Dominick is sitting up with tubes coming out of him and a bandage over his right eye. I'd seen all that brain matter on the car, so I figured this guy must be scrambled eggs. So I says, 'Dominick, do you know who I am?' He blinks at me with that one eye and says, 'Yeah, you're Chuck.' I fucking almost died. I was flabbergasted."

The likelihood of a leak within the Major Case Squad, the police equivalent of a double agent, changed the way Siriano conducted his work. A month after the Costa shooting, Siriano registered an informant after police arrested him shooting up a card game. Siriano avoided writing any reports, relying instead on the Manhattan DA's office to process the case. "I wanted nothing to go onto paper" in the Major Case Squad, Siriano said, "because I knew there was something wrong someplace. I didn't know it was Caracappa. It could have been anybody. I started keeping my eyes open after that."

Siriano noticed that his new method of processing paperwork outside the Major Case Squad irked Caracappa. "It really pissed Steve off," he said. "He said, 'What are you doing? Why won't you talk about it?'"

Meanwhile, Dominick Costa recovered. For the rest of his life his right eye drooped. A walnut-sized bump bulged from his forehead. He suffered seizures, but otherwise functioned normally. He was well enough, in any case, to serve as a key prosecution witness in the trial of five Bypass Gang confederates.

In late 1992, Costa entered the Witness Protection Program. He lived under a new name, Vincent Carbone, on a stipend of $1,381 a month in Chisholm, Minnesota, a backwater mining town two hundred miles north of Minneapolis. He gave up all ties to friends and family. He was essentially a man without a past, a swarthy stranger conspicuous for his thick Brooklyn accent and a New Yorker's reliance on taxis in a wide-open land where everyone drove great distances.

Safecracking was to Costa what gambling was to Burt Kaplan: an irresistible vice. Even in his new life as Vincent Carbone, he could not stop himself from assessing the flimsy security of local banks, though a break-in might cause a judge to revoke his plea deal and lead to his expulsion from the Witness Protection Program. Whatever the risks, the temptation was simply too great. Safes dangled like candy. Costa even relocated to a small apartment across the street from the First National Bank. "The banks are just on their knees, begging to be robbed," he said. "This is like heaven."

In April 1993, Chisholm police arrested Costa and an accomplice on suspicion of burgling the First National Bank and a law firm upstairs. The break-in had all the earmarks of the Bypass Gang: Costa cut the phone lines and circumvented the alarm system in order to enter the law firm through a broken window. He cut a hole through the floor and lowered himself into the bank. In the end he couldn't access the bank vault, but he stole $40,000 from the law firm's safe.

A week later a cabdriver told a local detective that Costa had bragged about the break-in, saying he had robbed banks back East. Police raided Costa's apartment, where they found precious coins removed from the law firm safe, as well as articles about the break-in clipped from a Chisholm newspaper. After his arrest, Costa told local detectives his true identity. He pleaded guilty to third-degree burglary and went to prison for fifteen months.

So far, Eppolito and Caracappa had earned their pay by helping Casso unmask a string of informants and locate those who would harm him. The detectives also provided invaluable details of law enforcement's aggressive new campaign to collect evidence with bugs and phone taps.

In late 1988, for example, Casso sent a Lucchese capo named Alphonse "Little Al" D'Arco to warn a second capo, Peter "Fat Pete" Chiodo, that a consortium of government agencies was investigating corrupt practices in the waste industry, including their business, Tiger Management, which trucked medical waste and construction debris from New York dumps to Ohio and other outlying states. While the Lucchese men were out celebrating St. Patrick's Day in March 1989, agents had surreptitiously placed bugs under the floor of the beat-up trailer parked in an industrial backwater by Newark Airport that Tiger Management used as an office. They also tapped its phones. As a result, agents could listen in as Chiodo gave orders, and they watched him come and go from a hotel room down the street.

Eppolito and Caracappa tipped Casso off. He then told D'Arco to "go get that fat bastard [Chiodo] and tell him that phones are bugged in there and the place is bugged," D'Arco later recalled. "And tell him the [authorities] got it bugged and you're going to get pinched if you don't watch your mouth. . . . Go tell him now."

D'Arco dutifully went to Chiodo's social club on McDonald Avenue in Brooklyn. "I took [Chiodo] down in the back of the club," he said. "There was plenty of noise in there and I talked low because I figured the place was also bugged. . . . I told him don't use the phones."

A short time later, on the afternoon of April 19, 1989, an investigator with the New Jersey Attorney General's office named Victoria Vreeland was watching the Tiger Management trailer from a surveillance station set up in a hotel room when a man wearing a grungy T-shirt and fedora pulled up in a mobile home. He got out and crawled under the trailer, where wires led to the listening devices. He then pulled his mobile home up to a nearby telephone pole. "He stood there and he was looking up at wires and then at some point he actually climbed on top of the mobile home and was playing with the wires on the telephone pole," she said. "He got back in the mobile home and proceeded to drive down the street a little bit to the next pole. . . . He actually repeated that pattern all of the way down the street, stopping at every telephone pole."

The phone taps fell silent that day, followed by the bugs. Casso had succesfully shut down the eavesdropping based on information about wiretap locations shared by Eppolito and Caracappa. "For the most part the investigation was over," Vreeland said. "We realized that we had been detected."

On a late December afternoon in 1988, just before Christmas, Sal Avellino, the Lucchese operative known as The Golfer, who had chauffeured the family boss, Tony Ducks Corallo, in his Jaguar in the years before

Corallo went to prison, left his home in Nissequogue, New York, on the North Shore of Long Island. He drove fifty miles to meet Gaspipe Casso at the Surfside Motel, across from a strip mall in Howard Beach, Queens. Casso had called the meeting to discuss the two intransigent Long Island garbage haulers, Robert Kubecka and his brother-in-law, Donald Barstow, who had held out against the corrupt union for seven years in spite of a steady stream of threats. The two had secretly assisted the Organized Crime Task Force since 1982. Robert had testified in criminal and civil investigations. Eppolito and Caracappa alerted Kaplan, and by extension Casso, that the garbage haulers were now cooperating with the FBI. They would testify the following month in a federal RICO suit.

Robert and Donald played a key role in the blockbuster conviction of the top eight Mafia bosses in the 1986 Commission Case by wearing wires while meeting with corrupt union officials and by encouraging investigators to bug Avellino's Jaguar, a brilliant gambit that yielded a critical trove of damning recordings. Robert and Donald had declined to enter the Witness Protection Program; they did not wish to uproot their families. They relied instead on the protection of the task force, though they did not always feel protected. No policemen stood guard outside the homes they shared with their wives and children. No security cameras recorded who entered their workplace. They kept a gun in the office safe, but never handled it.

Cooperating with the task force under threat of violence was either valiant or foolhardy, depending on one's point of view. The two garbage haulers may have reassured themselves that they had endured years of sabotage and intimidation, but no physical harm. They were small-time, and perhaps not worth hurting. Though that would change, now that Eppolito and Caracappa had informed Casso that Robert and Donald planned to testify in a federal racketeering suit.

At the Surfside Motel, Avellino argued that now was the time to kill them. Casso agreed. "We can't let these guys walk around," he said. "They testify against us, and we let them get away with it? No, get rid of them."

Eight months later, on the evening of August 9, 1989, Robert Kubecka received a threatening phone call, the latest of many, before leaving the office for a family gathering. We cannot know what the caller said, only that Robert was concerned enough to call a task force investigator in Connecticut who urged him to alert Suffolk County police. An officer came by to collect information. He promised to follow up the next day.

Ten trucks pulled out for their daily routes before dawn the next morning, leaving Robert and Donald alone in their cramped office on the quiet edge of East Northport, New York. At 6:15 A.M., Robert called 911. "I've been shot," he said. "Two people have been shot. Send help."

In the last conscious hour of his life, Robert and an ambulance dispatcher had the following exchange:

KUBECKA: I'm going to pass out. Please help...I can't keep my consciousness.
DISPATCHER: How old are you?
KUBECKA: I don't know.
DISPATCHER: Just stay with us. They're coming down. How badly are you bleeding?
KUBECKA: Bad.
DISPATCHER: What were you shot with?
KUBECKA: Gun.
DISPATCHER: A gun? A rifle? A handgun?
KUBECKA: Handgun. Left side of chest.
DISPATCHER: Left side of chest?
KUBECKA: Mmmh.
DISPATCHER: How badly are you bleeding?
KUBECKA: I'm passing out.
DISPATCHER: Hello? Hello?

Police arrived within seven minutes. They found Donald Barstow dead in a hallway near the front door. Blood smeared his hands, suggesting that he had raised them instinctively to shield himself. Down the hall, Robert sat slumped across a desk, barely conscious. He died on the way to Huntington Hospital.

Casso would dismiss the shooting as the unavoidable price of doing business, like rent or insurance. Robert, he said, was "helping the FBI. So, you know, in the life we were in, there was no other way but to kill the guy." Robert Kubecka and Donald Barstow were two of many who died in these unsettled years as a direct result of information shared by Eppolito and Caracappa.

The killings followed hard upon each other. These were not murders so much as executions. Casso and Kaplan referred to them euphemistically as "a piece of work."

In early 1990, Burt Kaplan sought Eppolito and Caracappa's help locating Anthony DiLapi, a short, frog-faced Lucchese loan shark who wore big tinted glasses and answered to the picturesque nickname "Blue Eyes over the Bridges," or, more simply, "Fat Anthony." DiLapi was justifiably wary to the point of paranoia. At his home in the Bronx, he hid money and guns in hollowed-out books and concealed them in compartments built into windowsills.

DiLapi had influence within the Lucchese family. His uncle, Tom Mix Santoro, was a former underboss who ran family operations in the Bronx until his conviction in the Commission trial. DiLapi himself had served two five-year terms for labor racketeering. When the parole board granted DiLapi's release, Casso summoned him to review the accounting for his bookmaking operations, a standard request to ensure that DiLapi paid proper tribute, or payment, to the higher-ups. DiLapi, however, had not kept the books forthrightly, or so it appeared when he didn't show up.

Casso asked Caracappa to contact DiLapi's parole officer, who said Fat Anthony had washed up in Los Angeles. But where exactly? The Major Case Squad had, by chance, recently hosted detectives from the Los Angeles Police Department while collaborating on an unrelated case. Caracappa and the other squad detectives treated their West Coast counterparts to a series of meals in Little Italy, a few blocks from police headquarters. So Caracappa was well positioned to call in a favor.

Charles Howard, a new acquaintance in the Los Angeles Detective Bureau, told Caracappa that DiLapi was living with a girlfriend just off Beverly Boulevard, in Hollywood, while nominally working as a used-car salesman. Casso then dispatched a four-man team headed by Joseph "Little Joe" D'Arco, Al D'Arco's son, who was staying at the Los Angeles home of a porn producer. Casso sent him a gun by UPS.

On February 4, 1990, DiLapi walked into the shadow of a garage beneath his girlfriend's two-story Hollywood apartment building with an armful of dry cleaning. His daughter and grandson had a layover at Los Angeles International Airport that day en route from Hawaii to Salt Lake City. DiLapi had hoped to join them briefly between flights; he had never met his grandson. But his daughter, Mary Ann, discouraged him, for whatever reason. So he had planned to run errands instead.

Before DiLapi reached his car, Little Joe D'Arco stepped from the half-light and fired five shots into DiLapi's face, followed by four to his torso. He died faceup on the garage floor with his head resting near the rear fender of a Volvo station wagon. The police found him in a pool of congealed blood with his shirt hiked up to reveal his ample midriff.

Two weeks after DiLapi died, Louie Eppolito threw himself a retirement party at El Caribe, the mob-connected Mill Basin banquet hall. Six years after the Internal Affairs Division cleared him of suspicion, Eppolito would quit the force as a detective second grade and the beneficiary of a generous pension. He would pursue a second career as an actor, scriptwriter, and filmmaker.

Eppolito was more suited to Hollywood than he might have seemed. He was, after all, a fabulist by nature. From the beginning, his police life had been a form of fabrication—the Mafia son recast as a cop, or, conversely, the cop recast as a Mafia son. Full-time storytelling was not such a leap. He had always been the loudest voice in the room, the most flamboyant dresser, the attention seeker. Now he would cast himself as a star, or try to, by drawing from his life on the Brooklyn streets.

Eppolito retired from the police force on February 18, 1990. Stephen

Caracappa would eventually follow him into retirement, but not yet. For the time being, he would continue to show up for work in the Major Case Squad, fastidious as always, while living a double life as Casso's mole within police intelligence circles.

A few months after Eppolito retired, in late winter of 1990, a Benson-hurst addict known around the neighborhood as Crackhead Eddie sold a vending machine and a three-wheeled all-terrain vehicle, both freshly stolen, to a burly Colombo associate and part-time rapper named Frank "Frankie Steel" Pontillo for $200 cash.

Pontillo drove the ATV to a local gas station. He found the owner fuming over his missing vending machine. With a full tank, Pontillo cruised a weed-strewn strip of land between the Belt Parkway and Graves-end Bay, a neglected area within sight of city dumps where he often rode dirt bikes on crude trails.

This time Pontillo decided he would plow his own trail. "I started mowing weeds down, going a little farther, knocking down more weeds," he said, "then all of a sudden—I don't even know how it hap-pened—I was wedged upside down in a hole with the trike on top of me. I was lying there bleeding and covered in dirt and thinking, 'Who would put a hole here?'"

After extracting himself, Pontillo found shovels, a pickax, and beer bottles hidden under a cardboard sheet. He steered the ATV home to clean up. "I drove slowly, really slowly, because my left hand hurt. While I'm puttering along a car comes down the dirt road. I knew they were cops coming toward me because they drove an undercover car. A Gran Fury, dark blue. The two guys pull up. A skinny guy drives, dressed up nice, with a fat guy sitting in the passenger seat wearing a Hawaiian shirt. He looks like a street guy, a gangster. I see a badge."

Pontillo paused to tell the cops that he fell in a hole. They snapped to attention. The fat cop said they were investigating a band of devil worshippers sacrificing animals in the underbrush. He asked Pontillo to show him the hole. Pontillo assumed they'd drive the car down, but the fat one insisted on riding on the back of the ATV. They set off, two big men on a tricycle.

When they arrived at the hole, the fat cop "reaches down," Pontillo said. "In the corner of my eye I see him pull up his pant leg and pull out a gun from his ankle. That's all I had to see. My instinct was *run*! It just kicked in without my even thinking. I'm running for my life. I hear shots, more than three. I'm zigzagging through the tall cattails."

Pontillo reached a rocky shoreline with a steep pitch down to the wet sand. He hid behind a piece of hulking wood, the weathered remnant of a barge, until the afternoon sky darkened. Then, once it was dusk, he made his way northeast along the bay front, at one point wading across an inlet. "I looked like I was escaping behind enemy lines," he said. "I'm all muddy, like I've rolled out of a swamp." He crossed a bridge onto Coney Island and knocked on the door of an acquaintance's body shop on Cropsey Avenue.

Pontillo told a handful of friends what happened. He told their fathers as well, at least those connected to crime families. He discussed the episode with his own father, who was incarcerated in the Metropolitan Correctional Center. Their advice was unanimous: You're alive. Mind your own business. Keep your head down. Let it go.

That might have ended the matter, if not for one night a year later, when Pontillo went to Pastels, a Bay Ridge club where disco played until dawn. In the men's room he ran into Frankie Russo, a neighborhood dealer of stolen guns. On the spot Pontillo bought a Glock equipped with a red-dot laser scope. Pontillo waded back into the club crowd with his new Glock stashed in his waistband. At 1 A.M. or so, he and three friends went to the Vegas Diner on Eighty-Sixth Street for a late meal. At 3 A.M., he headed home but stopped on an impulse to test the Glock. He parked on a service road off the Belt Parkway and walked back to a secluded area near the hole he had crashed into a year earlier.

Pontillo emptied the Glock's clip. He felt pleased with his purchase and ready for bed. He started back to the Belt Parkway but froze when a car emerged from the darkness. He threw the Glock away and hid in the bushes. The car stopped. Its doors opened. Out stepped the two cops, the fat and skinny pair who had shot at him a year earlier. Pontillo watched as the two cops opened the trunk and pulled out a black bag with handles, the size of a body, and dragged it down the road toward the hole he fell in a year earlier. "I'm saying to myself I can get these two guys right now, but I got not one bullet on me and I threw the gun away. So I just sat there quietly." He had another gun in the trunk of his car. He considered fetching it but decided against a shoot-out. He slipped off unnoticed.

Rudy Giuliani had already imprisoned eight old-guard Mafia leaders in the Commission case. Now, four years later, he was angling to cripple their replacements, the next generation of Mafia bosses. Casso knew that his control over Lucchese operations, and possibly his life, depended on Eppolito and Caracappa.

In 1989, Casso dispatched the Lucchese captain Big Pete Chiodo to bully Jimmy Bishop, a Queens Democratic district leader and a top official of the local chapter of the International Brotherhood of Painters. The Lucchese family had controlled the union for more than a decade, bribing influential politicians, fixing contracts, and pocketing 10 percent of the income from painting subways, bridges, and schools.

Bishop was a stout sixty-year-old, just five feet, nine inches tall, known for cocky talk and hard drinking. He had served in the Marines before becoming a bridge painter, as his father had. He worked for years atop the city's highest perches without fear of falling.

Casso considered Bishop too unreliable. He ignored phone calls, and he repeatedly failed to enroll Lucchese men in no-show jobs—paid positions without work. Chiodo warned Bishop, on Casso's orders, that Casso would have his grandchildren killed if he didn't resign. Two days later, Bishop stepped down. In an act of pluck or folly, Bishop then went directly to the Manhattan DA's office and offered a gift: he was willing to share a comprehensive account of the union's dirty mob entanglements.

Bishop had a lot to share. He had spent his entire adult life in the union, dating back to the days when he hung from bridge pylons with a brush in his hand. He had brokered many of the corrupt deals himself while seated at the 19th Hole Bar—fees paid to avert labor strikes, bribes paid to union officials, contracts dictated by mob bosses.

Bishop's recollection of dates and details was "extraordinarily accurate," a prosecutor said. "He was a guy trying to make amends for many mistakes in his life." Prosecutors warned Bishop that his life was in danger, that Casso would come for him, but he ignored them. He was an ex-marine, he said, and a Bronze Star recipient from combat duty in Korea. He insisted on taking care of himself.

The particulars of the investigation crossed Caracappa's desk in the Major Case Squad. He alerted Kaplan, and therefore Casso, that Bishop had agreed to assist a state and city probe preparing indictments against corrupt union officials and their Mafia handlers. Bishop had specifically implicated Casso. The investigation showed that Casso and his associates had handpicked the leaders of the six-thousand-member painters' union and demanded kickbacks from contractors.

Casso convened his inner circle in a small room over a pizzeria at the intersection of Utica and Flatlands Avenues in Brooklyn, a five-minute drive from his home. He told them what Eppolito and Caracappa had shared: Bishop was now a cooperating witness. "Fucking James Bishop," Casso yelled.

Fat Pete Chiodo inspected Bishop's home in the Queens neighborhood of Malba and concluded that the winding neighborhood streets and cul-de-sacs might impede a quick escape. Bishop had a girlfriend, a schoolteacher, who lived two miles away in the Whitestone neighborhood fronting the East River. Chiodo decided to ambush Bishop there instead.

In early May 1990, residents of the girlfriend's apartment building noticed men waiting in cars at the edge of the residents' parking lot. "It appears the killers knew he had a routine of being at that building and were waiting for a chance to hit him," a detective later said. Bishop liked to sit by the pool at his girlfriend's building, playing cards and talking to the neighbors. He usually left by late morning.

At 11:30 a.m. on May 17, Bishop was found slouched against the wheel of his two-tone gray Lincoln Town Car outside the apartment building in Whitestone. He had been shot eight times in the head and chest with a .380 semiautomatic as he was backing out of a parking spot. He managed to put the car in gear and drive about 150 feet before hitting a wooden fence. He died before an ambulance arrived.

News of Bishop's death was received with mounting frustration up in the Major Case Squad's fluorescent-lit rooms at One Police Plaza. Detectives had stood by helplessly as a series of promising investigations abruptly fizzled. The Lucchese family was uncovering NYPD wiretaps and anticipating the timing of police raids with uncanny precision. More alarming still, law enforcement's painstakingly cultivated informants— Robert Kubecka, Donald Barstow, Otto Heidel, Dominick Costa, Victor Filocamo, and now James Bishop—had died one after another in a long, bloody season of setbacks and defeat. "You couldn't help but feel that the wise guys were on to us," said Robert Intartaglio, an investigator in the Brooklyn DA's office. "Leaks are the worst thing that can happen. And yet they kept happening."

It was now clear and indisputable: the Luccheses had a mole embedded within law enforcement. A few detectives held quiet suspicions about who might be doing the leaking.

The list of detectives casting a distrustful eye on colleagues included Frank Pergola, a Major Case Squad detective working temporarily as a homicide investigator for the US Attorney for the Southern District of New York. In 1983, Pergola had arrested Dominick Montiglio, a Gambino associate and heroin dealer who acted as an intermediary between his uncle, Nino Gaggi, and Roy DeMeo, head of the Gemini Lounge assassination crew.

After Montiglio's arrest, Pergola showed him photos of Gambino associates who would surely try to kill him before he could talk. "When we started throwing pictures of the crew in front of him," Pergola said, "he realized he was in trouble." Montiglio wisely joined the growing roster of defectors: he agreed to cooperate.

That winter, Pergola had escorted Montiglio, his wife, Denise, and their three children to a pair of trailers on the shore of frozen Lake George, in upstate New York. It was "a safe place that nobody would know about," Pergola said. "Me and my partner stayed with Dominick in one trailer with no heat. The family stayed in the trailer with heat."

A friendship formed in the trailer that would last thirty-eight years. Pergola, the detective, and Montiglio, the Mafia associate, were raised blocks apart in the Bath Beach neighborhood of Brooklyn. Pergola's mother had grown up with Montiglio's father. They had attended the same schools. They spoke the same language. They laughed at the same jokes.

While Pergola and another detective watched out for their safety, FBI agents debriefed Montiglio. He gave them a long, unvarnished account of how he returned from a tour of Vietnam with the Green Berets; how he and Denise escaped Mafia entanglements by moving to Oakland, California, where he dabbled in music; how, in a sentimental moment, they returned to Brooklyn after seeing *The Godfather*; how they moved into his Uncle Nino's house; how Montiglio inevitably fell into a series of illicit chores for his uncle—collecting loan shark payments, trafficking in stolen cars, selling heroin, and, ultimately, participating in Gambino hits.

After ten days in the trailers, the FBI agents received a panicked call from the New York field office. "They said get out of there right now," Pergola said. "They know you're there."

Somebody had leaked their location to the Gambino family. Pergola assumed that assassins were driving north to get Montiglio. Within hours he relocated Montiglio to the safety of a Connecticut jail while Denise and the children stayed in a hotel under protective guard until they could enter the Witness Protection Program. Caracappa, as conduit of all records, likely spotted Pergola's Lake George location in his paperwork. Years later, a colleague told Pergola that an FBI wiretap had picked up a conversation confirming that Caracappa leaked the location to Casso, who forwarded it to Montiglio's Gambino bosses.

While working temporarily for the US Attorney for the Southern

District of New York, Pergola made a point of stopping by to keep up with old acquaintances in the Major Case Squad. During one visit in 1983, after the Montiglio episode, he placed his leather briefcase on a table while chatting with Caracappa. The briefcase contained files on homicide investigations resulting from information Montiglio had shared in his Lake George debriefings—including a file on Michael "Mikey Muscles" DiCarlo, who was murdered after his Lucchese associates discovered that he was pimping and raping underage boys.

Pergola interrupted his talk with Caracappa to use the men's room, leaving his briefcase on the table. He then left for a meeting at the Midtown North Precinct, on West Fifty-Fourth Street. He parked his Datsun 240Z about a block from the precinct house, with his briefcase in the trunk. When Pergola got home that night, the briefcase was gone; somebody had broken into the Datsun while it was parked outside the precinct house. Agents dusted the car for fingerprints, but found nothing. Pergola told FBI agents that he suspected Caracappa. "He must have called somebody," he said, "and told them where I was going."

Detectives often possess the power of intuition. They know things before they can prove them. So it was with Pergola when he suspected Caracappa of leaks.

In May 1990, Eppolito phoned Burt Kaplan to convene an emergency meeting at a rest area on the Long Island Expressway. Standing by the highway, Eppolito delivered pressing news: Caracappa had seen a confidential report indicating that a federal grand jury in Brooklyn had indicted Casso and his friend, the Lucchese boss Vic Amuso, along with more than a dozen others on charges of corrupting and controlling the $143 million contract to replace windows for the city Housing Authority.

Amuso immediately heeded Eppolito's warning; he dropped out of sight on May 15. He would spend the next fourteen months secluded in Pennsylvania. Casso lingered another week.

There was no shame in hiding. Many underworld figures had fled arrest, an all-star list that includes Dutch Schultz and Albert Anastasia. Still,

Casso could hardly bring himself to leave. He considered his departure an indignity, a reversal of hard-won prestige and a demeaning acknowledgment that New York's crime families were ceding ground to advancing prosecutors.

He also hated to abandon his vanity project, a waterfront home in Mill Basin. Except for a few aging godfathers residing behind walled estates on Long Island or in New Jersey, organized crime figures favored the inconspicuous. The more discreet, the better. By contrast, the home Casso built for himself and Lillian, on a block between the Kings Plaza Shopping Center and Jamaica Bay, was a pure expression of gangster flamboyance. Casso hired Anthony Fava, an architect and contractor who acted as a kind of in-house designer for Mafia projects. The gray stucco house stood out as an eccentric postmodern confection, tricked out with a tiled fountain animated by sculptures of dancing children, a gym, solarium, greenhouse, two dining rooms, and a patio leading to a private dock on a tidal channel. The imported front doors alone cost $40,000. The *New York Daily News* called the house "three floors of mob chic."

Most of all, Casso dreaded parting from his daughter, Jolene, eighteen, and son, Anthony, fifteen, and Lillian, his companion since childhood. He had grown up in a four-story brick building on Union Street with the rattle and clang of streetcars outside his window. Lillian was the nice Italian girl down the block, with ample lips, doe eyes, and a cloud of wavy brown hair. They were born three months apart. They grew up going to movie palaces and riding the subway to Coney Island. He could not remember a time when they were apart.

Caracappa warned that the arrests would come on May 30. Casso spent his last days of freedom tying up loose ends so that Lucchese operations could continue without him. He broke the news to Lillian over dinner at Da Noi, a Midtown Manhattan restaurant, and celebrated his forty-eighth birthday with his family. Six days later, he arranged a late-night meeting with Al D'Arco, the capo chosen as acting Lucchese boss in his and Amuso's absence.

Casso asked D'Arco to meet him by the cannon. He was referring to John Paul Jones Park, a grassy waterfront compound with a massive black nineteenth-century cannon guarding the Narrows, the gateway to New York Harbor. The park was the kind of outdoor location mafiosi favored for sensitive meetings where they could not be bugged. Gangsters called them "walk and talks."

D'Arco did not fit the profile of a mob boss. He was just five feet, seven inches—a short, balding man who lived with six family members in a four-room apartment on Spring Street, in Little Italy, with flocked wallpaper and a reinforced steel door. He rarely drank and never smoked. Mobsters of rank usually kept girlfriends, or *gumars,* on the side, but D'Arco, by all accounts, had remained faithful to his wife, Dolores, since meeting her in a Flatbush nightclub in 1953. Casso sarcastically called D'Arco "The Professor" for his dim wit.

D'Arco had joined the Lucchese family almost by inertia, as if it was the only option. He had grown up watching a mob-connected bookie do business from a storefront above his father's basement garment dye shop, a few blocks from the Brooklyn Navy Yard. Gangsters, he said, were "always around my neighborhood. It's like you're in a forest. The neighborhood is the forest and all the trees in it . . . were organized crime men. It was a way of life."

D'Arco joined the trees at age fourteen without much thought, though he was perhaps better suited to cooking in the kitchen of his family restaurant, La Donna Rosa, in the Soho neighborhood of Manhattan, where he helped prepare wild rabbit–stuffed ravioli and other recipes inherited from his Sicilian grandparents. La Donna Rosa was one of a dozen restaurants where oblivious tourists ate fish soup or stuffed calamari while gangsters dined at the next table.

D'Arco was like an unappreciated middle manager who reliably got the job done. He dutifully spent six years in jail on a heroin charge with his mouth closed, and he consistently earned for the Lucchese family with hijacking, drug deals, burglary, counterfeiting, arson, and armed robbery—everything but pimping and pornography, which he considered unsavory.

If D'Arco did not fit the exact profile of a mob boss, so much the better for Casso. A weak surrogate would be all the more pliable, more easily directed from afar. D'Arco, the mob traditionalist, would throw no curveballs, or so Casso assumed.

While Brooklyn slept, the two men met among the battlements of John Paul Jones Park, with the heaving harbor tide sloshing against a bulkhead and the low twinkling profile of Staten Island across the black water. Casso gave D'Arco a list of addresses for public pay phones in Brooklyn, Queens, and Long Island. A messenger would periodically tell D'Arco when to be at a specific phone to receive a call from Casso with instructions for family business.

The walk and talk was all logistics, until the final goodbye. Then Casso, the mob boss with the coldest heart, surprised D'Arco. "He told me, 'I'll see you, I'll be in touch,'" D'Arco said. "Then he got all choked up, emotional, and he started crying that he's going to leave, grabbing me, all that stuff."

Then Casso got in a black Jeep Cherokee, stolen for his use, and drove to New Jersey. His family and associates acted as if he were leaving for no more than a respite, that he would return as soon as pressure eased.

The arrests came after Memorial Day Weekend, on May 30, just as Caracappa had warned. At 9 A.M., six agents arrived with a warrant. They knocked on the door of Casso's home on East Seventy-Second Street. Lillian had no choice but to admit them. They searched the house, but eventually left, satisfied that Casso was not there, not anymore.

Meanwhile, that same morning, the FBI rounded up twelve union officials and high-ranking figures from four crime families, alleging they illegally controlled the window replacement business for public housing. One by one the suspects came before a US magistrate for arraignment, including Genovese boss Vincent "The Chin" Gigante, who wore a plush purple bathrobe to court. His appearance was in keeping with eccentric behavior that was either a sign of dementia, as his lawyer claimed, or more likely a ruse to avoid legal responsibility.

The suspects made a point of acting unconcerned, as mafiosi often did under such circumstances. "I feel terrific," John Gotti's brother, Peter, told reporters while handcuffed. "I just wish we had some coffee."

The indictments nonetheless landed with explosive force. Prosecutors were advancing now like an army confident that it could knock its foe backward, that it could send the five families reeling. "The mafia is not the entrenched, well-insulated organization it once was," said Jules Bonavolonta, the FBI agent who had helped make use of the RICO laws. He was now a supervisor in charge of organized crime probes. "It's getting weaker and weaker."

The next morning's newspapers reported that Lucchese leaders Vic Amuso and Gaspipe Casso had unaccountably slipped the dragnet. They had vanished with uncanny timing, thanks to advance word from Eppolito and Caracappa.

Casso knew that if he wished to maintain his iron grip from hiding, along with his heaping profits, he would have to rely on Caracappa to act as his eyes and ears within the emboldened forces of law enforcement, though it was unclear how much longer he could depend on Caracappa as he inched toward retirement. His crystal ball might decamp, leaving him to his own devices.

9

GASPIPE IN EXILE

WHEN NEW YORK GANGSTERS WENT INTO HIDING—
when they "lammed," as they called it—they tended to set themselves up comfortably in some far-flung spot where officials would not think to look, a place where locals met them without recognition. In 1936, Lucky Luciano loitered at racetracks and baths in Hot Springs, Arkansas. A Murder, Inc., gunman named Gangi Cohen hid in Hollywood, where he played tough-guy parts under an assumed name. Oddly enough, Albert Anastasia joined the US Army.

Gaspipe Casso, however, traveled no more than sixty-five miles, to central New Jersey. He stayed close to more easily manage Lucchese operations in absentia, and to surreptitiously visit Lillian. The FBI determined that Casso occasionally met with capos in Brooklyn, and with Vic Amuso in Pennsylvania, but they never managed to catch him. Though they did find the portions of his fortune, including a safe-deposit box registered in Lillian's maiden name, Delduca, containing a ten-and-a-half-carat diamond ring worth $500,000 and $200,000 in cash stuffed in a cereal box.

Back in Brooklyn, life continued without Casso. Lillian opened a women's lingerie shop in the Flatlands neighborhood. Their son, Anthony Jr., became a Lucchese underling.

For more than two years, Burt Kaplan intermittently drove Lillian from Brooklyn to New Jersey to meet her husband for weekend trysts in a dreary roadside hotel. As he made his way along the Belt Parkway,

Staten Island Expressway, and New Jersey Turnpike, Kaplan habitually checked his mirrors for Plymouth Gran Furys or other models favored by law enforcement.

On Sunday afternoons, Kaplan delivered Lillian back to Brooklyn. Casso returned to his temporary quarters in a hilly, wooded area just outside Mount Olive, a small suburban town of wholesome disposition where families picnicked in Turkey Brook Park and walked dogs along the banks of Budd Lake.

Lillian may have been lonely, but her husband was not. Casso neglected to tell Lillian—he likely told no one—that he was living at the brown split-level home of Rosemarie Billotti, a high school girlfriend whose parents owned a candy store with a jukebox where Casso and his friends once danced and hung out. Her parents had wanted Casso to marry her. He chose Lillian instead. Now Casso had moved in with Rosemarie. Even Casso's secret life held an inner secret.

Casso had been married to Lillian for more than twenty years. By all accounts she loved him, but like most Mafia wives, she chose not to confront her husband about where he spent his late nights or how exactly he earned the rolls of cash he carried. She must have known that he conducted after-hours business in bars and restaurants, and his notoriety made him attractive to a certain kind of woman. "Most all men in my life, everyone I know, had girlfriends," Casso said. "It goes with the territory. Women are drawn to us, the power, the money, and we're drawn to them. But only in passing. Some guys treated mistresses better than their wife, but that's a fucking outrage. No class. Only a *cafone* does that. I never loved any woman but Lillian. She and my family always, always come first."

Casso and his partner, Vic Amuso, would relinquish only limited control to Little Al D'Arco, their stand-in and substitute. From Rosemarie Billotti's house, Casso employed an elaborate system of messengers who directed D'Arco to a list of pay phones, each assigned a code number, at highway rest stops in Queens and Long Island for prearranged discussions of

Lucchese business—how to divide profits, develop new rackets, settle disputes. Casso also made monthly trips in a blue van with tinted windows to a Brooklyn safe house to meet with D'Arco and Kaplan. He disguised himself with a beard and glasses.

Today Casso might be diagnosed with obsessive-compulsive disorder. He meticulously organized everything in his presence, including a card file he kept on hundreds of Lucchese members, with code names and records of their operations. He insisted that D'Arco adhere to the same strict sense of order. "I used to accumulate the money with no records and put it in a bag and send it on," D'Arco said, until Casso insisted on proper bookkeeping. Casso perpetually believed that he was on the verge of returning. "I'll be able to come home because the government will never be able to prove its case," Casso told D'Arco in a phone call intercepted by the FBI. "When I come home, I'm going to have a party and invite all the creeps I want to kill. Then I'll kill them all."

Like an exiled king who had lost his bearings, Casso tried to murder his way out of trouble, with help from his crystal ball. From his Mount Olive bolthole he ordered seven of the more than thirty killings he would later confess to, starting with the death of Bruno Facciolo, the owner of a small Italian restaurant admired for its meat sauce and a veteran family enforcer who, according to Eppolito and Caracappa, had joined the growing list of Lucchese men who betrayed their oath. The detectives relayed word that Facciolo had furnished prosecutors with the names of the men who shot Anthony DiLapi in his girlfriend's Hollywood garage. Facciolo's thirty years of faithful and profitable service to the family counted for nothing.

D'Arco dutifully arranged matters for Casso, as he always had. He ordered a burly soldier named Louis "Louie Bagels" Daidone to ask Facciolo to introduce him to a friend. The meeting would take place in a car repair shop in Canarsie. Facciolo fled when he realized the meeting was a setup, but Daidone dragged him back. Before he died, Daidone later said, Facciolo "begged to be able to see his daughter one last time." Daidone refused. He held Facciolo down while a pair of accomplices stabbed him and shot him in both eyes.

On August 24, police found Facciolo's body in the trunk of his car parked on East Fifty-Fifth Street in Brooklyn after residents phoned the Sixty-Third Precinct complaining of a stench. The late-summer temperature had touched ninety degrees; the corpse had become bloated and begun to decompose. As a final touch, Daidone had stuffed a dead canary in Facciolo's lifeless mouth. Casso had specified the canary as a lurid warning to those who might sing.

The FBI later said that Facciolo had never informed. For whatever reason, Caracappa had passed bad information, as they had with Nicky Guido.

As an addendum, Casso ordered the murder of Facciolo's friends Larry Taylor and Al "Flounderhead" Visconti, after Caracappa reported that a law enforcement bug planted in their Canarsie social club had captured them discussing plans to avenge Facciolo's death. Taylor was shot three times as he sat in his Oldsmobile at 10:30 P.M after a party. Visconti died in the lobby of his apartment building. His assassin shot him four times in the face and once in his penis. Visconti was believed to have been gay. In Casso's mind, his sexuality had shamed the family.

Casso's appetite for revenge knew no expiration date. Even now, in mid-1990, he sought to punish those involved in assassinating Paul Castellano without the Commission's permission, a list that included a short, tough forty-eight-year-old Gotti lieutenant named Eddie Lino.

Five years earlier, Casso might have tapped Frank Santora to kill Lino. Or he might have assigned the job to any number of Lucchese gunmen. But Santora was dead and the Lucchese ranks had proven untrustworthy. Instead, he gave the job to Eppolito and Caracappa. They asked for a gun and a Crown Victoria.

On the evening of November 6, 1990, Detective Mary Dugan of the NYPD Crime Scene Unit arrived to find the area surrounding Lino's Mercedes on the shoulder of the Belt Parkway taped off by precinct police. She could see that Lino had been shot through the open driver's-side window. No glass had shattered to the ground, indicating that he had rolled the window down to speak to whoever had shot him. The only piece of hard evidence found was a black-faced Pulsar quartz wristwatch with a broken band lying fifteen feet from the Mercedes, where it might have slipped from the shooter's wrist. The yellow hands had stopped at 7 P.M., about the time of the shooting.

The day that Eddie Lino died, Burt Kaplan had surgery for a detached retina, his third, at the New York Eye and Ear Infirmary, in Lower Manhattan. At 10 P.M. that night, Eppolito stepped into the hospital room where Kaplan lay sleeping with a patch over one eye. He tapped Kaplan on the foot. "I've got good news," he said. "We got Eddie Lino." Eppolito recounted how they waited for Lino to leave the social club, how they followed him onto the Belt Parkway, how they pulled him over, how Caracappa squeezed the trigger nine times.

"How come Steve shot him?" Kaplan asked.

"Steve's a much better shot,'" Eppolito said. For all his bully talk, Eppolito deferred to Caracappa at moments of critical violence. A few days later, Casso sent a courier with a cake box containing $70,000 in hundred-dollar bills to Kaplan's front door. Eleanor invited him in. He refused. Kaplan forwarded the box to Eppolito and Caracappa.

In the Major Case Squad offices, Detective Chuck Siriano unwittingly joked with Caracappa about the shooter's ineptitude. "I was talking to Steve and I said, 'Well, that's the gang that couldn't shoot straight. The stupid guy left his wristwatch behind.' I'll never forget the look on Steve's face."

Mob bosses customarily retained a driver who also acted as bodyguard, gofer, and confidant. The man at John Gotti's side, day and night, was forty-seven-year-old Bobby Borriello, a six-foot-three Gambino stalwart and seasoned hit man who might pass as an Italian American Elvis Presley.

Casso knew that Gotti and his men had ordered the bungled attempt on his life at the Golden Ox. It could not have surprised Casso, then, when Eppolito and Caracappa produced a police cassette tape containing a covert recording of Borriello discussing the failed hit. Casso immediately recognized Borriello's voice when Kaplan played him the recording on a tape deck he kept in his kitchen. "These guys missed with Casso," Borriello said on the recording, "and they better take care of this thing or I'm going to get mad and I'll drive right into his driveway and kill him and his whole family."

Casso now added Borriello to his assassination list. In March 1991, Borriello's wife, Susan, answered the door of their three-story shingle house on Bay Twenty-Ninth Street, an area of well-tended middle-class homes in the Bath Beach section of Brooklyn, where the couple had recently moved with their children, ages two and eleven. A heavyset man she later recognized as Eppolito introduced himself as a detective. "He showed up alone, said he was a detective, showed a badge, pushed his jacket back to show a gun, did not give his name, but asked, 'Does Bobby Borriello live here?'" she said later. "I told him my husband wasn't home, and he said he'd be back, but he never returned."

At 7:30 P.M. on April 13, a Saturday night, Borriello pulled into his driveway after spending the afternoon at Aqueduct Racetrack. Susan was inside feeding Bobby Jr., their two-year-old. Their other son, Patrick, was at a movie.

Borriello's twenty-one-year-old nephew stepped outside after hearing a series of loud bangs. He found his uncle lying on his left side beside his new Lincoln Town Car. Big Frank Lastorino, a member of Casso's crew, had shot Borriello twice in the head and five times in the torso, then drove off. Susan came outside to see her husband "next to the car, all full of blood and holes." She collapsed when he was pronounced dead.

Police found ten shells from a .38-caliber semiautomatic pistol scattered about the driveway and a framed oil portrait of Gotti in the back of Borriello's car.

A few days later, Caracappa showed up to ask the neighbors what they knew about the murder. His questions might have seemed like a routine follow-up. Caracappa was more likely assessing who might have witnessed the murder, if anyone had, and who might be talking to the police.

Borriello was buried the old way, with a three-day wake at Raccuglia Funeral Home on Court Street and a bronze casket carried into 125-year-old St. Stephen's Church, where the Reverend Michael Carrano asked the Lord to "care for our brother Bobby." Outside, where television reporters queried locals, an elderly woman shrugged and said in Italian, "You talk, you die."

The sidewalk crone had recited an ancient Mafia credo. Casso had certainly done his part to enforce it. But by the spring of 1991, the two-fisted rules Casso grew up by on the Brooklyn docks had begun to lose their grip. The dictates had come to seem outmoded, even quaint. Nobody, not even Casso, could stop the rush of defectors and informants who chose to start life afresh in the Witness Protection Program. Associates and capos reacted like schooling fish. One by one they chose an advantageous moment to uncouple themselves from their crime families, to take their chances as cooperators. Their education rarely exceeded grade school, but they could shrewdly read the equation of risk and reward, as a card player might.

On May 8, 1991, the Lucchese capo Fat Pete Chiodo pulled into Pellicano's, a gas station a few blocks from a toll booth on the Staten Island side of the Verrazzano-Narrows Bridge, to investigate a knocking sound in his engine. He and a mechanic lifted the hood and peered in.

Chiodo was called "Fat Pete" for a reason. Jimmy Breslin, the newspaper columnist, called him "the fattest guy in world mafia history," an impressive claim considering the competition. At his heaviest, Chiodo weighed close to five hundred pounds. He was said to weigh himself with an industrial scale at a Staten Island freight terminal. He had a full head of black hair, thick tinted eyeglasses, and at least two chins.

The engine knocking may have alarmed Chiodo, given his tenuous standing in the Lucchese family. Chiodo was facing RICO charges in the Housing Authority windows case, the labor-racketeering investigation that drove Casso into hiding. The government case was so solid, and the likely sentence so lengthy, that Chiodo chose to plead guilty. However, he neglected to first ask permission from Amuso and Casso, the family bosses. Chiodo's plea convinced them that he had struck a deal and turned informant, though that was not the case.

A blue Chevrolet Caprice pulled up while Chiodo tightened his fan belt. Two men opened fire with a .38 caliber and 9-millimeter pistol. Chiodo made a massive target. The shooters could hardly miss: they hit him in the chest, stomach, legs, and arms as he stood with his head under the hood. "You should feel the breeze a bullet makes going past your ear," Chiodo later said.

Chiodo pulled his own gun and returned fire while retreating backward into a mechanic bay. After taking twelve bullets, Chiodo collapsed on his back like a wounded buffalo. "I happened to see the man that fell," a witness later told the police. "He was in a pool of blood." At that point, an attacker's gun jammed. He and his accomplice assumed they had done enough to kill anyone. They drove off.

Chiodo passed out from blood loss, but lived. His fat absorbed the bullets like pebbles dropped into a bowl of pudding. His girth saved his life.

After learning that Chiodo had survived, Casso sent a member of Chiodo's own crew, a man named Richard "Richie the Toupee" Pagliarulo, to Chiodo's lawyer to deliver a message: if Chiodo testifies in the windows case, we'll kill his wife. "While I lay in a hospital bed more dead than alive," Chiodo said, "they said my wife would be next."

Pagliarulo also tracked down Chiodo's father and told him the entire family would die if Chiodo cooperated with the government. The threat hardened Chiodo's disaffection. "I've come to a different outlook on a lot of things since the shooting," he said.

If Chiodo needed new friends, the charismatic and colorful Assistant US Attorney Charles Rose was happy to oblige. He showed up at Chiodo's bedside with a large pizza. Chiodo lay nearly incapacitated in his hospital bed. He was swaddled in bandages and encumbered by intravenous tubes. But he could smell the savory aroma of tomato and mozzarella filling the room.

Rose apologized for eating in front of Chiodo. He had had no time for dinner.

"I could go for a slice," Chiodo said.

"Oh, I don't think the doctors would like that," Rose said. "How could I justify it? 'Federal prosecutor feeds forbidden food to gravely wounded mafioso.' My god, I'd be in terrible trouble."

"Listen," Chiodo said. "What the fucking doctors don't know won't hurt them. So we'll eat a little pizza, and, you know, talk."

Chiodo was unable to feed himself. So Rose held a slice to Chiodo's mouth while arguing that the gas station ambush should annul his obligations to the Lucchese family. Whenever Chiodo warmed to the prospect of severing his mob ties, Rose fed him more pizza.

By the time Rose left the hospital that night, Chiodo had agreed to cooperate. He would recount all he knew about the Lucchese family. In return, the government would waive murder charges against him and enroll Chiodo and his family in the Witness Protection Program. Though it's hard to imagine many things harder than hiding a 435-pound gangster.

Four months later, Chiodo testified against his former associates accused of rigging $148 million in contracts to replace windows in public housing projects from Washington Heights to Flushing. A federal judge moved the trial to Westchester for three days to accommodate Chiodo, who was recuperating in an undisclosed hospital nearby. A phalanx of police and federal agents carrying machine guns and wearing bulletproof vests rolled Chiodo into the courtroom in an extra-wide wheelchair.

When Charles Rose, the prosecutor, asked about the blood oath sworn at his Mafia induction, a ceremony conducted above a Brooklyn funeral home, Chiodo repeated the vow: "If I ever betray my sacred oath, may my soul burn in hell." Chiodo wiped sweat from his brow. His right hand began to tremble so violently that Rose rushed to support him. After a recess, Chiodo was describing bribes that contractors paid to unions when he faltered again. "I'm really dizzy, your honor," he said before his ham-sized head dropped unconscious into his hands.

Casso could not punish Chiodo for his testimony as long as the government hid him, but he could exact revenge on those family members who chose to forgo protection. At 7:40 A.M. on March 10, 1992, Chiodo's thirty-seven-year-old sister, Patricia Capozzalo, stopped her Oldsmobile Cutlass Supreme at a red light in Bensonhurst after dropping one of her three children at school. A stolen black van with tinted windows pulled up beside her. Two Lucchese gunmen wearing ski masks got out and fired through the driver's-side window. Two shots hit Capozzalo in the neck and back, but she managed to duck under the dashboard for protection. She survived. After recovering, she and her husband joined the rest of the family in witness protection.

By attacking Capozzalo, Casso again broke a Mafia commandment: never harm uninvolved family, particularly women. Edward Wright, chief investigator for the New York State Organized Crime Task Force, called the ambush one of the "last desperate acts" of an underworld leader who may be "sending a message to subordinates saying whether you go into the Witness Protection Program or not, your relatives are fair game, whether they be men or women."

Less than a year later, on a cold February afternoon, a patrolman was preparing to tow a black Acura abandoned at Vermont Street and Flatlands Avenue, in the East New York neighborhood of Brooklyn. As a matter of routine, he checked the trunk before the tow truck rolled away. Inside he found a black plastic bag. Within the bag lay the frozen body of Chiodo's sixty-eight-year-old uncle, Frank Signorino, who had been missing for three days. He had been strangled and stabbed more than forty times.

Nobody obeyed the old order more faithfully than Little Al D'Arco, the titular head of the Lucchese family installed by Casso on his way into hiding. He was the good soldier, the steadfast fighter who found himself stationed above his natural level. He was nothing if not faithful. For eight months D'Arco had done everything Casso asked, though he later said that some of Casso's murder schemes were so paranoid that he found a way to ignore them.

Now, in this long season of disarray and uncertainty, even D'Arco was glancing over his shoulder. During the summer of 1991, his intermittent phone calls with Casso gave him cause to worry. He knew that Casso blamed him for the failed gas station attack on Chiodo and Chiodo's subsequent defection. D'Arco now detected a wind shift. Old friends grew standoffish. He sensed that he might be the next one found moldering in a car trunk.

D'Arco's apprehensions were warranted. Casso announced that a four-man committee would replace D'Arco as acting boss. D'Arco could take comfort in the knowledge that he would be among the four. Still, it was a humiliating demotion and a worrisome sign that Casso had lost faith in him.

On the night of September 18, D'Arco met with his fellow panelists at the Kimberly Hotel in Midtown Manhattan to discuss plans to exert control over the market for cardboard boxes used by grocery stores. The atmosphere in the room struck him as unusually tense. He noted with alarm the unexpected arrival of Mike "Big Mike" DeSantis, a Lucchese hit man. "I knew something was wrong," D'Arco later said. "Mike DeSantis had a funny-looking shirt on—like a bulletproof sweatshirt made of stiff material." He could see that DeSantis carried a gun concealed in his waistband, in the small of his back. D'Arco greeted him nonchalantly. "Hey, Mike, how you been?" he said, shaking hands. DeSantis's hand was "ice cold and clammy."

D'Arco noticed that DeSantis returned from the bathroom without the gun, which meant that anyone could retrieve it from a bathroom hiding spot, a standard ploy. The next man to use the bathroom might come out shooting.

D'Arco made a quick departure. "I'm leaving," he said. "I've been here too long." He stepped briskly from the hotel room and out onto Fiftieth Street. His driver was missing, further evidence of a trap. He walked off into the Midtown crowds.

D'Arco's break was clean and complete. He sent his wife, Dolores, and four of their five children to the safety of Hawaii. Meanwhile, he and his son Joseph hid at his mother's home in Bayville, a blue-collar

Long Island village sandwiched between the high-WASP enclaves of Locust Valley and Centre Island.

"That's it," he later recalled. "I washed my hands of the whole thing."

At 7 P.M. on the evening of September 21—three days after he fled the Kimberly Hotel—an intermediary phoned the FBI's New York field office on D'Arco's behalf and asked to speak to a veteran agent named Robert Marston. The switchboard operator checked with Marston, then put the call through to his suburban Connecticut home, where he was halfway out the door with his wife and children. They were going to a church fair with neighbors.

The intermediary came on the line. After a brief introduction he passed the phone to D'Arco, who asked Marston if he knew who he was. He did. Marston had learned of D'Arco's role in the Lucchese family while investigating a landfill operator who split proceeds with organized crime.

"I was told you were someone I could talk to," D'Arco said.

D'Arco began to speak in anxious, disjointed phrases about unspecified people trying to kill him. "His tone was highly agitated, very stressed and aggressive sounding," Marston said. "I'm sure he was sizing me up, and I was trying to size him up and figure out what the phone call was about."

D'Arco told Marston that he had weapons on hand and would use them if gunmen arrived. "I'm an hour away," Marston said. "If you're in imminent danger you need the local police to come out. I can call them for you. He said, 'No, I'm okay for now.'" D'Arco felt confident that he could defend himself. He had done so his entire life, under the toughest circumstances. But he could not protect his extended family if Casso came after them, as he might.

To calm the mood and promote trust Marston shared a bit about himself—his wife, his family, his posting in the FBI's New Rochelle office. He promised D'Arco that he would never lie to him. He would be candid when he didn't have an answer.

"I tried just to be a good listener and be myself," he said. "I had worked on enough cases with violent people who eventually cooperated to know not to be confrontational or challenge his power or strength. I knew it was unprecedented to be having that kind of conversation with someone at that level in the organized crime world. I just tried to be calm and listen as much as I could and be appreciative of what he was saying."

After he and D'Arco developed a measure of rapport, Marston indicated that he wanted to continue talking, if D'Arco did, but first he would have to consult with his FBI associates. They adjourned so that Marston could place calls. They were back on the phone by 8:30 P.M. Marston told D'Arco that he now had approval to bring him and his son to a safe location.

Marston and three other FBI agents pulled up to D'Arco's mother's modest house on a Bayville back street a little before midnight. Two additional agents waited in a second car down the street. D'Arco insisted that Marston be present for the FBI's arrival. In return, Marston stipulated that D'Arco and his son leave their guns inside. They stepped out front carrying only gym bags. "I didn't pat them down," Marston said. "I didn't look in their bags. Management might not have approved, but I thought it was a way to build a little trust. I followed my instinct."

The agents first drove D'Arco and his son to the FBI office in New Rochelle. They stopped long enough to arrange matters by phone, then went on to a hotel near Marston's home in southern Connecticut. As they drove through the darkened commuter towns of Greenwich, Stamford, and Norwalk, Marston spoke to D'Arco of minor matters to advance trust. It was, Marston said, "a surreal experience" to make small talk with a crime family boss as he pivoted away from his lifelong allegiance.

The FBI kept D'Arco and his son in the hotel for a week. He was under no obligation to stay, and at times he threatened to leave as the stress of his circumstance undid him. On at least one occasion, Marston walked D'Arco around the hotel parking lot until he calmed down.

At week's end, D'Arco signed a cooperation agreement in consultation with a lawyer the FBI hired on his behalf. At that point the FBI took his pager and reviewed his communications, including phone numbers and coded messages. They moved him to a rented home, a safe house, in northern Westchester, where he and his son lived under guard for months while agents debriefed him. The house was made secure with infrared sensors crisscrossing the perimeter. After long, tedious days of questioning he relaxed by cooking the agents dinner from his repertoire of Sicilian dishes. They shared a table laden with pasta and seafood. One evening Marston watched the Mafia classic *Goodfellas* with D'Arco, who provided a running commentary. He had worked closely with many of the real-life characters depicted in the movie, and had attended events the actors re-created.

As acting boss of the Lucchese family, D'Arco became the highest-ranking mafioso to cooperate with the government. "I'm going to tell you what I know," D'Arco said, "and how I know it." And he knew a lot. Marston and his fellow agents were pleasantly surprised to find that D'Arco had nearly complete recall of Lucchese affairs amassed over a long career of racketeering, loan-sharking, payoffs, and murders. He stood on intimate terms with the bosses and capos of all five families.

Among other things, D'Arco knew who was on Casso's assassination list. Agents discreetly approached the surviving targets to alert them. They showed the potential victims a photo of D'Arco holding Marston's FBI credentials to prove that the warning was not a trick—that it came from a credible source. In some cases, D'Arco wrote them a personal note. "Usually the answer was, 'Okay, thanks very much. I appreciate that,'" Marston said.

One day, shortly after an incarcerated mafioso died of cancer, D'Arco spoke to Marston privately about the routine blood test inmates take to screen for diseases. D'Arco began by pointing to his finger. "When guys from our crew get arrested and go to prison they get the blood test," he said.

Marston nodded, unsure of D'Arco's point.

"That's when they get injected," D'Arco said. He listed mafiosi who had died of cancer while imprisoned.

"In all seriousness, he and the people around him believed that when they got blood tests we injected them with cancer cells. To me, it was telling because it shows what an enormous leap it was for him to go from acting boss of a crime family to joining people he thinks are capable of injecting him with cancer."

After his long debriefing, D'Arco and ten relatives vanished into the Witness Protection Program. Before leaving, D'Arco gave Marston a few handwritten recipes, including a dish he called *Al's zuppa di pesce*.

D'Arco lived the rest of his life under a new identity, resurfacing under his real name to testify for the prosecution in fifteen mob trials. "For the rest of his life Al expressed remorse for things he had done while on the streets," Marston said, "and wondered if his years of testifying would compensate for his prior deeds."

D'Arco's flight into federal protection presented a grave threat to Eppolito and Caracappa. D'Arco was aware that Casso received inside information from detectives. Now that he was beholden to the government, D'Arco would not hesitate to share what he knew about Casso's crystal ball with agents, prosecutors, and, eventually, a jury.

On March 15, 1991, the television show *America's Most Wanted* profiled the fugitive Lucchese bosses Vic Amuso and Gaspipe Casso, who had been hiding for almost a year. As always, the show invited viewers to offer anonymous tips on a toll-free hotline.

Four months later, the FBI received word that Amuso regularly fielded phone calls at a public pay phone in a shopping mall in Dickson City, Pennsylvania. Agents arrested him outside a Thriftway pharmacy in the mall complex on July 28. They cuffed him, marched him to a black Dodge, and took him away.

Prosecutors charged Amuso with racketeering, extortion, fraud, bribery, and nine murders. Assistant US Attorney Charles Rose called him "a deadly don." In the weeks leading up to his trial, Amuso asked the judge to stop federal marshals from walking him into hearings dressed in his orange prison jumpsuit. He found it humiliating. The judge refused.

The marquee prosecution witness was Al D'Arco. He carried all the physical menace of a midlevel insurance executive, but his words stung. For three straight days he spoke slowly and clearly of drug deals, loan-sharking, extortion, and murder—all under the gaze of his former friend seated at the defense table.

Asked if he was testifying as retaliation for the plan to murder him in the Kimberly Hotel, D'Arco answered: "Yes, I am."

The jury convicted Amuso on all fifty-four counts. Minutes after the judge dispatched him with a sentence of life without parole, Amuso walked out of the courtroom smiling. But his wife, Barbara, confronted prosecutors in the hallway. "There's been an injustice done," she screamed. "You should hide your head in shame."

Amuso was the second Mafia boss convicted in Brooklyn that year. John Gotti, head of the Gambino family, was found guilty in the same courthouse six months earlier. He too received a life sentence.

Amuso's conviction deepened Casso's isolation. Now stripped of his closest ally, he continued to run the Lucchese family remotely, from Mount Olive, with a queasy awareness that D'Arco and other informants were sharing sordid details about him with investigators.

At 9:30 A.M. on September 20, 1991, a passerby noticed the body of Anthony Fava, the architect of Casso's Mill Basin home, laid out across the back seat of a stolen Oldsmobile Cutlass parked in Bensonhurst. He had been stabbed, shot, and stripped to his boxer shorts. His body was wrapped in a plastic sheet. His family had reported him missing two days earlier.

Meanwhile, the extravagant house Fava had designed for Casso on a waterfront corner in Mill Basin sat unoccupied. Casso had never moved in. Weeds sprouted in the yard. Vandals broke two picture windows. Newspapers reported that Casso ordered Fava killed because he had the audacity to send Casso an invoice. The Long Island newspaper *Newsday* offered a different explanation: Fava died because he was conducting an affair with Lillian, Casso's wife, while Casso was in hiding. The paper cited an anonymous government source. For whatever reason, Casso concluded the source was Charles Rose, the assistant US attorney, and planned his revenge.

The mist rose from Budd Lake, near Mount Olive, New Jersey, in the morning, as it did every year when the autumn air cooled. The leaves turned yellow and red on the rounded hills of Allamuchy Mountain.

Casso's surroundings were serene, even as his circumstance grew dire. By 1992, federal prosecutors had decimated the Lucchese ranks. Half of its men had been jailed, murdered, or flipped. He had almost no one left to rely on, except for his steadfast moles Eppolito and Caracappa.

With Amuso now incarcerated in rural Connecticut and strings of defectors headed into the Witness Protection Program, the FBI intensified its search for Casso, a last big fish loose in the sea. Agents felt confident that they would catch him soon. Though they wondered if they might find him dead. Casso had spent years arranging the deaths of informants, thanks to Eppolito and Caracappa. Now, as his capture became more likely, his own troops might turn their guns on him to prevent him from talking about them.

"We're getting closer, and [Amuso's] conviction will turn [Casso] up soon," said Don North, an agent who helped supervise the FBI investigations. "The question is whether it will turn him up alive or dead."

10

OPERATION GANGPLANK

CRIMINAL INVESTIGATIONS CAN BE LIKE WEATHER
patterns swirling over unfamiliar terrain. The topography comes into
view at its own pace, depending on how the wind blows.

Federal and state law enforcement knew all about the fugitive
Gaspipe Casso's criminal life and his psychopathic bloodthirst. They
knew his dark chapters, most of them anyway. But they could not
puzzle out how Casso had anticipated so many of their investigative
maneuvers—arrests, raids, wiretaps, bugs, informants—with such accuracy and foreknowledge. Nor did they grasp that Burt Kaplan, the
major league drug trafficker and inventive Lucchese adjunct, helped
Casso stay a step ahead of the law by relaying inside information supplied by Eppolito and Caracappa.

This part of the story—the alliance of convenience and profit forged
among Casso, Kaplan, and the detectives—was still unknown to investigators. It would remain so until a group of dogged DEA agents made
the connection almost by accident after a seven-month probe of a Staten
Island drug syndicate.

In the late 1980s, a big, bully-tempered Bonanno associate named
Freddy Puglisi sold pot from a corner grocery store called Piks on Flatlands Avenue in the Canarsie section of Brooklyn. Piks was the kind
of thinly concealed pot dispensary found in most New York neighborhoods before gentrification erased the city's seedy vestiges. Any shopper
could walk out with paper towels, cat litter, and a dime bag.

Puglisi was a big man, six feet four and a paunchy 240 pounds—a minor operator with grand ambitions. "Freddy was a nobody selling nickel and dime bags," said a DEA agent, "but he was a climber. He wanted to be a mobster."

Puglisi haggled bitterly with his supplier, a heavyweight dealer unwilling to grant Puglisi a chance to elevate his standing in the competitive drug market. Puglisi eventually scouted for an alternative, a source capable of raising him to the next level. Puglisi's underling, Rob Lucchese (no relation to the Lucchese crime family), introduced him to an acquaintance whose cousin attended Arizona State University in Tucson. The cousin, along with two other students, used a connection to import pot from Mexico. The students offered to supply Puglisi. As a test, Puglisi sent a $500 money order by Western Union. In return he received a five-pound sample of acceptable quality. The next day, Puglisi and two sidekicks flew to Tucson to set up a supply chain.

At first Puglisi sent cash to Arizona stashed in packages of toys. In exchange, the students mailed five- or ten-pound parcels of pot by US Postal Service and Federal Express. To divert attention from Puglisi, they addressed the deliveries to half a dozen friends and family members scattered about the bayfront neighborhood of Canarsie. By dividing the deliveries into small portions—ten pounds or less—Puglisi reduced the risk of jail.

Puglisi collected the packages and paid the recipients for their trouble. He could afford to. He paid $500 for a pound of pot and sold it for more than twice that. He was on his way to building a moneymaking machine, but he was insatiable. He wanted more.

By 1989 he had set up an additional supply chain: a handful of couriers flew to western cities with as much as $100,000 hidden in luggage. They returned by Greyhound bus or Amtrak hauling suitcases stuffed with pot. The couriers included Marie Molini, the mother of one of Puglisi's sidemen, and her sixty-something friend Edith Minkoff, both devoted gamblers. Puglisi paid them fifty dollars for every pound they brought home, plus an added perk: if they traveled through Las Vegas, he paid for a two-night stay, plus a gambling stipend.

The buses and trains proved an imperfect way to move substantial quantities of pot across the country. In July 1991, police detained Rob Spinelli, a Puglisi associate, and his sister Maryann in Chicago while transporting two suitcases of pot by train. The police found the pot in Maryann's bag, but Rob took responsibility and faced minor drug trafficking charges.

When Puglisi merged with an operation run by Rob's brother, Lucchese associate Mike "Baldy Mike" Spinelli, he inherited a more professional method: nine or so couriers flew west with stacks of hundred-dollar bills. They drove back to New York in Mercedes sedans with two hundred pounds of pot packed in Tupperware sealed with silicone to hide the odor. A San Diego lawyer had advised that Mercedes was the brand of car police were least likely to stop. For the same reason, the cars were registered in California; New York plates invited too much notice in the heartland.

Puglisi and his helpers met the couriers in empty Staten Island parking lots after 2 A.M. to transfer hundreds of pounds into the hands of waiting street distributors. The leftover bundles went to safe locations, known as stash houses. A repair shop called Guy's Tires cleaned the cars after each trip to eliminate incriminating scents. A car-carrying trailer then transported the Mercedes west so the couriers could do it all over again. So it went, month after month.

The supply operation was intricate and risky. On December 4, 1991, a Kansas highway patrolman named David Heim noticed a cream-colored Mercedes swerve across the painted lane line on an exit ramp off I-70 just outside Salina. He pulled the car over. The driver was a Puglisi courier named Sal Romano, though he claimed to be a San Diego resident driving to visit family in Brooklyn. Heim asked if the car contained any guns or narcotics. Romano said no, but he grew fidgety and shifty-eyed. Romano walked to Grandma Max's restaurant in a nearby truck stop for a bowl of soup while Heim brought in a dog for a sniff search. In the trunk Heim found clothes, a shaving kit, and two hundred pounds of pot wrapped in plastic. A lawyer flew in. Romano walked out on bail. And that was the end of it.

When Heim searched Romano's car he also found a map showing a zigzag eastbound route. Like all couriers, Romano followed a path that dipped south and veered north through the Midwest. The San Diego lawyer designed the route so the couriers would traverse states with lenient possession laws and counties too shorthanded to stop many cars. Puglisi had shrewdly limited the deliveries to about two hundred pounds, not enough to warrant serious legal consequence.

Over three and a half years, from January 1989 to mid-August 1992, Puglisi imported a total of forty-five tons, roughly a ton a month, from Mexico, Arizona, California, and Canada for a profit of more than $45 million. As a Bonanno associate, he was obliged to share a percentage of his profit with his capo, Frank Lino, cousin of Eddie Lino, the Gambino capo who died when Eppolito and Caracappa pulled him over to the shoulder of the Belt Parkway.

Pot arrived by the carload, but Puglisi still could not satisfy the demand. He turned to another supplier capable of helping him fulfill his ambition to become New York's biggest dealer: Burt Kaplan, the Brooklyn drug dealer and financial fixer.

Puglisi met Kaplan in 1990 through Mickey Sutter, a respected Lucchese associate. In return for the introduction, Puglisi agreed to pay Sutter $25 for every pound bought from Kaplan. The volume was so great that Sutter's cut totaled as much as $75,000 a month. For Puglisi, the added expense paid off. Kaplan's bounteous supply elevated Puglisi to a position near the top of New York's mob-controlled drug trade.

Buying from Kaplan was safer, too. Puglisi no longer worried about patrolmen pulling couriers to the highway shoulder in Texas or Ohio. Kaplan's pot arrived at the door of Puglisi's new Staten Island home as reliably as Chinese delivery. What's more, Kaplan's pot was high grade. The street couldn't get enough.

Kaplan delegated the logistics of supply to Tommy Galpine, the assistant he treated as a son. Galpine arranged for tons of pot to cross the border, bundled with knockoff clothing, to Café DiNova Italia, a restaurant he and Kaplan owned in El Paso, Texas.

Every few weeks, Galpine and a helper packed the pot—cut, compressed, and weighed—in the restaurant's basement. They stowed it in Rubbermaid containers hidden among boxes of counterfeit clothing loaded onto a truck. Galpine paid a driver $10,000 to deliver the containers to New York. The clothes went to Kaplan's Staten Island warehouse. He stored the pot in freezers installed in a second warehouse on West Thirty-Sixth Street, in the Garment District of Manhattan.

Galpine regularly loaded a dozen boxes of pot from the warehouse into the back of his Ford Bronco and crossed the Verrazzano-Narrows Bridge to Puglisi's home on Dent Road in Staten Island. He timed his deliveries for off-hours—before 6 A.M. or late at night. On one occasion, Puglisi went to Galpine's Brooklyn home to find a thousand pounds of pot spread across the living room floor. "Take what you need," Galpine said.

Puglisi delivered payments to Kaplan's Staten Island warehouse under carefully scripted terms: He paged Kaplan beforehand. Kaplan called back from a pay phone. Puglisi's driver waited in the car; it was understood that Puglisi would enter the warehouse alone, and that he and Kaplan would conduct transactions one-on-one. No witnesses, no hangers-on.

Kaplan supplied Puglisi with so much pot over eighteen months that he single-handedly swayed the street price. Stoners who bought a nickel bag in, say, Washington Square Park or any other open-air drug market of the time likely benefited from Puglisi's distribution chain.

As Puglisi's business grew, so did the risks. He protected his operation by surrounding himself with mob associates and made men. Once, when a buyer reached for a bag of pot stored in a basement freezer, Puglisi stopped him. "Not that one," he said, "that's the one with the head in it." A man suspected of stealing drug profits from Puglisi's home was strangled with a rope—the so-called Sicilian necktie—and dumped in Jamaica Bay inside a metal tool locker.

Puglisi eventually expanded his dealings with Kaplan to include stolen clothing and heroin. As the men grew closer, professionally if not personally, Puglisi learned that Kaplan had his own means of protecting his considerable interests from unwanted notice and intrusion: he received a steady stream of detailed information from his secret source, his crystal ball.

Puglisi and his band of drug dealers might have gone undetected if not for an indiscreet customer. In the spring of 1991, an undercover Pennsylvania state trooper bought six pounds of pot and two ounces of cocaine from an electrician named Joe Forlenza, who had moved from Staten Island to Stroudsburg, a picturesque town in the Pocono Mountains. Forlenza made a conspicuous target; he swaggered about the drowsy mountain village like a gangster. He had also cultivated a barroom friendship with the local police chief, which aroused the attention of state officials.

When state police tapped Forlenza's phones they found that he regularly peddled modest quantities of pot and cocaine. It was clear to investigators that Forlenza was supplied by his New York mob connections, though their exact identities remained murky. The recordings contained only nicknames—"Big John," "Little John," and "Bubblegum," among others.

On January 16, 1992, the Pennsylvania Attorney General's office contacted the DEA, which traced the nicknames back to overlapping circles of drug traffickers in Manhattan, Brooklyn, and Staten Island, a group centered on Puglisi. Two weeks later, the DEA launched Operation Gangplank to investigate Puglisi and his extended crowd of accomplices and abettors. ("Gangplank" referred to the migration of Italian Americans from Brooklyn to Staten Island.)

Puglisi's house proved tricky to watch because it stood back from the street on a low stretch of Dent Road. To see the house—to monitor its comings and goings—agents had to park in a conspicuous spot. "You're sitting on a slight incline and that's where they could easily see us," said Frank Drew, a veteran agent who had grown up a few miles away, across a narrow sliver of water called Arthur Kill, in Carteret, New Jersey. "It was a little easier in the winter with no leaves. We'd do drive-bys once in a while, but not too often or they'd recognize the car."

Drew had a reputation for relentless work, following his subjects for as much as seventeen straight hours. He had spent seven years in the FBI, three of them shadowing Eastern European counterintelligence agents operating out of United Nations consulates. He spied on spies.

Now, with the DEA, Drew led surveillance efforts in Staten Island. The DEA staffed Operation Gangplank with ten or so young agents, several just six months removed from a twelve-week training course in Quantico, Virginia. Drew was the guide, a street-seasoned veteran who showed the way.

Drew would position an agent in a car, known as the eye car, within sight of the subject's home or workplace, with one or two backups parked blocks away. "Frank had surveillance expertise," said Agent Mike Foldesi. "He was always orchestrating our positions. 'Hey, go set up over *there*. You go set up over *there*. You can look down *here*.'"

Drew and the other agents sometimes sat in parked cars watching Puglisi's home from 8 A.M. until 11 P.M., taking brief bathroom breaks at a nearby firehouse and fetching gas station coffee. To avoid detection, Drew regularly swapped one unmarked DEA car for another, drawing from a fleet the agency seized from drug dealers. Staten Island's hilly terrain complicated the observation by intermittently blocking signals when agents stationed nearby spoke by handheld radio.

Puglisi and his crew proved easy to watch. For all their thuggery, they were homebodies. "We knew their regimens," Drew said. "If we came by Puglisi's house and his car wasn't there we knew where to find him. We knew where they ate. We knew where their girlfriends lived. They were all home by a certain hour."

For Puglisi, the routine included beating his wife, Jackie, or so it appeared to Drew. The agents never saw him hit her, but they saw her coming and going wearing oversized sunglasses to hide bruises. Puglisi's associates later confirmed his abuse, and said they had considered interceding.

At 7:30 P.M. or so on the evening of January 21, 1992, Drew and Foldesi scouted a drab condo near the railroad tracks in the Oakwood section of

Staten Island. The condo belonged to John Silvestri, a Colombo family associate nicknamed "Bubblegum" because he accepted his first murder-for-hire assignment at the tender age of seventeen. He had moved into the condo after getting out of prison four months earlier and immediately began trafficking pot with Puglisi.

Drew and Foldesi drove by that day to see how they might set up surveillance in the awkward, alley-like lot outside Silvestri's condo. Five minutes after Drew parked, Silvestri unexpectedly came outside to walk his pit bull. "Silvestri stood on a little landing on the steps leading up to his front door," Drew said. "He looked left and right and suddenly his head darted back to the right. I thought, oh shit, he's looking at my car."

Silvestri walked over and tried to peer in, his face practically pressed to the glass. Drew and Foldesi slumped in their seats. Fortunately for them, the car, seized from a Queens drug dealer, had dark-tinted windows. "I hated those windows," Drew said, "but thank God for them. He never saw us."

Not surprisingly, Drew concluded that he would be too conspicuous watching Silvestri's home from a parked car, as he did elsewhere. Two months later, Drew met with a priest at Monsignor Farrell High School, more than a block from Silvestri's condo, to ask if the DEA could borrow space for an observation post. The priest said nothing. He simply handed Drew a set of keys and told him to use any unoccupied room. Over the following days Drew mounted a camera on a telephone pole overlooking Silvestri's front door. A transmitter beamed video a quarter mile to a receiver set up in an unused bedroom in a house where faculty lived on the school grounds. While students studied calculus and Latin downstairs, Drew and his colleagues watched Silvestri come and go.

On April 6, Drew and Foldesi followed Silvestri to Miller Field, a beachfront park with nine softball diamonds. Drew considered inviting Silvestri to play catch. If he accepted, Drew might propose that he become a DEA informant. "I knew he was into softball and I played softball at the time," Drew said. "I was just going to start bullshitting with him and just talk to him like a regular guy. At the end I'd say, hey, this is who I am. This is what we've got on you. You don't want to go back to jail. What do you want to do? And see what he said."

In the end, Drew's colleagues dissuaded him. They judged Silvestri unlikely to cooperate. Five months later, agents told Silvestri about Drew's plan. "I wish you had," he said. "I'd have rolled in a minute."

The ten or so agents assigned to Operation Gangplank initially wire-tapped John Silvestri's and Freddy Puglisi's home phones. A young agent named Eileen Dinnan and a handful of colleagues listened live from the DEA's Tenth Avenue office, in a factorylike building in the Chelsea neighborhood of Manhattan, where newly arrested drug dealers sat in detention cells facing a sign that read: "Home of the world's finest investigators. Enjoy your stay."

In law enforcement parlance, the agents "worked the wire," deciphering the encoded references to money, drug deals, and women. (The dealers lightly disguised their banter by referring to cocaine as "rock" and pot as "that thing.") The wire room agents learned to parse one voice from another, and to alert the field agents to departures and arrivals.

"Whatever they got they relayed out to us," Drew said. "They would call us out on the street and tell us so-and-so got a call, or somebody's coming over." The field agents, in turn, told the wire room who showed up so they could match an unfamiliar voice to a name.

As a matter of routine, the agents checked the identity of every phone number the drug dealers called and received. By spring 1992, technology had changed the game. The wire room agents increasingly found calls going to a pair of cell numbers as Puglisi and his friend Bobby Molini traded their pagers for a clunky precursor to flip phones.

Tapping landlines was hard enough, cell phones trickier still. With a judge's authorization, agents could direct phone companies to grant the wire room eavesdropping access to specific cell numbers. The trickiest part was getting close enough to record the tiny frequency number inscribed on the side of the phone. It required a measure of audacity and daring.

On May 17, Drew and his partner, Agent Foldesi, followed Puglisi and two sidekicks as they drove in Bobby Molini's stolen Mercedes convertible to the Colonnade, a suburban diner a few blocks from the softball diamonds at Miller Field. Foldesi went inside to watch from a distance as Puglisi and Molini ate in a rear booth.

When Drew walked by Molini's convertible he noticed Puglisi's phone, an OKI Pioneer, lying on the front seat. After confirming with Foldesi that Puglisi could not see the car from his booth, Drew photographed the phone. A DEA photo technician printed the photo large enough, and with enough clarity, to read the frequency number. By June 22, agents stationed in the wire room began listening to Puglisi issue orders on his cell phone.

A week earlier, on June 15, Drew had reluctantly met three NYPD detectives at the DEA office in Manhattan to brief them on the investigation. The detectives listened as he summarized in deliberately vague terms how he and fellow agents surveilled Puglisi and his crew. He told them that they had tapped landlines, and they had applied to the Department of Justice for approval to tap cell phones as well.

Drew shared this information grudgingly. Almost nobody outside the operation's immediate circle of agents knew about their work. Drew preferred to keep matters contained and confidential. However, a former NYPD detective, now a DEA intelligence analyst, had asked him to come in and describe his work in Staten Island. The analyst had helped Drew in the past, and Drew felt obliged to reciprocate. Still, Drew left the DEA field office with unease. The briefing was purportedly held to discuss overlapping interests, but it wasn't clear what they might be. The detectives introduced themselves, but Drew didn't retain their names. Who were they, he wondered, and why did they care about Operation Gangplank? He later suspected that Stephen Caracappa sat in. His attendance would help explain what happened next.

On the morning of June 23, Drew and Foldesi drove in separate cars as they followed Puglisi on errands—a phone call at a Shell gas station and a quick meeting at a Nathan's hot dog stand in Brooklyn, then back to Staten Island. At 10:10 A.M., they stopped at the Staten Island Mall on Richmond Avenue. Drew watched Puglisi from a Sanitation Department parking lot across the street. Foldesi parked on the far side of a Burger King. Both had clear views, from different angles, as Puglisi got out carrying a white plastic supermarket bag and scanned the parking lot from the Burger King entrance. Across the lot a short, slightly stooped older man wearing glasses and a windbreaker emerged from a black Buick with Florida plates and headed to the door. Drew and Foldesi joked on their two-way radios about the old codger coming to Burger King to yak with his friends over coffee. They stopped laughing when the old man paused to speak with Puglisi.

"Agents quickly realized this is a very unusual meeting," Drew later wrote in an official account.

Puglisi, in a rare show of deference, was "quietly standing with his hands in his jacket pockets not saying a single word, just nodding his head in agreement as he looked down at this man," Drew wrote. "This older man was doing all the talking, looking up towards Puglisi and occasionally pointing his finger at him. This goes on for about five minutes with Puglisi, normally the center of attention, not interrupting him at all as he quietly stands there."

Puglisi then handed the old man the plastic bag, which the agents assumed contained cash. He dropped it in his Buick and entered the Burger King with Puglisi. They talked at a table near the door for twenty minutes. The agents followed the old man's Buick back to a warehouse on Port Richmond Avenue on Staten Island. Foldesi ran the Florida license plate number through the Department of Motor Vehicles database, but nothing came up. The plates were not registered. "We had no idea who this guy was," Drew said, "or how he fit in or what he did."

Three weeks later, Foldesi was parked outside the warehouse, waiting for the old man to appear. When at last the man got in his car, Foldesi flashed police lights and pulled him over on a trumped-up claim that his car matched a black Buick carjacked half an hour earlier. Around his neck Foldesi wore an NYPD badge he bought in a police supply store. Foldesi asked the man for his license and registration to identify him.

"The old man was Burt Kaplan," Drew said. "We knew that Freddy [Puglisi] was showing him respect, so we knew he was somebody of significance. But we didn't know anything about him. We had other things to worry about. He was not yet a priority. So he got pushed to the side." Drew would not fully grasp Kaplan's importance to a larger investigation for another five weeks.

The cell phone wiretaps had gone live the day before Kaplan met Puglisi at Burger King. Kaplan likely learned of the wiretaps from his NYPD source—Caracappa—and summoned Puglisi to warn him that the DEA was now eavesdropping on his calls. It is also possible, though not confirmed, that Caracappa learned of the wiretaps when Drew briefed the detectives at the DEA office and passed that information along to Kaplan, who then alerted Puglisi.

Either way, Puglisi had now caught on to the DEA investigation thanks to Kaplan. On July 11, nineteen days after the phone taps went live, the DEA team intercepted their last call on Puglisi's cell phone, a conversation with his mistress, Susan Ehrlich, who happened to be engaged to his friend Bobby Molini.

Two days later, Drew was following Molini's Mercedes convertible when Puglisi called to remind him: "Don't use that cell phone anymore." Molini agreed, but continued making calls while delivering pot to customers in Brooklyn. He was in the center lane of the upper level of the Verrazzano-Narrows Bridge heading back to Staten Island when Puglisi called back:

PUGLISI: Did you get rid of that cell phone?
MOLINI: Yeah.
PUGLISI: Then how the fuck am I still talking to you? . . . I swear I'm surrounded by people with the IQ of house plants. . . . Get rid of that fucking phone!

Drew watched from a few cars back as Molini responded to Puglisi's order: he extended his left arm and dropped the phone. It bounced on the road and rolled under the front wheel of Drew's car.

With that, the two tapped phones fell silent. Meanwhile, Puglisi's associate John Silvestri had moved because he suspected, correctly, that officials had tapped his landline. Though the agents still had one last unlikely listening post: a housing police sergeant reported that his wife had installed a baby monitor in their newborn's nursery which, by a quirk of the airwaves, clearly picked up Silvestri, their new neighbor on Michelle Lane, speaking to drug buyers over a wireless house phone. The baby fell asleep to the sound of dealers arranging buys.

It hardly mattered that Puglisi had silenced the phone taps. By summer's end, the DEA had collected enough evidence to plan the arrests.

At 6:45 A.M. on September 9, 1992, a dozen DEA agents arrested Freddy Puglisi and twenty-three others in his orbit. Agents knocked a panel out of Puglisi's front door with a battering ram to find him fixing breakfast in his underwear. They laid him on the floor next to his dining room table and handcuffed him.

The sweep extended as far as Iowa and Florida. Defendants in Brooklyn and Staten Island were handcuffed and taken to an ad hoc processing facility set up in a spacious open room used by the National Guard in Fort Hamilton Park. They were photographed and fingerprinted, then sent to the US District Court in Cadman Plaza for arraignment.

The DEA agents could tell that somebody had warned Puglisi's team to expect the arrests. At least one explicitly said so. When Drew arrested Bobby Molini at his fiancée's apartment in the Tottenville neighborhood of Staten Island, he gave Drew a smirk. "We knew you were coming," Molini told Drew. The drug dealers had their secret source of information—Stephen Caracappa—and he was not above rubbing it in.

Puglisi had also anticipated the arrests. When agents searched his home on Dent Road, they found no sign of drugs or cash.

More than a month later, Drew and four other agents knocked on his parents' door in the small upstate town of Grahamsville. They arrived with a warrant at 9 P.M. and asked to come in. Puglisi's father, Freddie, Sr., feigned ignorance. What money? I don't know what you're talking about, he said. You should leave before my wife becomes upset.

Puglisi's mother, Emma, did become upset—so upset that she collapsed into a kitchen chair after a bout of crying and screaming. Her husband tried to calm her while talking to the agents. He eventually gave up. *Alright, here!*, he said. He slid a bookcase aside, revealing a hidden closet. Inside the closet sat a black briefcase. *This is what he gave me. I don't know what's in it. Take it.* The briefcase contained $188,000.

Puglisi happened to call from the Metropolitan Correctional Center, the federal jail in downtown Manhattan, at the exact moment that the agents found the briefcase. *Freddy, they're here*, Emma said. *They're searching. What are you doing to us?*

Puglisi's father took the phone. *Freddy, they've got a warrant. Your mother is upset, so I gave them the briefcase.*

From across the room Drew could hear Puglisi bellowing on the other end of the line. *You did what? You gave them the fucking briefcase? What the fuck!*

Frank Drew and the other DEA agents assigned to Operation Gang-plank assumed the twenty-four arrests conducted in the early hours of September 9 marked the beginning of the end of their investigation. Aside from pulling on a few final threads, they were done. Or so they thought. Drew had no way of knowing that a last line of inquiry, one that he might easily have ignored, would launch an entirely new avenue of investigation that would uncover Burt Kaplan's secret role as a broker of police information and, eventually, Eppolito and Caracappa's deceit.

"The [Puglisi] case was major news in organized crime circles," Drew said, "but at this point we didn't know the full scope of it."

The twenty-four arrests included John Silvestri's sister, thirty-five-year-old Andrea Giovino, who had grown up on the fringes of the mob. When she was little, their mother, Dolly, hosted a Gambino-controlled craps game in the dirt-floor basement of their Brooklyn home two nights a week. The house, Giovino later wrote, "smelled like a combination of antifreeze, dirt, the ocean, and corn chips. If poverty smells like anything, that would be it." Her mother taught her, at age five, to steal morning deliveries of bread, bagels, and milk from a nearby deli to help feed her nine siblings.

Giovino grew up to be a modern-day moll, a feral young blonde "addicted to the kind of high that came with being with [Mafia] guys." Armed with silky charms and ardent ambition, she capered through a series of high-rolling boyfriends. "The bigger the criminals, the better the life," she later said. "That's what we were taught."

When a judge sentenced her latest boyfriend, a Gambino heroin trafficker, to 260 years without parole, she didn't miss a beat. Within months she had blithely moved on with John Fogarty, a six-foot-four dealer known as Big John, who had grown up tough in Hell's Kitchen and Staten Island.

"He had the chiseled features—the high cheekbones, prominent, craggy jaw, and the dazzling smile of an actor," Giovino wrote. "I think what charmed people most about John was his eyes—blue, the color of an Alaskan husky's, and so penetrating that sometimes if you didn't know him well, he might scare you."

Like a lot of gangsters, Fogarty ran a legitimate side business, in his case an excavation firm, but his main job was trafficking cocaine. Pushed by Giovino, Fogarty cultivated more robust suppliers and expanded his operation. He took bolder risks, made bigger deals. Giovino, who became his common-law wife, was not about to cast her lot with a middleweight.

As his operation thrived, Fogarty came to embody the popular conception of the big-time cocaine dealer. "He was the kind of guy who would rent a limo," Giovino said, "and drive to Atlantic City with a ton of cocaine."

Fogarty liked cocaine a little too much, as it turned out. The dealer became a hardened user. By the time Giovino was pregnant with her fourth child—her third with Fogarty—his behavior had grown erratic. At Christmastime in 1988, he disappeared for three days. A friend of Fogarty's stopped by the house. He told Giovino where to find Fogarty: a drug den in the Dongan Hills section of Staten Island.

Fogarty eventually checked himself into a twenty-eight-day rehab program run by Seventh-Day Adventists in Bowling Green, Kentucky. He returned home before his wife gave birth to Keith, their eight-pound baby son.

In rehab Fogarty had befriended a drug counselor named Loren Peterson, who warned Fogarty that a fellow patient worked as a confidential informant for a Tennessee task force. Months later, in September 1991, the informant offered to sell Fogarty a hundred pounds of pot for $100,000. Fogarty confronted him about Peterson's claim, but the informant managed to deflect the accusation. Fogarty needed the supply to seed his growing operation, so he was willing to overlook the risk in order to sell the pot to Puglisi back in Staten Island.

A little after 1 A.M. on the morning of November 7, 1991, Fogarty and a friend, Scotty Brennan, arrived at the rendezvous, a mall parking lot in Franklin, Tennessee, carrying $100,000 in a plastic bag. The informant was waiting. Fogarty showed the cash; the informant showed the pot. Brennan judged the pot, based on its appearance, to be of shoddy quality, and said so. But there would be no haggling. The Tennessee task force closed in and arrested both men. Fogarty pleaded guilty to drug trafficking to keep his wife, Andrea, from facing charges. The Tennessee authorities had damning evidence against her: phone recordings of her negotiating the price. But they readily accepted a deal that would spare the mother of four children. The judge sentenced Fogarty to eight years in a state prison.

The brothers Mike and Rob Spinelli traveled to Nashville to assassinate the informant. When they arrived at the restaurant where he worked, a manager said he had quit the previous day. "He knew enough to know that these people were real," Drew said.

John Fogarty had served less than two years of his eight-year sentence when the DEA swept through the boroughs on the morning of September 9. An agent phoned Andrea Giovino minutes before arriving at her house, possibly in deference to her four sleeping children. He asked her to open the door before they broke it down.

Giovino ran downstairs in her underwear and looked out a window. "I thought my neighborhood had been converted into a movie set," she said. "The flashing lights of police cars striped the trees and houses." Agents in DEA windbreakers stood in the driveway. An agent speaking through a megaphone issued a warning: open the door or we'll break it down. When she swung the door open, a dozen agents entered. They read her Miranda rights: "You have the right to remain silent. Anything you say can and will be used against you in a court of law. . . ."

The DEA knew that she played no direct role in selling pot and cocaine, but she handled the finances and negotiated the terms. They had watched her house for six months and tapped her phone. She immediately, and without prompting, told agents that her husband, John Fogarty, would cooperate. She knew that Burt Kaplan had a source inside the NYPD; she could trade on that information as a get-out-of-jail card.

At 11 P.M., Giovino was arraigned before a US District Court judge. She used the deed on her house to pay the $100,000 bail and took a car service home to Staten Island. "There was no question that she went home that night and told [Fogarty] what he was going to do," Drew said. "She knew what he did and what he knew. She was no dope. She was not going to spend a night in jail."

Five days after the arrests, Fogarty called from jail to ask Agent Drew—begged him—to come to Tennessee to talk about a cooperation deal. "You've got the wrong people," he said. "You don't know what you've got."

Drew was skeptical, but willing to listen. "I didn't feel like going down to talk to him," he said. "I assumed he was just getting an earful from his wife. But he was persistent. We had no idea that this was about to take a whole other turn."

The following afternoon, Drew and his colleague, Agent Dinnan, flew to a tiny airport in Blountville, Tennessee. The next day Drew and a Tennessee deputy sheriff named Barry Kincaid drove an hour to the Northeast Correctional Center in the remote town of Mountain City. Officials had relocated Fogarty and Brennan from the Franklin County Jail after they had abused inmates who mistook them for pushovers. "Scotty was a kickboxer, and a legitimate tough guy," Drew said. "Fogarty was a big guy too. These people apparently thought they were going to push these New Yorkers around, but, to quote the sheriff, they took over that jail within hours. They were beating up so many inmates that they had to split the New Yorkers up. Scotty stayed local to Nashville and they sent Fogarty across the state."

The warden escorted Fogary from solitary confinement to a meeting room. He walked in—a big man wearing a prison jumpsuit. He immediately told Drew and Deputy Sheriff Kincaid how much they had yet to learn about the Puglisi operation. Puglisi and his crew "knew you were coming," he said. "You guys missed everything. You don't know what you've got."

Drew pressed Fogarty for details. He said he was reluctant to speak further until Drew relocated him. "Nobody wants to talk in prison," Drew said. "They don't want to be labeled a rat." But Fogarty's presumption strained Drew's patience. He told Fogarty that he was not going anywhere. If Fogarty did not start talking, Drew said, he would leave. "We are going back to New York," he said, "and your wife can go to jail."

Now Fogarty grew forthcoming. Puglisi, he said, ran a nationwide operation that distributed vast quantities of pot and employed organized crime figures, some of whom, now in DEA custody, had committed murders.

After an hour of talk, Drew and Deputy Kincaid drove to a small country store. Drew asked a woman behind the counter for a pay phone.

She listened to his New York accent uncomprehendingly. He asked again. She didn't respond until Deputy Kincaid interceded. The woman pointed to an ancient booth with a rotary phone in the corner.

Drew called Assistant US Attorney Ross Pearlson of the Eastern District of New York to fill him in. Pearson urged Drew to press Fogarty for more detailed information so that he had a more complete background as he prepared charges against the defendants arrested on September 9.

When Drew emerged from the booth, Kincaid laughed. "That girl ain't ever heard anyone talk like you," he said.

Drew and Dinnan, accompanied by a supervisor from the Pennsylvania Attorney General's office, traveled to a federal courthouse in Greenville, where a court order signed by Judge Leo Glasser arrived from Brooklyn by fax. The US marshal, however, was reluctant to hand a Tennessee prisoner over to a federal agent with a funny New York accent until Drew, now out of patience, loudly threatened to bring him before Judge Glasser in New York to explain why he had defied the order. Drew then drove the seventy-three miles back to Mountain City to extract Fogarty from prison. On the return drive to Greenville, Fogarty expressed his relief at leaving rural Tennessee. "Wild animals, people with no teeth," he said. "This is a scary place."

The agents debriefed Fogarty that afternoon on the understanding that his statements would not be used against him later. Those terms, known as a proffer, required that he have legal representation. Thomas J. Wright, a local lawyer appointed to represent Fogarty, put his cowboy boots up on a conference room table. He addressed the New Yorkers with a thick Tennessee twang and a wagging finger. "I don't know what kind of games you people are playing here with Mr. Fogarty, but I want to tell you that you will not take advantage of my client just because he's not in New York. You'll keep this in line and anything that I think is out of line, this thing is over."

For the next ninety minutes, Fogarty recounted in graphic detail the distribution and sale of hundreds of thousands of dollars in high-quality pot. He cataloged several murders and agreed to show Drew where to find the body of a Cuban cocaine dealer shot to death with a

.44 Magnum on Staten Island by the Spinelli brothers, Mike and Robert, so that Fogarty could avoid paying him $200,000.

Drew asked how Puglisi and his men had learned the DEA had them under surveillance. How did they know the DEA had tapped their phones? How did they anticipate the arrests?

"They knew you were coming through Burt, Burt Kaplan," Fogarty said. "Burt has a source."

But who was the source? "No one knows," Fogarty said. "It's Burt's crystal ball." The crystal ball's identity remained a mystery, even to Fogarty. The only way to find out would be to squeeze the information out of Kaplan himself.

At 3:30 P.M., after Fogarty's disquisition, the US marshals escorted him from the room. The New Yorkers looked at Wright, Fogarty's court-appointed attorney, for his reaction.

"My god, I've never heard anything like that in my entire life," he said. "Do you believe him?"

"Every word," Drew said.

11

DESERT RETIREMENT

LOUIE EPPOLITO AND STEPHEN CARACAPPA HAD spent a collective forty-four years on the police force by the time Eppolito retired in 1990 and Caracappa followed in November 1992. Eppolito's pension paid more than $5,000 a month. Caracappa got nearly $4,000. It was enough to live on, but not extravagantly. Both planned to supplement their pensions with other work.

Eppolito had a new vocation in mind. He hoped to parlay his tough cop demeanor into a movie career. In 1989, he played the first of more than a dozen small parts, including a hit man on the television show *Kojak*. In 1990, he landed a cameo in the Martin Scorsese movie *Goodfellas*. As the camera panned across a Polynesian-themed nightclub called the Bamboo Lounge, the actor Ray Liotta named the mobsters at their respective tables and bar stools—Pete the Killer, Freddy the Cop, Nicky Eyes, Jimmy Two Times, and a hanger-on named Fat Andy, played by Eppolito. At 230 pounds, he looked the part. Warner Brothers paid Eppolito $19,000 for his cameo.

Eppolito also coached the *Goodfellas* actors on Mafia etiquette. Twenty-five years after Scorsese released the film, Ray Liotta told talk show host Jimmy Kimmel that to prepare for his wise guy role the producers "gave me a guy who used to be a cop, his family was in the mob, and he later went mob." One day, Eppolito offered Liotta pointers over lunch. When Liotta reached for the check he found his wallet missing. Minutes later, as they walked outside, he spotted it on the sidewalk. "All of a sudden, boom, there's my wallet," he said. "There's no question [Eppolito] took it from me. Then he threw it on the street and said, look, there it is."

Kimmel asked why Eppolito would take his wallet.

"Because he's a douche," Liotta said.

Eppolito later said that he met the actor Joe Pesci on the *Goodfellas* set, and that Pesci had helped him land small parts in *Predator 2, Bullets over Broadway,* and *Lost Highway.*

Eppolito no doubt appealed to casting directors because he fit a particular profile, a cartoonish tough with an authentic Brooklyn accent and the jowls of a man who favored osso buco and other heavy Italian classics. It is easy to imagine him schmoozing his way into small parts.

Eppolito was astute enough to know that he could play a certain kind of role in someone else's story, but he might also draw on his own life. He wrote a self-pitying memoir, co-authored with veteran reporter Bob Drury, titled *Mafia Cop: The Story of an Honest Cop Whose Family Was the Mob.* In its pages Eppolito portrayed himself as the conflicted son of Fat the Gangster. He was, he wrote, an abused boy who grew up burdened by an awareness that his father killed for a living. He nonetheless dedicated the book to his father: "For my father Ralph. Thanks for making a man that no other man could break."

In his self-serving depiction, Eppolito forged an against-all-odds career as a decorated patrolman and detective, only to be framed by police officials suspicious of his connections to Italian South Brooklyn. He came across as a salty but honorable man, devoted to family and friends, who fell victim to a smear campaign by his own colleagues, only to be gloriously exonerated. One of Eppolito's former partners called the book "a bunch of horseshit."

If Eppolito was, as his dedication claimed, "a man that no other man could break," it was still possible for him to break himself by heedlessly publishing incriminating material. "This moron moves to Vegas and does a book, basically talking about himself," Sammy Gravano told a reporter. "He put a light on himself. I thought at the time it was weird. . . . You can't do that kind of stuff, bragging like that whether you're a cop or a gangster. I thought to myself, 'These cops aren't going to like what you did.'"

Caracappa had the same concern. The book included a photograph of him and Eppolito in a relaxed pose during their tenure on the Robbery Squad, both smiling at the camera. Eppolito's tie hangs undone, as always. The caption identifies them by name—"two Godfathers of the NYPD."

When Caracappa saw the photograph, he recognized a danger that Eppolito had overlooked, out of arrogance or obliviousness. By identifying himself and Caracappa in a published photograph, he made it possible for any witness to their illicit work for Casso—shooting Eddie Lino, for example, or abducting Israel Greenwald and Jimmy Hydell—to put names to their faces. Caracappa fumed. His best friend had published a smoking gun.

The list of people who could now identify Eppolito and Caracappa included their Mafia employer, Gaspipe Casso, who until then had only known them as "the crystal ball." Burt Kaplan, acting as intermediary, had shrewdly withheld their identities for mutual protection. Now that Casso knew their names he could, in theory, implicate them should he join the growing list of cooperators.

In 1992, Eppolito promoted his book on the *Sally Jessy Raphael* daytime talk show. He sat in a guest chair with a pompadour and mustache dyed an unnatural black, verging on purple, with a red tie and matching pocket square worn over a black shirt. He looked like a sad sack casino washout eager to make a flush appearance. His face furrowed into a sad-eyed puppy dog frown as he described how his abusive father broke his nose at age six after he failed to show sufficient interest in boxing. "My dad is dead twenty-six years," he said. "I'm still scared of him."

Eppolito portrayed himself on camera as the agent of righteous violence—a one-man vigilante who set police procedure aside on behalf of the injured and helpless. When he said that he routinely dared abusive husbands to hit their wives in front of him and face the consequences, the middle-aged women in the studio audience clapped. When he mentioned shoving a gun in the mouth of a mobster who had threatened his own mother, they applauded louder still.

Shortly after *Mafia Cop* was published in 1992, Eppolito sent a copy to Hugh Mo, the former deputy commissioner in charge of police trials, who nine years earlier had acquitted Eppolito of passing a confidential police file to Rosario Gambino. Mo said that he was shocked to find that Eppolito had mentioned him in the dedication, as if he had gone out of his way to bend matters on Eppolito's behalf. "I was taken aback," Mo said. "He tried to make me look like a hero. I'm no savior. I was only doing my job."

Eppolito had a new career, and soon a new home 2,500 miles from Brooklyn. He and Fran had moved to a four-bedroom house with a terra-cotta tile roof, white stucco walls, and a swimming pool in a gated community on the sandy edge of Las Vegas. They shared the house with Fran's mother, Nina, a sizable gun collection, and Eppolito's menagerie of pet snakes.

After Caracappa retired in November 1992, he and his wife, Monica, moved into a comparatively modest house directly across Silver Bear Way from the Eppolitos.

During a rare visit, Eppolito's son from his first marriage, Lou Jr., was surprised to see Caracappa enter the house unannounced. "Out of nowhere, here comes Steve Caracappa walking in the door. I'm like, 'Why is Steve here?' I thought that was so strange. Now I know why. He needed to keep watch on my dad. My dad talked a lot and said too much stuff."

Caracappa was like Eppolito's shadow, quietly accompanying him. He found work as an assistant chief of security at a women's prison on the outskirts of Las Vegas, a typical job for retired cops. Even in a city famous for sin he rarely stayed awake past 9 P.M.

For a decade Eppolito and Caracappa had pursued a double life on the assumption that their law enforcement colleagues could not catch them. Now that the Nevada sun warmed their backyards and the neon light of the Vegas Strip shone on their faces, their work for Gaspipe Casso may have felt like ancient sins, old enough for them to believe in their desert absolution.

A year had passed since they pulled Eddie Lino over on the Belt Parkway. But even now, as they settled into legitimate new careers, they could not resist striking up with the local Gambino associates. They were open to whatever gifts of fortune the underworld might send their way.

"We come out to Vegas, we're New York guys," Caracappa said over dinner with a new acquaintance. "I mean, we're stupid when we come out here. We don't have any of the connections we have in New York. . . . We're really not bad guys, we're legit guys, but on the other hand, don't fuck with us."

12

GRABBING GASPIPE

EVERY WEEKDAY MORNING GASPIPE CASSO'S WIFE, Lillian, unlatched the front door of her lingerie shop in the Flatlands neighborhood where she spent her days selling hosiery, garters, and satin slips to Brooklyn housewives. While she commuted to work, her husband woke up fifty-five miles away in Rosemarie Billotti's bed. Casso had made himself comfortable in her Mount Olive home, though it could as easily be called his. Billotti held the title, but he paid the bills.

Mount Olive was a pleasant enough town, and Casso had improved the grounds with a pool, hot tub, decks, and landscaping. But it was still not home. By December 1992, Casso, now fifty-two, had skulked in hiding for thirty-one months. He had missed two consecutive Christmases with Lillian and their children, Jolene and Anthony Jr., with a third holiday weeks away. Casso had always assumed that he could wait things out, that the charges against him would eventually evaporate and the FBI would turn their attention elsewhere. If anything, the opposite was true: By the fall of 1992, investigators had turned up the heat on America's most wanted mobster. Sixteen months earlier, the FBI had arrested Vic Amuso, Casso's friend of twenty years and partner in running the Lucchese family. Amuso now loitered in federal prison, faithfully following the constraints of omertà. He did not speak. He did not cooperate.

Not so with the other Lucchese leaders. Al D'Arco, Casso's reliable adjutant, had abandoned his oath and allied himself with the government.

If Casso were caught, D'Arco would be among the first to testify against him—followed by Fat Pete Chiodo. Both had told federal agents entire chapters of Lucchese history, including the string of murders committed on Casso's orders. Based on information they provided, federal prosecutors indicted Casso in absentia on new charges. They accused him of executing eleven men in the Lucchese orbit since 1988 and conspiring to kill three others.

"He is the most dangerous, cunning and ruthless Mafia leader left on the streets," said Andrew J. Maloney, the United States Attorney for the Eastern District of New York. "He is No. 1 on our hit parade of wanted criminals."

Federal authorities now intensified their search for Casso. D'Arco told investigators that the Lucchese capo Big Frank Lastorino had likely replaced him as Casso's main contact back in Brooklyn. (Lastorino was the gunman who shot Bobby Borriello to death outside his Bensonhurst home.) NYPD detectives found that Lastorino owned a pair of cell phones, clunky early models equipped with a small antenna. With the FBI's help, detectives determined that Lastorino had exchanged calls with somebody in a particular cell grid in New Jersey. They traced the calls to 79 Waterloo Road in Mount Olive, a split-level house owned by a single woman who had moved from Brooklyn.

On Friday, January 16, 1993, Burt Kaplan drove Casso's wife, Lillian, to meet her husband at the Rockaway Mall in central New Jersey. They would spend the weekend together, shopping, eating, and retreating for spells to a hotel room Kaplan had booked for them in his name. When Kaplan picked Lillian up on Sunday night, Casso hugged and kissed her goodbye.

On Monday morning, authorities listened in as Casso called Lastorino and directed him to send three dozen roses to a Staten Island address with a note that said, "Happy Birthday, Mom, from your son Anthony."

Casso was unaware that the FBI had gathered in the woods outside his door. At 11 A.M., twenty-five agents armed with shields, helmets, and Kevlar vests watched from a distance as Billotti drove off in a Jeep

Cherokee. They then pulled into her driveway and took up positions surrounding the house so that Casso could not slip out the back. They closed in with automatic weapons raised.

An agent banged—*thump, thump, thump*—at the locked door, shouting, "FBI!" When nobody answered, they broke the door open with a battering ram and stomped their way inside with guns cocked. Casso called from the upstairs landing to say that he heard them. He came downstairs dripping wet, with a towel tied around his waist and his hands held high. "He didn't have his gun in the shower like in the spaghetti westerns," an FBI agent said.

Agents might not have recognized Casso from old surveillance photos. He had grown his hair and wore a mustache and glasses during his years in hiding. New York's most dangerous Mafia leader, a fugitive akin to Billy the Kid and John Dillinger, surrendered with meek compliance.

Agents handcuffed Casso and led him to a car. Inside the house they found a rifle, two briefcases containing $340,000 in cash, bookkeeping for Lucchese family operations, a card catalog index of Lucchese men, and a list of proposed new members. When Billotti returned, agents arrested her and charged her with harboring a fugitive.

The next day's newspapers declared Casso's arrest the latest, and most dramatic, in a series of aggressive crackdowns on the New York Mafia families. "Another day, another don," said Agent James M. Fox, head of the FBI's New York field office.

Casso used his one permitted phone call to contact Lillian. By now she knew that FBI agents had arrested him at a girlfriend's home. She told him to drop dead and hung up.

Agents took Casso to the Metropolitan Correctional Center, a featureless twelve-story federal holding facility standing incongruously among the cluster of civic buildings near City Hall. In the third-floor receiving office he was fingerprinted, photographed, and stripped. Corrections officers looked in his mouth and ran fingers through his hair. They handed him a bedroll consisting of two sheets and a blanket. Pillows were forbidden.

The next day Casso, cleanly shaven and dressed in blue prison clothes, pleaded innocent to a sixty-seven-count indictment at an arraignment before Judge Eugene H. Nickerson in Brooklyn federal court. The indictment accused him of ordering fourteen murders, drug trafficking, gambling, loan-sharking, labor racketeering, and other crimes. If convicted, he faced life in prison. His lawyer did not bother to request bail. Casso was silent throughout. He turned to wave at his son and daughter, now in their early twenties, who sat in the front row of the empty courtroom. Lillian chose not to attend.

Casso's new life progressed according to rigid jailhouse routine. He woke in a metal-framed bed in his eight-foot-long cell at 6 A.M. under fluorescent lights, followed by a 6:30 breakfast. He mingled with inmates in the caged rooftop yard—a perch so high that Casso could almost glimpse his South Brooklyn neighborhood across the East River. Otherwise Casso had nothing to do but pace in his cell like a shark trapped in a dirty tank. He waited for a letter or phone call from Lillian. They never came.

If the Metropolitan Correctional Center offered Casso any consolation, it lay in the camaraderie of other wise guys housed together on the eleventh floor, also known as Mafia Manor. (Corrections officers boarded them together to minimize clashes with inmates of other backgrounds—Black, Puerto Rican, and Irish.)

The eleventh-floor cells were filled with operatives from all five crime families netted in the federal crackdown on organized crime. The Gambino capo Gregory Scarpa, Sr., nicknamed "The Grim Reaper," was in residence. So was Anthony "The Greek" Spero of the Bonanno family, along with Mike Spinelli and Bobby Molini from the Puglisi crew in Staten Island. All awaited trial. All faced life sentences. The Italians ate together and played gin rummy. They drank smuggled wine and smoked cigars.

Casso was like the mayor of the eleventh floor. When he entered the mess hall or rooftop recreation area, the others received him with handshakes and shows of respect. He was the powerful underboss who had dodged the FBI for almost three years.

The Metropolitan Correctional Center was the most degrading of federal penitentiaries. It stood two blocks from City Hall, but subjected inmates to gulag squalor. In summer the metal-lined cells baked like pizza ovens. Frosted glass filled the slit-shaped windows so inmates rarely saw daylight or glimpsed the outside world. They jammed wads of toilet paper in their ears to prevent cockroaches from crawling in while they slept.

Casso felt that he could not abide these conditions for the months leading up to his trial. Nor could he accept that, once convicted, he would likely live out his days in a federal penitentiary. He knew that escape was possible, at least in theory. In 1981, a couple hijacked a helicopter and tried to pluck a drug dealer from the rooftop. The scheme failed when the inmate was unable to cut through a wire screen covering the rooftop recreation area. Nine years later, two drug suspects escaped by lowering themselves from a second-floor window on an electrical cord ripped from a floor polisher.

Casso bribed a guard named Thomas Moore $500 a week to deliver daily hot lunches from a restaurant seven blocks north, in Little Italy, which he and his friends washed down with bottles of wine and brandy. "We were eating great when Gaspipe bribed the guards," said Frankie Steel Pontillo, who was awaiting a prison transfer after a murder conviction.

When Moore proved trustworthy, Casso recruited him for his own escape plan. At 6 A.M. on a Saturday, a guard came to Casso's cell to say that a lawyer was waiting to meet him in a third-floor conference room. In fact, there was no meeting. Moore had sent the guard from the prison control room, where he was working that morning. The guard escorted Casso to an elevator. From the control room Moore redirected Casso's elevator from the third to the ground floor. Underneath his prison jumpsuit Casso wore smuggled street clothes. As the elevator descended, Moore sent a guard stationed on the street to check on a bogus problem elsewhere in the complex.

The plan was for Casso to shed his jumpsuit and open a side door with a duplicate key and walk free in his street clothes. However, a guard happened by just as he exited the elevator. He was caught steps from freedom. Two guards escorted him back to his cell. "That was the end of plan one," Casso later told a reporter. "It all happened so fast and unexpected."

In February 1993, Casso tried a modified version of the same plan, this time with help from the Bypass Gang, the safecracking crew. Casso was to call the gang on a smuggled cell phone as he rode the elevator down. They would seize the street guard and handcuff him, leaving Casso free to walk to a waiting car. This variation might have worked, except that a few days before the scheduled breakout, terrorists bombed the parking garage beneath the World Trade Center. Security in downtown government facilities was redoubled.

On his third try, Casso arranged for the Bypass Gang to intercept the US marshal's van carrying him from a Brooklyn court. A cement truck was supposed to block the street. For whatever reason, it never showed up.

The bungled third try ended Casso's escape attempts, but not his scheming. He hatched an audacious plan to delay his trial, or force a mistrial, by murdering Eugene Nickerson, the seventy-nine-year-old US District Court judge presiding over his case. Casso's scouts told him that Nickerson boarded the Long Island Railroad in Roslyn, Long Island, for his daily commute to Brooklyn. He forwarded notes on Nickerson's schedule to members of the Colombo family with a request to assassinate him at the train station or while traversing the plaza outside the US Courthouse, but the scheme never materialized.

About this time, assistant US attorney Greg O'Connell met alone in a Long Island hotel with a source who claimed that Casso had also planned to kill O'Connell himself, along with his close friend and colleague, assistant US attorney Charles Rose. Casso hoped that one or all of the assassinations would delay his trial long enough for Chiodo and D'Arco, the key witnesses against him, to die of natural causes. Both men suffered serious health issues. The source, O'Connell said, "was sweating profusely on his forehead. He had a strained look on his face and he was shaking. He was incredibly anxious."

Rose and O'Connell alerted the US marshals, who advised them to switch up their daily routines. FBI agents escorted them to and from work.

Casso later said that Rose alone was his target. In keeping with his brand of scorched-earth retaliation, he asked Eppolito and Caracappa to surveil Rose. For the second time in less than a year, Casso had violated the ancient Mafia prohibition against harming family members and public officials—not to mention the audacity of killing a federal prosecutor.

By all accounts, Rose shrugged off the threat. "Was it something I said?" he joked. His fiancée, Elaine Banar, took the threat more seriously.

Banar was a special agent for the US Customs Service. She had met Rose a year earlier when he, in his role as prosecutor, sat with her at the Bridge Café, in Brooklyn, covertly observing an undercover agent dining across the room with the target of an investigation. She had not wished to babysit an assistant US attorney during a delicate undercover operation, but Rose was so charming, and told such amusing stories, that she momentarily forgot about the undercover operation in progress across the room. He had to remind her.

Now, as his fiancée, she made a point of carrying her government-issue pistol when she met Rose for dinner. And she made sure to sit with her back to the wall so that she could survey who entered the restaurant.

In the end, the threat came to nothing. Casso assigned a trusted hit man, Georgie Neck Zappola, to follow up on Eppolito and Caracappa's surveillance of Rose's apartment building. By mistake, Zappola watched over the home of Charlie Rose, the television talk show host. Charles Rose, the prosecutor, lived some blocks away, on East Eighty-Fourth street in Manhattan, with two cats, a retired bomb-sniffing dog adopted from the NYPD, and a dwarf rabbit he had rescued from Central Park. To his menagerie he now added bodyguards.

Like all the inmates housed in the Metropolitan Correctional Center, Casso had closely followed the news, on television and in tabloids, of

Sammy "The Bull" Gravano, the stocky, blue-eyed Gambino underboss who switched sides after prosecutors played him FBI recordings of his boss, John Gotti, secretly taped in the Ravenite Social Club in Little Italy. Speaking privately, Gotti had belittled Gravano, called him greedy, and blamed him for three murders.

Gravano took Gotti's disparaging words—insults spoken behind his back—as betrayal. He responded in kind. "I want to jump from our government to your government," Gravano told a federal prosecutor. He agreed to tell all he knew in return for a reduced sentence. He later delivered devastating testimony leading to a series of convictions. His damning accounts helped imprison Gotti for life. In exchange, Gravano was granted early release and enrolled in the Witness Protection Program.

If the government gave Gravano a favorable deal to entice other potential cooperators, it worked. The message was clear: no matter how many heinous crimes you commit—no matter how many murders—federal prosecutors could get you off with a light sentence and a safe sinecure as long as you agreed to testify against your friends. Gravano's decision to change sides made it possible for others to do the same.

Like every seasoned mobster, Casso denounced the arrangement. He had spent his life condemning informants—the hated rats, squealers, and canaries. But now, trapped in his stripped-down cell, Casso began to reconsider the fundamental Mafia precepts. He had slowly, painfully, come to accept that he could not escape, that he would almost certainly serve a life sentence without parole. If so, he would never again walk home in the summer evening light to eat dinner with his children or kiss Lillian or drink espresso with friends in a Brooklyn café or steer his runabout on the choppy waters of Jamaica Bay. He had discussed with his lawyer, Mike Rosen, the possibility of pleading guilty, but even then he would serve at least twenty-two years.

Loyalty demanded that Casso keep quiet, but loyalty to what exactly? The Lucchese family lay in tatters after Fat Pete Chiodo and Al D'Arco flipped. Indictments and defections had decimated its senior ranks. The surviving associates were little more than a collection of street hoods without fealty or discipline. The family's grip on industries and unions had loosened.

With each new arrest, with each headline indictment, the old Mafia, the Mafia Casso grew up with, lost authority and moved incrementally closer to dissolution. Half the Lucchese men were now either dead or incarcerated. He had come to distrust them anyway, all the vipers and *cafones*.

In January 1994, US marshals escorted Casso to the Brooklyn US Attorney's Office to provide handwriting samples in the presence of FBI agents. The samples would be used to match him to incriminating documents found in the Mount Olive house. Casso refused to sign. He was then made to appear before Judge Nickerson, who fined Casso $5,000 a day, up to a maximum of $1.2 million, until he complied. After initially holding out, Casso told his lawyer, Mike Rosen, that he would provide the handwriting sample after all.

By Casso's account, Rosen sent an associate, Jean Marie Graziano, to the US Attorney's Office to attend the handwriting session in his place. While Graziano got coffee, Casso sat handcuffed to a chair. In her absence he spoke to Richard Rudolph, an FBI agent who had helped arrest him in New Jersey. "If you guys make me a good offer," Casso said, "I'll work with you."

"Excuse me?" Rudolph said. "You're willing to cooperate?"

Rudolph walked down the hall to the office of Charles Rose, the same assistant US attorney whom Casso had plotted to kill months earlier with Eppolito and Caracappa's help. Stepping into Rose's office, Rudolph reported Casso's unexpected overture: the notorious Gaspipe, the man Rose's colleague Greg O'Connell nicknamed "Lucifer," was prepared to cooperate in exchange for leniency. The deal was consummated with a handshake before Graziano returned with coffee. Casso withheld his decision from her, and from Michael Rosen, because he knew they would disapprove. Rosen had a reputation for defending mobsters with bare knuckles. Representing a turncoat would hurt his practice.

After a decade of the long, punishing, low-pay grind in the US Attorney's Office, Rose and O'Connell had earlier decided to resign and enter the more lucrative field of criminal defense. They planned to join their new partner, another former assistant US attorney, in private practice, but Casso's arrest led them to delay their departure. They could not resist one last splashy mob trial before leaving the Department of Justice.

But now, with Casso cooperating, they had little reason to stay. There would be no trial after all. What's more, they doubted Casso could serve as a viable witness in other mob trials, given his history of violence and deception. Still, the FBI held out hope that Rose and O'Connell could use Casso as a prosecution witness alongside D'Arco, Chiodo, and Gravano—a dream team of mobster turncoats. Though technically an underboss, Casso was among the most powerful underworld figures, the architect of hundreds of intricate schemes and dozens of murders. He was capable of sharing the names and details of entire chapters of Mafia machinations dating back to the 1960s.

For Casso's protection, the federal prosecutors went to great lengths to keep his change of status secret—so secret that Casso's own lawyer, Michael Rosen, knew nothing about his defection. When Rose and O'Connell called to break the news Rosen assumed they had contacted him on a matter of courtroom logistics. He suggested they discuss details at the courthouse later that day.

"Don't knock yourself out," O'Connell said. "Mr. Casso no longer needs your services. He's got a new lawyer. He's on Team America now."

Casso's reversal blindsided Rosen. His client had always talked like a tough guy, like a faithful follower of omertà. The prosecutors arranged for Matthew Brief, a former federal prosecutor, to replace Rosen as Casso's lawyer.

On the morning of March 1, 1994, two guards led Casso from his cell. His removal may have aroused suspicion. Guards routinely retrieved inmates for court hearings, but they also transferred them to isolated units for their protection after they struck a cooperation deal. US marshals drove Casso to Brooklyn Federal Court in a van with five Colombo defendants also charged with racketeering and murder. During the twenty-minute ride over the Brooklyn Bridge, he made a point of telling them that the judge had summoned him to provide handwriting samples in advance of his trial. It was a ruse. In reality, Casso was en route to a closed hearing in the courthouse basement where he would finalize his cooperation deal by pleading guilty to seventy crimes including racketeering, extortion, and fifteen murders. The agreement required him to provide "complete, truthful and accurate information and testimony, and [not to] commit, or attempt to commit, any further crimes." In return, the government agreed to place him in protective custody.

US marshals drove Casso to LaGuardia Airport immediately after the hearing. He was flown by government jet to La Tuna, a federal prison twelve miles north of El Paso, Texas, where Casso would reside in a wing reserved for cooperating witnesses. For his own safety, he could no longer mix with the general prison population.

By chance or irony, prison officials assigned Casso the two-room cell once occupied by Joe Valachi, a soldier in the Genovese family who, in 1963, famously divulged a series of Mafia secrets while testifying before a congressional committee on organized crime. Valachi was the poster child of Mafia defectors.

Casso's debriefing began immediately in a cinder-block room of dorm-like austerity. The agents took note of Casso's obsessive neatness. He organized every detail of the room—pencils, comb, water glass—in keeping with his need for scrupulous order. He arranged his blanket and bed sheet just so. If a coffee cup left a stain, he wiped it with urgency.

As Casso spoke, his FBI handlers wrote longhand notes, known as 302s, that document the progress of a case. FBI agents never knew how forthcoming a new informant might be, and on what subjects they might choose to elaborate or demur. They might divulge sensitive secrets, particularly for the purposes of revenge, or they might issue hollow boasts and misdirections. The pair of case agents huddled with Casso recognized from the first hour that he would share without restraint. Casso was "extremely forthcoming," a law enforcement official told the *New*

Detective Louie Eppolito earned commendations from the NYPD while exploiting his wide-ranging family connections to the Mafia. *(Charles Frattini/ NY Daily News via Getty Images)*

(Below) Detectives Stephen Caracappa (left) and Eppolito (right) began their careers as partners in the Brooklyn Robbery Squad. They moonlighted for the Lucchese crime family, passing sensitive police information and facilitating murders. *(Spencer A. Burnett)*

(Above) In a case of mistaken identity, Lucchese gunmen shot Nicky Guido outside his family home, on Christmas Day, after Eppolito and Caracappa misidentified him. *(Linda Rosier/*NY Daily News *via Getty Images)*

(Above) The skilled bank burglar John "Otto" Heidel was shot to death near Marine Park, in Brooklyn, after Eppolito and Caracappa revealed him to be an FBI informant. *(*NY Daily News *via Getty Images)*

Eppolito and Caracappa accepted murder contracts, including the assassination of Eddie Lino, a Gambino capo, shot nine times on the shoulder of the Belt Parkway. *(*NY Daily News *via Getty Images)*

By the early 1990s Eppolito was an aspiring screenwriter, director, and actor with small tough-guy parts in a dozen movies. *(NY Daily News via Getty Images)*

(Below) Eppolito promoted his book, *Mafia Cop,* on the *Sally Jessy Raphael Show,* an appearance that would eventually resuscitate the long-dormant investigation into crimes he committed with Stephen Caracappa. *(YouTube)*

(Bottom) Lucchese underboss Anthony "Gaspipe" Casso (right), shown in an FBI surveillance photo, hired Eppolito and Caracappa to surveil the Gambino underboss Sammy "The Bull" Gravano (left). *(The Federal Bureau of Investigation)*

SAMMY GRAVANO

ANTHONY CASSO

DEA Agents Frank Drew (left) and Mike Foldesi (right) investigated a Staten Island drug ring, which uncovered Eppolito and Caracappa's connection to the mob. *(Frank Drew)*

Months from retirement, Detective Tommy Dades chanced on evidence that he would use to restart the probe into Eppolito and Caracappa's wrongdoings. *(Tommy Dades)*

After leaving law enforcement, Tommy Dades coached aspiring young boxers, including four Golden Gloves champions. The gym, he said, "is a dream factory." *(Tommy Dades)*

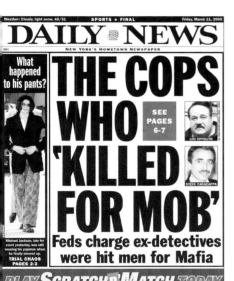

(Above) FBI and DEA agents found more than a hundred guns in Eppolito's home after arresting him in a Las Vegas restaurant. *(Drug Enforcement Agency)*

On March 11, 2005, the *Daily News* reported that Eppolito and Caracappa had been charged with kidnapping, money laundering, and participating in eight murders, among other crimes. *(NY Daily News via Getty Images)*

(Below) After FBI agents arrested him in his mistress's home, Gaspipe Casso would implicate Eppolito and Caracappa, only to disqualify himself as a cooperating witness with a series of jailhouse crimes. *(The Federal Bureau of Investigation)*

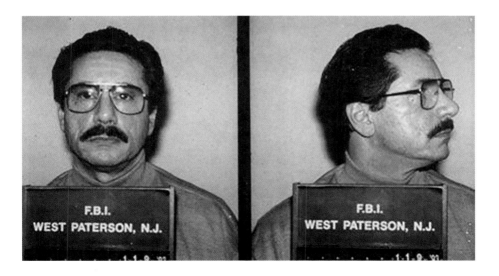

(Top) Barry Gibbs spent nineteen years in jail after Eppolito arrested him for the murder of a prostitute. *(Zoe Potkin)*

Gibbs, with the Innocence Project lawyers Vanessa Potkin and Barry Scheck, moments after a State Supreme Court judge dismissed his sentence. *(Debbie Egin-Chin/NY Daily News Archive via Getty Images)*

Brooklyn Assistant DA Mike Vecchione was poised to prosecute Eppolito and Caracappa for murder if the federal RICO case unraveled. *(Michael Albans/NY Daily News via Getty Images)*

G. Robert Blakey drafted the RICO law as a tool to vanquish organized crime once and for all after decades of half measures. A federal judge would question its application to Eppolito and Caracappa. *(Steve Marcus/*Las Vegas Weekly*)*

Eppolito leaves Federal Court for lunch with his wife, Fran, during closing arguments. *(Carolyn Cole/* Los Angeles Times *via Getty Images)*

Codefendant Stephen Caracappa outside court with his brother Dominic (left) and attorney Rae Koshetz (right) after a judge granted bail. *(Louis Lanzano/AP)*

Andrea Eppolito became her father's most vocal defender, speaking daily to the press gathered in Cadman Plaza. He "loved being a cop . . . he was so proud of all the things he did for this city." *(Todd Maisel/*NY Daily News *via Getty Images)*

Defense attorneys Edward Hayes (left) and Bruce Cutler (right) staged an attack on the government witnesses, calling them "lowlifes" and "reprobates." *(Todd Maisel/*NY Daily News *Archive via Getty Images)*

Assistant US Attorneys Mitra Hormozi and Robert Henoch brought RICO charges against Eppolito and Caracappa, despite the judge's doubts about the statute of limitations. *(Debbie Egan-Chin/*NY Daily News *Archive via Getty Images)*

York Daily News. "Casso knows a lot of specifics about a lot of crimes." He was alternately jocular and chilling in his descriptions.

At his plea hearing, Casso had confessed to fifteen murders. Now, in the debriefings, he surprised agents by expanding his inventory well beyond the earlier tally. He had participated in thirty-seven murders in all, he said, twenty-two more than the FBI count.

After Casso confessed to plotting Judge Nickerson's murder, federal agents put the judge under protective guard for months. "It was only talk at that point," a law enforcement source told *Newsday,* "but who knows, [he] and his people are zany enough to have carried it out."

Casso impressed his interrogators with his matter-of-fact way of recounting murders, as if recalling a golf outing. He remembered, for example, how, after the Coast Guard seized a drug-smuggling ship in 1978, he resolved to kill the captain's son, whom he considered unfit to withstand police interrogation. Casso invited the boy on a fishing trip in the Florida Everglades. "When the kid showed up I took my gun out and shot him," Casso said. He laughed as he recalled how irritated he became when the victim bloodied up his car. Then, as Casso shoveled dirt on the grave, the boy regained consciousness and tried to climb out. Casso hit him in the mouth with the shovel. When the boy fell backward, he buried him alive.

Asked if the episode disturbed him, Casso said no. "It had to be done."

Casso would eventually share the details of his elaborate racketeering and drug smuggling in their entirety—all of it poured into the 302s. But his catalog of confessions dimmed in comparison to a single disclosure. In the early days of debriefing, he offered thunderous news: he claimed to have kept on his payroll a pair of moles within the NYPD. For seven years, he said, two high-ranking detectives fed him streams of confidential police intelligence that he used to protect friends and punish enemies. More shocking still, they helped commit a series of murders on his orders, in at least one case pulling the trigger themselves. While Casso routinely paid them for their services, he did not know their names until relatively recently.

Burt Kaplan, the intermediary, had withheld their identities for six years. Casso had glimpsed the detectives across the Toys"R"Us parking lot when they delivered Jimmy Hydell, handcuffed in the trunk of a car, but he didn't learn who they were until 1992, when he recognized them in a photograph published in *Mafia Cop,* Eppolito's memoir. Their names appeared beneath their beaming smiles: Louie Eppolito and Stephen Caracappa. Over the coming days, Casso returned to Eppolito and Caracappa over and over, elaborating on all their labor on his behalf.

The news both shocked Casso's debriefers with the jolting force of an earthquake and, on consideration, made perfect sense. How else could he have deftly sidestepped so many raids and wiretaps—most conspicuously in May 1990, when he and the Lucchese boss, Vic Amuso, disappeared hours before their planned arrests? How else could he have executed secret informants with pinpoint accuracy? Casso's divulgence also fit with the prolific rumors that Eppolito had unsavory underworld dealings, which Eppolito consistently denounced as a low slur against a decent Italian American cop.

Casso's disclosure might have the ring of truth, but his word alone would not convict Eppolito and Caracappa. Casso, after all, was a notorious criminal and a liar. But it was a start. "He's told us who they are," a law enforcement source told Jerry Capeci, dean of the organized crime reporters. "Now we are going to have to prove it."

13

A FENCE IN HIDING

SECRETS HAVE A WAY OF SLIPPING OUT, EVEN FROM the depths of a federal prison hard against the Mexican border.

On March 26, 1994, Jerry Capeci reported in the *New York Daily News* that Casso had named two high-ranking detectives as mob accomplices. A bold, black-lettered headline—"Hero Cops or Hitmen?"—commanded the front page, accompanied by a photo taken from Eppolito's book, *Mafia Cop,* of him and Caracappa from their days as successful and respected detectives.

"A celebrated hero detective who dubbed himself Mafia Cop in his autobiography has been fingered as a mob executioner by a top gangster turned informer," Capeci wrote. Eppolito was assisted, Capeci continued, "by a former partner on the Brooklyn police robbery squad, Stephen Caracappa."

Capeci called Las Vegas to collect Eppolito's rote denials. "I don't know anyone in [the Lucchese] family," Eppolito told him. "I don't know why [Casso] would say that. I don't know anything about it. I never hurt anybody in my life."

News of Eppolito's corruptions would surprise no one. But to secretly work for Gaspipe Casso, the man dubbed "Lucifer"? It did not seem possible. And nobody imagined Caracappa, an administrative leader of the Major Case Squad, could involve himself in such atrocities.

Caracappa's Major Case colleagues reacted with varying degrees of disbelief. "I looked at [the newspaper] and said, 'Is it possible?'" Detective Joe Piraino said. "A lot of guys didn't believe it, didn't *want* to believe it." Though Piraino recalled how Caracappa referred to himself as the consigliere of the Major Case Squad. He had an odd tendency to use Mafia terminology.

On the day news broke that Eppolito and Caracappa were alleged to work for the mob, Mark Feldman, head of the organized crime section in the US Attorney's Office in Brooklyn, and Kenny McCabe, an investigator in his office, invited Detective Chuck Siriano of the Major Case Squad to meet them at a Fulton Street bar in Brooklyn.

"Eppolito didn't surprise me at all," Siriano later said. "He came from an organized crime family. I don't even know how he got on the [police force], to tell you the truth. But I was upset about Caracappa. I said, I can't believe it. It can't be true. Steve keeps a gun on his ankle and I don't even know if it works. I never saw him take his gun out. I never saw him go to the [shooting] range. He's such a wimp. I thought there's no way he did this." Siriano came to understand that Feldman and McCabe had met with him to persuade him, for his own sake, not to mar his reputation by speaking up on Caracappa's behalf.

"We were sitting at a small table," Siriano said. "Kenny grabbed both my hands and pulls me across the table. He looks me straight in the eye. He says, 'Chuck, I interviewed Casso. Caracappa did it. He's guilty. He did it.' I sat back in my chair. I was completely stunned."

Burt Kaplan had learned of Casso's change of allegiance a week before Jerry Capeci broke the story in the *New York Daily News*. He was in the bathtub when his lawyer, Judd Burstein, called to say that he had heard through the gossipy circle of criminal defense attorneys that Gaspipe Casso had flipped—or "gone bad," to use the mob term.

We may have a problem, Burstein said.

Kaplan rose from the tub in a state of alarm. "You have no idea how big a problem," he answered.

"He was upset," Burstein later said. "I didn't have to be Sherlock

Holmes to figure out that if Mr. Casso was a cooperating witness, Mr. Kaplan might have some difficulties."

Kaplan could easily imagine the nature of the difficulties to come. He knew that federal attorneys would not draft a cooperation agreement unless Casso was prepared to serve up a wealth of allegations to use against others in court. He felt sure that the government wouldn't "take a guy like Casso, who had so much baggage, unless he could give them something spectacular back." Once Casso started talking he would almost certainly describe the list of illegal schemes he had conducted with Kaplan, including drug smuggling and murder.

Burstein advised Kaplan not to flee. To do so would constitute what lawyers call consciousness of guilt, and his disappearance would disqualify him for bail if authorities caught him. "There was nothing illegal about him leaving New York," Burstein said. "There were no charges against him. On the other hand, I thought it was a very stupid thing for him to do."

Kaplan ignored his lawyer's advice. He decided, without hesitation, to disappear before the FBI could arrest him. He would go that very day. He told Burstein that he might hide in China, where he had an ownership stake in a company called China Rising.

Three hours after stepping from the bathtub, Kaplan showed up, unannounced, at Caracappa's apartment on East Twenty-Second Street. Caracappa had not yet moved to Las Vegas. On his last stop before slipping out of New York, Kaplan warned Caracappa "that we've got a real problem . . . I told him Anthony Casso went bad and that I'm going on the lam . . . and I wanted him to know that I didn't go bad and he could rely on me."

Kaplan then expressed concern that Eppolito might be too boastful and undisciplined to safeguard the secrets they held in common. "I always felt Louie was a little flamboyant," he said. "Can you control Louie? Can you take care of the situation with him?"

"Louie's been my partner and I trust him," Caracappa said. "Don't worry. Louie will be fine. I'll take care of it."

With that, Kaplan disappeared. He did not go to China, as he led others to believe. Instead, his assistant, Tommy Galpine, arranged for their pot-smuggling partner, a man they knew only as "Dave," to escort Kaplan from San Diego to Mexico.

Kaplan lived in Ensenada, seventy miles south of Tijuana, for five months under the alias Barry Michael Meyers, then moved to Portland, Oregon, and eventually to a complex of rental condos in Las Vegas so forgettable that he would later remember the community only as "Paradise something."

In Las Vegas, Kaplan manufactured coats and dresses designed for women employed by casinos and hotels. He lived the life of an elderly garment executive, cruising the casinos in the evening with an extramarital girlfriend named Louisa. He looked like just another sallow-skinned retiree blinking in the glare of the Strip.

All the while, Galpine sent Kaplan periodic care packages, delivered by Federal Express, containing as much as $25,000 in large-denomination bills bundled in clothing.

Kaplan ran his new garment business in Las Vegas, but his main purpose was making sure Eppolito and Caracappa stayed off the list of government cooperators. The retired detectives may have viewed Kaplan with the same suspicion. The three men "were much like tarantulas circling each other," a judge would later say, "afraid that any one of them would poison the others."

In late summer 1994, Kaplan found Eppolito's number in a phone book. He asked an acquaintance to call because he "did not want to put my voice on the phone because I felt that there was [likely] surveillance on his phones." Kaplan arranged to meet Eppolito at Smith's, a supermarket near Eppolito's home. Kaplan played slot machines in the vestibule until Eppolito arrived.

"We started walking in the fruit department while I wheeled the cart," Kaplan said. "This was the first time I'd seen him since the problem happened with Casso and I went on the lam and I asked [Eppolito] what was going on, is he all right, is he under any pressure, is he getting any heat. He said the press was awful but he had hired an attorney."

Eppolito received a generous NYPD pension, but exceeded his means.

He had bought a five-thousand-square-foot house in a subdivision, Spanish Palms, the kind of overnight tract development that ends abruptly at open desert. Then he decided he wanted a bigger house nearby. Along the way he got into a dispute with a builder. Eppolito confronted him with a hatchet. "I will personally kill you, and I'll do it in front of your mother and father," Eppolito said. "And then I'll kill them."

During their supermarket walkabout Eppolito told Kaplan that he needed a bridge loan, just enough to tide him over until he moved into the new house. He asked Kaplan if he could arrange for him to borrow $75,000 from a loan shark. He was willing to pay the inflated interest, the vig, which would come to $750 a week.

Kaplan figured that he would serve his own interests by keeping Eppolito solvent and safely confined to his new life in Las Vegas. So he asked Galpine to send $75,000 from their drug proceeds. The money arrived in stacks of hundred-dollar bills bound with rubber bands packed in Christmas presents. Kaplan gave Eppolito thirteen envelopes containing a total of $65,000. (Eppolito paid back $55,000 within a year. Kaplan forgave Eppolito the balance because, Kaplan later said, "he was my friend.")

Kaplan kept $10,000 for himself. Las Vegas offered a degenerate gambler no respite. His entire life, and the lives of those close to him, accommodated his steady accumulation of gambling debt. Bitter lessons should have taught him to bet only what he could afford to lose, but like any addict, he persisted on a blind belief in providence. In this case, he took the $10,000 and bet on the Super Bowl, and he won.

14

A MAN WITHOUT A COUNTRY

THE DROVES OF MAFIOSI WHO SIGNED COOPERATION agreements with federal prosecutors in the 1990s tended to obey the rules and restrictions of their new lives as government protectorates. Small-scale smuggling and bribery were commonplace in federal penitentiaries, but by and large the informants abided by their agreements. Their pact with the government was, after all, an invitation to a new life, a fresh start.

Gaspipe Casso was the exception. Even after signing his cooperation agreement, he continued to commit crimes—flagrantly and extravagantly. He was temperamentally incapable of following rules, even when his violations jeopardized his standing and threatened his long-imagined reunion with Lillian and their two children. He had no off switch, no guardrails.

Casso bribed guards and other prison staff with cash, theater tickets, and car tires. In exchange, he received contraband vodka, wine, sushi, steak, and other delicacies. According to Jerry Capeci, the *New York Daily News* reporter, Casso also used his considerable charm—the manipulative charm of a sociopath—to convince a secretary to lend him the use of a prison telephone.

Corrections officials consented to smuggling as an innocuous offense. They might have tolerated Casso's contraband, but not his violence. He had a lengthy feud with Salvatore "Big Sal" Miciotta, a 350-pound Colombo family capo who, after flipping, admitted to five murders. His debriefing led to the arrest of seventeen of his Colombo associates.

Miciotta accepted a cigar and a snack from Casso, then cozied up to prison officials by reporting that Casso hoarded contraband. In other words, Miciotta snitched on a snitch. By way of revenge, Casso walked up an elevated walkway behind Miciotta while he played cards on New Year's Eve. He leaned through a railing and beat Miciotta on the head with a rolled-up magazine. "Since this was not a very efficient weapon and Big Sal is a very large man, this did not render Big Sal helpless," a law enforcement source told the *New York Daily News*. Miciotta easily reached through the railing and grabbed Casso's shirt. He beat Casso until guards pulled them apart. By Casso's account, he saved face by flogging Miciotta after guards left him handcuffed in the showers.

The assistant US attorneys Charles Rose and Greg O'Connell had postponed their move to private practice in order to prosecute Casso. They now reversed course and flew to La Tuna to see if he would hold up as a witness in upcoming mob trials. They doubted any prosecutor would call him to the stand, given his sordid history, but they agreed to interview him.

Casso welcomed them into the bare sitting room beside his sleeping cell. Rose goaded Casso by rearranging objects on a shelf, knowing that Casso, with his obsessive insistence on order, would impatiently restore them to perfect alignment.

Casso admitted to asking Eppolito and Caracappa to scout Rose's apartment to assassinate him. Casso said that he believed Rose had leaked a rumor to *Newsday* that his wife, Lillian, was conducting an affair with the architect of his Mill Basin home.

"I forgive you, Anthony," Rose told him. "Let's continue."

Rose knew Casso's type. As a college student, Rose had tended bar at the Playboy Club in Midtown Manhattan, where the flush mafiosi swaggered in late at night with tarted-up women, all cleavage and teased hair, and handed him ten-dollar tips peeled from wads of cash.

It did not take long for Rose and O'Connell to confirm their doubts about Casso's suitability. Every mobster-turned-witness dating back to at least the 1930s faced skeptical juries. Why, after all, should jurors trust the word of career criminals and fraudsters? The credibility gap was especially wide for Casso due to his outlandish history of violence and deception. It would be hard for prosecutors to present a witness who had plotted to kill both an assistant US attorney and a district judge. "Charles [Rose] and I didn't want to sign him," O'Connell said. "I didn't see how you could credibly present a guy like that. You're going to stand there and say here's why the jury should believe this guy? He continued to lie and lie and lie."

In the eyes of the assistant US attorneys, Casso damaged his standing most inexcusably by maligning Sammy Gravano, the Gambino underboss who, after becoming a cooperating witness three years earlier, had played a prominent role in the conviction of John Gotti, his former boss. Casso sent federal prosecutors a letter via his lawyer, Matthew Brief, disputing the testimony of both Gravano and Al D'Arco in high-profile mob trials. In particular, Casso asserted that Gravano lied in the Gotti trial when he testified that he never sold drugs. Casso claimed to have sold Gravano commercial quantities of pot in the 1970s, and he said that Gravano had offered to sell him $160,000 worth of heroin.

Casso was always a dubious witness. Now it appeared that he might deliberately embarrass justice officials. If federal prosecutors called Casso to the witness stand, his 302s, all five hundred pages, would be made available to defense lawyers who would no doubt find specific instances where Casso contradicted Gravano and called him a liar. Defense lawyers could then ask for mistrials or file appeals. Gotti could be released. All the prosecutors' work could be undone.

"I found out that they didn't want me to say anything negative about Gravano," Casso said. "If I said something negative about him my debriefers would literally get up and walk away, or they would say, 'We'll discuss that later.'"

After visiting Casso, O'Connell wrote a memo urging his superiors in the Department of Justice to remove Casso from the list of cooperating witnesses. Then, in the summer of 1994, O'Connell and Rose finally left for private practice, about a year later than planned. The question of what to do about Casso now fell to their replacements—George Stamboulidis and Valerie Caproni. Though there was little doubt about where they stood: Casso had already disqualified himself.

That summer, Caproni and Brief, Casso's attorney, drove two and half hours from Brooklyn to meet with Casso in the witness protection unit of a federal prison in Fairton, New Jersey, south of Philadelphia. In his authorized biography of Casso, Philip Carlo called the meeting "stiff, formal and unfriendly—Casso sensed trouble in the wind." On the return drive Caproni said, "We can never use Casso as a witness."

On August 8, 1997, Stamboulidis wrote Brief to say that Casso had violated his cooperation agreement by bribing guards, by "brutally" attacking a fellow inmate, and by fabricating "derogatory information" about other witnesses. Due to Casso's infractions, Stamboulidis said, the Justice Department would not submit a petition, known as a 5K1.1, asking a judge to reduce his sentence. In other words, the government would rescind its promise of leniency, and it would not afford him the protections normally due a cooperating witness.

Casso was now a man without a country. He had betrayed his Mafia friends and could expect from them the violent retaliation due a defector. Nor could he count on government protection, since the Eastern District prosecutors had cast him aside. Worst of all, Casso's cooperation agreement had obliged him to plead guilty three years earlier. As a result, he would have no trial, and could not pursue whatever slim chance of acquittal a trial afforded. Instead, he would go straight to sentencing. At fifty-eight, his face bore the grooved lines of middle age. His black mane was flecked with gray. He would spend the rest of his life looking out for assassins in maximum security.

Casso asked Judge Nickerson for a hearing, arguing that the US attorneys had singled him out for retribution after he questioned the credibility of Al D'Arco and Sammy Gravano, their prize witnesses. Yes, he had bribed prison officials, Casso said. Yes, he attacked Miciotta. But other inmates had committed similar offenses, and worse, without forfeiting their standing as protected witnesses.

Normally it would fall to Judge Nickerson to accept or reject Casso's motion to uphold the cooperation agreement, but Nickerson had recused himself nine months earlier after the FBI disclosed that Casso and members of the Colombo family had once conspired to kill him. He was replaced by US District Court Judge Frederick Block, who upheld the prosecutors' decision.

"Simply put, criminal behavior by cooperators should be condemned, not condoned," Judge Block said. Casso became the first Mafia defector ejected from the program. "They're railroading me," he told a *New York Times* reporter as he was led from a courtroom.

Nine days later, Judge Block sentenced Casso to thirteen concurrent life terms without parole, or 455 years. He went directly to ADX Florence, a hundred miles south of Denver, the so-called Alcatraz of the Rockies. His new home was the most secure prison in the federal system, an escape-proof high-tech "controlled unit" designed to incarcerate inmates too treacherous for the general prison population.

"I help them and I get life without parole," he said. "This is really a fucking joke."

The underworld received word of Casso's banishment with almost unanimous relief and undisguised schadenfreude. As a Lucchese boss, he had ruled with a brutality rare even by Mafia standards. As a defector, he threatened to implicate without distinction between allies and antagonists.

Nobody benefited from Casso's banishment more than Eppolito and Caracappa. Casso had told FBI agents every detail of their crimes and betrayals, all of it dutifully recorded in his 302s. But without Casso's testimony, federal prosecutors saw no point in indicting Eppolito and Caracappa. For now, their deeds would remain an open secret within law enforcement, a shameful episode that would, most likely, go unpunished.

So Eppolito and Caracappa were free to pursue their new lives as police pensioners with closets full of desert leisurewear and backyard pools shaded by palm fronds. All their crimes receded into a half-forgotten past, as if they had never happened.

15

THE LAST TRUE BELIEVER

AS IT TURNED OUT, CASSO WAS NOT THE ONLY INSIDER capable of implicating Eppolito and Caracappa. A second path of investigation would lead, via circuitous and unexpected means, to their exposure in court.

By September 1993, Frank Drew and the other half dozen DEA agents assigned to Operation Gangplank had arrested Freddy Puglisi and his circle of drug traffickers and murderers. They now turned to a second phase: following up on John Fogarty's bomb drop in a Tennessee courthouse that Puglisi's main supplier, Burt Kaplan, had a secret source of information within law enforcement.

The DEA had learned almost nothing about Kaplan in the year since Drew and Foldesi spotted him talking to Puglisi outside the Staten Island Burger King. But as Puglisi sidekicks flipped, one by one, after their arrests and unburdened themselves to debriefers, the agents came to understand that Fogarty was right: Kaplan was a mastermind with a well-placed mole. "We began to see that he's got a source somewhere," Drew said. "He's got a hook somewhere."

Drew and his fellow agents were entirely unaware that the FBI were watching Kaplan for their own reasons. Nor did they know that Gaspipe Casso, in his debriefings, had identified Kaplan as his connection to Eppolito and Caracappa.

Based solely on their own suspicions, the DEA agents observed Kaplan come and go from his Staten Island warehouse. "We suspected something was going on there," Agent Foldesi said. "There was always some dude standing in the loading dock just looking around all the time."

Kaplan's warehouse discouraged easy surveillance. Port Richmond Avenue was so desolate that any decent-looking parked car invited notice. Drew and Foldesi considered setting up an observation post on the second floor of an abandoned two-story building, a former dry cleaner, directly across the intersection. But first they would need the owner's permission. Con Edison, the utility company, provided the owner's home address, an apartment on West Street, across from the World Trade Towers. They found the owner to be a Chinese American who spoke only splintered English. When Agent Foldesi explained their plan, the man grew agitated. He looked around the room and offered no answer. Drew asked: Is somebody else using that building and asked you not to say anything? The man relaxed. He smiled and said yes. (The agents would later learn that the Manhattan DA's office was using the house to surveil Kaplan.)

Weeks earlier, a Puglisi underling, now an informant, had told the agents how they might learn more about Kaplan. "If you want to get Burt, grab Rich Sly," he said. "He knows about him."

Sly was a major pot and hashish dealer, a Kaplan customer, who had so far escaped arrest. Drew and two other agents descended on Sly as he walked down a street in Mill Basin. They expected resistance; instead, Sly welcomed the arrest. "He couldn't have been happier," Drew wrote in a memo. "Sly immediately falls to the ground and begins crying as agents put the cuffs on him. 'Thank you, thank you. I'm so glad it's you guys. I thought they were going to kill me.' Sly continues to thank agents as he is processed."

Sly disclosed the inner workings of Kaplan's drug trade, including the key operational role played by his assistant, Tommy Galpine, who he mentioned happened to be conducting an extramarital affair. With this, agents saw an opportunity. They hoped Galpine could lead them to Kaplan, now missing for almost a year.

At 6:30 A.M. on February 20, 1995, Foldesi stationed himself in a car outside a 7-Eleven at the corner of Utica and Fillmore Avenues, down the street from the home Galpine shared with his wife, Monica, in Mill Basin. Galpine had met her when Kaplan first employed Galpine as an errand boy and she was working as a nurse in a psychiatric hospital. Drew waited on Coney Island Avenue, near the Belt Parkway. A third agent stood by to intercept Galpine if he exited the Belt Parkway at Cropsey Avenue, as he often did.

The agents had been trailing Galpine's white Bronco for almost three years, ever since he began delivering bundles of pot to Freddy Puglisi's house on Staten Island. They had by now memorized Galpine's routines, though familiarity did not always make the job easier. Galpine would "drive like a total maniac, constantly on the lookout for surveillance," Drew said. "His speed would vary from very high to a slowdown to a complete stop within seconds. . . . The closer he got to the Verrazzano-Narrows Bridge, the worse he got."

The agents took up their positions twenty minutes before the sun rose that winter morning. They waited more than four hours before Galpine left home. At 10:45 A.M., he drove to the 7-Eleven to pick up a large coffee, as he always did. After two stops on Flatbush Avenue, he merged onto the Belt Parkway headed west. He slowed at Cropsey Avenue but didn't get off. Instead, he accelerated to more than ninety miles an hour across the Verrazzano-Narrows Bridge. In Staten Island he resumed a normal pace en route to Georges Lane, a dead end with a row of modest homes facing train tracks. Galpine entered the last one on the left, a beige two-story stucco-and-brick house with a generous patio. Drew and the other agents did not know for sure what Galpine might be up to, but they could guess. He stayed inside for more than four hours, then drove to Kaplan's warehouse. He returned to the house the following days, each time staying for hours.

Agent Foldesi retrieved the account details for 19 Georges Lane from a utility company: the resident was a woman named Clarissa Colon. Agents spotted her for the first time on February 16, an attractive dark-haired woman with a young son.

Four days later, Drew and Foldesi asked the minister of St. Mark's United Methodist Church, located two hundred feet or so across the railroad tracks from Colon's home, for permission to mount a surveillance camera on its pyramidal steeple. The minister said he might consent if the DEA contributed generously to the church maintenance fund. Drew said federal agencies were not accustomed to making donations. With that, the minister simply said no and walked away.

On February 20, six days after Galpine was first followed to Georges Lane, Drew parked a surveillance van in the St. Mark's lot without consulting the minister. From there, agents photographed Galpine and Colon walking her son to the school bus stop on the corner. It was an unusually warm February day. Galpine and Colon lingered outside, hugging and kissing.

Fifteen or so months later, in the spring of 1996, the informant, Rich Sly, called DEA agent Eileen Dinnan to say that Galpine had moved out of his home. His wife, Monica, was filing for divorce. Dinnan then called Drew, who had recently been reassigned, to ask if he recommended showing the incriminating photographs of Galpine and his mistress to Galpine's estranged wife. "Are you kidding?" Drew said. "Show her! She'll be pissed."

The DEA agents were aware of Monica's reputation as a volatile personality. She would call the Kaplan house late at night claiming Galpine abused her. She also expressed resentment at her husband's devotion to Burt Kaplan and the constant coddling of Kaplan's daughter, Deborah, whom she facetiously called "the princess." The Kaplan women, mother and daughter, wore fancy clothes and drove expensive cars. Where, Monica demanded, was her share of the spoils?

One afternoon the following month, Dinnan and William Oldham, an investigator for the Eastern District, invited Monica Galpine to meet them at the Floridian, a diner on Flatbush Avenue. They were seated in a corner booth when Monica entered. She was, Oldham later wrote, "nearly good-looking but not quite. She was a bottle-blonde with big hair . . . she was tough-looking, a neighborhood girl."

Monica sat so that only the back of her head would be visible to other customers and lit the first in a series of cigarettes. She said she was afraid that Kaplan and Galpine would take revenge on her for talking.

"Burt's got connections," she said. "He's got power and money. . . . Burt had cops. Tommy had cops." She was referring, of course, to Eppolito and Caracappa.

Dinnan showed Monica the photographs taken from the surveillance van in St. Mark's parking lot—the photos of her husband with his arm around Clarissa Colon. It surprised no one when Monica then agreed to cooperate. She eventually shared everything she had heard or witnessed in Kaplan's empire—how week after week, month after month, the trucks loaded with pot and counterfeit clothing rolled in from Mexico, how she drove to Kaplan's house with Galpine and waited in the car while he went inside to pick up envelopes of cash for the detectives who did favors for Kaplan.

She did not know the detectives' names, she said, but she and Galpine once ate at the New China Inn, a restaurant on Flatbush Avenue, where Galpine pointed out a framed headshot of a jowly man with a mustache. "That's one of our cops," Galpine had told her. "He's got his picture on the fucking wall."

The New China Inn had closed years earlier. The framed photo presumably disappeared into the Brooklyn landfills. In a memoir, Oldham explained that after hearing Monica's story, he found the former restaurant owners living in the Sunset Park neighborhood of Brooklyn. They identified the policeman in the photograph as Louie Eppolito.

Years later, Kaplan would say: "It was Monica who sunk us."

At 7 A.M. on September 9, 1996, Agent Dinnan and a colleague walked the six steps leading to the front door of Kaplan's two-story brick home on Eighty-Fifth Street in Bensonhurst. They could see a security camera trained on them as they knocked. When Eleanor Kaplan cracked the door open, an agent inserted a foot. They entered to find Kaplan lying sick in a back bedroom. He had a monitor for the front-door security camera set up by his bedside. Agent Dinnan handed him an arrest warrant. They led him to a car in handcuffs.

Kaplan and his assistant, Tommy Galpine, were charged with trafficking twenty-four tons of marijuana and forty-four pounds of cocaine, plus related counts of tax fraud. Afterward, Kaplan instructed his wife to dispose of his copy of Eppolito's book, *Mafia Cop*, which Eppolito gave him with the inscription: "To my good friend Burt."

As soon as Kaplan was in custody, the FBI pressed him to say what he knew about the detectives. Kaplan refused. He made clear, without equivocation, that he would not cooperate. Not now, not ever. "No disrespect," he later recalled, "and they respected that."

At Kaplan's bail hearing, Assistant US Attorney Judith Lieb tried again. She asked Kaplan's attorney, Judd Burstein, if Kaplan might be willing to testify against Eppolito and Caracappa in return for a reduced sentence, or no sentence at all. Burstein, in turn, asked Kaplan, who complained that prosecutors had singled him out for arrest simply to pressure him into testifying against the detectives. He refused.

Kaplan resisted every government effort to win his cooperation. He consequently went to trial on May 5, 1997, in US District Court in downtown Brooklyn. The prosecution produced Bobby Molini, Freddy Puglisi's flunky, who testified that Kaplan imported vast quantities of pot from Mexico. To dramatize his account, the government wheeled in a shopping cart full of pot that filled the courtroom with its tangy aroma.

Monica Galpine told the jury that Kaplan was the surreptitious mastermind behind scores of illegal schemes. She did not leave the stand without taking the opportunity to call Kaplan's daughter, Deborah, "spoiled."

Deborah, now a legal aid attorney, called Monica Galpine a drunk who was "incapable of telling the truth."

Privately, Deborah and her mother pressed Kaplan to make a deal that would spare him extended prison time. He refused. "My wife and daughter had been asking me to cooperate from that first day," he said, "and I didn't do it."

A jury convicted Kaplan of conspiracy to distribute marijuana. The judge sentenced him to twenty-seven years, practically a life sentence for a sickly sixty-two-year-old. "We're both men," Kaplan told Tommy Galpine, his codefendant, moments after the sentencing. "We've got to do what we've got to do."

He went to the federal penitentiary in Allenwood, Pennsylvania, to serve his time, a stooped bald man in horn-rimmed glasses. He was frail, but walked into the penitentiary with pavement-hard resolve to stand firm against law enforcement. "He is probably the last true believer in the code of the mafia, the omertà," Burstein told Jimmy Breslin, the newspaper columnist.

For all their vainglorious talk of loyalty and honor, for all their macho posturing, a string of Mafia chieftains, culminating with Casso, had caved and signed plea agreements when faced with lengthy incarceration. Kaplan was the rare operative to steadfastly refuse, even though, as a Jew, he would forever stand on the Mafia's margins. Nothing would make him talk, he said. He was unmovable. And so the federal agents gave up and left him alone to serve his time.

The government by now had a general sense of Eppolito and Caracappa's crimes, but agents and prosecutors nonetheless shelved their investigation for lack of evidence. They had no case without Casso or Kaplan. The two retired detectives went about their lives as Vegas retirees. They walked in the Nevada sunshine without cause to look over their shoulders.

PART II

16

A CASE REVIVED

BY THE LATE 1990S, TEN BOXES CONTAINING RECORDS
of the moribund Eppolito-Caracappa investigation, now overlooked
and half-forgotten, gathered dust in the US Attorney's Office in Brooklyn. They might have moldered there forever if not for Tommy Dades,
a tall, generously tattooed detective with a lean, athletic build and an
engaging smile, who stumbled onto the case by accident months before
his retirement. Like any devoted detective, Dades hated an unresolved
case. His involvement began with a simple phone call from a grieving
mother.

In the years after Jimmy Hydell took on the risky job of ambush-
ing Gaspipe Casso outside the Golden Ox restaurant, and after Casso
tortured Hydell into confessing in Jimmy Gallo's basement, Hydell's
younger brother, Frankie, fashioned his own criminal career consisting of low-level burglary, drug sales, and petty extortion. He and his
crew, operating loosely under the auspices of the Gambino family, used
crowbars and fishing gaffs to steal from thirty or so bank night boxes
where, in the days before ATMs, customers deposited cash or checks
after hours. Across his upper back Frankie wore a tattooed repudiation
of his brother's killer: "Casso is a rat."

Bottom scroungers like Frankie rarely avoided jail for long. They
were expendable, and the higher-ups left them to their bleak rewards.
In 1987, at nineteen, Frankie pleaded guilty to attempted manslaughter.

He served six and a half years in Attica and elsewhere, then resumed his illicit rounds in South Brooklyn.

In the course of his duties as a Gambino lackey, Frankie, by then thirty-one, was recruited to help scare a union official and construction foreman named Frankie Parasole, who foolishly tried to put a mob associate named Lenny DeCarlo to work pumping water and razing walls on a job site. It was understood that mobsters in control of construction unions benefited from no-show jobs. They pocketed paychecks without actually dirtying their hands.

DeCarlo planned to school Parasole in Mafia protocol by inviting him to a Super Bowl party at Club Duvo, a two-room Dyker Heights social club. Parasole had spent the weekend with family in the Pocono Mountains. He dropped his wife and children at home, in Sheepshead Bay, and drove to the club in time for the pregame show. As commentators weighed the relative merits of the Green Bay Packers and the New England Patriots, DeCarlo and more than a dozen others slapped Parasole around in the back room. Frankie watched the beating, watched Parasole buckle to the floor, but stayed his hand. Then DeCarlo fired a bullet into Parasole's substantial buttocks. DeCarlo intended the shot as an admonition, an innocuous flesh wound that would send a message: never flout mob rules. Instead, the bullet pierced the femoral artery. Blood pooled onto the club floor. Everybody took off, except Frankie. He loaded Parasole into his Jeep so that police would not enter Club Duvo. He stopped at a bus stop a few blocks away and called 911 on a pay phone. Parasole bled to death in the ambulance.

Frankie would not be charged as an accomplice to murder since he was no more than a witness. But the police now had a recording of his panicked plea for help on the 911 call. He had unwittingly revealed himself to be a Gambino associate, and therefore worth investigating.

A short time later, a Pakistani shopkeeper complained to police that Frankie was shaking down his cigarette and candy store on Thirteenth Avenue, a strip of grocers and butchers running like a spine through Borough Park and Dyker Heights. Frankie paid weekly calls to demand payment for "protection." In the process, he had violated parole. He now faced two additional years in jail. The Brooklyn DA's office proposed a deal. Frankie would become an informant; in return, the state would waive the extra time. Frankie confronted a mafioso's gravest choice: stay loyal to his street friends or inform on them to avoid incarceration. He had to decide if he was a loyal family affiliate or a nation of one.

Frankie took the deal. A short time later, he sat with FBI agent Matt Tormey in a secure apartment known as a safe house. Over the course of a single session Frankie and Agent Tormey finalized their agreement. Frankie would serve as a confidential informant. The FBI would pay him cash for whatever secrets he shared.

Frankie at first resisted the requirement that he also share information with Tommy Dades, the NYPD detective. For Gambino street associates like Frankie, Dades was a day-to-day adversary, an impediment to his livelihood. "You know that everybody hates your fucking guts," Frankie told Dades when they met. "Both you and your motherfucking partner. You guys are destroying the whole neighborhood, locking everybody up, breaking chops for no reason."

Dades, however, was practiced at swaying reluctant informants. He was a good talker, and a good listener. He had a lot in common with South Brooklyn tough guys. He grew up drinking, joking, and fighting on the same streets, in the same bars. He had friends among them.

Dades refrained from arguing with Frankie. Instead, he slowly, gently coaxed him into seeing how they might both benefit. If Frankie named names and identified crime operations, the government would reward him. "I guess when Frankie saw that I was just doing my job and got to know me," Dades said, "we kind of liked each other." Frankie liked Dades enough, in any case, to warn him about John Pappa.

Pappa was a loud-mouthed twenty-two-year-old Colombo drug dealer, an up-and-comer whose mother had tried to draw him away from the mob life by relocating to New Jersey. The move did nothing to reform Pappa. After high school he crisscrossed South Brooklyn with an arsenal stashed in his car. He dressed the part with a tight tank top, Champion sweatpants, and high-top Nike sneakers. He tattooed the Roman battle motto *Morte prima di disonore* ("Death before dishonor") across his upper back.

Pappa's self-proclaimed honor did not stop him from murdering close friends to advance his standing within the Colombo family. "He was just a stone-cold killer," Dades said. "He killed people for no reason."

In 1997, Dades teamed up with FBI agent Matt Tormey to investigate Pappa for five murders. Pappa became uncomfortably aware that Dades shadowed him. He showed up to question Pappa after three arrests, in part to ask if Pappa might consider flipping. "He's in a cell and I start talking to him and hinting to him that we know about all the things he did," Dades said. "He was not receptive whatsoever."

The Colombo bosses warned Pappa not to threaten Dades. It would only invite trouble. But he ignored them. "Frankie Hydell and another informant told me that Pappa felt that if he killed me, that would be the end of anyone looking into him," Dades said, "which was ridiculous."

In one of their first meetings, Frankie Hydell told Dades that Pappa "sat on your house for two days. He saw your wife and kids go in your house. He was waiting for you to come home and then he was going to kill you in front of them."

Sure enough, Dades's neighbor in the Tottenville section of Staten Island had noticed a man in a red car parked by Dades's house. The car pulled out when the neighbor approached. By surveilling Dades's house, Pappa broke an inviolable street rule that applied to both mobsters and law enforcement: leave families alone. "It was a little too personal," Dades said, "when it involved my kids."

The police wired Dades's house with security cameras and a panic alarm. A radio car sat out front. With his home secured, Dades set about taking Pappa off the street.

Frankie told Dades and Agent Tormey that Pappa's close friend Sal Sparacino would marry his fiancée within weeks. "We had a hunch," Dades said, "that Pappa would be in the bridal party."

They guessed right. Sparacino had asked Pappa to serve as an usher. Sparacino, the groom, was unaware that Pappa had helped kill his twenty-four-year-old brother, John, three years earlier for taking unearned credit for a murder. One of Pappa's friends shot John once in the back of the head with a .22 as he scrounged inside a refrigerator. Pappa and his crew then sliced John's genitals off with a steak knife and inserted them into his mouth. Afterward, they drove his body to Howard Avenue, in Staten Island, and torched the car.

Dades and Agent Tormey guessed Sal Sparacino's wedding venue based on his address. Tormey then asked the church for the date and time of the rehearsal without revealing his identity.

On a clear Friday afternoon, Dades and Tormey sat in an unmarked SUV parked across from Saint Ann's Church in Staten Island. The bride, groom, and their bridal party had assembled inside with the priest for a 3 P.M. rehearsal, all except for Pappa. Dades and Tormey waited another half hour. They were about to give up when Pappa pulled up with his girlfriend. He walked to the church ahead of her. Dades and Tormey paused until Pappa was climbing the marble church steps. They waited in order to narrow Pappa's avenue of escape.

"We both jump out of the car," Dades said, "and we got our guns out and I yell my name to him so he knows it's me. 'It's Tommy Dades, John. Freeze.' He looks at me and bends down on one knee and says, 'Yeah, right.'" Pappa reached for his waistband.

"He's got a gun," Dades yelled to Tormey.

Pappa spun upright, holding a 9-millimeter handgun. "He pulled out this cannon with fifteen in the clip, one in the chamber and the safety off," Dades said. "I don't have a bulletproof vest on. Tactically, I should have shot him right there."

But Dades chose not to. Pappa never pointed the gun directly at him. Dades paused long enough for Pappa to open the church door and step inside. Dades followed. He held the door open with his foot, his finger pressed lightly on the trigger of his handgun. "I might [have been] seven feet behind him," Dades said. "I've got my gun pointed at his head. I don't shoot him. All I see is people. I don't see his gun but I hear it hit the tile floor. . . . I yell to Matt, 'Loose gun right of the pews.'" Tormey retrieved the gun before a member of the wedding party, all of them Pappa's close friends, could retrieve it.

Pappa then ran up the aisle, weaving among ushers and bridesmaids. The church rang with screams. Dades leapt and tackled Pappa just short of the altar. He leaned his knee into Pappa's head and leveled his gun at him. "I started screaming as loud as I could, 'Don't anybody fucking move! Don't move! I'll kill anyone that moves!' I didn't know who any of these people were. All I knew is that they weren't friends of mine. 'Everybody get down!' I yelled. I ended up putting the priest on the floor."

Dades sat beside Pappa in the back seat as an FBI agent drove them to the Sixty-Eighth Precinct in Brooklyn for booking. He noticed Pappa sliding to the door as they rode over the Verrazzano-Narrows Bridge, as if angling to go out. "He never got his hands on the door handle, but he's inching away from me," Dades said. "I'm like, if you think I'm going to stop you from opening the door and jumping out, be my guest. Goodbye, take care."

Meanwhile, Tormey stayed at the church to handle the bridal party's outrage. The groom, Sal Sparacino, fumed at the disruption. He demanded Dades's badge number. But his anger subsided when he learned that Pappa had been involved in his brother John's murder. "They're saying, 'We want to know who that crazy detective is,'" Dades said. "And Matt says to the groom, 'That crazy detective just locked up the guy that killed your brother.'"

Dades attended Pappa's entire trial in Brooklyn Federal Court. When the jury retired for deliberations, Pappa glanced back from the defense table. "He looked at me and pointed his finger like a gun," Dades said. "He winked at me and pulled the trigger. My words to him were, 'You better hope you get convicted because if you come back after me, I'm going to kill you.'" Marshals escorted Dades from the courtroom.

Dades had no need to fulfill his promise. The jury convicted Pappa for four murders, drug dealing, and illegal possession of a gun. The judge sentenced him to two life terms, plus sixty-five years on firearms counts and drug trafficking. He was twenty-one years old.

By the time Pappa entered the federal penitentiary in Allenwood, Pennsylvania, Frankie Hydell, the confidential informant who warned Dades of the danger Pappa posed to his family, had already paid the price.

Frankie had proven to be forthcoming. He revealed details of bank burglaries, pot shipments, and other crimes committed by more than a dozen mobsters, though he was selective about what he disclosed. "Frankie gave us what he wanted," Dades said. "He didn't want to go full bore, but he did give us good information about people that interested us. It was a good arrangement."

Like every informant, Frankie worried that his mob friends would uncover his deceit. He understood the risk: informants faced a death sentence, without exception.

Sure enough, in early 1998, the owner of a Bronx chop shop, a garage for dismantling stolen cars, warned the Gambino circle that Frankie was leaking word of their crimes to the authorities. (It is not clear how he knew.) When two Gambino associates confronted Frankie, he laughed off their accusation. But his government handlers, Dades and Tormey, were not laughing. "We begged him to come off the street," Dades said. "We said, 'We'll put you in the Witness Protection Program. Whatever you want, but you've got to get off the street.'"

Frankie refused. He believed the Gambino men were just testing him. "We were very uncomfortable with his decision," Dades said, "but you can't force somebody to leave."

Tormey talked to Frankie on April 27, the last day of his life. "We spoke around dinner time," he said, "and later that night he was killed."

The Gambinos recruited a friend to serve as a Judas goat. He invited Frankie to Scarlet's, a strip club in a stucco bunker two blocks from South Beach in Staten Island, where a boardwalk runs along an Atlantic-facing beach.

Frankie settled up and said goodnight a few minutes after midnight and walked across a parking lot aglow from Scarlet's neon-purple sign. He was shot three times in the head and chest moments after opening the door to his Toyota Camry. He died stretched out, faceup, between two parked cars.

Dades was at his desk in the Intelligence Division that morning when an FBI agent called to ask if he'd heard that Frankie died. Dades assumed he meant Frankie Saraceno, a Colombo associate killed two nights earlier under the Outerbridge Crossing, a bridge spanning a narrow strait dividing Staten Island and New Jersey. "I said, 'You mean the night before?' He said, 'No, Frankie Hydell.' I couldn't even let him finish talking. I hung up the phone. I was shaking. I called up Matt [Tormey], who was driving. Matt almost crashed his car. He took it very, very badly. We were in shock, we were in shock."

Dades and Tormey drove to Betty Hydell's house later that day. Hours after she learned of her son's death, they told her that Frankie had been cooperating with them: he died because they had made him an informant. He passed away on their watch. "That was tough," Dades said. "Betty was devastated. Jimmy had been on her mind for years. And now Frankie. But she was nice to us. She didn't blame us. She knew we were trying to solve Frankie's murder."

Tommy Dades had a particular gift for speaking with the mothers he encountered in the course of detective work. His own mother, Della, had struggled to raise him in a run-down apartment with abandoned cars out back at Forty-Eighth Street and Ninth Avenue, in the Sunset Park neighborhood of Brooklyn. "I'm not going to say we were dirt poor, but it was rough for a while," he said. "My mother did the best she could."

In the 1970s, Brooklyn was still a borough of distinct ethnic enclaves. Sunset Park was an exception. It was a ragged stretch of two- and three-story apartment blocks where kids of mixed backgrounds—Black, Puerto Rican, Indian, and West Indian—played pickup sports and jostled in the streets. In his younger years, Dades was the only white kid around. All were poor, in varying degrees. "We were lucky if we got a pair of sneakers once a year at Christmas," he said.

Dades never met his father, an immigrant from a small Greek hill town who did two tours in Vietnam with the Marines. His mother grew up in a Jewish household on the Lower East Side of Manhattan. "I felt like I didn't know where I came from or where I belonged," he said. "It was a confusing situation."

Dades's father was stationed in Germany when the couple split in 1963, leaving Della pregnant and broke. She supported Tommy by working full-time as an administrator in a Brooklyn hospital. He remembers her as a loving, attentive mother, but she was still young and attractive. Boyfriends and a taste for harmless gambling diverted her attention. "I was basically on my own from the time I was eight or nine years old," Dades said. "I could easily have gone the other way."

Dades grew up rough in a neighborhood thick with gangs and drug dealers. He received the first of eleven tattoos at age fifteen, a Tasmanian devil inked in a basement parlor at Albany and Lefferts Avenues. A tattoo artist known as Billy the Knife added two more later that year.

In the years before video games and iPads, the action was all on the streets. "I was a good kid growing up, a small kid but I was tough," Dades said. "I used to get my ass kicked all the time. The neighborhood was rough. There were a lot of fistfights, a lot of gangs. But I wasn't afraid of anybody."

Puerto Rican street gangs—the Dirty Ones, Spanish Lords, La Familia, among others—patrolled Sunset Park. When Dades was fifteen, seven members of the Dirty Ones cornered him and two friends on a subway car. One of Dades's friends hit an assailant over the head with a boom box as the train rumbled into a station. The blow bought them enough time to slip through the subway doors and run upstairs to Fourth Avenue.

If Dades had any steady male figure in his young life, it was his grandfather, Edward Schwartz, known as Blackie, who started as a newsboy in 1930 and rose to a position of standing on the production and distribution side of the *New York Daily News*. He came home late each night with a copy of the next day's early edition for his grandson Tommy. For most of his life Dades would read the *New York Daily News* every morning, front to back, paying particular attention to boxing coverage. He studied the long lineage of heavyweight champions—Jack Dempsey, Gene Tunney, Max Schmeling—in the 1968 and 1973 editions of *The World Almanac,* a gift from Blackie.

Blackie himself had boxed in the 1930s. "He still had pecs at age 79," Dades said. "He shadowboxed in his bedroom wearing his boxer shorts until the day he died."

For Dades, boxing would be a lifeline in a neighborhood full of bad choices. He and his friends made subway pilgrimages to the storied Manhattan gyms—Gramercy, where Cus D'Amato trained Floyd Patterson, and Gleason's, where the founder, Bobby Gleason, posted a quote from the poet Virgil: "Now, whoever has courage, and a strong and collected spirit in his breast, let him come forward, lace on the gloves and put up his hands."

Dades answered Virgil's call. Uncoached and unpolished, he sparred wearing gloves, but no protective headgear, with friends in basements and backyards. "I guess the scales began to change," he said. "People knew they might have a problem if they started with me."

Dades came to understand an ironic lesson of pugilism: the better his sparring, the less he relied on his fists. "When you have confidence that you can fight," he said, "that's when you don't fight." Fighting taught him how not to be tough.

By age sixteen, Dades and his circle of Eighth Avenue friends were drinking boilermakers—dollar shots chased by twenty-five-cent beers—at Flannery's, a bar up the block from his apartment, where a trio of bookies dominated the pay phone. "If you tried to use the phone there on a Sunday," Dades said, "you'd get your arms cut off." Flannery's became a second home. "It matured us," Dades said. "It gave us street smarts."

They also drank at Tali's, a small, dark Bensonhurst bar entered beneath a blue-and-white awning. Inside was a long wooden bar, a jukebox, and a few tables that would later serve as home base for the Gambino capo Sammy Gravano.

Dades came of age in 1970s Brooklyn. He and his friends wore tight, silky shirts and partied all night at 2001 Odyssey, the disco where John Travolta danced to the Bee Gees in *Saturday Night Fever.* They got into brawls. They ran wild.

In Sunset Park, the Mafia was a hovering presence—feared, but not envied. "We hated the wise guys," Dades said. "We didn't have two cents to rub together and their kids were driving around in brand-new cars. There was no love for them where I grew up. We knew about them."

Dades left school after ninth grade. "If I applied myself I was good, but I had a short attention span. I just wasn't a guy to be in a classroom." He wasn't alone. None of his friends graduated from high school. Of the limited options available to dropouts, Dades favored the Marines, but Della objected. "She was afraid I'd turn out like my father. She said why don't you go somewhere where you can come home if you want to."

Dades and a friend rode a Trailways bus sixty-three hours to Las Vegas, where they worked as busboys at the Sabre Room, a plush Middle Eastern–themed restaurant in the Aladdin Hotel. They stayed with a friend of Della's, a casino blackjack dealer, before moving to a furnished apartment off the Strip.

Las Vegas might seem an unlikely place to shelter a son from trouble, but the city's vices lay beyond his reach. "We were too young to get into the casinos," Dades said. "There wasn't much to do but work and walk back through the desert to our house." After clearing plates of chicken Kiev and coq au vin rouge for eight months, Dades used his earnings to fly on TWA back to Sunset Park.

For the next five years, Dades drove a truck for the *New York Daily News,* where his grandfather had presided over the loading docks. His shift started as the first papers printed at 11 P.M. He drove dark city streets until eight the next morning, delivering the day's lurid headlines to newsstands and bodegas.

The job was decent enough, but fraught with union politics. When the drivers went on strike in the early 1980s, a protective older friend took Dades aside. "He just said, 'Tommy, there's better things in this world for you. Find a way out of here.'"

Fortunately for Dades, he had studied for, and passed, the high school equivalency test at age eighteen, making him the first of his neighborhood friends to earn a high school diploma. "You'd have thought I graduated from Harvard," he said.

The GED qualified him to apply to the police, sanitation, and fire departments. Dades scored well on all three entrance exams. He was gunning for sanitation, but the police called first.

"Being a cop was the best thing that ever happened to me," he said. "It saved my life. Because most of the people that I grew up with went the other way . . . I was right there with them. But the day I put on that uniform, something good began happening for me. I put my life into it."

His early days walking a beat on the edges of South Brooklyn—Coney Island, Flatbush, Bensonhurst, and Sheepshead Bay—were not always encouraging. "You're standing on West 34th and Surf Avenue on a 4:00 P.M. to midnight. You're freezing and there's nowhere to eat and you're bored because nothing is going on. It's the dead of winter, day after day. It's not that I didn't like it. I just had a few second thoughts."

Dades graduated to the First Precinct, an hourglass-shaped square mile on the southern end of Manhattan, where he arrested a succession of dealers peddling nickel bags to Wall Streeters. In 1989, he was promoted to detective—"got his shield"—while working narcotics full-time in Brooklyn and Manhattan.

Dades lacked a "hook" in narcotics, in police lingo. He was without a connection to promote his career. As a result, he filled the department's most dangerous and stressful role: undercover drug buys. He put needle track marks on his arm with theater makeup and greeted dealers staked out on the street or selling from apartments. For Dades, undercover work was demanding but exhilarating. "In the morning, you're out there buying vials of crack, bags of heroin," he said. "You're looking all dirty and grungy, and later in the afternoon you change. You got a diamond ring on. You're driving a Caddy Seville going up to Roosevelt Avenue and buying kilos. It was fun."

Dades had a rare street sense. "Tommy was the kind of detective who had no problem going out and talking to people, finding information, and he enjoyed it," said Sergeant Joe Piraino, his boss in the Sixty-Eighth Precinct, where Dades worked after leaving Narcotics.

Piraino and Dades often rode in an unmarked police car around Bay Ridge and Dyker Heights scouting for wise guys. They studied the street from a parked car like hunters in a blind. "We'd watch for anyone who looked like they didn't belong, for something suspicious," Piraino said. "Tommy had an eye for those things."

Dades thrived. He knew how to converse with underworld suspects, both on the street and in detention. "Tommy knew the players and he was good at talking to them—associates, made guys, and bosses," said Piraino. "And they'd talk to him because he spoke their language."

In 1996, Dades landed in an organized crime unit within the NYPD Intelligence Division, then located in downtown Brooklyn, where he earned a citywide reputation as a hard-nosed, full-throttle street-level investigator. He was the kind of detective, a former federal prosecutor said, capable of producing exactly the right witness to rebut defense testimony on twenty-four hours' notice.

Many of the mobsters knew Dades, and they greeted him as he traveled the Brooklyn neighborhoods. "I would stop at Thirteenth Avenue to go to the B & A Pork Store to get steaks or veal cutlets to take home," Dades said, "and I'd walk right by everyone I was harassing all day."

In his off-duty hours Dades boxed on the NYPD team, known as the Fighting Finest, in assorted bouts. He was dedicated and disciplined enough to fight in thirty-five amateur matches. "I had a good chin," he said. "I could get hit a lot and never stop. I'd just come at you. I had more heart than skill. Nothing to brag about. I took a good beating."

Policing and boxing injuries led to ten surgeries. "I stopped counting," he said, "after five hundred stitches." When Dades removes his shirt, Detective Phil Grimaldi said, "he looks like Frankenstein."

The accumulated scars were not just physical. Dades had witnessed every grisly crime scene imaginable—decapitated bodies, two female police officers dead by suicide, one of them pregnant, a baby drowned in a bathtub, a body so decomposed and eaten by maggots that it had melted into a sofa, two drunks shot to death by police as they charged Dades with machetes, one of them swinging his blade just ten feet away.

"The worst part of being a detective was notifying a family that a loved one died," he said. "Especially if you were going there with a priest in the middle of the night . . . to hear the gut-wrenching screams of parents, I hated it." As tough as the job was, Dades might have soldiered on in his full-bore manner if not for 9/11.

His mother, Della, retired in 2000 after working forty years. Three months later, doctors diagnosed her with a grave illness. The condition was likely terminal, but Dades chose not to tell her. "She was my best friend," he said. "I dreaded the day she would leave."

Dades was prepping for an undercover gun buy in Staten Island when the first plane hit the Twin Towers at 8:46 A.M. on September 11, 2001. Like most New Yorkers, Dades and his team at first assumed that a hapless amateur pilot had caused a freak accident. They were driving on the Brooklyn-Queens Expressway when news of the second plane came over the police radio. They pulled off and watched the unearthly events—the jumpers, the purple-gray smoke plumes, the stomach-souring sight of the towers sinking into themselves, the scrambled fighter jets screeching low overhead—from an East River pier a block and a half from the Intelligence Division office.

Dades went to Ground Zero late that afternoon as part of an emergency response team. "When I got down there I couldn't even tell what street I was on. It was raining debris. People applauded as first responders drove down. We stood beside Ground Zero with all that shit raining down on us."

Dades returned home that night around 11:30 P.M. to find that his next-door neighbor, a Cantor Fitzgerald employee, had died in the towers. Dades had seen him leave for work at 6 that morning. Over the following days, Dades worked twelve-hour night shifts at Ground Zero.

At 6:45 P.M. on Saturday, four days after the attacks, Dades called Della before his shift. "She said, 'You be careful.' I said, 'Don't worry about me. You be careful. I love you. I'll talk to you in the morning.'"

By sunrise on Sunday, as he stood near Ground Zero, Dades found himself laboring to breathe. "I didn't have a clue why," he said. He drove back over the Brooklyn Bridge to the Intelligence Division, where a detective went upstairs and signed him out. Dades had intended to check into an emergency room, but headed home instead when his breathing briefly improved. He ended up at an urgent care center near his Staten Island home. He was there, filling out paperwork, when his wife, Roseanne, called to say that his mother had passed away at her Brooklyn apartment.

"She was dying," Dades said, "but we didn't expect her to die that soon. It was like a part of me had been ripped out." Roseanne went to his mother's house, along with a cousin. Dades could not bring himself to go. "Despite all the things I've seen in my life, I couldn't see my mom. I couldn't go back to the house." Dades took four bereavement days, then returned to Ground Zero for one more shift before resuming normal investigative work.

Four months after the Twin Towers fell, David Cohen, a lanky thirty-five-year CIA veteran with no police experience, joined the NYPD as a deputy commissioner. He arrived with a mandate to recast the Intelligence Division as a surveillance post searching for Al Qaeda sympathizers hidden in Muslim neighborhoods.

His plan was an end around of sorts. The CIA charter banned agents from spying on Americans. The NYPD Intelligence Division, however, operated under no such restrictions. Under Cohen, it became an unconstrained counterterrorism outfit—stopping random cars in Pakistani neighborhoods and employing informants, known as "mosque rakers," to listen for inflammatory sermons. The talk was of Baghdad, not Bensonhurst.

The long campaign to break the mob, energized by the RICO laws, now lost urgency. Backstreet shootings and grocery store shakedowns seemed unthreatening, almost picturesque, compared to the world-changing terror of jihad.

Cohen's "only concern was terrorism," Dades said. "Nothing else mattered. Terrorism, that was it. . . . We'd solved twenty-five murders. We'd put at least a hundred wise guys in prison. We'd established a better working relationship with the FBI and DEA than anybody in the history of the department. But the only thing this new boss wanted to know about my squad was when were we all retiring."

In September 2003, Dades was sitting in his cubicle when he received a call from Betty Hydell, the sixty-five-year-old mother of the murdered and missing brothers Frankie and Jimmy Hydell. Dades had struck up an unlikely friendship with her while investigating Frankie's shooting death in the strip club parking lot. He saw a mother's sweetness behind her tough demeanor.

Betty called Dades periodically. Sometimes to talk about nothing in particular, sometimes to complain about the NYPD's failures. "She would call me out of frustration," Dades said. "What's happening with Frankie? How come you can't do anything about Jimmy? She would holler at me. But she knew we were trying to work Frankie's case as best we could. I just told her all I can promise you is I'll try."

Even if Betty blamed Dades for the NYPD's failures, they nonetheless formed an almost familial bond. Dades cultivated relationships with the mothers he met in the course of his detective work—the mothers of victims and perpetrators. "Whether you're a good guy or a bad guy, a mother is still a mother," he said. "I saw the pain in their faces. I wasn't going to solve their problems, but I worked hard to give them closure."

He gave them his phone number and told them to call if they needed anything. He explained the intricacies of the judicial system, exchanged Christmas cards, and ran errands. More than anything, he charmed them with his big smile and street-funny Brooklyn banter. Almost without exception, they came to trust and rely on him.

"Tommy was a man of his word," said Joe Piraino. "If he told them that he was going to do everything he could to find who was responsible for the killing of their loved one, he did that."

Dades's thoughtfulness paid dividends. He knew from experience that mothers held secrets. And they would confide only in those who earned their trust.

As often occurred, Dades's conversation with Betty that September day focused on the unanswered questions about her older son, Jimmy, who was abducted in 1986, a month after his failed attempt on Casso's life outside the Golden Ox restaurant. His body had never turned up. Toward the end of the call, after expressing the usual frustrations, Betty offhandedly mentioned for the first time that she felt sure that she knew who had killed Jimmy. On the day he disappeared, she said, two plainclothes detectives had come to her Staten Island home looking for him—a fat cop and a thin cop. She was watching the *Sally Jessy Raphael* show one morning six years later when Louis Eppolito seated himself in a guest chair to promote *Mafia Cop,* his memoir.

Betty immediately recognized Eppolito as one of the two detectives who had come looking for Jimmy. "Oh my God!" she said aloud. Her son's kidnapper had the audacity to promote his memoir on television.

Betty bought a copy of *Mafia Cop* that day. She couldn't stand to read it, but she studied the photographs of Eppolito and his partner, Stephen Caracappa, whom she recalled as the second detective on the day of their drive-by. Betty told Dades that she called the FBI. An agent dutifully took a statement, but never followed up.

At first Betty may have kept quiet about Eppolito and Caracappa for fear that they might take revenge on Frankie, her second son. Of course, that no longer mattered now that Frankie was dead.

Betty assumed the detectives were untouchable. Eppolito, after all, was not just a cop but a *Mafia cop.* "She figured Eppolito was beyond the law, protected by cops and mobsters," Dades said. "So for all those years she sat on that crucial piece of information."

Dades had noticed Eppolito across the room at two Christmas gatherings with mutual police friends—he was too loud and obnoxious to miss—but they had never met. Even from a distance, Dades instinctively disliked

Eppolito, with his boasts and boorish manner. Like most detectives, Dades had heard stories about Eppolito.

Dades was picking up coffee from Dunkin' Donuts on the morning of March 26, 1994, when he saw the front-page *New York Daily News* report that Gaspipe Casso had fingered Eppolito and Caracappa as his moles and helpmates. "There were whispers around about them, but I didn't believe it," Dades said. "It just seemed too incredible." To be sure, patrolmen and detectives routinely received freebie meals and rounds of drinks. Petty handouts were an accepted form of small-scale corruption. A greedier contingent took cash bribes from drug dealers and mobsters, or pilfered from victims of violence. Eppolito and Caracappa stood accused of corruption of an entirely different order. The police rank and file was prepared to believe all manner of corruption, but not two detectives acting as contract killers on behalf of a mob boss. "I found it very far-fetched," Dades said.

Not everyone found it implausible. Days after former police commissioner Benjamin Ward died, in June 2002, Hugh Mo, the lawyer who presided over Eppolito's Internal Affairs trial eighteen years earlier, attended his wake. After paying his respects, Mo got a ride with Richard Nicastro, the chief of detectives, now retired, who had been obliged against his will to accept Eppolito back into the detective ranks after Mo dismissed the case. "I haven't forgotten what you did," he told Mo as they drove side by side through the rain. "You found that guy not guilty on some technicality—that was not right.

"You make your decision," Nicastro added, "and I make my decision, and I think Eppolito is dirty."

Nicastro had expressed the consensus among police veterans: Eppolito and Caracappa were dirty—though nobody yet knew the depth of their misconduct—but there was not much to be done since the Eastern District had dropped the investigation.

Now, as Dades listened to Betty, he began to wonder if her account linking Eppolito and Caracappa to her son Jimmy's disappearance might be enough to reopen the case. He called it "a small gold nugget of information."

Betty told Dades that she "knew" the two men had abducted her son Jimmy. "I told her I'd try" to build the case, Dades said, "but I didn't know where to start."

The next day, Dades walked unannounced into the seventeenth-floor office of Mike Vecchione, chief of the rackets bureau in the Brooklyn DA's Jay Street office and quarterback of a long list of high-profile prosecutions.

Dades had earned the right to intrude. He had a ten-year collaboration with Vecchione that functioned as the judicial equivalent of a relay race: Dades investigated homicides and other crimes in the Brooklyn streets, many of them half-forgotten. When he had amassed sufficient evidence he passed his findings to Vecchione, who brought a suspect to court.

"I used to say I was Tommy's D.A. and he was my detective," Vecchione said. "He was dogged. He left no stone unturned, and he had great rapport with witnesses. When he gave his word to a witness they knew he was not going back on it."

Dades could not have picked a worse moment to interrupt his friend. Vecchione was submerged in one of the most demanding cases of his career, the prosecution of Brooklyn Supreme Court justice Gerald Garson on bribery charges.

"And then Tommy walks in and tells me he's got this great case," Vecchione said. "I almost laughed. There is no way I had time for it, whoever it is. *No way.*" But when Dades told Vecchione that he had found an eyewitness linking Eppolito and Caracappa to the disappearance, and presumed death, of Jimmy Hydell, Vecchione paused.

"Are you kidding me?" he said. "Of course I'm interested. What have you got?"

Vecchione, too, had heard the rumors about Eppolito. "The word around the police department was that he was a dirty cop," Vecchione said, "but they just couldn't get him." He knew, as well, that the federal case against Eppolito and Caracappa had languished after Casso disqualified himself with his lies and jailhouse transgressions.

Dades told Vecchione "that he'd gotten a new piece of information that he thought might move the investigation along," Vecchione said, "and might allow us to reopen an investigation that had long been dormant. . . . For years people had talked about it but never done anything about it."

Vecchione called Mark Feldman, an assistant US attorney in the Eastern District. "I told him we were thinking of reopening the investigation," Vecchione said. "He did not seem impressed."

When the Eastern District broke off their investigation of Eppolito and Caracappa six years earlier, they had stored ten or so boxes of documents in William Oldham's office. With Feldman's blessing, Dades now retrieved the dust-covered boxes. He rolled them downstairs on a handcart over the course of several up-and-down trips and delivered them to a spare room, furnished with no more than a desk and phone, on the eighteenth floor of the DA's Jay Street office. The room sat off an open workspace used by the detective investigators who helped state prosecutors develop cases. Its obscurity helped Dades work discreetly. He mentioned the investigation to no one outside the DA's office. Nor did he requisition additional paperwork for fear that word would trickle back to Eppolito and Caracappa through the gossipy police channels.

Dades had earned the right to work as he wished without accounting for his whereabouts. He signed in at the Intelligence Division every morning at 8 A.M., then went to work at Jay Street. At 4 P.M. he returned to sign out. In this manner he loaned himself out to the DA's office as a full-time investigator.

Dades had climbed the ranks as a street detective, but for the next six months he was primarily a reader. He turned fresh eyes on the material, poring through the boxes, binder by binder, sheet by sheet, piecing together strands of evidence. He read FBI investigation summaries, crime scene reports, police logs detailing corruption allegations against Eppolito, Caracappa's search history within the NYPD's computerized files, their work schedule for specific dates retrieved from precinct storage rooms, and the transcripts of Gaspipe Casso's interviews with FBI agents. "It was overwhelming," he said.

The documents told a story of bureaucratic dysfunction, corruption, and foundering—most flagrantly by the NYPD, which failed to stop the detectives after repeated allegations and suspicions.

"[Eppolito] fooled a lot of people for a very, very long time," Vecchione said. "He fooled the entire police department for a long time. He fooled people who were his friends, his colleagues."

Even in 2003, Dades encountered doubters. "When I approached certain people—I won't mention their names—they basically laughed in my face," Dades said. "They said, what makes you think you can do this? I said, 'I don't think I can do this, I'm just looking to take a shot at it.'"

If some of Dades's NYPD colleagues dismissed him, others openly disapproved of his efforts to investigate two of their own. The animosity came, in particular, from older policemen—officers of Eppolito and Caracappa's generation—who devoutly believed in a code of silence, the police equivalent of omertà.

Eppolito and Caracappa "were respected by a lot of guys," Dades said, "and a lot of people didn't care for me very much because of [the investigation]."

Vecchione encountered more than hostility. His sister called him at the office on a day of crushing work pressure, the day an indicted judge was to surrender, to say that intruders had ransacked Vecchione's upstairs apartment in the Queens Village home he shared with his father after separating from his wife. When he got home, Vecchione could tell that the housebreakers had clearly targeted him. They hardly touched his father's downstairs apartment. After inspecting the wreckage, Vecchione retreated to a couch in their finished basement and wept. "It was horrendous," he said. "I didn't how know to handle it."

A month later, Vecchione stepped out of his home for his morning commute to find the back window of his government-issued car shattered. Repairmen found a stash of marijuana inside the car's roof. It was presumably planted to implicate him. This time the police installed round-the-clock bodyguards and cameras, and they asked him to wear a panic button on a lanyard that would summon police and emergency services.

Vecchione never determined who broke into his home and car, but he suspected that Eppolito and Caracappa's allies were trying to scare him off. "We were never able to prove it was or wasn't," Dades said, "but we assumed that word of the investigation had gotten out."

The probe continued, despite the resistance. Along the way Dades consulted Joe Ponzi, chief investigator for the Brooklyn DA's office and the guiding force behind more than a hundred criminal probes in some of the city's toughest neighborhoods. He began in 1977 as a polygraph examiner. Twenty-six years later, he headed all investigations. He was known in New York law enforcement circles as a figure of lofty professionalism, a man so diplomatic that he navigated the trickiest encounters without a ripple of conflict or confusion. "Even the killers he arrested had a hard time getting mad at him," wrote Jerry Capeci, the crime reporter.

Ponzi was one of a handful of higher-ups who had shaped how Dades approached his career and influenced his bearing as both a man and a detective. "If you don't have a father," Dades said, "you have to find one on the street."

Every day or so Dades sat facing Ponzi's desk in his work uniform—leather jacket, T-shirt, and big white sneakers. Ponzi sat opposite in a crisp suit with a neatly trimmed mustache and brushed-back hair. He wore a gold ring inscribed with his father's shield number. Emilio Ponzi was an admired detective sergeant who, by coincidence, had supervised Eppolito and Caracappa more than twenty years earlier in the Brooklyn Robbery Squad.

Ponzi made an effective sounding board for Dades, whose motors tended to race high with emotion and strength of will. Under Ponzi's direction, he began to make circumspect overtures and took statements from Betty Hydell and Al D'Arco—the former acting boss of the Luccheses, now an informant.

In 2003, Dades asked Richard Nicastro, the former chief of detectives, how Eppolito came to rejoin the force after leaving his fingerprints on the Rosario Gambino file. Nicastro was unwilling, or unable, to say why the police commissioner overruled him when he tried to bar Eppolito from the detective ranks, but he made clear that Dades was on the right track. "I hope you're calling to say you're going to lock that fat fuck up," he said.

Meanwhile, Dades continued to read through forgotten records. Detectives do not always make rigorous readers. Dades was the exception. He had an ability to digest documents and puzzle out how evidence fit. "I went over as much information as I could," he said, "to try and come up with a mistake that they made here or there."

By checking Caracappa's work logs, Dades determined that he had taken a day off on February 10, 1986, the day the diamond dealer Israel Greenwald disappeared.

While reading through the Lucchese family folder, kept in a locked filing cabinet in the Major Case Squad, Ponzi noticed that Caracappa wrote notes to himself concerning the Los Angeles whereabouts of Anthony DiLapi, the Lucchese defector, shortly before he took five bullets to the face in a Hollywood garage. Dades read, twice over, the five hundred pages of Gaspipe Casso's debriefings, his 302s. Whatever Casso's deceptions and grotesque wrongdoings, the transcripts acted as a map of Eppolito and Caracappa's long history as secret Mafia agents. Dades "always believed Casso's information about Eppolito and Caracappa," he said. "It just had the ring of truth." He spent his days methodically corroborating everything Casso had said about the detectives.

Casso told agents, for example, that Eppolito and Caracappa had delivered Jimmy Hydell bound in the trunk of a car to the Toys"R"Us parking lot near the Belt Parkway. Casso then drove the car to the home of his friend Jimmy Gallo, on East Seventy-Seventh Street in Canarsie, while he was away. Casso dragged Hydell to Gallo's basement and shot him more than a dozen times.

In late winter 2004, Dades and Bobby Intartaglio, his colleague in the DA's office, obtained a search warrant for Gallo's home, which had changed ownership twice since Jimmy Hydell died in its basement. Dades chose not to involve the NYPD crime scene unit because he wanted to keep the investigation quiet. Instead, he recruited a forensics team from Bellevue Hospital. They spent a full day in the renovated basement, ripping down mirrored walls and pulling up floorboards in search of bullets and traces of blood for DNA testing. "It was something we had to do," Dades said. "We tried everything, but nothing came of it."

Then, the morass of material yielded the first in a series of breaks. Like all detectives, Caracappa had to submit his name and tax ID to request digitized police records, along with the subject of his investigation. As Dades read line by line through the minutiae of Caracappa's search history he could see exactly, and exhaustively, what information Caracappa had sought. "No matter when you use the code," Dades said, "even ten years later, it still leaves a computer breadcrumb trail, a paper trail."

Dades found that on November 11, 1986, Caracappa had requested a computer search for Nicky Guido, one of three men who attacked Gaspipe Casso outside the Golden Ox. What's more, Caracappa had assigned his search a fake case name. "That was the moment," Dades said, "when I knew I was on the right track."

Caracappa had no lawful reason to search for Guido's particulars; he was not the subject of an investigation. Nonetheless, Dades found that Caracappa had retrieved details on a Nicky Guido born on February 2, 1960. Address: 499 17th Street in Windsor Terrace.

Dades now had an inkling of why Casso's gunmen shot the wrong man. He asked the assistant chief investigator to find the birthdate of the Nicky Guido who had helped Jimmy Hydell fire shots at Casso. "I'm just sitting there waiting for it to come up," Dades said, "and praying that the birth dates are different."

They were. Casso's intended target—the Nicky Guido who helped attack him—was born on January 29, 1957. The discrepancy proved that Caracappa, in a case of mistaken identity, had come up with the wrong man and passed his address to Casso for execution. As a result, an innocent young man died forty-four days later.

From the reams of records Dades had extracted hard evidence linking Caracappa to a murder committed because of information he provided. The discovery also corroborated the version of events Casso had shared with his debriefers. "That was the first thing I saw," Dades said, "that proved Casso was right."

As it turned out, Guido was only the first in a series of victims whom Casso located with Caracappa's help. "Caracappa would type in his code, do a search for a certain guy," Dades said, "and then a month later he'd be murdered."

The investigation gained momentum. "Now we knew that we had something," said Vecchione. "We knew we were on the right track."

Betty Hydell's assertion that Eppolito and Caracappa hunted down her son Jimmy on the day of his abduction and the computer search tying Caracappa to the Nicky Guido murder qualified as breakthroughs, but they were not enough. "I said to the guys, listen, we need somebody who either gave the order or was there when they killed," Vecchione said. "We need somebody on the inside."

By early spring of 2004—eight months after Dades began reading documents—Joe Ponzi, chief investigator for the Brooklyn DA, had sequestered himself in his office to review the amassed evidence. His concentration was so intense, he said, that he "could almost hear the bullets zipping by as I turned the pages." Only when he deemed the evidence sufficient would he pass it along to Vecchione—and ultimately to a grand jury.

The problem for Ponzi was this: Betty Hydell's word alone would not convict the detectives. Prosecutors needed a central galvanizing witness, a participant who could tell the whole story. But who might qualify besides the disqualified Gaspipe Casso?

After weeks of discussion, Ponzi and the investigative team arrived at a conclusion: the only feasible way forward was to make Burt Kaplan a cooperating witness. "We needed somebody on the inside," Vecchione said. "When we couldn't get Casso, the next best thing was to get Kaplan."

The inconvenient impediment was Kaplan himself. He sat in jail resolutely refusing to cooperate. He would not yield, no matter how many times prosecutors had pressed.

17

THE RELUCTANT WITNESS

AT AGE SEVENTY-ONE, BURT KAPLAN SHUFFLED about the grim institutional halls of the federal penitentiary in Allenwood, Pennsylvania, like an arthritic pensioner. During his nine years of confinement he had suffered a stroke (his second) a detached retina (his third), arthritis, prostate cancer, and Raynaud's disease, a disorder that constricts blood flow to the fingers and toes. Age and illness had reduced him to a sickly codger staring out at his dreary surroundings through thick dark-framed glasses.

If served in full, his sentence would keep him in jail another fifteen years. He was resigned to living out the balance of his sentence, or however long he lived, within Allenwood's drab walls. As a Jew, he could never formally join any wing of New York's five crime families. He stood forever outside the ranks of capos and consiglieri, but he nonetheless obeyed the traditional Mafia code of silence as devoutly as any Sicilian. Kaplan stood firm. He would not discuss his crystal ball.

There would be no deal, Kaplan insisted. He would spend his remaining days on the few paltry diversions available to him—walking laps around the outdoor track, playing pinochle with old-timers, and betting cigarettes on football games. Though he did not smoke, the cigarettes, won and lost, fed his lifelong gambling compulsion.

In January 2004, Kaplan and other inmates sat around the television watching the full schedule of NFL playoff games. They saw the Tennessee Titans beat the Baltimore Ravens with a forty-six-yard field goal, and they watched a fifty-two-yard interception return put the Green Bay Packers over the Seattle Seahawks. Through the divisional rounds and conference championships Kaplan wagered one-on-one against a six-foot-six heroin dealer named Andrew Lawson. As always, they bet cigarettes, the jailhouse currency. The betting line for the Super Bowl made the New England Patriots seven-point favorites over the Carolina Panthers. Neither Kaplan nor Lawson wanted to bet against the indomitable Patriots. And who could blame them? The Patriots had running back Kevin Faulk and quarterback Tom Brady.

For once, Kaplan suggested they refrain from betting. He held firm even when Lawson offered to take the underdog Panthers, plus the seven points. Kaplan still declined. On February 1, the Patriots' Adam Vinatieri put his head down and kicked a forty-one-yard tiebreaker with four seconds remaining to edge the Panthers 32–29.

After the final whistle Lawson demanded his cigarettes. Kaplan refused. He reminded Lawson that he had turned down the bet. Lawson persisted. Kaplan invited a third inmate to mediate. The arbiter sided with Kaplan, which further provoked Lawson. They scuffled. Kaplan was no match for Lawson. He ended up with a cut on his neck.

Retribution, Kaplan later said, is "part of what prison life is all about." With help from an outside friend, he paid Mexican inmates $1,000 to corner Lawson in a snow-covered prison yard and beat him with a combination lock swung in a tube sock. In response to the beating, prison officials moved Kaplan to the Metropolitan Detention Center, on the Brooklyn waterfront, until they could arrange a transfer to another federal penitentiary.

Shortly after Kaplan arrived in Brooklyn, Tommy Dades received a call from William Oldham, the Eastern District investigator. Oldham had earlier visited Kaplan at Allenwood in hopes of persuading him to cooperate. Kaplan rebuffed him, as he always did. Oldham planned to try again now that Kaplan was in the borough. "The old man is in Brooklyn and I'm going to go see him," Oldham told Dades. "Want to come with me?" Dades knew that Kaplan had rejected every overture. He doubted Oldham could persuade Kaplan when others had failed. Dades declined.

Oldham phoned over to the DA's office again on May 26, 2004. This time he spoke with Joe Ponzi, the chief investigator. Ponzi had noted Kaplan's intransigence in the interview notes written after his arrest. How did Kaplan feel now? Ponzi wondered. Might nine years in prison have rubbed the edge off his resolve? If Kaplan harbored any hidden inclination to implicate Eppolito and Caracappa in return for a reduced sentence, Ponzi believed he could draw it out of him. As a polygraph interrogator he had coaxed more than a hundred suspects into confessions and cooperation deals. "Ponzi had a silver tongue," said Bobby Intartaglio, the investigator.

Kaplan was a federal prisoner. Ponzi could not meet with him without an accompanying federal agent. Oldham's invitation therefore presented a rare opportunity. Ponzi immediately agreed to meet Oldham downstairs on Jay Street, for the short trip over to the Metropolitan Detention Center. Ponzi did not have time to prepare. He relied instead on his instincts as a seasoned interrogator.

Within the hour, Ponzi, Oldham, and a second federal investigator, Joe Campanella, were waiting in a meeting room. Kaplan walked in, a withered man in baggy orange prison garb and owlish eyeglasses. Oldham invited him to sit.

Kaplan made clear from the outset that his presence in the meeting room endangered his life: the longer they talked, the more likely his fellow inmates would suspect him of dealmaking with authorities—and give him the rough treatment a rat deserved. "Mr. Oldham, I told you we can't be doing this," he said. "We tried this before and I can't be seen here like this, talking to you."

Ponzi knew that seducing a potential informant required patience and a particular chemistry of trust. If Dades was the street-smart detective who spoke to mobsters as one neighborhood kid to another, Ponzi was like his polished uncle. "Ponzi could develop a good rapport with that kind of witness," Vecchione said. "He had a different persona. He was not threatening in any way. He was always very well dressed. And he had learned a lot from doing polygraph tests."

Ponzi explained that the Brooklyn DA's office had uncovered new evidence implicating Eppolito and Caracappa. They were working, he said, in conjunction with federal investigators. He made the case for co-operating: Kaplan could linger in his diminished life at a federal prison until he died in a lonely hospital ward, or he could cooperate and return home to Eleanor.

Kaplan listened before repeating his standard rebuff: he would never cooperate. "With all due respect," he said, "I've been down this road with Mr. Oldham before. The night I got arrested for the pot case . . . that night I got pitched by the FBI, the DEA, the DA, every chief and inspector from the police department. I had more business cards from law enforcement in my pocket than I ever seen in my life. Every one of them told me I could go home that night. . . . I told them, and I'll tell you now, no disrespect . . . I've done nine years and I can do the rest."

Now Ponzi toughened his stance. He tried to coerce Kaplan by reminding him that his relatively comfortable standing in federal prison could change. "No disrespect to you," Ponzi said, "but I don't want you to think I'm here now and then I'm going to ride off into the sunset. You know, you could very well find yourself at Rikers Island tomorrow, written out of the federal system and into the state system."

"Young man, don't do that," Kaplan answered. "Don't try to threaten me. I could overmedicate myself any time I want. Believe me, I will commit suicide before you put me in some cell at Rikers."

The discussion continued, with Kaplan now agitated. He paced the room, saying he must go. He banged on the door to summon a guard. With Kaplan standing at the door Ponzi posed a last-ditch query: Look me in the eye and tell me Eppolito and Caracappa had nothing to do with the death of Nicky Guido and you'll never see me again, he said. Kaplan bore partial responsibility for the death of an innocent man, since he had brokered the arrangement that led to the mistaken identity. Kaplan could accept that his underworld acquaintances met grisly ends; they chose the mob life. He had less stomach for the death of an innocent. He paused at the door. He turned around. He walked back to the table and sat down.

"Mr. Kaplan, I don't purport to know everything or anything," Ponzi said. "But I think *you* do. I think you do and I want to hear it from you. Why don't you tell me what I don't know?"

Kaplan considered himself to be among the last honorable mobsters. He was unsure if he could adopt the role he most despised: a rat. But he agreed to consider the possibility. He had family to think about, including a grandson, and the lingering possibility that Eppolito and Caracappa might testify against him if he chose not to implicate them. "I told them I wanted some time to think this over," Kaplan later said, "and speak to my attorney."

That summer, the Police Athletic League hired Tommy Dades to train teenagers at the Park Hill Boxing Gym, a new facility on the first floor of a notoriously tough low-income housing project in Staten Island. The gym was dedicated to two local detectives murdered a year earlier during an undercover gun buy. A plaque in their honor hung on a wall, alongside old fight posters and photos.

Drawing on his amateur career, Dades spent his evening hours showing teenagers how to adopt the right footwork, how to lower their weight into a fighting stance, how to keep their chins down, how to turn their hips and bring their fists back to their face after every punch. His raspy Brooklyn voice shouted pointers above the smack of the mitt sessions and the *thump, thump, thump* of speed bags.

"Law enforcement is a dirty business," he said. "Everyone has their agendas. There's a lot of backstabbing and jealousies, and what some of the perps do is unforgivable. At this place," he added, referring to the gym, "there is none of that. The kids are pure, and the boxing is pure." He called the gym "a dream factory."

Dades was focused on boxing, but he was not quite done with the investigation. On July 30, 2004, he retired from the police department after twenty years and joined the Brooklyn DA's office as a civilian investigator. He would stay on in his new capacity long enough "to put the fin-ishing touches on what would be the most rewarding case of my career."

The case hung in limbo while Kaplan weighed his options from a fed-eral penitentiary in West Virginia. In the meantime, ten or so investiga-tors and prosecutors met weekly at the US Attorney's Office beside the courthouse on Cadman Plaza. A calm, highly organized assistant US attorney named Robert Henoch doled out assignments from the head of a conference table. At forty-two, Henoch had tried a dozen street gang cases in the Manhattan DA's office before joining the US attorney's staff in Brooklyn. He had just returned from deployment to the Persian Gulf as a lieutenant colonel in the army reserves.

Henoch first learned of the case when William Oldham put Eppoli-to's book, *Mafia Cop,* down on his desk and filled him in on the inves-tigation. "I thought it was insane," Henoch said, referring to Eppolito's criminal history. "It couldn't possibly be true."

Henoch now had the tricky job of forming a cohesive team out of his colleagues in the federal office and their counterparts in the Brooklyn DA's office, who routinely viewed each other with suspicion. As long as anyone could remember, the two sides—state and federal—had com-peted for the big crime cases, and the attendant publicity, coming out of mob-heavy Brooklyn. The state prosecutors viewed the feds as arrogant and high-handed. They tired of playing the role of little brother.

In August, a contingent that included Ponzi and Henoch flew to West Virginia. After some negotiation, they reached a final deal: Kaplan would cooperate fully, as his wife and daughter had urged him to do for more than a decade. In return, prosecutors agreed to ask a judge to grant a more lenient sentence. He received one extra benefit: "The gov-ernment helped me get some teeth," he said.

Kaplan signed his cooperation deal days later, pleading guilty to kidnapping, money laundering, obstruction of justice, racketeering, and murder before a federal judge in Brooklyn, an appearance kept secret to ensure his safety.

Kaplan, who had spent his adult life shuttling to and from prison, would never return to the cellblock life. He moved for now to Fairton, a witness protection facility in southern New Jersey. "If Italian inmates saw him in Brooklyn," said Bobby Intartaglio, "they'd kill him. We had to take him out of the city."

When officials removed an inmate's name from the Bureau of Prisons website, mobsters assumed that he had flipped. They consequently listed Kaplan as "in transit" for months. They also guarded his wife, Eleanor, and their daughter, Deborah.

After signing his cooperation agreement, Kaplan asked Ponzi to relay word to his assistant, Tommy Galpine, in a federal penitentiary in Loretto, Pennsylvania, that he too should cooperate.

Tabloids later attributed Kaplan's change of heart to a toddler. His daughter, Deborah, a newly appointed criminal court judge in Manhattan, had adopted a son from Eastern Europe. The boy was now two and a half. News reports depicted Kaplan as eager to leave jail in order to hold his grandson—to dote on him and help raise him.

Kaplan later said that he based his turnaround more on survival than familial sentiment. No doubt he would delight in meeting his grandson, but by his account he had accepted a deal out of fear that Eppolito and Caracappa might flip if he did not. If so, they would surely point a condemning finger at him. In his mind, the choice came down to this: inform or be informed on. Better to sit in the witness chair than at the defense table.

"I wanted someday to be able to spend some time with [my grandson]," he said. "But I can't honestly say I did this for my family. I did it, in all honesty, because I felt that I was going to be made a scapegoat in this case."

Kaplan's agreement marked a turning point: For the first time since federal prosecutors disqualified Casso from testifying, it looked as if Eppolito and Caracappa might be indicted. If the detectives went to trial, Kaplan, the enfeebled fence and Mafia confidant who held their secrets, would serve as the marquee witness. Kaplan could almost single-handedly convict his own crystal ball.

Once or twice a week for more than a year, Assistant US Attorney Robert Henoch rose at 5:30 A.M. and drove to Fairton, the federal detention facility in southern New Jersey, to lead caffeinated eight-hour debriefings held in a lunchroom furnished with little more than a vending machine. "[Kaplan] had an incredible amount of information because he knew everything about everyone," Henoch said. "He was like an encyclopedia and never forgot anything."

On off days Bobby Intartaglio helped to corroborate Kaplan's account by driving him to the places he had met Eppolito and Caracappa—the cemetery near Caracappa's mother's home and a rest stop by the Long Island Expressway. He also drove Kaplan's wife, Eleanor, out for visits.

As the debriefings continued, the tension between the state and federal factions escalated. At one point Henoch refused to let Intartaglio and Josh Hanshaft, a prosecutor in the Brooklyn DA's office, into the room with Kaplan. They waited in the hallway for hours. When Ponzi arrived, he went inside to speak with Henoch. In the course of their keyed-up conversation Henoch called Kaplan "my witness."

Ponzi was known for his calm demeanor, but Henoch's presumption provoked him. "My witness? What do you mean, '*my witness*'?" Ponzi recalled saying. "I'm the one who turned this guy."

For his part, Henoch felt obliged to limit access to Kaplan to prevent investigators from inadvertently feeding him information about the case. If they did, the detectives' defense team could irreparably damage Kaplan's credibility by showing that he had based his testimony on facts taken from his government handlers, not from his honest memory of events. In legal terms, Henoch wanted to avoid "leading the witness."

"At that point the case is done and Eppolito and Caracappa are back on the street," Henoch said. "I micromanaged the preparation of Mr. Kaplan for trial. Maybe some of the investigators did not like that, but that was the way it had to be. I didn't let any of them ask questions without running the questions by me. It wasn't personal at all. I knew how careful you have to be when your case turns on the word of a career criminal."

Kaplan had warned of his failing memory, though, in fact, his memory proved nearly infallible. He calmly, deliberately led his questioners back through the half-forgotten byways of deception and duplicity— back to 1982 when his jailhouse friend, Frank Santora, first mentioned his cousin Louie; back to 1986 when Kaplan hired Santora and the two detectives to kill Israel Greenwald; back to the $4,000 monthly retainer paid in exchange for tip-offs and police intelligence. He recalled how Casso had paid extra for the detectives' help in eight murders; how they extracted Anthony DiLapi's location from the LAPD; how they shot Eddie Lino on a service road off the Belt Parkway. Kaplan's accounts roughly matched those Casso had related a decade earlier in his own debriefings with FBI agents. In addition, Kaplan filled in a great many blanks in law enforcement's map of the underworld.

Now, at last, prosecutors could move forward with a solid central witness, the reliable insider they'd always lacked since expelling Casso a decade earlier. With this in hand, investigators sat on folding chairs around a Formica table to consider how, and if, they might have enough to finally charge Eppolito and Caracappa.

18

THE UNDERCOVER ACCOUNTANT

ON A WARM LATE SPRING JUNE DAY IN 2002, A heavyset fifty-five-year-old certified public accountant with thinning combed-back hair and intemperate tastes named Stephen Corso was driving from his home in suburban Ridgefield, Connecticut, to his Fifty-Seventh Street office in Midtown Manhattan.

Corso was a partner in the accounting firm Merdinger, Fruchter, Rosen & Corso. As he navigated the southbound commuter traffic that day, his cell phone rang. An office manager was calling to say that FBI and IRS agents had entered with a search warrant. They were confiscating boxes of Corso's files. He made a U-turn and drove home.

The raid could not have entirely surprised Corso. The impounded files contained evidence of Corso's history of embezzling from clients, including longtime friends. For years he had told clients what taxes they owed and asked them to wire the funds to his own account. Instead of paying the government on the clients' behalf, he kept the money. Meanwhile, he told the government the clients qualified for refunds. He kept those too.

By 2002 he had misappropriated $5.4 million used to finance, in his words, a spree of "girlfriends, jewelry, and going out." He had also amassed gambling debts—he owed casinos $600,000—while leading a hidden life in Las Vegas, where he helped his firm expand its West Coast presence. Not surprisingly, the IRS eventually caught on. If a jury convicted Corso of tax evasion and mail fraud, as seemed likely, a judge could sentence him to as much as seven and a half years.

Corso was a dealmaker by nature. He made a living by trading in shortcuts and dodges. His instincts led him to quickly accede when federal prosecutors offered a way out: they promised to ask a judge to reduce his sentence if he agreed to plead guilty and work undercover in Las Vegas, where the FBI surveilled organized crime figures.

The FBI opened a six-room office suite, wired with hidden microphones and cameras, where Corso offered dodgy clients solutions to tax problems, both legitimate and illicit. The FBI paid him $5,000 a month for his undercover expenses and granted him permission to file fraudulent tax returns for his new clients—strippers, bartenders, bouncers, and mobsters. All of them, Corso said, "substantially understated the level of income they were earning."

Starting in the spring of 2003, Corso mingled at mob gathering spots, including the Crazy Horse Too, a strip club a few blocks off the Las Vegas Strip, and a storefront social club operated by a Lucchese soldier named John Conti, who hosted Thursday lunches where bronzed old men with potbellies and comb-overs bragged of their friendships with John Gotti and Paul Castellano. "[Conti] told me he ran Vegas for the mob," Corso said.

Corso was a smooth talker with a natural touch for the criminal workaround. He knew how to talk, how to joke. He drank with his new friends, caroused with them, and offered financial advice—all while wearing a recording device the size of a cell phone tucked inside his neatly tailored suit. In his two years undercover, Corso filled nine hundred tapes of boasting and banter. "We came across anything and everything," said his handler, FBI agent Kevin Sheehan.

In October 2004, Michael DiBari, a Gambino associate using the casinos to launder money, asked Corso to meet with a friend named Louie Eppolito, who, he explained, was a retired detective trying to raise enough money to produce his screenplay. Corso knew nothing about Eppolito. Agent Sheehan had not mentioned him as a figure of interest.

A week later, an associate of the Bonanno crime family named Mike

Frate and his son, John, gave Corso a copy of *Murder at Youngstown*, Eppolito's screenplay. Agent Sheehan instructed Corso to say that he was reluctant to meet with Eppolito because he was a former detective. "Mike Frate said that he understood my concern," Corso later said, but that Corso "shouldn't worry" because "Lou was one of us."

Corso asked Agent Sheehan how to proceed. "He said to me hang tight," Corso said. "Do not meet with anyone and I'll get back to you within a couple days."

Agent Sheehan knew Eppolito and Caracappa by reputation. The older agents who preceded him in the Las Vegas field office had mentioned the two retired detectives with shady reputations who, Sheehan noted, lived across the street from each other. "They really weren't on my radar," Sheehan said. "It wasn't as if either was public enemy number one in Las Vegas. So I didn't have high hopes. But I thought if they want to talk, let's see what they have to say."

Tommy Dades had no way of knowing that the FBI was already watching Eppolito and Caracappa in Las Vegas. So, in the thick of his investigation for the Brooklyn DA's office, he arranged his own surveillance. "We wanted eyes on what was going on out there with these guys," said Mike Vecchione, the assistant DA. "We had to cover all our bases."

In October 2003, Dades called Frank Drew, the DEA agent who had investigated Freddy Puglisi's pot network on Staten Island. Drew referred Dades to his colleague Timmy Moran, group supervisor for the DEA in Las Vegas.

Dades wanted to confine the ongoing investigation of Eppolito and Caracappa to a closely held circle. "Friends and friends of friends," he said. "People I trust." Moran fit the bill.

Moran was taking his daughter to Irish dance practice when his phone rang. Dades was calling from Brooklyn. Moran knew of Dades, but they had never met. After introducing himself, Dades explained that investigators in the Brooklyn DA's office and their federal counterparts in the Eastern District had revived the dormant probe into the two former detectives now living in Las Vegas. Moran knew nothing about Eppolito and Caracappa, aside from noticing Eppolito's book, *Mafia Cop,* in a bookstore.

Moran's work in Las Vegas mostly involved tracking suspicious visitors from Mexico and South America and monitoring a cell of Israelis who were importing ecstasy from Belgium. Moran agreed to watch Eppolito and Caracappa for signs that their criminal behavior continued in their desert retirement. The next night, Moran drove over to Silver Bear Way to see Eppolito's home. "Typical Vegas house," Moran said. "They all look the same."

A few weeks later, Moran flew east on a Sunday red-eye. Dades picked him up at Kennedy Airport early on Monday morning. On the way to Dades's house on Staten Island, Moran, bleary-eyed, noticed the Mount Loretto Church, where Francis Ford Coppola had filmed a baptism scene for *The Godfather.* Moran just had time to shower before they met with Assistant US Attorney Mark Feldman at 9 A.M. in the Eastern District office. Dades needed a federal official's blessing to keep the case with the DEA in Las Vegas. Feldman agreed. Moran would be the agent of record in Las Vegas. They made these arrangements unaware that the FBI was already surveilling the detectives.

Moran concluded that watching the mob cops mostly meant watching Eppolito, since Caracappa rarely left home at night. One evening Moran trailed Eppolito to a New York–themed pizza restaurant decorated with Yankees memorabilia and photos of the Twin Towers. Eppolito went inside. Moran followed. "My first thought was, Louie, you've got to stop dying your hair. My second thought was disappointment at seeing a former law enforcement guy adopt the persona of a wise guy walking down Mulberry Street," said Moran.

Moran and his DEA associates followed Eppolito and Caracappa everywhere—to meals with washed-up Vegas mobsters, to strip clubs and restaurants. "I don't know why they didn't burn me," said DEA agent Kenny Luzak, meaning detect his hovering presence. Luzak trailed the detectives so closely, and so often, that their gazes occasionally met.

Looking into Caracappa's eyes, Luzak said, "was like looking in the eyes of a shark. Pure evil. That guy creeped me out."

Meanwhile, unbeknownst to Agent Moran and the DEA, the FBI was poised to send Stephen Corso, their undercover accountant, into Eppolito's house to record the first in a series of conversations.

On December 7, 2004, Corso pulled into the driveway of the four-bedroom white house with a terra-cotta roof that Eppolito had bought partially with pot proceeds loaned by Burt Kaplan. A five-foot-high fountain trickled on a patch of lawn.

In Las Vegas, Eppolito had assumed a bigger version of his earlier self. He had always been the loudest, flashiest man in the room, but now he drove a Cadillac and collected snakes and a hundred or so guns, including a snub-nosed handgun engraved with the words "Mafia Cop Louis Eppolito." In the city of second chances, he bet that a movie career would pay for a life that exceeded the modest comforts his $5,000-a-month police pension afforded.

He had some success. Between 1986 and 2005 he played small roles in more than a dozen movies. In addition to *Goodfellas,* he appeared in *State of Grace* and *Lost Highway.* Without exception, he played a gangster or cop. Casting directors no doubt hired him for his cartoonish tough guy physique and Brooklyn accent. His presence lent authenticity.

Corso entered the house through two white pillars and introduced himself to Eppolito, a tub of a man with a conspicuous display of rings and medallions, and his wife, Fran. They drank espresso in the kitchen before retiring to the den Eppolito had fashioned for himself in the garage. Eppolito sat behind an oversized desk surrounded by two NYPD medals, two medals of merit, and photos of himself posed with Joe Pesci, Robert De Niro, and other actors.

Eppolito explained that he was trying to raise the $5 million required to produce *Murder in Youngstown.* He had a young Australian actor named Costas Mandylor in mind for the lead. Mandylor had appeared alongside the former lightweight champion Ray "Boom Boom" Mancini in *Turn of Faith,* Eppolito's previous screenplay. The film was made, but never released to theaters.

Eppolito had tried to raise funds by appealing to the vanity of his Las Vegas acquaintances. He offered to write screenplays based on their lives for a fee of $75,000. The investor was entitled to half of whatever income the screenplay might produce. "I says, 'Put up seventy-five thousand dollars. I don't care where you get it from, and you and I will both own the script,'" Eppolito told Corso.

He had at least one taker, a long-retired casino call girl named Jane McCormick, who in her saucy prime had entertained Frank Sinatra, Dean Martin, Peter Lawford, and other Rat Pack types. She wrote an unpublished memoir, *The Confidence Game,* detailing a life sullied by molestation, rape, and sex for pay. She hired Eppolito, at a discounted rate, to turn her story into a screenplay. "I haven't trusted a man in I don't know how long," she said, "but I trusted him." She shouldn't have. Eppolito charged her $45,000, but never delivered.

Eppolito turned to Corso for help raising the balance of the movie money. Corso told Eppolito of an unnamed (and fictitious) client who might hire Eppolito to write a script, but the $75,000 payment would likely come from Florida drug sales. Would Eppolito object? Eppolito said he "didn't give a fuck" if an investor was the "biggest drug dealer in the United States. But don't ask me to transport drugs for him. I don't do that."

And would Eppolito balk if the investor signed the contract with a false name? "He could sign it fucking John Wayne," Eppolito said. "I don't fucking care what name he uses." Corso's tape recorder took it all down.

While Stephen Corso sat inside the Eppolito house discussing fictitious investors on behalf of the FBI, DEA agents watched the house from the street. Neither agency knew of the other's presence.

Timmy Moran (DEA) called Kevin Sheehan (FBI) that night to say that he and his agents were surveilling two retired detectives. In fact, his agents were outside Eppolito's house at that very moment. "We need to talk," Sheehan said. Within twenty minutes the two agents met at a bar. They figured out that their respective teams were following the same two men: Eppolito and Caracappa. Then Sheehan "explained to me that they had a source into these guys," Moran said, referring to Stephen Corso. "I said, great. Let's work it together."

The twin surveillance efforts came together by chance just as prosecutors in New York intensified their efforts to develop a case against Eppolito and Caracappa.

"It was divine intervention," said Robert Henoch, the assistant US attorney.

Stephen Corso may have felt like a marionette: two federal agencies now dictated his undercover maneuvers.

Two nights after their introductory meeting, Corso joined Eppolito for dinner at Valentino, a garish Italian restaurant with salmon-colored walls inside the Venetian Resort and Casino. As the meal wound down, Corso asked Eppolito about the eight men he had boasted of killing in the line of duty. "Did I ever feel bad about killing?" Eppolito said. "No. I never lost a minute's sleep. Problem is, if I knew where they were I'd go back and kill them again."

Corso would meet Eppolito more than twenty times over a series of substantial steak and pasta meals washed down with rounds of chianti, despite Eppolito's recent double bypass surgery. All the while DEA agent Kenny Luzak watched furtively from the restaurant bar.

Corso dangled promises of quick cash and a plan to enrich Eppolito by taking his production company public, though Eppolito himself did most of the talking. He unknowingly recorded an unending series of obscenities and slurs and details of his tax arrears and his suspicion that investigators were examining his affairs. "Because of who my family was back in Brooklyn," he said, "they're still coming after me." He claimed, with good reason, to have seen men watching his house from a parked car.

Along the way, Corso led Eppolito to believe that he had interest in his daughter Andrea, an Italian-American beauty with dark eyes and long brunette hair. If the movie money came through, Eppolito said, he would encourage his daughter to date Corso. In other words, he used his daughter as a bargaining chip.

On New Year's Eve, Caracappa joined them at Il Mulino, another brassy Italian restaurant, this one tucked within a shopping arcade in Caesars Palace. Eppolito showed up in a dark shirt with shirttails out. As always, Caracappa wore a suit.

Caracappa didn't attend all the dinner meetings with Corso, but he was a watchful presence. He lived with his wife, Monica, in a relatively modest house directly across Silver Bear Way from Eppolito. He had situated himself near his closest friend, a friend who required watching. The two may have supposed they were in the clear. Thirteen years had passed since their last known crime, the shooting of Eddie Lino beside the Belt Parkway. But there was still the chance—a good chance—that Eppolito would slip up.

Eppolito gravitated to the thousand-watt Vegas limelight. Caracappa leaned the other way: Monica complained that in a city of all-night revels her husband fell asleep after dinner. The desert playground had not changed his sullen demeanor. He looked as gaunt and reserved as ever. His two indulgences were taking in stray animals and accompanying Monica for strolls through the subdivision where residents rarely walked.

"You couldn't ask for better neighbors," said the husband of a resident who served on the homeowners association board. "Steve is one of the kindest people you'll ever know. These are real stay-at-home people."

When Caracappa joined Eppolito and Corso for dinner, he did so in his capacity as vice president of DeAntone Productions, Eppolito's production company. He likely vetted Eppolito's scripts to make sure they revealed nothing about their underworld employment.

So far, Corso had taped Eppolito boasting about Mafia connections and declaring his willingness—his *eagerness*—to take money laundered from shady sources. His words compromised him, but they were not enough to demonstrate an ongoing criminal enterprise, as the RICO laws required.

At a meeting held on February 3, 2005, Corso was more explicit about the money's illegal origins: "This is drug money that's coming, okay?" Eppolito consented. Corso explained that it would come in increments of $10,000 or less to avoid detection. Later that day, a DEA agent wired $9,000 into Eppolito's bank account from a fictitious account set up at Bank of America, followed by another $5,000 three weeks later.

A new possibility emerged when, at a February 8 meeting, Caracappa spoke of drug dealing as a plausible, even admirable pursuit. "It's like anything else," he said. "If you look at it as business you could make a lot of money. A lot of legit guys, a lot of ex-cops, get into the business. They made their money and they got out. Back in the late '70s, if you had the balls to do it, you could have made millions."

If Corso, coached by his handlers, could catch Eppolito and Caracappa in an illegal drug sale, federal prosecutors back in the Eastern District office might make the case for a continuing criminal enterprise.

On February 15, Corso, as instructed, told Eppolito and Caracappa over bruschetta appetizers and drinks that he had lined up a group of potential investors. "They're Hollywood punks," he said. "Some of them are famous." The fictitious investors were meant to play on Eppolito's weakness for celebrities. They were flying in from Los Angeles in a few weeks, Corso said, and they wanted to buy party drugs. "These guys, being young, like to party," Corso said. "And they do things that . . . I have no knowledge about. And basically that's designer shit, designer drugs."

"Tony can take care of that for you," Eppolito said, referring to his tall, dark-haired twenty-four-year-old son. Tony, he added, could "bring them to all the places, the top places."

Corso steered the topic back to buying drugs. "They don't want to go to places . . . they want me to get them either ecstasy or speed."

"You've got to ask Guido," Eppolito said, referring to Tony's close friend Guido Bravatti, who came from a family of Sicilian circus performers and eked out a living on the margins of Vegas nightlife. Eppolito called Corso later that night and gave him Bravatti's phone number. Corso met Bravatti and Tony Eppolito for dinner the following evening. Corso explained that his clients wanted an ounce of crystal meth and eight or so ecstasy pills. The two younger men agreed to help. They would do anything, they said, to help Corso find investors for Eppolito's movie. "Because you're my dad's friend," Tony Eppolito said, "there is no way anybody you bring us would get screwed, believe me." Corso asked them to deliver the drugs to his office, where the FBI and DEA could videotape the transaction.

Tony Eppolito and Bravatti arrived the next day, as planned, and handed Corso a foil envelope containing 24.4 grams of meth. They delivered slightly less meth than requested, and no ecstasy. Corso nonetheless thanked them and paid $900 in hundred-dollar bills. "A pleasure doing business," he told them.

Agents Sheehan and Moran watched and listened from the adjacent room. When the two men left, Sheehan called Corso and asked him to pick up the envelope with a tissue and bring it next door.

On March 3, Corso ate a tense dinner with Eppolito at BOA Steakhouse inside Caesars Palace, where Eppolito's daughter Andrea worked as a hostess. After Andrea seated them, Eppolito said that he had received an anxious phone call from Tony, who expressed concern about the drug sale. "I got a panicky call from my son," Eppolito said, "and I'm very fucking upset. Don't call him or Guido anymore. No more." Though Eppolito relaxed when the drinks came and the meal got underway.

It didn't matter anymore what Eppolito thought of Corso, or anyone else. Corso would record his last conversation with Eppolito that night. His undercover work was done. He had helped deliver what prosecutors required: hard evidence of Eppolito and Caracappa committing a crime. The statute of limitations imposed by the RICO laws was no longer ticking down. After dinner, Corso said his goodbyes and drove off. Eppolito and Caracappa would not see him again for another year, in a courtroom 2,500 miles away.

19

A CASE DIVIDED

ONE WINTER DAY IN 2005, JOE PONZI ENTERED MIKE Vecchione's office in the Brooklyn DA's Jay Street office to update him on the investigation. In the course of their discussion, Ponzi casually mentioned that a DEA agent had testified before a federal grand jury impaneled to indict Eppolito and Caracappa.

"What are you talking about?" Vecchione said.

"Don't you know?" Ponzi asked.

Vecchione did *not* know. The US Attorney's Office for the Eastern District, which had once shelved the Eppolito-Caracappa case, now intended to proceed without the investigation's prime movers in the Brooklyn DA's office. "They never said a word to us," Vecchione said. "I was shocked because they never let on. I was beside myself."

In the year since Burt Kaplan flipped, Tommy Dades and other state investigators had met weekly with their federal counterparts in the Eastern District offices beside the federal courthouse. The two sides had a history of competing for the same high-profile cases. Awkward as it might be, they nonetheless proceeded on the understanding that the Brooklyn DA's office would charge Eppolito and Caracappa for their part in the murder of Jimmy Hydell. This was in keeping with normal practice: most murder cases were tried in state court. Meanwhile, Robert Henoch and his Eastern District colleagues would pursue a separate racketeering case. At least that's how Mike Vecchione understood their agreement.

G. Robert Blakey designed the RICO laws to convict members of criminal conspiracies, but within a time limit. The defendants had to have committed a crime within five years of their indictment. The statute of limitations posed a problem for Henoch and his team of prosecutors. Defense lawyers could plausibly claim that Eppolito and Caracappa's criminal careers had ended when Caracappa retired from the police department in 1992; or when the FBI apprehended Casso in 1993; or when the DEA arrested Kaplan in 1996. In any of these cases, the five-year statute of limitations would have expired. In order to bring a RICO charge, the feds would have to reset the clock with a more recent crime.

Now Vecchione learned that federal prosecutors had quietly concluded that the drug sale put them safely within the time limit. They could seek a RICO indictment. The feds were forging ahead on their own. (Vecchione would have had no advance knowledge of the federal grand jury because they convened in secret.)

He immediately called Assistant US Attorney Mark Feldman. "I can't believe you're doing this," he said. "We had a deal, Mark. We agreed that we would take Hydell, you would take the RICO if you could make it."

"That's not really the way I remember it," Feldman said. "I think I said that if there was a RICO *we* would take it. Well, there *is* a RICO."

"Yeah, you *did* say that," Vecchione said. "But you said we would have the murder, and you would have the RICO. I went out on a limb and told my boss that we had a deal."

Feldman tried to defuse the matter by calling it a misunderstanding. "No, but I think maybe you misread me," he said. "I don't think I ever said that."

Now Vecchione was furious. "C'mon, what are you, kidding me? That's exactly what you said. I don't understand how you can deny it. We went through it several times."

Feldman asked for time to craft a compromise, but Vecchione expected no conciliation or accommodation. Burt Kaplan was a federal witness. Without access to him, the Brooklyn DA's office could not proceed with a murder charge against Eppolito and Caracappa.

In desperation, Vecchione asked associates to think of ways to file a writ in federal court to force the Bureau of Prisons to hand Kaplan over to New York State so they could put him before their own grand jury. Or maybe, he suggested, they could tell a judge that the Eastern District was obstructing governmental administration by withholding a witness. Neither suggestion gained headway. They were expressions of frustration more than plausible options.

A few days later, Feldman came to the Brooklyn DA's office to tell Vecchione, in person, that Robert Henoch and other federal prosecutors planned to proceed with their RICO case in its entirety. We want to tell the story from beginning to end, so we need to use everyone, Feldman said. If you take out Hydell, he added, you remove a big piece of the case. It just doesn't make sense to do it that way.

Feldman also argued that if Vecchione called Kaplan to the stand in a state murder trial, defense attorneys could use Kaplan's testimony against him in the later RICO trial. In other words, the defense could ambush Kaplan in cross-examination, citing any lapse or inconsistency between his two appearances as evidence of falsehood and duplicity. No, Feldman said, better for Kaplan to appear before the jury fresh, with his credibility intact.

Vecchione was livid, but he slowly, begrudgingly, came to accept Feldman's logic: the kidnap and murder of Jimmy Hydell marked the beginning of Eppolito and Caracappa's seven-year service to Casso. Vecchione acknowledged that the crime should not be spliced out and addressed in a separate trial. The detectives' many corruptions and depravities should be told together, in a single devastating narrative.

Vecchione agreed to cede the case to the Eastern District in its entirety, provided that Feldman's boss, US district attorney Roslynn Mauskopf, credit the Brooklyn investigators with breaking the case and developing it to this point.

"As I thought about the case, I came to agree that the greater good is to have these two convicted," Vecchione said. "That's why we capitulated."

Tommy Dades was not so conciliatory. "Didn't I tell you right from the beginning they were going to fuck us?" he told Vecchione. "So, they fucked us. What do you expect?"

Robert Henoch, the assistant US attorney who would lead the prosecution, said his office had at no time intended to share the case. "It was never going to Brooklyn," he said, "because [Kaplan] was never Brooklyn's witness."

Feldman and a colleague came to the Brooklyn DA's Jay Street office to reclaim the borrowed boxes of evidence, the records Dades had used to build a case. "They came in aggressive," Dades said. "I saw red. Ponzi gave me a look like 'Don't start with them.'" Dades was so embittered that he asked for a receipt. He worried that the Eastern District might later accuse him of withholding evidence.

With the issue of who would try the case at last resolved, it would now go forward with all the weight of RICO laws exerted in federal court. But first the authorities would have to apprehend their suspects.

20

CUFFED AT PIERO'S

PREPARATIONS FOR THE ARREST CAME TOGETHER
in the twenty-four days after Eppolito's son, Tony, and his friend Guido
Bravatti sold Corso the 24.4 grams of meth. In fact, the Eastern District's
office had arranged matters faster than expected, or wanted, because news
of the grand jury indictment had leaked. A producer for the CBS news
show *60 Minutes* called the Eastern District's office to say they planned to
send a crew to film the arrest. In response, Mark Feldman told CBS that
any reporter or cameraman who came to the arrest scene would themselves be arrested and prosecuted for impeding a federal investigation.

Tommy Dades stayed out of it, except to call Betty Hydell, the mother
of two dead sons, the night before. "I gave her the good news," he said.
"It was like a weight off her shoulders."

At 7 P.M. on March 9, 2005, a black SUV with tinted windows pulled
up to the portico entrance of Piero's, a restaurant with dark wood panel-
ing, muraled ceilings, and U-shaped leather banquettes—a style known
as Mob Vegas. A garish red neon sign spelled its name above a team of
parking attendants. Five or so agents, along with Bobby Intartaglio of
the Brooklyn DA's office, waited inside at the bar. Agent Kevin Sheehan
parked nearby. Agent Moran rode with a team following the SUV, reporting its position by radio. The surveillance team could see their targets, an obese sixty-three-year-old with a gaudy display of rings and his
slender sidekick, get out and hand the valet some bills. Agents in three
cars pulled in, blocking the SUV from escaping.

As Eppolito and Caracappa approached the host, a dozen agents swarmed them. Caracappa put his hands in the air and circled around for the pat down. "Eppolito flexed hard and we forced him to the ground," said Agent Kenny Luzak. "It's been a long time coming," he said to Eppolito as he removed a loaded .45-caliber semiautomatic handgun from his waistband.

"Yes, it has," Eppolito said.

A source told the *New York Daily News* that "Louie was trying to be brave, but Caracappa was really shaken."

As the agents walked the two men away in handcuffs, the Piero's host said, "Well, I guess *they* won't be needing their table."

Two hours after the arrests, agents broke down Eppolito's front door with a battering ram. Eppolito's son, Tony, was walking downstairs. He sat on a step when he saw them enter. Fran Eppolito arrived minutes later. "She was yelling at us," Agent Luzak said. "'You've got the wrong fucking house. Get off out of my house. You don't belong here.'"

Agents placed items in evidence bags: photographs documenting Eppolito's ties with mobsters and 116 guns locked in a pair of safes, including two AK-47 assault rifles, a sawed-off shotgun, and the .38 revolver with "Mafia Cop Louis Eppolito" inscribed on its side.

Agents also found a framed letter from Hugh Mo, the deputy police commissioner who had cleared Eppolito of departmental charges after the FBI found his fingerprints on confidential police files seized at the home of heroin trafficker Rosario Gambino. Mo wrote to thank Eppolito for sending a copy of his book, *Mafia Cop,* and wished him good luck with his Hollywood career.

Agents arrested Eppolito's son, Tony, on charges of distributing methamphetamine. Later they broke down the door of Guido Bravatti's apartment across town. They found him inside with a naked girlfriend.

In the hours after the arrest, Agent Moran entered Eppolito's cell in a DEA lockup. "I said for the most part you've been a gentleman through this, and I appreciate that," Moran said. "So I'm going to be up front with you. We've got your kid in that cell right there. The blood just drained out of his face."

Moran also introduced himself to Caracappa, who mentioned law enforcement acquaintances they had in common, as one might at a party. "Here's a guy who just got arrested under RICO," Moran said. "He's going away for the rest of his life, and he's talking to me like it's a reunion."

The twenty-seven-page indictment, unsealed the next day in Federal District Court in Brooklyn, accused Eppolito and Caracappa of participating in a racketeering conspiracy that began with the abduction of Jimmy Hydell in 1986 and ended with the meth sale six days before their arrest. According to the indictment, they participated in eight murders, two attempted murders, kidnapping, and money laundering while working for the mob. As secret associates of the Lucchese family, they were charged with compromising state and federal investigations and disclosing the identity of secret informants, three of whom were killed.

Eppolito had been suspected of mob ties for at least sixteen years, but nobody imagined the enormity of the crimes. Newspaper columnists and public officials agreed that the allegations might qualify as the most abominable acts of police corruption in NYPD history.

The crimes were "stunning," said Brooklyn US District Attorney Roslynn Mauskopf, who announced the indictment at a press conference in the Eastern District's office. "These corrupt former detectives betrayed their shields, their colleagues and the citizens they were sworn to protect. . . . They used the confidential files of the NYPD as their personal yellow pages."

Tommy Dades watched the press conference live on NY1, a cable news channel, from the family room in his Staten Island home. When Mauskopf said that federal investigators had never given up on the case, he turned the television off. Brooklyn District Attorney Charles Hynes declined to attend, choosing to hold his own press conference afterward.

Newspaper readers might have been shocked by the allegations, but many of Eppolito and Caracappa's former colleagues in the detective ranks were not. "From a law-enforcement point of view, I have two words: *embarrassing* and *predictable*," said Joe Coffey, who headed the Organized Crime Task Force until 1985.

Two days after the arrest, Eppolito and Caracappa filed into a Las

254 BLOOD AND THE BADGE

Vegas courtroom wearing baggy orange jumpsuits. A pair of hastily hired local lawyers recited the two men's achievements in uniform and argued all but one of the alleged crimes had occurred more than a decade earlier. They asked a federal magistrate to release them on house arrest with electronic monitoring. The magistrate was unmoved. He ordered them held without bail until federal marshals could transport them to Brooklyn for arraignment more than a month later.

The news vans had congregated outside the Federal District Court in Brooklyn by midmorning on April 21, 2005. They were too late, as it turned out. Eppolito and Caracappa had arrived hours earlier. They sat handcuffed and shackled in the back of a black SUV that delivered them to a discreet back entrance. At noon they entered a sixth-floor courtroom to plead not guilty to every charge. They looked haggard and unwell after six weeks in jail; the anticipation of a trial had sapped them of swagger.

Eppolito turned from his place at the bar to blow a kiss to his twenty-eight-year-old daughter, Andrea, who sat with other family members. She wore lip gloss and a pantsuit with a neckline that was more Bellagio than Brooklyn. "My father loved being a cop," she told reporters outside the courthouse. "He was so proud of all the things he did for this city. . . . Now it's time for someone to protect and serve him."

The *New York Daily News* ran a full-page photograph of her looking beautiful and defiant, a tough-talking mob daughter, on the next day's front page. "You Leave My Dad Alone," the headline said.

Nicky Guido's family had never come to terms with his death in the eighteen years since Casso's gunmen shot him outside their Windsor Terrace row house on Christmas Day 1986. "If my brother had died because of a beef on the street, it would have hurt," Mike Guido said. "But at least I would have understood it."

Guido's father died shortly after Nicky. His mother was now a seventy-seven-year-old widow living alone in Florida when she heard her son Nicky's name mentioned in connection with the arrest of two retired detectives on the television news. She didn't grasp the arrest's significance until her surviving son called from New York. "We never thought eighteen years later this would turn up," he said. "We had left it alone."

Barry Gibbs, the postal worker and crack addict convicted of the murder of a prostitute found dead by the Belt Parkway, was lying awake in his jail cell in the Eastern Correctional Facility, a maximum-security prison in upstate New York, when he heard a 5 A.M. radio news report: authorities had arrested two former NYPD detectives in Las Vegas on racketeering and drug charges. Louie Eppolito was one of them. "There is a god," Gibbs yelled.

Gibbs had served almost nineteen years of a twenty-to-life sentence after Eppolito, then a detective in the Sixty-Third Precinct, arrested him for murdering the prostitute Virginia Robertson. "They took everything from me," Gibbs said. "I lost my identity. I lost my son. I lost my family and I lost my dignity and I lost my honor. [Eppolito] destroyed me, totally destroyed me."

It had taken Gibbs three years to adjust to the Byzantine codes and conduct of jailhouse life. "Whatever you learn out here, whatever's normal with relationships, how to talk to people, it's completely the opposite inside. It's a 360-degree turnaround."

Gibbs visited the prison law library almost daily. He applied for parole every two years, but parole boards favor inmates who express remorse. Gibbs felt none; he considered himself a victim, not a perpetrator. "I thought I was going to die in prison," he said, "because I knew I could never admit to the parole board to a murder I did not commit."

Gibbs had promised his son he would come home. By 2005, he was convinced he would not. "I started to make plans to die in jail," he said. He arranged for a cemetery plot on Long Island and a life insurance policy. He granted a friend power of attorney over his affairs.

Gibbs had exhausted his options, until Eppolito's arrest. When federal agents searched Eppolito's home on Silver Bear Way they found the nineteen-year-old file for the Robertson homicide, the crime Eppolito pinned on Gibbs. Eppolito took the file when he retired, a violation of police procedure. His breach raised suspicions about Eppolito's handling of the case.

When Vanessa Potkin of the Innocence Project learned of Eppolito's arrest from newspaper reports, she contacted the US Attorney's Office in Brooklyn. "We reached out to say that we represent a person who we think is innocent," Potkin said. "We want you to look into this case."

The US Attorney's Office brought Gibbs to Brooklyn for questioning. Meanwhile, FBI agents tracked down Peter Mitchell, the primary witness, who, under questioning, recanted his testimony. "He broke down as soon as they came," Potkin said. "He said, 'I've been waiting for you to come here.'"

Mitchell acknowledged that he never saw Barry Gibbs at the crime scene; he never believed Gibbs was involved. Mitchell had only identified Gibbs in the lineup and testified against him, he now said, after Eppolito threatened him and his family. A Black man with a felony conviction and a parole violation was poorly equipped to resist a detective's threats.

On September 29, 2005, Barry Gibbs, now fifty-seven, stood before Judge Michael Gary, wearing a maroon sweater and baggy blue jeans. He was barrel-chested and unkempt, with a tousled white beard. When Judge Gary threw out his 1988 conviction and life sentence, Gibbs raised his hands over his head, then rubbed them together under his chin as if in prayer. "Mr. Gibbs," Judge Gary said, "the case is over."

Gibbs walked out of the State Supreme Court a free man after eighteen years, ten months, and fourteen days in jail. He had almost no money. His mother and ex-wife had both died during his incarceration.

Riding downstairs in a courthouse elevator, Gibbs said what he really wanted was a good cup of coffee and a hot bath, luxuries unknown in jail. He walked outside with his right arm around Vanessa Potkin and his left around Barry Scheck, a founder of the Innocence Project. "Thank god," Gibbs said. That evening, Gibbs got his hot soak in the bathroom of Scheck's loft in the DUMBO neighborhood of Brooklyn. "I'm scrubbing, and I'm crying," Gibbs said. "I wanted to get the jail off me."

Afterward, Gibbs met Scheck's dog, Barney. "I was looking at Barney and Barney was looking at me and I decided to kneel down. As I went to kneel down, Barney started to move closer to me. I got all the way down and Barney came all the way up to my face and gave me a kiss. That is when I knew I was free, after a kiss from that dog. It was the most uplifting day I ever had."

One thread of investigation had had to wait until after Eppolito and Caracappa's arrest, lest the witness face retaliation.

In his debriefings Burt Kaplan told FBI agents that in 1986 he hired his jailhouse friend, Frank Santora, and Santora's cousin, Louie Eppolito, along with Eppolito's partner, Stephen Caracappa, to kill the diamond dealer Israel Greenwald. Kaplan could not, however, provide specifics of the murder. He had distanced himself from the crime, as he always had. Santora told Kaplan that Greenwald had died in a garage on Nostrand Avenue, nothing more.

But where on the avenue? Nostrand runs more than eight miles, a north-south spine from Williamsburg to Sheepshead Bay, with dozens of garages along its route. Investigators could not know which garage might contain Greenwald's body until Joe Campanella, a federal investigator, thought to search the half-forgotten file on Frank Santora's homicide. He had been shot to death seven years earlier while walking with his friend Carmine Varriale. Along with ballistics analysis and the medical examiner's report, Campanella found an address book removed from Santora's pocket at the death scene. The book contained a number for a Pete Franzone. They did not know who he was, but figured he might be connected to another address book listing: Pete's Towing at 2232 Nostrand Avenue. Could Pete's Towing be the garage where the detectives, along with Eppolito's cousin Frank Santora, killed Israel Greenwald?

After Eppolito and Caracappa's arrest, Pat Lanigan and Bobby Intartaglio, investigators in the Brooklyn DA's office, went to the towing garage on Nostrand Avenue, where a new owner directed them to Franzone's home. Franzone's wife, in turn, sent them to a public housing complex in Sheepshead Bay where Franzone now worked maintenance.

Nineteen years earlier, Franzone had helped bury Greenwald's body against his will, but now, in a moment of panic, he denied any knowledge of the incident. "I was afraid," he later said. "I didn't know if [the investigators] worked for Louie Eppolito."

Franzone looked for a lawyer the only way he knew how: in the yellow pages. Franzone had quit school after sixth grade. He could barely read. But he managed to find the lawyers listing and read down as far as "Abramson, Alan."

Franzone eventually told Abramson what happened—how Santora and Caracappa had walked into a garage with a man wearing a yarmulke while Eppolito kept watch in a car; how Santora brought Franzone inside, where the man's body sat motionless; how Santora had forced Franzone to help bury the body in a five-foot hole and fill it with lime and dirt covered with a fresh layer of cement.

Abramson urged Franzone to tell investigators what he knew, and made arrangements for Franzone to share the details of Greenwald's murder over a series of debriefings. Meanwhile, Franzone and his wife were moved to a secure living arrangement until they could enter the Witness Protection Program.

Franzone could not remember which one-car garage contained Greenwald's body. So, on March 31, 2005, an FBI team simply picked one at random and went to work. They set up an excavation grid with stakes and string, as archaeologists would, and dug through sandy soil, first with a backhoe, then with pointed garden trowels. They poured the excavated dirt through wire mesh screens, sifting for tiny bits of evidence.

The first two days uncovered nothing but a four-inch sewer pipe. As the crew burrowed under a third garage, they saw signs of loose soil beneath a layer of concrete. As they dug deeper they found pasty white flecks, remains of the lime thrown on Greenwald's body to hasten decomposition. At about five and a half feet they uncovered a bit of blue fabric from a pin-striped suit. Dr. Brad Adams, a forensic pathologist from the medical examiner's office, touched the clothing and felt a shoulder blade.

The unearthed skeletal remains were balled up in a fetal posture with hands bound and a ShopRite plastic bag over the head. Greenwald sat just as he had in the moments after his death nineteen years earlier. The skull, still covered by a threadbare yarmulke, revealed that Greenwald had been shot twice in the back of the head. His wallet, including his identification, was mostly intact. The remains of a visa or some other travel document showed a portion of his name—"Green . . ."—faded, but legible.

The next day, Greenwald's widow, Leah, walked home from her job as an elementary school teacher. As she neared her apartment building, FBI agent Geraldine Hart stepped up and showed a badge. A DEA agent accompanied her. Leah invited them upstairs. She assumed the agents had come to discuss a letter she had sent requesting the entire FBI file on her husband's disappearance. Agent Hart broke the news: the FBI suspected they had found her husband's body. They had yet to verify his identity with tests. They would need to take a swab from one of her daughters to match the DNA. But they were pretty certain it was her missing husband.

News of the unearthed body resolved nineteen years of excruciating uncertainty. Without a body, she could not claim life insurance and other benefits normally due a widow. Worst of all, the enduring mystery of her husband's disappearance had caused Leah to drift from job to job, home to home, dislocated and untethered. By lurid coincidence, in the early 1990s, she and her two daughters had rented an apartment two blocks from the Nostrand Avenue garage where his body lay five and a half feet underground. "I lived there for two years," she said. "I parked my car right across the street. We were looking for him, and now that we know, it is simply unbelievable that he was so close."

Two months after the forensic team raised the body, Leah and her daughters buried her husband in a cemetery outside Tel Aviv. He lies below a white stone slab engraved with an epitaph in Hebrew: "A charitable and kind man, big hearted and a good friend . . . killed by the hands of evil people in New York on Feb 10, 1986 when he was only 34."

Through the spring of 2005, Eppolito and Caracappa stayed in the Metropolitan Detention Center in Brooklyn. Their six-by-eight-foot cells contained only a toilet and a metal bed topped by a thin mattress. They had no windows or bars to look through, only cement walls and steel doors with a slit for metal food trays.

On July 7, they shuffled into the US District Court in Brooklyn for a bail hearing. They appeared stubble-faced and frail after four months in detention. Caracappa had the stupefied bearing found among those emerging from solitary confinement. Eppolito looked as if he had lost weight but gained years. His hair had turned a whiter shade of gray.

The bail hearing was like a movie trailer, a preview of the drama to come, with defense lawyers claiming their clients had no mob ties. They were merely innocuous storytellers sharing exaggerated yarns drawn from the New York streets. "He's not an outlaw, he's not a gangster," Eppolito's lawyer, Bruce Cutler, told the judge. "He is a creator of stories, of canards, of apocryphal stories. The gangster's genre is the genre that sells and that's what Mr. Eppolito was writing."

In response, the lead prosecutor, Robert Henoch, read passages from Eppolito's book, *Mafia Cop,* in which he described beating a man with a pipe and submerging another man's head in hot water mixed with ammonia. "Words are important, your honor," Henoch said, "because words are windows into what's in someone's mind."

As if that wasn't grisly enough, Henoch quoted from a portion of the tapes Corso had secretly recorded in which Eppolito boasted about threatening to kill his contractor with a hatchet when construction of his home fell behind schedule. "Killing is imbedded in me," Eppolito had said.

Jack B. Weinstein, the Brooklyn federal judge assigned to the case, granted bail after satisfying himself that Eppolito and Caracappa presented a minimal flight risk. He would postpone their release for two weeks so they had time to post $5 million bonds secured by family properties and get fitted for electronic monitoring anklets to be worn on house arrest.

Neither man seemed to react after Judge Weinstein announced his ruling. Eppolito blinked a few times. Caracappa stared straight ahead without expression. The clutch of reporters gathered for the hearing had no doubt expected to update a straightforward story about corrupt cops getting a comeuppance. What happened next complicated the plotline.

Judge Weinstein chose this moment to cast doubt on the government's RICO conspiracy case. By law, prosecutors had to show that the sale of 24.4 grams of meth to Stephen Corso in 2004 constituted an ongoing organized crime conspiracy. Without it, the five-year statute of limitations would have expired in 1997 and Judge Weinstein would be obliged to dismiss the charges.

"The charges seem to me to be relatively stale," Judge Weinstein told the prosecutors, "and the statute of limitations problem is going to be a serious one. I'm suggesting it's a weak link in your allegations." He had fired a warning: he would not allow federal prosecutors to get away with a cute legal contrivance.

The entire question of the statute of limitations could have been avoided by trying the two detectives in state court. Tommy Dades, speaking to a reporter by phone from the Staten Island gym where he trained teenage boxers, promised that prosecutors from the Brooklyn DA's office would be waiting on the courthouse steps to arrest Eppolito and Caracappa on murder charges if Weinstein dismissed the federal case. "Which is how I envisioned this case from the beginning," he said. "If it becomes a state case again, the feds would hand over Kaplan as a witness, along with Betty Hydell and several other witnesses, [and] these guys are dead."

Federal prosecutors had amassed a substantial inventory of evidence, but the defendants could take a modicum of encouragement from Judge Weinstein's expression of doubt over the statute of limitations. Eppolito appeared heartened, in any case, when, on July 21, he and Caracappa were finally released on bail. He changed into street clothes in a courthouse restroom, then carried his prison clothes balled up in a bag to deliver to his brother-in-law as a souvenir.

"This is the first step of my trip home," Eppolito told reporters as he and his family stood outside the courthouse waiting for a ride to his sister Sheila's split-level house in Plainview, Long Island, where he would stay for the duration of the trial. Eppolito would celebrate his fifty-seventh birthday there the following day. He and Caracappa could leave house arrest only to meet with their lawyers.

Eppolito hoisted his pant leg so reporters could admire his electronic ankle bracelet. "I did none of these crimes, neither did Steve," he said. "All of my life I have held my head high . . . that is how I was raised. I just hope the public doesn't rush to judgement."

By contrast, Caracappa left the courthouse unsmiling and mute on his way to his ninety-four-year-old mother's Staten Island home. A short time later, Lizzie Hydell, sister of the abducted and tortured Jimmy Hydell, drove to Mrs. Caracappa's house. "I knocked on the door," she said, "and I was getting back in the car when he came around from the back of the house. I said, do you know who I am? I said, you're going to rot in hell. He just stood there. And I got in my car and left."

In the interminable back-and-forth—the relentless motions and maneuverings—the defense petitioned Judge Weinstein to dismiss the indictment altogether, but he refused. After weighing more than an hour of arguments from both sides, he set a trial date. He agreed with the prosecution's contention that charges brought by a grand jury should not be dismissed before a trial. Besides, he added, the public deserved to hear evidence of egregious police dereliction. Corruption should be entered on the public record.

"This case *has* to be tried," Judge Weinstein said, "and it *will* be tried."

At the end of December, while the lawyers filed motions and sparred for favorable footing, Eppolito and Caracappa retired for the holidays, unsure if this would be the last Christmas spent with family.

21

JUDGE WEINSTEIN'S COURTROOM

EVERY TRIAL IS THEATER. THE PRINCIPALS AND BIT players, benign and bellicose alike, assemble for the daily showing as the case works its way, however ponderously, toward a final decision. Interrogators and truth tellers play their assigned roles.

Unlike theater, however, a trial's outcome is never preordained. The script can veer to the unexpected, and often does.

United States v. Eppolito and Caracappa might also have been considered an awkward reunion, with the families of defendants and victims sitting, day after day, in uneasy proximity. A long succession of violent acts had brought them together for an uncomfortable reckoning. Allies and antagonists mingled in the hallway. They smoked cigarettes in Cadman Plaza and ate lunch at the Park Plaza Diner, a short walk from the courthouse.

As the trial got underway, Eppolito, seated with Caracappa at the defense table, perspired in a baggy blue suit. Once brawny and imposing, he now looked shabby and obese. He turned occasionally to speak with his wife, Fran, and their daughters, Andrea and Deanna, who occupied front-row seats marked "family members." They dressed in black and held rosary beads.

Two rows behind Fran and her daughters sat Lou Jr., Eppolito's estranged son from his first marriage. He was the half brother Andrea and Deanna barely knew. Lou was a year old when his father left him and his mother, Teresa, in 1970.

As a child, Lou Jr. looked forward to his father's custodial visits. Eppolito would pick him up on a motorcycle and ride with him to Long Island for weekend stays in the home he shared with Fran. "He would run red lights and speed, but nobody would bother him," Lou Jr. said. "He was a decorated cop. To me, he was a hero."

The mood changed when Eppolito and Fran had children of their own. Lou Jr. felt a chill from his stepmother, and he never again felt entirely welcome. "Something as simple as looking in the fridge seemed awkward," he said. "I just felt out of place. She made it very difficult."

Eppolito barely mentioned Lou Jr. in his memoir. "He has a son who walks around with his name," Lou Jr. told the *New York Daily News,* "but I felt ignored, invisible." Eppolito had moved to Las Vegas without even telling his son.

Now Lou Jr. was thirty-five, a thoughtful, soft-spoken supervisor at a New Jersey vitamin warehouse. He faithfully attended the daily proceedings with his partner, Rob, seated beside him. The Eppolitos never invited Lou Jr. and Rob to join them in their back booth of the Park Plaza Diner during lunch breaks. In fact, they barely exchanged a word. "They wouldn't look at me," Lou Jr. said. "They didn't even acknowledge me."

Unlike Andrea, who was her father's unwavering and sometimes strident supporter, Lou Jr. kept an open and honest mind: he wanted to attend the trial in order to gauge his father's guilt for himself. "I need to be there," he said. "I need to hear the facts and evidence."

Stephen Caracappa sat impassively by Eppolito's side. For the duration of the trial he ate lunch alone in a third-floor courthouse lunchroom.

Jane McCormick, the former Las Vegas call girl, sat in the fourth row, wearing a red rhinestone-spangled cowboy hat. She eagerly told reporters how Eppolito had swindled her by charging $45,000 to write a screenplay based on her life, then failed to deliver. "I just came down here to look him in the face," she said.

Behind McCormick sat a pack of reporters with pens and pads in hand waiting to record the indelicate details of what could be the last great mob trial. Bland white-collar crimes had dominated the recent docket. Now came a trial that promised the noir spectacle of old gang-land days—decorated detectives leading double lives, a geriatric drug trafficker brokering favors for the mob, an accountant turned under-cover agent, a kidnapped hit man screaming in a car trunk, a mob boss hiding out with his mistress, a dead mobster with a canary stuffed in his mouth. The story was tantalizing enough to draw celebrated reporters, including the columnist Jimmy Breslin, who had recently retired from newspapers after fifty years to write books. With tousled hair and a neck-tie pulled loose, he looked like a rumpled reporter played by a stage actor.

Breslin found the gentrified city of Mayor Michael Bloomberg short on book-worthy lowlifes and gangsters. Great underworld figures like John Gotti and Joe Bonanno were gone. Breslin had come to the court-house hoping to find a yeasty character for a book.

Tommy Dades did not attend a single trial day. "Everything went sour because of how [the US Attorney's Office] took the case away," he said. "I just figured, why antagonize anybody? Let them do their job. I stayed away."

The light of media attention shone on the trial well before Judge Jack Weinstein gaveled it into session. "The whole thing exploded," Dades said. "Agents were knocking on my door and calling me like crazy. Deals were flying all over the place."

Ed Bradley, a correspondent for the CBS news show *60 Minutes,* had interviewed Gaspipe Casso at the Metropolitan Correctional Center, in downtown Manhattan, back in 1998, but CBS held the segment back until a month after the Eastern District had indicted Eppolito and Cara-cappa. Casso's story of detectives on the Mafia payroll was too outland-ish to accept on its own without supporting evidence.

Then, in January 2006, two months before the trial, *60 Minutes* aired an interview with Caracappa in which he stiffened with indignation. "Totally ridiculous," he said of the charges. "Anybody who knows me knows I love the police department. I couldn't kill anybody. I shot a guy once on the job and I still think about it. It bothers me. . . . I'm fighting for my reputation. I want to be vindicated of this. And, I'm mad. I'm angry."

Caracappa was known as the quiet one, the cryptic sidekick, but he had made a convincing impression on camera, leading to speculation that he and Eppolito might testify in their own defense, a move that would expose them to potentially crushing rounds of cross-examination.

If any judge could manage the circus quality of the coming trial, it was hawk-faced Jack Weinstein, an eighty-five-year-old jurist and legal scholar known for his strong hand and insistence on fairness and common sense. A Yale Law School professor had called him a "benevolent despot" after Judge Weinstein presided over a class-action suit by Vietnam veterans made ill by the use of the defoliant Agent Orange. If jurisprudence had a Mount Rushmore, Weinstein would be on it.

By coincidence, Judge Weinstein grew up in Bensonhurst, the homeland of organized crime. At age eight, he had acted on Broadway, appearing as one of the so-called Dead End Kids in Sidney Kingsley's play about boys growing up on the New York streets. Ten years later he was a submarine lieutenant in World War II. Now, at eighty-five, he was a strong-voiced judge with an almost cultish following in judicial circles. His book *Evidence, Cases and Materials* is an authoritative text found in every law library.

"Sitting in the Brooklyn federal courthouse," Jimmy Breslin wrote, "Weinstein for all his life has been a lighthouse in the fog."

If Judge Weinstein was a steadying presence, the two lead defense lawyers were the opposite. Bruce Cutler (for Eppolito) and Edward Hayes (for Caracappa) entered the early proceedings as famously flamboyant, attention-grabbing fixtures of New York courtrooms. While prosecutors dressed in drab civil servant wardrobes, Cutler and Hayes wore Italian suits, power ties, and butter-soft Italian shoes. They greeted each other with hugs and double-cheek kisses. In contrast to the earnest and efficient young assistant US attorneys assigned to the case, Cutler and Hayes were like two entertainers living off their reputations.

Of the two, Cutler was better known as a tabloid character, having defended John Gotti in a courtroom down the hall fourteen years earlier. He looked just as a casting director might conjure a mob lawyer: bald and bull-necked, with a ready sneer. Like a high school football coach, he tended to speak several pitches louder than anyone else in the room. Hayes, his friend and fellow defense counsel, wrote that "Cutler talks like a guy who gargles Brillo for breakfast."

Hayes was the more refined of the pair, at least in appearance, with monogrammed shirts and silk pocket squares. His clients included Anna Wintour, Jennifer Lopez, and Robert De Niro. "I can get you out of anything," he once told Andy Warhol. Newspaper profiles rarely failed to mention that Hayes had served as the model for the slick, street-smart defense attorney Tommy Killian in his friend Tom Wolfe's book *Bonfire of the Vanities*. *The New York Times* described Hayes as "like a guy holding Shea Stadium nosebleed seats, though he's got a town house on the Upper East Side."

Both Cutler and Hayes tended their reputations as colorful New York characters, but they also intended to win—and they had a clear notion of how. "I think there will be some surprises," Hayes said, "and I certainly have a few."

Before the two-week parade of witnesses commenced—before the drug dealers, mistresses, and Mafia gofers had their say—both sides made opening statements. This was their moment to make first impressions on the jury, to introduce the general arguments to come before the trial bogged down with DNA samples, surveillance photos, and under-cover recordings.

In the morning on Monday, March 13, 2006, Assistant US Attorney Mitra Hormozi rose from the prosecutor's table. A slim thirty-seven-year old, she looked young enough to intern with Bruce Cutler, though she had already helped convict Bonanno crime boss Joseph Massino. In a fifty-minute opening, she told the jury that Eppolito and Caracappa were worse than conventional mobsters: they were corrupt detectives who used the authority of their badges to help commit eight murders. "The defendants went into business together, and the business was crime," she said. "Even worse, the defendants com-mitted many of these crimes while sworn to protect the very people they preyed upon. . . . They were able to do murders because they were cops. . . . For years, the two defendants effectively armed one Mafia family, and one treacherous man within that family, with the power of the city of New York."

Now it was Cutler's turn to step onto the stage. Speaking in his Bensonhurst baritone, he said that Hormozi's opening was one of the most effective he had ever heard. He then struck back at the prosecution's vulnerable spot: he warned the jury that the government's case rested entirely on the dubious veracity of Burt Kaplan and other informants who, he said, were no more than "lowlifes" and "reprobates" who "can never be trusted."

These Mafia men, these once swaggering adherents of omertà, Cutler said, had capitulated and turned on their own friends as soon as the government squeezed them. "They called each other tough guys, goodfellas—until the jail door shut," Cutler sniped. "Then they wet their pants and called Mommy—the government."

Cutler had a way of speaking in loud, forceful repetitions, as if rapping. He described the government witnesses as men who "kill, kill, steal, sell drugs, make money, beat up, steal, kill, kill, make money . . ." They are, he said, "the lowest form of life." Collectively, he added, the government witnesses accounted for "at least ten murders, and maybe twenty, five arsons, four building explosions, six tons of marijuana, seventeen heroin transactions, one kidnapping, and fourteen thefts." His strategy was immediately clear: demean the witness, then the next one. Then the next one. At times he enunciated with a deliberate slow-motion cadence, as one might in the moment before shoving an adversary.

If the defense could not win on the evidence, as appeared to be the case, it could perhaps sway the jury with political sentiments. Cutler argued that the government had succumbed to a "spiritual and moral cancer." In all its abusive power, the feds had exalted the violent criminals who made up their witness list while persecuting upstanding detectives like Eppolito and Caracappa. At least Eppolito was honest enough to acknowledge that his father and uncle were in the mob, Cutler said. "He had the courage to say no to that life."

Cutler gave way to Hayes, the other celebrity defense lawyer, who stood behind his client rubbing Caracappa's shoulders, as if they were a couple. "Steve Caracappa has spent his whole life risking his life for other people," he said. "What happened here is that gangsters learned that the best thing they could do . . . is turn on the people that were investigating them."

He held up his keys and jangled them, saying the Mafia informants knew that testifying for the government was the key to their own escape.

With the opening statements concluded, Hormozi began the prosecution with a bang. She projected onto a screen large-scale photographs of the eight alleged murder victims, then described each murder in stomach-souring detail. She progressed in chronological order, starting with Israel Greenwald, the diamond dealer, killed in 1986 and buried beneath Peter Franzone's garage on Nostrand Avenue. "They used the power of their position to get Israel Greenwald to walk voluntarily to his own execution," Hormozi said. "Eppolito stood guard while mobster Frank Santora and Caracappa walked Greenwald in, tied his hands and tied a bag over his face with his necktie." Santora then told Franzone, "Start digging or I'll kill your family," Hormozi said. "Franzone felt he was digging his own grave."

She added, "Until now, they've gotten away with it."

Hormozi showed Bruno Facciolo with the lifeless canary stuffed in his mouth, Eddie Lino slumped dead in his car beside the Belt Parkway, and the body of twenty-six-year-old Nicky Guido, the victim of mistaken identity, shot to death in his new Nissan on Christmas Day 1986, wearing the bloodstained white jacket he received as a gift that morning.

Of the eight murders, Nicky Guido's was the most disturbing, and the most likely to disquiet jurors. In a wrenching follow-up to the murder scene photo, Hormozi called Guido's now-elderly mother, Pauline Pipitone. "I really wasn't going to court and telling my story," she later wrote, "but I was told the prosecutors could make me if I didn't come on my own."

The courtroom quieted as she walked to the witness stand, a fragile-looking white-haired woman. She hesitated as she made her way, as if she hated to make the trip. She could barely look up when Hormozi showed her a photograph of her son, but under questioning she managed to describe the moments after his shooting—how she ran outside. "His heart was bleeding," she said. "The blood was on the white jacket."

Hormozi asked Pipitone if her life was ever the same. She said no. After Nicky's death, her husband succumbed to illness and depression. He died three years later.

After Pipitone stepped down, Judge Weinstein called a recess in order to privately scold the prosecutors for attempting to sway jurors with a needlessly graphic account. "I don't want witnesses like this brought in the case unnecessarily," he said.

The first public clash came when prosecutors called Al D'Arco, the former acting boss of the Lucchese family, who surrendered to the FBI in 1991. At seventy-three, D'Arco now "looked more grandfatherly than Godfatherly on the stand," according to the Associated Press.

Fifteen years in the Witness Protection Program—fifteen years living an invented life in an outlying state—had not softened D'Arco's Brooklyn accent. He spoke the language of backstreet Bensonhurst in the formal mahogany courtroom surroundings. He sounded like a black-and-white-movie mobster as he detailed the five-year period when Gaspipe Casso relied on information from his secret police sources, his "crystal ball," to unmask traitors and informants within La Cosa Nostra. More often than not, Casso relied on D'Arco to arrange murders of the disloyal. Mitra Hormozi led D'Arco down the list of victims—Bruno Facciolo, Anthony DiLapi, Al Visconti, and Larry Taylor.

D'Arco described meeting Casso just before he slipped into hiding at the end of his savage run as Lucchese underboss. "I said, 'What are you doing here? Get on the lam. Vic [Amuso] went on the lam already, why are you over here? Get out of here now.' [Casso] says, 'No, no. I got until Monday, then I'm going.'"

D'Arco explained that Casso knew the day of his arrest because his two police sources had given him advance notice. D'Arco said he never knew the identity of the detectives on the Lucchese payroll until the story became public.

The day ended with Cutler, in cross-examination, sparring with D'Arco like two bullies from the old neighborhood. Judge Weinstein was forced to intercede.

> D'ARCO: Keep your voice down, pal.
> CUTLER: I am not your pal.
> D'ARCO: You are not mine either. . . . I'm not answering you if you're a loudmouth in here.

The back-and-forth grew screechy and insulting. Within minutes D'Arco noted that Cutler had a reputation for freeloading in a Mafia restaurant on Mulberry Street, in lower Manhattan:

> D'ARCO: Do you want an answer or do you want to hear yourself talk? Do you want to keep talking forever, Mr. Cutler . . .
> CUTLER: Mr. D'Arco, did you . . .
> D'ARCO: . . . like you did in Taormina when you sat down with all the crew in there and drank with them and ate with them and never picked up a tab. Is that the Mr. Cutler I know, huh?

Cutler raised his own voice to match D'Arco's. "Would you agree with me . . ."

"I wouldn't agree with you on anything," D'Arco snapped.

As his exasperation swelled, Cutler bellowed at D'Arco, his neck muscles bulging, his face florid and his fingers stabbing the air.

"I don't know what the hell you're talking about," D'Arco yelled back, rising from his seat. "You're not making any sense to me."

Cutler recognized that the exchange had gone too far. With a lowered voice he apologized to Judge Weinstein.

"Why should I be upset?" Weinstein answered sarcastically after dismissing the jury. "You not only raised your voice, you screamed repeatedly and stomped throughout the court . . . I told you I didn't want that.

I'm not going to have an exhibition at this trial." With that, he brought down the gavel and adjourned for the day.

During the next day's lunch break Mary Ann DiLapi, a forty-seven-year-old mother from Salt Lake City, sat on a park bench outside the courthouse trying to hold back tears. She had flown to New York in order to testify about the death of her father, Anthony DiLapi, who had been trying to distance himself from the Lucchese family when Eppolito and Caracappa tracked him down in Los Angeles. She was in the courtroom a day earlier, when Al D'Arco described how Gaspipe Casso had ordered him to assassinate her father in a garage. "Five in the head," she told a reporter, "four in the body."

The prosecution team crossed her off its witness list after Judge Weinstein reprimanded them for putting Pauline Pipitone on the stand. DiLapi lingered in the park hoping for a glimpse of Eppolito on his way to or from the Park Plaza Diner before she flew home. A reporter asked if she might speak to Eppolito. "Whatever I would say wouldn't be very ladylike," she said.

The second day belonged to Burt Kaplan, the critical prosecution witness. His arrival was its own reunion of sorts, since Judge Weinstein had presided at Kaplan's trial for selling stolen clothes thirty-four years earlier.

Kaplan did not resemble a lifelong criminal. To Alan Feuer, a crime reporter for *The New York Times,* Kaplan looked more "like a man that one might find playing shuffleboard on the Lido Deck of a Carnival cruise ship."

He perched on the witness stand like a frail bird, thin-faced and arthritic, inspecting the courtroom through black-framed glasses. He might be geriatric, but for four days he spoke with precision in a steady, measured voice. He came off as a man resolved to speak the blunt truth, without contrition or regret.

Under questioning, Kaplan recalled how he befriended Eppolito's cousin, Frank Santora, while serving time at Allenwood in the early 1980s. "Frankie approached me and said his cousin was a detective and, if I wanted, his cousin could get me information and could help me if I had problems," Kaplan said. Santora also "offered to murder" if Kaplan "had serious problems in the street."

Kaplan told the jury he was at first reluctant to work with any detective, even Santora's trusted cousin. "I felt it was something that could come back to haunt me," he said.

Despite his reservations, Kaplan eventually gave Santora and the detectives $30,000 to kill Israel Greenwald. Kaplan explained that he took up the role of intermediary after Santora died. For six years he met the detectives three or more times a month—surreptitious late-night meetings at his home, at a Staten Island cemetery, an apartment belonging to Eppolito's mistress, and a Long Island Expressway rest stop. Whatever the location, Kaplan handed the detectives monthly cash payments of $4,000 in return for confidential information culled from police files. In total, they were connected to twelve murder plots. It was the first time a witness directly implicated the two defendants.

Kaplan's grisly portrayals, strangely at odds with his schlubby appearance, electrified the courtroom. Among other things, he was a gift to the reporters seated in the back. The *New York Post* called him "the convict canary."

The investigator Bobby Intartaglio sat next to Jimmy Breslin as he scribbled down Kaplan's words. "He couldn't write fast enough," Intartaglio said. "He's saying, 'Oh, this guy's good!'"

Breslin would loosely base an entire book, *The Good Rat*, on Kaplan. "An unknown name steals the show," he wrote, "and turns the proceeding into something that thrills: the autobiography of Burton Kaplan, criminal."

Breslin found the defendants, Eppolito and Caracappa, "dreary and charmless." Kaplan, by comparison, "talks about designer jeans and dumping a body in the Connecticut River—because the ground was too frozen—in the same tone of voice. . . . I'm so enamored of him. . . .

The minute he sat down in the witness chair he started talking and that was it."

Kaplan testified that he had decided to cooperate after serving nine years of a twenty-seven-year sentence for marijuana trafficking because he suspected that the detectives would talk if he did not.

Kaplan said that he lost confidence in Caracappa's assurances that Eppolito would keep quiet if investigators questioned him about the murders, as Kaplan believed they eventually would. "I didn't think that [Eppolito and Caracappa] would stand up," he said, using the Mafia term for holding out against government pressure, "and I was tired of going to jail by myself."

Had Kaplan not cooperated, he said, "I would be at the defense table now and Louie and Steve would be up here." While Kaplan spoke, Eppolito drummed his fingers. Addressing reporters afterward, he called Kaplan's statements "stupid, stupid answers to stupid questions."

On his second full day, Kaplan delivered six hours of morbid recollections, detailing the murder of Israel Greenwald, the first victim of his nineteen-year collaboration with Eppolito and Caracappa, and the abduction of their second victim, Jimmy Hydell. Kaplan paused, his voice breaking with emotion, as he recalled how, by Casso's account, Hydell had begged him to dump his dead body on the street so his mother, Betty, could collect life insurance. "Casso didn't do it," Kaplan said. "He hid the body. He took pleasure in telling me he [killed Hydell] himself."

The arrangement paid off, Kaplan said, until he and Eppolito argued, leaving him to liaise with Caracappa. "I always liked Steve," Kaplan said, looking directly down at him from the witness stand. "I still do."

Before stepping down for the day, Kaplan inspected photographs of his daughter Deborah's 1985 wedding shown on a courtroom monitor. He identified executives from Calvin Klein and Gloria Vanderbilt as guests he knew from the legitimate portion of his clothing business. They mingled with a dozen or so Mafia stalwarts, including Gaspipe Casso.

Kaplan said that he had invited his Mafia contacts in order to help his daughter who, he assumed, would become a defense lawyer. It was not a preposterous move: she had worked briefly for Gerald Shargel, a noted defense lawyer who represented a series of mob figures, including Kaplan.

On the days that Kaplan testified in US Federal Court in Brooklyn, his daughter, Deborah, by now a civil court judge, was handling a drug case in Manhattan Criminal Court. The Honorable Deborah Kaplan stood on the opposite side of the law from her father, but she had supported him without sullying her reputation. For years she had disavowed any knowledge of her father's crooked affairs. In 1973, as a twelve-year-old, she had pleaded with Judge Weinstein to reduce her father's four-year sentence on a theft conviction. She had served as a character witness in his 1997 drug trial, though she and her mother privately pressed him to cooperate.

Father and daughter were by all accounts unusually close. "I think she loves me," Kaplan said during cross-examination the next day. "But I think she lost a lot of respect for me. . . . In my mind, I'm very embarrassed by what I did to my family." His acknowledgment came as one of the few times when Kaplan lost his composure.

"You failed her, didn't you?" Hayes asked during cross-examination.

"Yes," Kaplan said. He could say no more.

Kaplan's admission that he invited Lucchese family members to Deborah's wedding, and claimed to have done so on her behalf, was more than she could accept—even from her father. In a statement released by her spokesperson, she said that she was "very offended that my father thought he could help my career by inviting criminals to my wedding. . . . My father's actions continue to be very painful to our family."

Kaplan choked on emotion when asked about his daughter, but otherwise withstood the four-hour cross-examination unruffled. He did not waver or stumble. Speaking in his usual measured tone, he cataloged and confessed to his own long list of crimes, though, he said, he had witnessed no murders.

The cross-examination, held on Kaplan's third day of testimony, was the defense's opportunity to erode his credibility. At the critical moment, however, the two defense lawyers floundered. They came across as manic and directionless. Bruce Cutler led the jury on a long excursion, never quite arriving at coherent questions. Along the way he touched variously on a friend who had attended West Point, the views from the federal prison in Lewisburg, and Brooklyn high school football. Cutler was so discursive that Judge Weinstein found it necessary to intervene. "If you continue your rambling way," he said, "I'm going to have to limit you."

Ed Hayes was no better. He flitted among subjects so abruptly that Kaplan struggled to follow. When Hayes tried to portray Kaplan as tricky and duplicitous, Kaplan drew laughs from the jurors. "I'm being honest," he said. "I'm a criminal."

Hayes asked if Kaplan worried that Eppolito and Caracappa would silence him, as they had silenced others. "Believe me, that was on my mind," he said, but he decided it was unlikely. "I believed they loved me."

During the lunch break that day, Lizzie Hydell, sister of the murder victim Jimmy Hydell, left the spectator gallery and walked to the Park Plaza Diner. Eppolito happened by as she ate lunch. "I walked up to him," she said, "and said, 'How does it feel to fry slowly?'"

Mike Guido, brother of the victim Nicky Guido, restrained himself from confronting Eppolito in the diner. "He was five feet away, eating with his wife and daughter, his family intact," he said. "I'd do anything to be able to sit down and have a meal with my family. Instead, all I have left is a mother who cries every single day, a woman who lives in a state of perpetual grief."

The defense lawyers had a last chance to undercut Kaplan at his final appearance the following Monday. Cutler came at Kaplan with his usual long-winded windup. At one point Cutler implored Kaplan "to please just stay with me, please stay with me for one second" as he tried to ask, in fits and starts, about the money Kaplan loaned Eppolito. Robert

Henoch, the prosecutor, eventually stood up and asked, "Judge, can we have a question from the lawyer?"

Cutler pressed Kaplan to admit that he felt no regret or repentance for all "the misery, the death, the destruction" he had caused. He implied that Kaplan had fabricated stories implicating Eppolito and Caracappa on the assumption that he would in return receive a reduction in his sentence. "The reason you signed the cooperation agreement," Cutler said, "and the reason you pleaded guilty to things you weren't even charged with is that you hope, and your expectation is, that you would get out of jail. Isn't that what you're hoping?"

Kaplan maintained his composure. "Anybody that's in jail," he said, "hopes to someday get out. . . . I agreed to cooperate with the hope of someday going home sooner than I would have." A judge would review his sentence at a later date, but Kaplan said he made no assumptions. "Mr. Cutler," he said, "I've been before judges before and I've never been lucky . . . whatever happens, happens."

Cutler suggested that Kaplan might testify to whatever prosecutors wanted since he and his wife, as guests of the Witness Protection Program, would depend on government generosity. Not so, Kaplan said. So far the government had paid for nothing more than his dentures and storage for his family's furniture. "I have no money hidden away," he said, "and if I had the ability to take care of my wife at this point I gladly would. I don't want the government to spend any money on me."

For the second time in the trial, Judge Weinstein cut off Cutler's cross-examination, in this case for mentioning that Kaplan had failed a polygraph test. The jury was not supposed to know since Kaplan had passed a subsequent test. The reproach did not seem to bother Cutler. "Judge Weinstein knows better than I do when I'm finished," he told reporters outside the courtroom.

On March 21, the sixth day of testimony, the geriatric drug dealer was followed by a deep dive into police records. Steven Rodriguez, a detective in the vast police archive known as the Criminal Records Division, reviewed the half dozen instances when Caracappa searched the department's proprietary database for addresses, photographs, and other biographical information useful to Casso. Rodriguez noted that in every case Caracappa obscured the subject of his inquiry—Nicky Guido, Anthony DiLapi, and the rest—by bundling the name among others.

On cross-examination, Edward Hayes said Caracappa had followed police regulations and would not have been so stupid as to search for a name later associated with murder. "You would have to be a falling down moron," Hayes said, "to not know that any inquiry into these records was going to be kept in perpetuity by the Police Department."

Nonetheless, the evidence showed that Caracappa made a practice of using the police records for his own needs. Mitra Hormozi produced a 1985 printout showing that Caracappa had run a criminal history check on his fiancée. Hayes tried to excuse his client's breach as innocuous, the kind of harmless lapse anyone might commit. "If a middle-aged man was about to be married and he wants to do a check on his future wife, would that shock you?" he asked Rodriguez.

"Yes, it would," Rodriguez said.

"Even if the boss said it was okay?" Hayes pressed.

"It would still bother me," Rodriguez said.

Caracappa suffered another blow when the prosecution showed a 1989 black-and-white photograph of him with a cigarette dangling from his lips. The image was a frame taken from a personal video shot by Joe Piraino, a colleague in the Major Case Squad, at a gathering to celebrate Piraino's promotion to sergeant. Piraino knew that Caracappa was skittish about the attention. "He was civil about it, but you could tell he didn't want to be on film," he said, "but too bad, he was on film anyway."

In the photograph, the cuff of Caracappa's white dress shirt is pulled up to reveal a wristwatch identical to the Pulsar quartz watch with a black square face and yellow numerals that a police officer found near the Mercedes where Eddie Lino lay dead in 1992. The Pulsar's glass face was broken. The time had stopped at 7 P.M., about the time Lino died.

Fortunately for Caracappa, an FBI laboratory could not conclusively match a hair found on the watch with a DNA swab taken from Cara-cappa. For that reason, Judge Weinstein ruled the wristwatch inadmissible. "There are several million people in New York City that would meet that test," he said. "It's not coming in."

In the trial's late stage, the prosecution corroborated Kaplan's testimony with supporting witnesses. They took the unusual step of calling his former attorney Judd Burstein who, by coincidence, was already in the process of volunteering himself. In order to question Burstein, prosecutors had to ask Kaplan to waive attorney-client privilege. He agreed, allowing Burstein, a veteran defense attorney, to become a prosecution witness. As expected, Burstein confirmed that Kaplan had admitted to acting as an intermediary between the mob and the detectives after Burstein called with news that Casso had flipped. Burstein quoted Kaplan as saying, "This is a big problem for me. I was the go-between."

Every morning, Lou Eppolito, Jr., and his partner, Rob, took their seats in the second or third row, just behind his stepmother, Fran, and his half sisters. Lou Jr. spoke periodically during the trial with two reporters—John Marzulli of the *New York Daily News* and Zach Haberman of the *New York Post*. He expressed his honest ambivalence: He loved his father, he said, but he would remain open to whatever the evidence might show. His openness aroused resentment among the relatives seated in front of him, who expected family to close ranks.

The tension led to a blowup one afternoon when Lou Jr. and Rob encountered Lou's father, stepmother, and half sisters in a parking garage near the courthouse. "Then my stepmother decides to open her mouth, and she comes over waving an umbrella and she's yelling and saying things in my face. It was a really bad situation with us yelling back and forth. My father, believe it or not, was the one who said, 'Get in the car and let's get the hell out of here.' Because he didn't need that. He was on bail. He didn't need more drama in the parking garage."

In his opening remarks, Bruce Cutler, speaking on Eppolito's behalf, had called Stephen Corso, the crooked accountant working undercover for the FBI, "one of the most repulsive and disgraceful human beings you will ever see in a courtroom."

Disgraceful or not, he took the stand on the afternoon of March 21, conspicuously tan, pomaded, and dressed in a designer suit, to recall how, with coaching from his FBI handlers, he had insinuated himself into the Las Vegas underworld, cultivating friends at the Crazy Horse Too and John Conti's social club. He made himself a useful adjunct, a conveniently shady accountant capable of finessing fraudulent tax returns for bouncers, strippers, and semiretired mob associates. He traveled with a miniature recorder, taping hundreds of hours of incriminating conversations.

By the time Corso's new Mafia friends introduced him to Eppolito in late 2004, he said, Eppolito was desperate to raise the remaining $5 million needed to produce *Murder in Youngstown,* so desperate that he would gladly accept illegal drug money. "He didn't care about the source of the money," Corso told the jury. "He just wanted the money." Corso added that Eppolito also spoke openly, and at length, about the sums he hid from the Internal Revenue Service.

The twelve jurors put on twelve pairs of headphones in order to hear a short portion of the recordings in which Corso said his Hollywood clients and potential investors in Eppolito's movie had requested recreational drugs for an upcoming visit to Las Vegas. And they heard Eppolito say, "Guido can handle it," referring to his son Tony's friend Guido Bravatti.

On cross-examination, Cutler asked Corso if the FBI had encouraged him to inject the request for drugs into the dinner conversation to entrap Eppolito and Caracappa, or simply incriminate them. "The FBI did not tell me to inject," he said. "They told me to throw it out there and see what happens."

Also captured on video was the drug transaction—$900 exchanged for 24.4 grams of meth—which took just two minutes and nineteen seconds. Not a blockbuster sale, but enough to establish an ongoing criminal conspiracy dating back to the 1980s, or so the prosecution claimed.

Whatever else they revealed, the recordings also gave jurors an unvarnished sense of Eppolito's coarse commentary and low calculations. For example, he could be heard explaining why he preferred to do business with Jews. "There's no better way," he said. "The Jews say, *you're* Jewish, *he's* Jewish, *he's* Jewish, *he's* Jewish. There's four of us, that's a quarter each, we all get a quarter. [The way] Italians do it is, I want 65 cents, I'll give you a dime, I'll give him three cents, I'll give him seven, but I make sure I get the most. . . . Italian people for some reason, and I don't know the reason why, they almost feel, 'How am I getting fucked? Where am I getting fucked?' It's like their assholes are always puckered."

In response, the defense demeaned the witness, as usual. Cutler bore down on Corso as a debauched government stooge.

CUTLER: You dishonored yourself and your profession and this country when you [stole money from clients], you agree with me?

CORSO: I certainly dishonored myself and all those things that you said, yes.

CUTLER: You stole for the worst reasons . . . indifference, callousness, profiting, greed?

JUDGE WEINSTEIN: Is that a question?

CUTLER: Yes, sir.

JUDGE WEINSTEIN: You may answer.

CUTLER: Are those adjectives apt?

CORSO: I stole because I had a gambling problem and what I did was absolutely wrong.

In her cross-examination, Rae Koshetz, part of Caracappa's defense team, asked Corso about his feelings for Eppolito's daughter Andrea. Over the course of a dozen lengthy Italian dinners with Eppolito, Corso had made no secret of his attraction to Andrea, despite a twenty-year age gap. "Aren't you interested in dating Eppolito's daughter?" she asked.

Corso looked uncomfortable. He acknowledged that he was. "The impression that I received was that if the deal went through," Corso said, "if the [movie] money occurred, Lou would suggest to his daughter that she date me."

"You're saying that Eppolito was using his daughter as a bargaining chip in this business deal?" Koshetz asked.

"I'm just stating to you what he said to me," Corso said.

Judge Weinstein ruled the taped conversation about Andrea inadmissible. He would spare her the humiliation. By doing so, he denied the newspaper reporters their titillation.

The prosecution argued that Koshetz's line of questioning opened the way for the jury to hear the recorded conversation about Andrea, despite Judge Weinstein's earlier objection, but the judge stood firm. "We're keeping the daughter out," he said. Andrea's mother, Fran, nodded her approval from her front-row seat.

Fran wouldn't be nodding for long. The prosecution's next witness was her husband's former mistress, his *goumada*. Cabrini Cama practically brushed against Fran as she walked up the aisle in a snug pantsuit and four-inch heels. She wore her dark hair in bangs with magenta highlights. In a deposition, Fran said that "Louis was unfaithful to me and I was aware of it during the relationship. What does it say to you that I am still here today?"

Cama testified that her "relationship" with Eppolito began in 1982 and ended when he moved to Las Vegas. "He was a nice guy," she said.

Cama was a bit player whose only role, aside from embarrassing Eppolito and his family, was to confirm that he and Caracappa met with

Kaplan in her Bensonhurst apartment about ten times to exchange confidential information for cash.

By the ninth day, the pace quickened. Prosecution witnesses cycled in and out with the purpose of further corroborating Kaplan's accusations. The government called the trial's second grieving mother, Betty Hydell, to identify Eppolito and Caracappa as the detectives spotted in a car outside her Staten Island home on October 18, 1986, the day her son Jimmy disappeared.

Now sixty-seven, she took her place on the stand dressed in black, with white hair and glasses. As she began her testimony, an image of her late son appeared on the overhead monitor. In a trembling voice, she explained that Jimmy rode with a friend to Brooklyn that morning because his brother, Frankie, needed Jimmy's car. (Jimmy kept a second car in Brooklyn.) Frankie returned minutes after leaving to report that two men had followed him. Betty told the jury that she looked out the window and saw them, two detectives passing slowly by in an unmarked powder-blue car. She told Frankie to drive around the block; she circled the block the other way in her own car. "I wanted to see if they would follow him," she said. Sure enough they did. "I wanted to see who they were." She knew something was wrong, she said, when Jimmy failed to come home for dinner.

The defense declined to cross-examine Betty. Nor was she asked to identify the defendants in the courtroom, but she did describe the men she saw twenty years earlier. "One was the big one," she said, with "black hair, white shirt on, black jacket, gold necklace." The "little one," she said, "had very dark hair, thin face." That was enough.

On the twelfth day, another round of minor players buttressed the prosecution with supporting details and amplification. A retired detective testified that the burglar-turned-informant Otto Heidel had secretly taped conversations before Casso's assassins gunned him down as he changed a flat tire on Avenue U. An FBI agent recalled that the diamond merchant Israel Greenwald was poised to cooperate with the bureau when he disappeared. Frank Santora's daughter, Tammy, described Eppolito and Caracappa furtively conferring with her father at her sweet sixteen party.

The newspapers glossed over these testimonies, focusing instead on Tommy Galpine, Burt Kaplan's forty-nine-year-old errand boy. As a witness for the prosecution, he described how he and Kaplan trafficked in stolen designer clothes and illegal drugs.

Kaplan employed Galpine for twenty years, right up until the DEA arrested them both in 1996. Like his boss, Galpine served nine years before cooperating with the government. He confirmed much of what Kaplan had said, sometimes verbatim. He said that Kaplan explained that Eppolito and Caracappa—he called them "bulls," the mob term for detectives—fed him police intelligence, and that Kaplan routinely forwarded that intelligence to Gaspipe Casso.

Galpine recalled how Kaplan contacted him, prison to prison, to warn that Clarissa, a woman Galpine described as "my paramour, my mistress," had fallen behind on mortgage payments. The two men arranged for Clarissa to move in with Kaplan's wife, at their Eighty-Fifth Street home, to ease her financial burden. The drug dealer's wife now hosted the gofer's mistress.

The newspaper reporters relished the story, of course. Though what followed had more legal bite: Galpine was able to place Eppolito and Caracappa at Kaplan's Brooklyn home in 1987 or 1988. "I was in the habit of stopping over at Burt's house just about every night to go over what happened that day or what we were going to do the next day," he said. "I don't remember exactly when it was, but it was in the evening. Burt met me at the door. He told me, 'Tommy, I can't let you in now because those cops are here. I don't want them to see you. I don't want you to see them.'"

Galpine made the nature of Kaplan's arrangement with Eppolito explicitly clear: "Burt [Kaplan] was getting information from Louie

[Eppolito], a New York city cop, and passing it off to Anthony Casso, who was a mobster." Galpine also detailed the sums Kaplan paid for information. He recalled Kaplan sending him to meet Eppolito on a Brooklyn street corner a few blocks north of the Belt Parkway in order to deliver $5,000 in cash. Eppolito was standing beside a white car when Galpine pulled up. Eppolito hugged him and took the thick envelope.

On cross-examination, Cutler called Galpine "a thief, a liar" and "errand boy" who followed Kaplan, "a Fagin character," on a "spiral to perdition, to hell." Galpine appeared baffled by Cutler's language. "What's the question?" he asked.

The prosecutors saved the grisliest for last. Peter Franzone, the barely literate tow truck driver and reluctant gravedigger, had kept a secret for nineteen years. He was too frightened of Eppolito to tell anyone what he saw. "I was scared, because who is going to believe me if I mentioned a cop was involved? I figured [Eppolito] would kill me or arrest me and put me in jail and have somebody else kill me."

Franzone broke his long silence on the trial's thirteenth day. He recounted how, in 1986, Frank Santora and Eppolito escorted a man wearing a yarmulke into a single-car garage on Franzone's Nostrand Avenue lot while Eppolito kept watch; how only Santora and Caracappa came out; how Santora led him back into the garage. He saw a body flopped against the wall. Santora forced him to dig a five-foot hole, or face death himself. He described how they rolled Greenwald's body into the grave. The victim lay in a fetal position as they filled the dirt in around him.

On March 31, Mitra Hormozi entered the final piece of evidence: a statement from Leah Greenwald, which neatly brought the jury back to her husband, the murder victim Hormozi cited in her opening remarks. "After the morning of February 10, 1986," Hormozi said, "Leah Greenwald never saw her husband again." Then, after a methodical fifteen days and twenty-five witnesses, the prosecution rested its case.

Gaspipe Casso, the spurned witness, had hovered about the trial like a specter, present in thought if not in body. Witnesses had invoked his

286 BLOOD AND THE BADGE

name, over and over, as the Lucchese underboss who paid Eppolito and Caracappa.

Two weeks before the trial convened, Casso contacted the US Attorney's Office in Brooklyn. He offered to disclose the location of Jimmy Hydell's long-missing body. In return, he asked the government to cap his life sentence at twenty years. It was as if Casso could not stand to loiter in supermax, scorned and forgotten, while the impending trial earned headlines. His proposal was roundly rejected.

Then, a month later, Casso threw the proceedings into turmoil from a distance of eighteen hundred miles. In a March 4 letter mailed to Assistant US Attorney Mark Feldman, Casso claimed Eppolito and Caracappa were innocent. The letter came as a head-spinning reversal: Casso was the first to implicate the detectives after turning government witness in 1994. Now, in a letter neatly handwritten in block letters, Casso sought to clear them of all wrongdoing, saying he and Kaplan alone had committed the crimes. "I, Anthony Casso," he wrote, "hereby confess to have personally participated, as part of a three-man team, that shot and killed Eddie Lino in Brooklyn's Gravesend section. Detectives Eppolito and Caracappa are falsely being accused of this crime." The letter also said, without evidence or corroboration, that Eppolito and Caracappa played no role in the death of Israel Greenwald, that Casso could "honestly prove" that they had nothing to do with kidnapping Jimmy Hydell and never supplied the Lucchese family with "confidential information." He said that he and Kaplan "cooked up a scheme to frame these cops." Casso wrote "sworn statement" as a letterhead, as if to lend credence.

Henoch acknowledged that the US Attorney's Office had received Casso's letter back in early March, but had not shared it with the defense, as procedure requires, since his claims were so far-fetched and clearly inadmissible. Henoch assumed that Casso was intent only on disrupting the trial to get back at the US Attorney's Office for dumping him as a cooperating witness a decade earlier. Nonetheless, "It is not the prosecutor's province to decide what they should and what they shouldn't share," said Rae Koshetz of Caracappa's defense team, "or to make an independent evaluation of his credibility."

The court recessed a few minutes before 1 P.M. on March 30 so that two defense lawyers, Rae Koshetz and Bettina Schein, along with their clients, could speak by phone with Casso, who called in from the super-max prison in Florence, Colorado. (Cutler and Hayes conspicuously abstained, presumably to avoid conflicts with other mob-related clients.)

On the phone, Casso claimed that he and Kaplan had fabricated a plan to frame the two detectives by passing messages to each other from their respective prisons via Lillian and Eleanor, their wives. He said that he and two associates, not the detectives, killed Eddie Lino, and that the detectives never tipped him off. "I wish you luck," Casso told Eppolito and Caracappa at the end of the call.

Meanwhile, Cutler and Hayes settled themselves on benches beside a concrete chessboard in Cadman Plaza, outside the courthouse. It was an unusually warm afternoon for late March. Cutler ate a ham and Swiss cheese sandwich. Hayes drank a smoothie. In conversation with a reporter for *The New Yorker* magazine, they presented themselves as two outer borough guys, a long-running shtick. "I'd rather be doing this than sitting in La Grenouille," Hayes said, though he had no doubt spent many evenings eating at La Grenouille, or its equivalent.

"The greatest lunches I had," Cutler said, "were on construction gangs."

A man traversing the plaza recognized Hayes from the dust-jacket portrait printed in his memoir, *Mouthpiece: A Life in—and Sometimes Just Outside—the Law,* published two months earlier. While Hayes stood to shake hands, Cutler explained his grievance against those who would extinguish everything ragged, raw, and glorious about the New York of his childhood. "It began in 1980, when Reagan took over, and when Giuliani was the U.S. Attorney in the Southern District, and brought an unprecedented war on the underworld. He used the RICO statutes to take out all the old-timers."

In their lunchtime interview with the reporter, as in the courtroom, Cutler and Hayes put forward their view of an intolerant and overreaching federal government. "The concept of the US, what this country was based on, was individual rights," Hayes said. "It's a big part of the

American myth: cowboys, trial lawyers. You really find a war on that kind of thing today, the myth of the individual. Thank god the jury can still look you in the eye and say, 'Go fuck yourself.'"

Afterward, Cutler and Hayes pressed Judge Weinstein for a mistrial based on the government's failure to share the letter from Casso recanting his original allegations. Casso's contentions, however far-fetched, would have infuenced their strategy, the defense lawyers claimed, had they known about it. "Mr. Casso gives a completely exculpatory account of what happened," Hayes said.

The next day, Judge Weinstein ruled that Casso's last-minute disclosures were not cause for a mistrial, as the defense had argued. He acknowledged that the government did not share the letter from Casso, or even notify the defense of its arrival, but he deemed the letter "of no significance . . . it's a completely pallid letter."

Cutler and Hayes, he added, were free to call Casso as a witness at any time. They could have questioned him on any topic. But they chose not to "because, in effect, he was a wild cannon." He warned the defense lawyers that calling Casso could backfire. "When he gets here and gets on that witness stand . . . he may have other things to say that he won't tell you on the phone that he will say under oath here before this jury in order to curry favor with the government, which is the only organization that can help him."

Still, Judge Weinstein would allow the defense to call Casso if they were willing to take that risk, though it would require that US marshals rush Casso to New York encumbered by heavy security. Hayes and Cutler declined. Casso was indeed mercurial, just as Judge Weinstein said. Besides, in their phone call he offered no concrete evidence that would call into question the testimony of Burt Kaplan and other witnesses. As a result, Casso would stay in the harsh confines of Florence, unheard and disregarded.

The next morning, the defense began its case. Earlier in the trial Hayes had indicated that he might call his client, Caracappa, to testify. Caracappa had spoken publicly only once since his arrest, on *60 Minutes*, and made a convincing impression. But in the trial's final days Hayes reversed himself and removed his client from the witness list. "He sort of wanted [to testify]," Hayes told a reporter, "[but] I don't want him to. I think there's a lot of problems with the government's case and I don't need to put him on."

Oddly enough, the defense began its case without Edward Hayes. He had unaccountably left for Los Angeles on the defense's most critical day to meet with federal prosecutors on behalf of another client, a *New York Post* gossip columnist accused of accepting bribes from investor Ron Burkle to keep his transgressions off Page Six. Hayes's cocounsel, Rae Koshetz, tried to explain that he "had a very important meeting."

"I don't care what he had," Judge Weinstein said. "He's not in California with my permission. I have important matters to take care of with your client."

When a court clerk got Hayes on speakerphone, he explained from his room at the Hotel Bel-Air that he could not "be available over the next six or seven hours because I'm in this meeting with the U.S. Attorney in Los Angeles."

"You *are* available," Judge Weinstein said. "Tell the United States Attorney in Los Angeles that the meeting is at an end."

Filling in for Hayes without advance warning, Koshetz called just three witnesses: a former colleague of Caracappa's in the Major Case Squad testified that they worked thirty-two straight hours after the murder of the militant rabbi Meir Kahane in a Manhattan hotel, suggesting Caracappa would have been too exhausted to shoot Eddie Lino the next day; an excavator expressed doubt that Peter Franzone could have dug Israel Greenwald's grave in the frozen ground in February, as he said he did; and, finally, a money-laundering expert questioned Kaplan's credibility.

Cutler had already decided against calling Eppolito. His constant exaggerations, falsehoods, and slurs would hurt his case. Instead, for the jury's consideration, Cutler submitted eighteen commendations, plaques, and honorable mentions awarded to Eppolito during his police career. Cutler pulled them, one by one, from a Home Depot cardboard box and handed them to a court clerk.

"We rest," Cutler said after submitting the dust cover of Eppolito's book, *Mafia Cop*. Cutler's entire defense took just thirteen minutes. After listening to prosecution witnesses for four weeks, the defense concluded its case by 11 A.M. "Ex-Detective's Defense Rests Without Breaking a Sweat," *The New York Times* pronounced.

A few minutes after 10 A.M. on Monday, April 3, Judge Weinstein resumed his place on the bench. The twelve jurors filed in and took their seats in the jury box, the same seats they had occupied for sixteen days. Daniel Wenner rose and walked to a lectern. At thirty-four, he was the youngest of the three assistant US attorneys. Shifting his gaze between his notes and the jurors, he delivered a three-hour summation.

In most trials, the summation is a culmination, a crescendo of both evidence and emotion designed to consolidate the jurors' loyalty and sweep away doubts. In Wenner's hands, however, the summation was more clinic than climax.

Using PowerPoint, Wenner systematically reacquainted the jurors with the testimony and evidence logged into the record over the previous weeks. He reminded the jurors, as if any could forget, that Eppolito and Caracappa worked as double agents for the Lucchese family in exchange for $4,000 a month, that they participated in at least eight homicides, starting with Israel Greenwald in 1986 and ending with Eddie Lino in 1992, and that they had leaked critical police intelligence about investigations and surveillance.

"It is one of the bloodiest, most violent betrayals of the badge that this city has ever seen," he said. "The defendants Stephen Caracappa and Louis Eppolito, motivated by nothing less than pure greed, unleashed and facilitated a wave of violence in the 1980s and 90s. These corrupt men . . . led double lives. They did nothing less than arm the homicidal maniac Anthony Casso with the motive and the means to leave an avalanche of death in his wake. . . . They gathered and sold information to the mob. They kidnapped for the mob. They murdered for the mob."

Wenner walked the jury through all the charges—money laundering, obstruction of justice, murder conspiracy, murder for hire, and drug distribution—and pointed them to specific evidence supporting each charge, including Frank Santora's address book, Caracappa's search records, the exact angle of shovel marks in a grave. He tied up loose ends.

Wenner's summation was thorough, if lumbering. He parsed the evidence, bit by bit, showing how one witness corroborated another. He spoke of "predicate acts" and "subpredicate acts." When Judge Weinstein noticed jurors flagging during a discussion of phone numbers and code names, he called a ten-minute break so they could stretch and refresh.

Every lawyer in the room knew that however scrupulous the government team might be, the five-year statute of limitations imposed by federal RICO laws could still derail their case; it hung over their argument like a curse. Wenner tried to forestall the issue by emphasizing the sale of methamphetamine to Stephen Corso in late 2004. He maintained that the transaction extended the detectives' pattern of criminal behavior practically to the day of their arrest. "Don't be fooled into thinking that the conspiracy ended when the defendants retired from the force," he said.

Wenner closed with the image of Eppolito arrested at the entrance of Piero's restaurant in Las Vegas. As he clamped on the handcuffs, DEA agent Kenny Luzak said it's been a long time coming. Eppolito said, "Yes, it has."

"He knew he was finally caught for what he had done," Wenner said. "We spent the last several weeks proving to you that these defendants were conspirators in an enterprise that obstructed justice, committed kidnapping, murder, bribery, money laundering, and other crimes. . . . It is now up to you. Convict them proudly."

Hayes followed with a sentimental portrait of Caracappa as an honest working-class New Yorker, a retiring Vietnam veteran who rose by means of dogged toil to the rank of first-grade detective and served as a stalwart of the elite Major Case Squad. "The fact of the matter is that

Stephen Caracappa went out every day and made sacrifices and took risks that very few people ever do," Hayes said. "And this is what he got for it? This is the price he paid?"

Hayes appealed to whatever resentment the jury members might feel toward the federal government, in all its arrogant power, persecuting an honorable man, a Brooklyn civil servant, simply for its own aggrandizement. "Why bother having a jury system?" Hayes said, with broad sarcasm. "Why not let Washington call us up and say: 'Hey, this is the result'? This is going to get us great publicity and take away all the other foul-ups that the Justice Department has had."

Caracappa, Hayes said, was an honest crime fighter with "no vices. He doesn't have a secret life. . . . What would possibly motivate him to betray everything? Nothing."

Hayes then turned the summation over to his cocounsel, Rae Koshetz, who contended, once again, that the statute of limitations had long since expired. This was the defense's silver bullet, or so they hoped.

To be sure, she said, the government came to court armed with lurid allegations that they could "stir into a conspiracy casserole and serve warm in federal court." But prosecutors still must account for "that pesky five-year statute of limitations." In other words, to convict Eppolito and Caracappa, the government had to prove that they continued to commit crimes beyond the statute of limitations date of March 9, 2000, five years before their indictment. No such crime had occurred, Koshetz said. For one thing, the defendants could no longer use their standing as detectives to disguise their activities once they retired in the early 1990s. Besides, she added, their employers, Kaplan and Casso, had long since gone to prison.

"Was there any way to revive a dead RICO conspiracy allegation and bring it within the statute?" she asked. The answer was the contrived meth sale. The problem, Koshetz said, was that the sale was an isolated act, not a pattern, in which Eppolito and Caracappa played only a marginal role.

"Neither Lou Eppolito nor Stephen Caracappa negotiated a drug deal, set a price, talked about identity, quality, or quantity of drugs or handled any drugs or money," she said. "Ladies and gentlemen, they sold nothing. They conspired to sell nothing. At the end of the day this conversation was nothing [more than] a failed government effort to drag that old Corso allegation into a new century and bring it within the statute of limitations."

The drug sale was, she added, "a Johnny-come-lately artificially grafted onto the case by the government to avoid the problem of the statute of limitations. It's like wearing a straw hat with a winter coat. It doesn't fit."

The next morning, Bruce Cutler stood up from the defense table and buttoned his suit coat. He rolled his shoulders, as a batter might before stepping to the plate, then delivered his last words in defense of Eppolito, a summation short on legal specifics or lines of reasoning. Instead, with arms waving and voice loudening, he let loose another name-calling attack on the witnesses. He proceeded as if locution, not logic, could win the day.

"Some, like myself, thought his closing was truly brilliant," the columnist Steve Dunleavy wrote in the next day's *New York Post*. "Others thought it was over the top, and at least one lady sitting next to me thought it was hilarious."

Cutler certainly did not intend hilarity. If anything, his tone grew more bellicose in the closing minutes. The government's case, he said, rested on "sweetheart pacts given to cretins and devils." He called Burt Kaplan a man who led "a double life, triple life, even a quadruple life." Stephen Corso, the cooperating accountant, was a "sophisticated, unctuous, polished, lowlife thief." Al D'Arco was "a miserable, desiccated, unrepentant villain."

He called the reluctant gravedigger, the five-foot-four Peter Franzone, "a subhuman gnome . . . he's a creep and a lowlife and liar." He paused to read the definition of "gnome" from the *American Heritage Dictionary*: "One of a race of dwarf-like creatures who live underground and guard treasure hoards."

To those who found his summation florid—one crime reporter called it a "tone poem"—he offered a half apology. "I've tried as best I can to use the English language in a precise way," he told the jury. "It was drilled into me as a boy."

As he had throughout the trial—throughout much of his career—Cutler portrayed the government as an unfeeling federal elite. "The FBI has an arrogance that comes with power," he said. "It is that mentality that I fight against, and I'll always fight against."

The prosecutors, he said, were "educated, sophisticated professionals" who came to court armed with "light shows and erudition." By contrast, Eppolito was an honest civil servant.

Cutler returned, as Wenner had a day earlier, to the moment of Eppolito's arrest at the entrance of Piero's. Most observers took Eppolito's acknowledgment that his seizure had "been a long time coming" as an admission of guilt. But Cutler spun it the opposite way. He depicted the arrest as a long time coming for a man harassed by law enforcement his entire adult life. "I know you have been after me," Cutler said, interpreting Eppolito's state of mind. "I know what happened as a result of my book. Come and take me."

He ended by telling the jury: "He is in your hands."

In the US court system, the last word goes to the government. So at the beginning of the trial's fourth week, in its final hours, Robert Henoch, the lead prosecutor, issued his rebuttal. He jumped on Cutler and Hayes for skirting the incriminating facts in favor of a vague anti-government grievance. "When you make a speech and don't go into the details," Henoch said, "then something is wrong."

In response to Cutler's depiction of the prosecution as federal elites, Henoch reminded the jury that "it's not a Washington case. We are in Brooklyn. We live here [so] don't tell us we are . . . somehow puppets of some evil Department of Justice scheme. Just stop."

He acknowledged that Cutler waged his summation with a "big voice, big words, big vocabulary." But no decibel level, he argued, could diminish the damning testimony of Kaplan and Corso. "These are two heavyweight champions," Henoch said, gesturing at Cutler and Hayes at the defense table, "and they didn't land a punch, not a scratch."

Henoch said Cutler and Hayes never explained why Eppolito and Caracappa had a relationship with a criminal like Kaplan in the first place. "The fact that Mr. Caracappa, a Major Case Squad detective, a first-grade detective in the Organized Crime Homicide Unit, knew Burt Kaplan has no innocent explanation," he said. "There is no reason for him to know that man. If he were an honest cop he wouldn't even want to be seen with Burt Kaplan."

In his testimony, Kaplan had demonstrated his familiarity with the defendants' domestic lives. How, Henoch asked, could Kaplan describe Eppolito's basement or Caracappa's black cat if they were not on close terms? Turning to Cutler, Henoch said, "You're the best lawyer in America, but you can't explain that away."

In parting, Henoch cast attention on the victims' families. He invoked Psalm 23, which Caracappa's lawyer, Rae Koshetz, had mentioned when she cross-examined Corso twelve days earlier. "The Lord is my shepherd; I shall not want," he said.

"You know when that psalm is recited?" Henoch said. "It's recited in church at funeral services. You know when it's recited? At a grave site in Jewish burials . . . It's relevant because twenty years after those men acting under color of law pulled Israel Greenwald off the road and they marched him into a lot and Stephen Caracappa and Frank Santora executed him while Louis Eppolito stood lookout. Twenty years later Leah Greenwald finally got to recite Psalm 23 . . . at the gravesite for her husband. . . . How dare they bring that into the courtroom the way they did? How dare they?"

He closed: "Make this a temple of justice. Hold them accountable. Hold them accountable."

Outside the courtroom, Leah Greenwald embraced Henoch. "You were amazing," she said. "You were so beautiful."

The nearly four-week excursion through the Brooklyn underworld, with its roadside shootings and bodies abandoned in car trunks, its cast of capos and consiglieri whispering orders, had come to an end with a simple prayer.

The jury broke for lunch, then reassembled at 2 P.M. The courtroom was uncomfortably warm, or maybe it just felt that way as Judge Weinstein read 134 pages of legal instructions after a long, draining day. When he noticed jurors nodding off, he asked a clerk to lower the thermostat and dismissed the jurors for a brief recess while the room cooled. During the break Caracappa talked with his brother, Dominic, at the defense table. Eppolito sat nearby with his daughter. Ed Hayes sat in the hallway discussing dinner plans on a cell phone.

When the jury reconvened, Judge Weinstein instructed them to decide the case solely on the evidence, and to consider whether a witness's testimony contradicted or supported another witness's words. He reminded them that the government must prove guilt beyond a reasonable doubt, and he defined conspiracy. When he came to the statute of limitations, he paused for a long moment, tapping his pen. Eleven days earlier, during Stephen Corso's testimony, Weinstein had warned Mitra Hormozi that the statute of limitations was a "ticking time bomb that can explode at any time."

Weinstein now laid down the parameters for the jury: "If you find that one or both of the defendants were at one time engaged in a racketeering conspiracy involving the charged enterprise but that the enterprise was no longer in existence as of March 9, 2000, you must acquit the defendants. . . ."

Weinstein dismissed the jury at 5:20 P.M. with orders to return at 9:30 the next morning to begin deliberations.

22

JUSTICE FORESTALLED

EDWARD HAYES LATER TOLD REPORTERS THAT HE could sense the guilty verdict coming.

He took it as a bad sign when the jury lingered over an unusually long lunch on the second day of deliberations.

That afternoon, word came that the jury had reached a verdict. They had deliberated only a day and a half—a total of ten hours—while sequestered in a small room behind the courtroom. The entire dramatis personae hastened to their places in the fourth-floor courtroom. Hayes could glean the guilty verdict in the way jurors avoided eye contact with him when they returned to the courtroom, and by their grave demeanor.

The jury stood as Judge Weinstein entered. Eppolito's daughter Andrea kissed a crucifix strung on a rosary. Her sister, Deanna, crossed herself.

At 2:10 P.M. the courtroom deputy, holding a verdict sheet, asked the jury foreperson, a middle-aged woman, "Proved or not proved?" seventy times. Seventy times she answered "proved" in a soft, almost whispery voice. For twenty full minutes she repeated "proved, proved, proved, proved, proved." "Through count after count, the word 'proved' was a tiny, frightening sound in the stillness," Jimmy Breslin wrote in the next morning's *Newsday*. "Nobody spoke or moved." Andrea wept quietly.

The jury found that Eppolito and Caracappa had murdered Israel Greenwald in Peter Franzone's garage on Nostrand Avenue and murdered Eddie Lino in his Mercedes beside the Belt Parkway. They found that the detectives had kidnapped Jimmy Hydell and handed him over to Casso to die.

Everyone looked at the defendants as the weight of the verdict settled upon them. Caracappa sat back, shook his head, and placed his hand on his chin. Eppolito stared straight ahead. Judge Weinstein thanked the jury and dismissed them. "Bail is revoked," he said. "The defendants are remanded. Marshals, take charge."

Bruce Cutler held his client in a bear hug. Hayes shook Caracappa's hand and kissed Eppolito's cheeks, then welled up in tears.

As detectives, Eppolito and Caracappa knew the procedure. Eppolito undid his belt and placed it on the defense table. He unknotted his yellow necktie. He handed his daughter his watch and a gold chain from around his neck and emptied his pockets. The lawyers watched as marshals led their clients through a back door to a holding cell where they would pause before proceeding to the Metropolitan Detention Center. "Dad, this is not over," Eppolito's daughter Andrea yelled as her father disappeared from sight.

US attorney Rose Mauskopf walked to the well of the courtroom and hugged Robert Henoch, the lead prosecutor. Relatives of the murder victims allowed themselves a subdued celebration. "Finally, after twenty years they get these people," said Leah Greenwald. "I knew they were guilty 100 percent, but in America you never know."

In the hallway, Jimmy Breslin asked the defense lawyers about their next move. "It's only the first round, Jimmy," Cutler said. "Only the first round of the fight."

Cutler and Hayes rode the elevator down in silence, fedoras in their hands, to a press gathering outside the courthouse door where Andrea Eppolito was already speaking to reporters. "People have called this the worst case of corruption New York has ever seen," she said, "but it was not on the part of my father and not on the part of Stephen Caracappa. It was on the part of the government."

When the Eppolito family dispersed, Mauskopf read a prepared statement blaming the detectives for "perverting the shield of good and turning it into a sword of evil. They didn't deliver us from evil. They themselves were evil personified. They did it as cops and they did it as Mafia cops."

Caracappa's wife, Monica, attended only the last three trial days. She learned of the conviction while watching CNN on a return flight to Las Vegas.

A day or so after the verdict, Edward Hayes and Rae Koshetz buzzed into a conference room within a protective housing unit in the Metropolitan Detention Center to meet with Caracappa. "I remember him standing up," Koshetz said. "His eyes started to water, and he sort of turned his back, because he didn't want me to see that he was crying."

The defense team immediately announced their intention to appeal. "It's the *appearance* of justice," Cutler said, "but it's *not* justice. It's just the beginning of the struggle, and I won't abandon it."

As it turned out, Cutler would abandon the struggle, like it or not. On his ninth day of isolation in the protective housing unit within the Metropolitan Detention Center, Eppolito complained by phone to John Marzulli of the *New York Daily News* that the two defense lawyers, Cutler and Hayes, had "abandoned" him and Caracappa. "They put up no defense for our lives," Eppolito said. "I believe you have to fight."

Eppolito resented Cutler for refusing to let him speak for himself from the witness stand, a long-simmering point of contention. Cutler suspected Eppolito could not answer questions without lying or offending the jury with racial slurs. By contrast, Eppolito believed himself to be a forceful, persuasive presence.

According to Eppolito, Cutler had failed to inform him of his constitutional right to testify. "I wanted to take the stand," Eppolito told Marzulli. "I begged them. I said, 'Put me in there. This is my life I'm fighting for.'"

Judge Weinstein agreed to hold a hearing to determine if Cutler should be replaced. Cutler responded with a letter to Weinstein saying he was prepared to withdraw in time for Eppolito to hire a new lawyer for his sentencing and appeal.

Eppolito came to the hearing on April 24 with an unkempt goatee and a faded white T-shirt stretched tight over his substantial belly. Judge

Weinstein looked across the courtroom in disapproval. "I don't want a defendant coming into my courtroom in that way," he said. "It's demeaning."

"I apologize, your honor," Eppolito said. "They gave me a shirt that had a hole in it and I had to beg for this one."

With the scolding concluded, Judge Weinstein proceeded to formally discharge Cutler from the case. Eppolito was accompanied by his new lawyer, Joseph Bondy, who by appearance and manner was Cutler's opposite—slim, precise, crisply articulate. Cutler called his replacement "a guttersnipe lawyer." (Following Eppolito's lead, Caracappa replaced Hayes with Daniel Nobel, a public defender.)

With the hearing adjourned and his responsibilities dissolved, Cutler left without speaking to his former client. Stepping from the courthouse, he paused long enough to call Greg Smith, a *New York Daily News* reporter, a bum.

Cornered by reporters in the courthouse hallway, Bondy said he was "not here to analyze the animus. I'm here to win the case." Winning, he added, would require attacking the prosecution's vulnerable point: the government's contention that the criminal conspiracy linking Eppolito and Caracappa to the mob was ongoing. Cutler, he said, made an egregious mistake by not formally challenging the government's right to bring racketeering charges. In an ominous sign for the prosecution, Judge Weinstein appeared to agree.

Eppolito asked his wife, Fran, and their children to skip the June 4 sentencing. By custom, the court invited the victims' families to stand, one by one, and pour their fury and resentment out in public. When everyone had their say, the judge would issue the sentence. Not surprisingly, Eppolito wished to spare his family the words of heartbreak and condemnation directed at him, the talk of lost childhoods and rage without end.

The testimonials were unsparing. Israel Greenwald's daughter Michal, now thirty, read from a typed statement held with trembling hands: "You took away our daddy and by doing so you took away our childhood. You took away our mother. You stole our innocence. You filled our nights with nightmares and our days with torture. . . . My sister and I would often turn to God, begging him to find our daddy and bring him home, begging him to let us know what happened so that we can try to heal."

Then she looked directly at Eppolito and Caracappa. "You thought you could get away with it and you almost did. . . . But you strongly underestimated the power of a child's innocent prayer."

Next came Betty Hydell, mother of Jimmy Hydell, the failed assassin kidnapped by Eppolito and Caracappa and delivered to Casso in the trunk of a car. "I was as close to you then as I am now and you deny it," she said of the day the detectives came looking for Jimmy at her Staten Island home. "I just wish you'd stay in jail the rest of your life and you die in jail alone."

The speakers did not include the mother of Nicky Guido, the twenty-six-year-old killed in a case of mistaken identity. She was too unnerved to attend. "My family and I have kept this to ourselves as much as we could," she wrote in a letter to Mayor Michael Bloomberg, "even though you could imagine how the press and newspapers are always interested in talking to me."

Caracappa remained stoic as always, though his composure cracked momentarily when his new lawyer, Daniel Nobel, cited a letter of support his brother Dominic wrote to the judge.

It would seem impossible for Eppolito and Caracappa to say anything in the backwash of so much grief and vitriol. Nonetheless, Eppolito rose to deliver the rambling self-defense Cutler had suppressed for weeks. He began with an awkward note of conciliation, saying he understood the families' pain. As a detective, for twenty-two years he had knocked on doors and delivered grave news. "I know the feelings of every family here today," he said. "I know how they feel inside their gut."

Eppolito thanked his own family, naming them one by one, though he neglected to mention his son Lou Jr., the only one in attendance. He insisted on his innocence, despite his conviction and the preponderance of evidence behind it. "I can hold my head up high," he said. "I never did any of these things." He then inexplicably invited the victims' families to visit him in jail, where he promised to prove his innocence.

During Eppolito's speech, a barrel-shaped man with a shaggy beard popped up from the gallery. "Mr. Eppolito," he shouted, "do you remember me?"

The interruption flummoxed Eppolito. "No," he said.

"I'm the guy you put away for nineteen years. I'm Barry Gibbs. You don't remember me?" Eppolito arrested Gibbs for murder in 1986. He was incarcerated for almost two decades before Peter Mitchell, the primary prosecution witness, recanted his testimony, leading to his exoneration and release.

"You don't remember what you did to me?" Gibbs continued as marshals muscled him from the courtroom. The families of the murder victims applauded Gibbs. "I had a family too. Remember what you did to my family?"

A hearing full of odd surprises grew odder still when it came time for sentencing. Judge Weinstein began by affirming Eppolito and Caracappa's guilt. "There has been no doubt, and there *is* no doubt, that the murders and other crimes were proven without a reasonable doubt," Judge Weinstein said. He would grant no leniency for the men convicted of "the most heinous series of crimes ever tried in this courthouse."

In the hearing's climactic moment, Weinstein issued a life sentence and a $1 million fine, the harshest penalty available, but he would not impose the sentence, he said, until after he conducted another hearing, on June 23, to determine if Eppolito and Caracappa had suffered deficient representation, as their new lawyers argued, and therefore would qualify for a mistrial.

As the hearing ended, Barry Gibbs stood outside the courthouse as a reminder of what Eppolito and Caracappa could soon endure. "Every day in jail is like a million years," he told reporters. "It's not a day, it's a million years."

For their part, Eppolito and Caracappa returned to their shared cell with a particle of hope: their conviction could still be overturned despite the judge and jury's insistence on their guilt.

The June 23 hearing added another swerve to the proceedings. For the first time in their lives, Cutler and Hayes would be made to take the stand in their own defense, as if they had traded places with their former clients. If Weinstein ruled that two of the best-known defense attorneys in the country had mishandled the case, their reputations, and their considerable vanity, would suffer accordingly.

"To accuse a fighter of walking away from a fight, that is what is so insulting, that is what is so galling," Cutler told a *Washington Post* reporter over lunch at the Four Seasons. "This is the most offensive thing that has ever happened to me in my life. . . . The stain is there. The cleaners are not getting this thing out no matter what happens."

The hearing began with Joseph Bondy calling his client, Eppolito, who, in wrinkled suit and sneakers, bad-mouthed Cutler, saying he declined to work through lunch and never explained the charges. In fact, Eppolito said, Cutler grew increasingly detached as the trial wore on. He refused to read the notes Eppolito passed during testimony and barely spoke to him. "Tell him he's annoying me," Eppolito quoted Cutler saying to a colleague, as if they were a feuding high school couple communicating through an intermediary.

When Eppolito followed Cutler to the Park Plaza Diner, he said, Cutler would "put up his hand and say, 'Don't tell me anything.'"

Bondy asked Eppolito where Cutler was during a meeting called to discuss the possibility of Casso testifying for the defense. "I believe he was doing an interview for a magazine," Eppolito said.

In the scrambled condition of the case, Robert Henoch, the lead prosecutor, found himself in the unlikely position of promoting the competence of the defense attorneys, the same men he had spent three weeks debating, in order to avoid a mistrial. He questioned Eppolito for more than three hours, a testimony so full of contradictions and slanders that no one in attendance could dispute Cutler's decision to keep Eppolito safely confined to the sideline.

Henoch played an audiotape of Eppolito bragging to the undercover accountant Stephen Corso about his continued influence with the Mafia. After listening to the tape, Eppolito said he was exaggerating in order to impress Corso.

"You'll tell a lie if it will help you?" Henoch asked.

"Yes," Eppolito said, "if it will help me get a movie made, yeah."

Bondy objected when Henoch asked about Eppolito's habitual use of racial slurs. Eppolito said he did use slurs—he called them "epitaphs" instead of "epithets"—not "to hurt their feelings. I just use it for slang." He acknowledged washing his hands after shaking hands with Black people.

"You use the N-word all the time?" Henoch asked.

"All the time," Eppolito said. "That's just the way I speak."

"You're a racist?"

"I guess you could say that."

Eppolito said he was "not a violent guy" just before Henoch read a passage aloud from Eppolito's book, *Mafia Cop,* in which he described punching a witness called Bugs until his arms hurt, then pushing Bugs's head into a bucket of diluted ammonia until "his face mutated into a giant purple blotch." Henoch also read Eppolito's account of inserting a shotgun into a man's mouth and feeling "this wonderful heady urge to pull the trigger" as the man befouled himself. In both cases, Eppolito said he was exaggerating for narrative effect. Most implausibly, Eppolito denied any connection to Burt Kaplan other than occasionally buying suits from his discount clothing outlet.

Henoch also asked Eppolito why he didn't exercise his right to testify if he wished to do so. "You're fighting for your life," he said, "but you didn't want to raise your hand and tell the judge you want to testify?" Eppolito said he was too scared. On the first day of jury selection, a crash on the Long Island Expressway had caused him to arrive late for court. Since then he was reluctant to anger Judge Weinstein. "I didn't want to tick off the judge," Eppolito said.

Eppolito's daughter Andrea also testified, condemning Cutler for taking his $250,000 fee before "cruising" through an ineffectual defense. Later, while fielding questions from reporters, she defended her father's use of racist language. "My father was raised on the street by a man who had a third-grade education," she said. "It was common vernacular on the streets . . . and that's the language my father adopted."

While Eppolito and his daughter testified, Cutler and Hayes waited their turn outside the courthouse. Hayes sat on a folding chair in the sun while Cutler spoke to a reporter. "It's just another attempt by the client to fight another day," he said of Eppolito's motion to have his conviction overturned. "But personal attacks on me I don't understand, and I don't cotton to."

On Monday morning, Cutler took the stand to forcefully defend his performance in the trial as "the best I ever did." When questioned by Eppolito's new lawyer, Joseph Bondy, Cutler denied any misgivings. "Did I make any mistakes? No," he said. "Did I lose the case? Yes. My intention as a defense lawyer is to pulverize the government case, to eviscerate the credibility of government-paid witnesses. . . . That is my defense: attack." Cutler expressed some pity for his former client, saying Eppolito "tried to play a gangster, which he wasn't."

When Bondy ended his questioning, Judge Weinstein interrupted to say that the government need not cross-examine Cutler. The judge had all but made up his mind: Cutler had provided his client "excellent representation," and argued his case in a "highly professional way." Judge Weinstein also lambasted Eppolito's "immorality and lack of credibility."

When Judge Weinstein finished castigating Eppolito, Bondy continued, despite growing evidence that Weinstein would reject the defense's motion for a mistrial. Bondy called Caracappa's former lawyer, Edward Hayes, as a witness, but Hayes was not in the courtroom. He had flown to visit his mother in Miami for the weekend and had not yet returned. A month earlier, Judge Weinstein had scolded Hayes for flying to Los Angeles on a critical trial day. Now Judge Weinstein was out of patience: he said he would sign an arrest warrant for Hayes if he failed to show up by 3:15 P.M. Bondy killed the time by reading aloud from Hayes's memoir. "I'm delighted that you filled the waiting time with reading," Judge

Weinstein told Bondy. But the memoir, he added, was "puffery. These books are written so that [lawyers] can claim high legal fees."

At 3:35 P.M., twenty minutes past the deadline, Hayes entered with a broad smile and a deep tan. He wore a pink polo shirt beneath a loud windowpane sport coat. He appeared not the least bit contrite. He was accompanied by his brother, Steven, who would serve as his lawyer.

For the remainder of the afternoon and the following day, Hayes described his legal strategy. He said Eppolito and Cutler squabbled throughout the trial, but that Eppolito had never demanded to testify in his own defense, as he claimed. For the second straight day Judge Weinstein sided with the accused lawyers. He found that Hayes, like Cutler, presented his case "in a highly professional manner."

Judge Weinstein had openly pooh-poohed the mistrial motion by signaling his support for the two fired defense lawyers. Caracappa's new lawyer, Daniel Nobel, warned his client that the motion stood only a "snowball's chance in hell."

The judge would not issue his written decision for another three days. If he denied the motion for mistrial, as everyone expected, he would immediately sentence Eppolito and Caracappa to life in prison. The process that began with their arrest almost sixteen months earlier would at last reach its conclusion. The victims' families—Linos, Guidos, Greenwalds, Hydells, and the rest—could leave the courthouse and cross Cadman Plaza for the last time assured that justice had been fulfilled, despite the strange setbacks and postscripts. City officials could brag that the courts had adjudicated the police department's worst corruption case, and federal prosecutors could add another takedown to their long campaign against organized crime. All the players would take comfort in knowing that in the end the system had worked. But it did not turn out that way.

On June 30, Judge Weinstein stunned everyone concerned, no one more than the defendants themselves, by vacating the convictions altogether on a technicality. The next day's *New York Daily News* ran its headline across the front page: "Getting Away With Murder."

In a seventy-seven page memorandum, Weinstein acknowledged

that prosecutors "overwhelmingly established" that Eppolito and Caracappa had "kidnapped, murdered and assisted kidnappers and murderers, all while sworn to protect the public against such crime." Weinstein
conceded their guilt, but he nonetheless acquitted them because the
five-year statute of limitations on federal racketeering charges had, in
his opinion, expired. He called it a "weak link in [the prosecution's] allegations."

Once the detectives retired to Las Vegas in the 1990s, he wrote,
the "conspiracy that began in the 1980s had come to a definite close. The
defendants were no longer in contact with their old associates in the
Lucchese crime family." Their "sporadic acts of criminality" in Las
Vegas, in his opinion, were unrelated to their earlier employment
with Gaspipe Casso.

He offered an analogy: "A retired contractor who opens a delicatessen in his retirement may encourage his old employees and clients to
buy their lunch at his new store, and time on the job sites may have
taught him what brand of pastrami those customers prefer; that does
not mean he remains in the construction business."

Judge Weinstein was known as a principled judge, and independent-
minded. He acquitted two guilty men based on the letter of the law in
spite of the inevitable backlash. "It will undoubtedly appear peculiar to
many people that heinous criminals like the defendants . . . should go
unwhipped of justice," Weinstein wrote. "Yet our Constitution, statutes
and morality require that we be ruled by the law, not by the vindictive-
ness or the advantage of the moment."

Robert Henoch, the lead prosecutor, was "stunned. It came out of the
blue. I didn't think he would do it."

By siding on principle, not punishment, Judge Weinstein may have
been making a sly sideways reference to the US Supreme Court ruling
a day earlier that the Bush administration's use of military tribunals
for terror suspects held at Guantánamo Bay violated a code of military
justice and the Geneva Conventions.

Joseph Bondy traveled to the Metropolitan Detention Center in
Brooklyn to deliver news of the acquittal in person. Eppolito wept and

embraced him. "I was afraid that I was going to spend the rest of my life in jail," he said.

In their Las Vegas subdivision, Monica Caracappa watched CNN coverage of her husband's reprieve with friends. "I know my husband will be unhappy that he's exonerated on a technicality," she said. "But I will take my husband home any way I can."

Across the street, at the Eppolito home, "it was like the world stopped," his daughter Andrea said. "We were stunned. We had not been given much reason to hope. . . . We were all crying, my mother and sister and me. It was like everything was in slow motion."

For their part, Cutler and Hayes took Judge Weinstein's surprise decision as vindication of their defense strategy. "I thought the government overreaching here was clear from the beginning, and I always said that," Cutler said. Nonetheless, he added, "If you ask me if I expected it, I didn't expect it."

The families of the murder victims did not expect it either. They reacted with a mix of bitterness and bafflement. "We thought this was over," said Betty Hydell. "I couldn't believe it. I couldn't see why the judge would do this. He called it a 'hideous crime.'"

The men and women of the jury also assumed they had come to a just conclusion. They sat through three weeks of testimony followed by deliberations over the complexities of racketeering law only to find their judgment discarded on a point of detail. "It was a like a slap in the face," one juror told the *New York Daily News*. "These guys may just get off, from the way it looks. And the thing is, they did it. They did it! . . . I know we didn't misunderstand it. The conspiracy went on. If they can't get a conviction on that, I give up on the system."

Jurors may not have understood that Judge Weinstein carefully gauged the timing of his ruling in order to give prosecutors a second chance. "I had the sense that he did it just to give us a poke in the eye," Henoch said. "He knew it would be reinstated."

Had Judge Weinstein granted the earlier defense motion to dismiss the charges, the government could not have appealed. The Constitution does not allow defendants to be tried twice for the same offense, a provision known as double jeopardy. By waiting until after the verdict to rule on the statute of limitations he had permitted the government to take the case to the Court of Appeals.

In the short term, Judge Weinstein offered the families, and jurors, a small measure of consolation by denying Eppolito and Caracappa bail. He judged them to be flight risks.

At least for now, Eppolito and Caracappa would spend their days in the same cramped compartment in the Metropolitan Detention Center, safely apart from the general prison population. They spent twenty-three hours a day in a seven-by-twelve-foot cell equipped with a bunk bed and little else. The ceiling above them leaked and their sink produced no water. They drank with hands cupped under a shower head. Eppolito was a slob; Caracappa was neat to the point of obsessiveness. In these close quarters, their twenty-seven-year friendship began to fray.

"I dare say most marriages would flounder under similar conditions," said Caracappa's lawyer, Daniel Nobel.

23

JUSTICE FULFILLED

THE LONG, TANGLED STORY OF EPPOLITO AND CARA-
cappa was told, and told again, even before it reached its ending. Book publishers pitched it to readers as both the darkest case of police corruption in New York history and an account of the Mafia's lurid death throes. William Oldham, the Eastern District investigator, was the first to tell it. In November 2006, he teamed with reporter Guy Lawson to publish *The Brotherhoods: The True Story of Two Cops Who Murdered for the Mafia.*

Detective Tommy Dades and Assistant District Attorney Mike Vecchione published their version, *Friends of the Family,* three years later, with movie rights sold to Warner Brothers. Eppolito himself was said to be writing a sequel to his memoir, *Mafia Cop,* though it never materialized. Seven years after *The Sopranos* first aired, Mafia nostalgia persisted. Everyone loved the bad old days.

Meanwhile, Eppolito and Caracappa lived in judicial limbo, acquitted but imprisoned in a shared cell while prosecutors appealed Weinstein's decision. "Mr. Eppolito and Mr. Caracappa now inhabit a strange piece of legal real estate," wrote Alan Feuer, who covered the proceedings for *The New York Times,* "one which might be labeled 'guilty but acquitted.'"

The waiting wore on the defendants. They spent months confined to their cell, with intermittent breaks for outdoor exercise. When an Associated Press reporter requested an interview, Eppolito responded with a two-page letter written in block letters objecting to Judge Weinstein's decision to deny bail. "As you know, this case was overturned by the judge, yet we linger in solitary confinement."

He blamed the press: "We were both crucified with each and every story that was written. It was proven to me by the press that they are not after the truth, but only to sell their newspapers with lies made to make us look like corrupt dirty cops, who were more like monsters than good family men which we are."

Eppolito supposedly shed a hundred pounds from his three-hundred-pound frame eating what Fran called "the incarceration diet." He was, she said, "thinner than when I married him." He now looked like a sad-eyed hound, with his once-rounded jowls drooping and his chin peppered with white stubble.

Even if the Court of Appeals affirmed Judge Weinstein's decision to toss the conviction, Eppolito and Caracappa would still face a federal drug trial in Las Vegas, where their discussion of the meth sale, and the transaction itself, were captured on audio- and videotape. The drug charges alone could send them to prison for ten years.

Lastly, if the acquittal held, the Brooklyn DA could still file state murder charges. If the murder charges reverted to the state, they would carry a measure of vindication for Assistant DA Mike Vecchione, who had reluctantly ceded the case to the federal prosecutors in the Eastern District. "I remember [Brooklyn District Attorney Charles Hynes] calling me and saying, well, now the case is yours," said Vecchione. "So we started to get ready. I delved back into material I hadn't touched in a long while."

However, murder charges were still only a possibility. They could not be filed until the Court of Appeals ruled on Weinstein's decision to overturn the convictions. The appeal had a round-two feeling, like an overtime period played to settle a deadlock.

At the hearing, held on October 18, 2007, the three-judge panel gave the two defense attorneys ten minutes each to convince them that Judge Weinstein was right, that the statute of limitations had expired. Mitra Hormozi got twenty minutes to argue the opposite: that the government had not overreached, and that the judges should reinstate the convictions.

"I will be praying for my husband," said Monica Caracappa. "I'm flabbergasted that no one has sympathy."

Monica's prayers appeared to pay off. At first the judges seemed skeptical of the government's case, pressing Hormozi about the statute of limitations and how the prosecution team defined an ongoing criminal enterprise. What linked the criminal behavior in Brooklyn and Las Vegas, Hormozi argued, was the desire for an easy illegal payoff and the inclination to keep their moneymaking secret. The judges expressed doubt. "I don't see the relationship of what getting designer drugs to impress a client has to do with the dreadful things they were doing in the 1980s," said Judge Robert Sack.

Not surprisingly, Eppolito's lawyer agreed. Bondy asserted that the drug sale and money were "completely sporadic disparate acts utterly unconnected to the New York acts."

The Court of Appeals for the Second Circuit took almost a year to pick over the complexities of the statute of limitations and reach a unanimous decision. In the meantime, Eppolito and his wife, Fran, resolved a charge of income-tax evasion based on their bogus 2000 filing. On February 5, 2008, they pleaded guilty in Las Vegas.

The United States v. Eppolito and Caracappa saved its biggest surprise for last. On September 17, the Court of Appeals reinstated the original convictions. For the second time, the two men were found guilty. More than three years after their arrest at the entrance of Piero's restaurant, their fate was now settled: they would go to prison after all, and for life.

In a seventy-page opinion, Judge Amalya L. Kearse called Judge Weinstein's interpretation of the statute of limitations too restrictive, saying the conspiracy continued years past the March 2000 cutoff. She noted that Eppolito gave Kaplan his pager number after moving to Las Vegas, an indication that he and Caracappa hoped to keep working for the Lucchese family. The two men, she wrote, "received money for each crime in New York, and they broke the law for money in Las Vegas." In each city their methods were "sufficiently similar in purpose." The Court of Appeals therefore reinstated the convictions.

The *New York Daily News* announced the reversal with the headline: "These Two Mafia Cops Will Rot in Jail."

Bondy said that he might appeal to the Supreme Court. Eppolito's unsinkable daughter Andrea declared the family's intention to fight on. "This isn't over," she said. "We're not done. My father's not done." The Court of Appeals' ruling nonetheless rang with finality. "Thank God a small measure of justice has been restored for the families of the victims," said Robert Henoch, the lead prosecutor, who had moved on to private practice.

Of the Eppolito and Caracappa families in attendance, only Lou Jr. seemed to accept the final verdict. "My father and Steve made a choice," he said, "and they will have to live with it."

After all the twists and turns, the testimony about missing bodies, mothers speaking for murdered sons, celebrity lawyers threatened by a judge, a beautiful daughter feeding reporters words of defiance, an exonerated convict shouting from the gallery, a conviction erased and restored, the case had reached its final chapter.

It was all over now except for the formality of a second sentencing back in Judge Weinstein's courtroom. At 2 P.M. on March 6, 2009, marshals escorted Eppolito and Caracappa into a tenth-floor courtroom through a side door. They appeared wan and hollow-eyed in baggy prison outfits. "They looked," wrote Jim Dwyer in a front-page story for *The New York Times,* "as if they had been shipwrecked." They had spent more than thirty-six months in lockdown waiting for a final resolution. Caracappa had asked to be excused from the hearing. Judge Weinstein required him to attend.

As at the first sentencing, almost three years earlier, family members rose to say their parting piece. "Twenty years ago these two lowlifes shot and killed my father," said Eddie Lino's son, Vincent. "May you have a long life in jail." Before returning to his seat he turned to them and said one word: "Rot."

Israel Greenwald's daughter Yael Perlman spoke directly to her father: "Daddy, I cannot even bring myself to imagine the anguish that you must have felt in your final moments of life, when you were kneeling in front of your murderers, these convicts in this court, with a plastic bag over your head, tied with your own tie. Your heart must have been screaming out from under that plastic bag, 'My children, my children, my wife, my parents.'"

Barry Gibbs, who had disrupted the first sentencing by shouting at Eppolito, now spoke in turn. "You are going to die every day in jail, Eppolito. Now you will know the hell you put me through. . . . They're going to love you in jail. And I'm going to love it too."

Finally, Judge Weinstein sentenced Eppolito to life in prison plus a hundred years with a $4.75 million fine; Caracappa received life plus eighty years and a $4.25 million fine. With that, Eppolito and Caracappa were led from the courtroom and into the federal penal system, never to return. All that remained were grief and anger.

Chief Investigator Joe Ponzi of the Brooklyn DA's office watched the sentencing from a back row reserved for law enforcement. Afterward, Jerry Capeci, the veteran organized crime reporter, showed Ponzi a press release issued by the US Attorney's Office that credited the FBI, DEA, and its own investigators and prosecutors—everyone but Ponzi and his associates in the Brooklyn DA's office.

Ponzi's colleague, the investigator Pat Lanigan, tried to make the best of the slight. "We don't need any pats on the back," he told Capeci. "We got paid to do a job, and we did it as best we could. And we're glad that Louie and Steve will be in prison for the rest of their lives."

Ponzi said nothing.

EPILOGUE

AS EPPOLITO AND CARACAPPA HEADED TO HIGH-security penitentiaries in Tucson, Arizona, and Butner, North Carolina, respectively, the key witnesses who testified against them faced their own legal reckonings.

On February 3, 2009, the US District Court of Connecticut sentenced Stephen Corso, the accountant who agreed to wear a wire, to a prison term of less than a year and ordered him to pay restitution of $5.4 million to his former clients in monthly installments of $4,000. His ex-wife, Beth Ann Corso, petitioned a federal judge to list her among Corso's victims and grant her a share of the disbursements. The judge refused.

After Corso's release, he chose not to enter the Witness Protection Program because, he said, he wanted to continue seeing his family. Instead of accepting government protection, he moved to Encinitas, California, and changed his name from Stephen P. Corso to Steven J. Corso. His accounting license was revoked. He had promised a federal judge that he would "never, ever" work as an accountant again. But in 2015, the Securities Exchange Commission accused him of providing accounting services to public companies, and companies hoping to go public, under his new name.

Burt Kaplan also earned a reprieve. Judge Weinstein reduced his twenty-seven-year prison sentence for drug trafficking to nine years, time already served. He spent the last three years of his life in an undisclosed location outside New York State. "I've been in a lot of jails," he said. "One is as bad as the other. The only advantage I have [in the Witness Protection Program] is there's less people." Kaplan died of prostate cancer in 2009. "The canary will sing no more," the *New York Post* announced in its death notice.

Jimmy Breslin, who loosely focused his 2009 book, *The Good Rat,* on Kaplan, suggested that Kaplan might have faked his death in order to escape adversaries on both sides of the law.

"Who says he's dead?" Breslin told *The Village Voice.* "I made a study of the man and I wouldn't believe him if he told me today was Wednesday. He might have a reason to want me not to know it was Thursday." If so, Kaplan's feigned death would be the latest in a lifelong series of dodges and trickery.

Eppolito and Caracappa's final sentencing brought a measure of resolution to those who had suffered. It also brought generous recompense. On June 3, 2010, New York City agreed to pay Barry Gibbs a $9.9 million settlement, the largest personal payout in city history. The deal came five days before jury selection was to begin in his $18 million civil rights lawsuit that claimed Eppolito "deliberately fabricated witness statements and police reports, withheld material, exculpatory evidence from prosecutors and intentionally failed to conduct an adequate investigation." He had already collected $1.9 million from New York State in a separate suit.

Gibbs was now sixty-two and battling colon cancer. He told the Associated Press that he planned to spend some of the money on medical bills and pay his three grandchildren's college tuition. "I had my freedom taken away from me and now I have it back," he said. "I'm going to live each day like it's my last." Gibbs died on March 23, 2018.

Meanwhile, the families of seven murder victims filed civil suits against the city for its failure to supervise and investigate Eppolito and Caracappa. For years the city tried to dismiss or delay the lawsuits. The proceedings moved so slowly that Mark Longo, a lawyer for Pauline Pipitone, the mother of Nicky Guido, accused the city's Law Department of stonewalling in hopes that she would die before a trial convened. "I've got a lady in her eighties here," he said. "The city really needs to step up."

The cases dragged on for so long that Pipitone made a direct appeal to Mayor Michael Bloomberg. "How could anyone believe that the city didn't know about how these detectives were operating," she wrote in a letter. "How they were using police information. How they were doing it over a long period of time and how they were being paid by crime people for the information only someone in their job could possibly have provided. It makes no sense to me and I am afraid that the delay that is caused while I am forced to wait for an appeals court to review the case again means that I won't be here to see justice done."

A federal district court allowed the seven families to consolidate their respective cases into one. In January 2009, a city lawyer deposed Pipitone. On page fifty-eight of the one-hundred-page transcript, he asked about the day her son was murdered as he sat in his Nissan outside the family home. Three pages later the transcript pauses, with the explanation: "witnesses crying."

"So he didn't make any sounds?" asked the city lawyer.

"What do you mean by 'sound?'" Pipitone answered. "He was dead."

On May 24, 2011, Hugh Mo, the former deputy police commissioner of trials, sat for a civil deposition hearing at Brooklyn Federal Court, where he declined to discuss the reasoning behind his 1985 decision to acquit Eppolito of Internal Affairs charges despite evidence that he had given a police file to Rosario Gambino, a mobster and heroin dealer. Backed by city lawyers, Mo argued that he was entitled to the same rights as a state or federal judge. "It is un-American as far as I'm concerned, for an adjudicating officer to go back and do a Monday morning quarterback," Mo said. But Nick Bustin, a lawyer for the Greenwald and DiLapi families, argued that Mo had no such rights, since he was acting not as a formal judge but as a police official presiding over a disciplinary proceeding. Bustin also asserted that Mo forfeited whatever privileges he might have by discussing the case with newspaper reporters and book authors.

For years the city tried to quash the lawsuit. The impasse broke in October 2014, when Judge Raymond J. Dearie of the Federal District Court in Brooklyn ruled the lawsuits could proceed, citing evidence that the killings would not have occurred had the NYPD fired or disciplined Eppolito after catching him sharing confidential police records. He said the NYPD's "inexplicable failure" to punish Eppolito likely emboldened him and Caracappa.

Judge Dearie also acknowledged a "systematic failure" to address corruption during Benjamin Ward's tenure as police commissioner in the late 1980s. He made reference to "powerful evidence" that the NYPD at that time "tolerated corruption to avoid bad publicity."

In the end, the city Law Department concluded that it was better to close the books on what might be its ugliest corruption case of all. In late January 2015, the city reached a $5 million settlement with Pauline Pipitone. "This tragic matter involves the murder of an innocent man," the Law Department said in a statement accompanying the settlement. "After evaluating all the facts, it was determined that settling the case was in the city's best interest."

Six months later, the city paid another $5 million to the family of Israel Greenwald. It settled for lesser amounts with the families of four other victims—Eddie Lino, Otto Heidel, Bobby Borriello, and James Bishop. In total, the city paid $18.4 million to settle seven lawsuits.

In June 2016, Caracappa petitioned Judge Weinstein for early release. "Please know I have been fighting the case in courts . . . I have stage 4 cancer and will not survive," he wrote by hand to the judge. "There is nothing I can do in your case," Judge Weinstein answered. Caracappa died ten months later at a medical detention center at age seventy-five.

Eppolito struggled with heart disease, but he outlived his former partner by more than two years. He died in his sleep on November 3, 2019, in a hospital near the Tucson penitentiary where he was serving a life sentence. He was seventy-one.

Gaspipe Casso, the psychopathic Lucchese underboss who sponsored the detectives' worst abuses—the fatal disclosures of police intelligence, abductions, and killings—never returned to Brooklyn. He spent twenty-six years in America's most secure prisons while sinking into ruinous ill health. In his last years, Casso suffered from prostate cancer, bladder disease, and pulmonary issues from a lifetime of smoking. In November 2020, in the thick of the pandemic, he contracted COVID-19 while housed in a high-security prison in Tucson. He died of complications from the virus on December 15.

AFTERWORD

TOMMY DADES LEFT HIS POST AS AN INVESTIGATOR
in the Brooklyn DA's office at the end of 2004, three months before
agents arrested Eppolito and Caracappa.

For the first time in twenty years he had no crime to puzzle out, no
informant to question, no clock to punch. Instead, he went to the Police
Athletic League gym in Staten Island five nights a week, from 5 to 8 P.M.,
to coach teenage boxers. "You're teaching them how to jump rope, how
to put gloves on, how to wrap their hands, how to hit the speed bag, and,
eventually, how to enter the ring for a slow pace of sparring."

Dades stepped into the ring himself for amateur bouts. He ended
his fifteen-year boxing career, a total of thirty-five fights, with a win in
a 2006 charity fight at the Sheraton Hotel in Manhattan against a taller,
heavier Los Angeles policeman. "After that I said, I can't do this anymore. I hurt all over."

His hiatus from policing did not last long. After three months, Mike
Vecchione and Joe Ponzi persuaded Dades to return to Jay Street to consult on a series of investigations in the rackets division. He worked from
an office down the hall from Vecchione and reported only to him. His
second chapter on Jay Street proved an imperfect arrangement. Dades
was accustomed to working with almost complete autonomy. As a detective first grade, he had earned the right to pursue cases as he saw
fit—in his own way, on his own hours. His post in the DA's office was
more political, and therefore hindering. After three years, Dades had

reached a personal terminus. He felt depleted and bereft—smothered by office maneuverings and grieving a recent divorce. He left the DA's office for the second and final time at the end of 2007.

Despite the media attention heaped on the federal agencies and assistant US attorneys who ultimately jailed Eppolito and Caracappa, Dades was the one who revived the case. For him, the outcome delivered gratification and bitterness in equal measure. "My whole life I went to work whistling," he said. "I went to work smiling. The police department saved my life. But in the end, I'd had it. I was physically and mentally exhausted. I came in on a Sunday and cleaned out my desk. I'd hit a point in my life where I just wanted to be left alone. So I disappeared for a while."

On the morning of April 23, 2022, Tommy Dades and DEA agent Frank Drew drove together to Joe Ponzi's funeral mass at Our Lady of Pity Roman Catholic Church on Staten Island. Ponzi had died five days earlier at age sixty-five. The service was a kind of reunion with old friends and acquaintances from all corners of law enforcement.

Ponzi had retired in 2014 after thirty-seven years as an investigator in the Brooklyn DA's office. It was the only job he ever held. In the quiet years before the onset of sickness, he bought a share in a racehorse, a thoroughbred named Sunset Louise, drank scotch with friends, smoked cigars, listened to Frank Sinatra, and played with his seven grandchildren.

Dades often called Ponzi his best friend, though he may have been more like a devoted older brother and guiding spirit—a figure of steady integrity and grace. "Joe broke a thousand hearts when he passed away," Dades said. "Every time I fell down in the sewer he picked me up."

Dades, now sixty-two, lives alone on a quiet suburban street outside New York with his dog, Skip, whom he named for Idrissa "Skip" Karama, a boxing protégé who won a Golden Gloves championship and later died of cardiac arrhythmia at age twenty-one. Dades keeps company, as well, with a full house of unsettled memories.

"If you hold things in for a long time, at some point in your life they're going to come out," he said. "I've been through a lot of sad things and I've gotten through them. I've adapted. I've thrown it all up in the sky and prayed."

Dades talks by phone almost daily with the men he worked with—Frank Drew, Phil Grimaldi, Mike Vecchione, and others. Even in the ease of retirement, they succumbed to the pull of unsolved cases. Like an old band on a reunion tour, they lent their expertise to an NYPD detective in charge of cold cases until he too retired.

They focused in particular on the unsolved case of the body that Frankie Steel Pontillo, the Colombo associate, saw Eppolito and Caracappa transporting to a hole they had dug in the no-man's-land between the Belt Parkway and Gravesend Bay when he wandered out at 3 A.M. to test-fire his new Glock. Dades first learned of the episode when he met Pontillo at a barbecue, and he found that his friend Detective Phil Grimaldi was working on the case. "I said, 'Wait, wait, Tommy,'" Grimaldi said. "'That's the homicide I'm always telling you about.'"

By their count, the murder would be the fifteenth involving Eppolito and Caracappa in some capacity. "If we were still on the job," Drew said, "we'd solve that case."

ACKNOWLEDGMENTS

Every book project is like a galley ship lined with oar pullers. I'm indebted to all those who pulled alongside me.

The deepest of bows to my exceptional editor Charles Spicer. Thank you for your staunch support and friendship.

I'm obliged, as always, to Joy Harris for her advice and advocacy.

I want to express particular gratitude to Tommy Dades and Frank Drew, who pulled back the curtain on a dark world I could otherwise not know and helped me to understand its strange doings, at least a little. They fielded endless calls, texts, and emails with great patience and good humor.

Thank you to Sara Thwait for making me look better than I deserve. And to Elisabeth Cannell for her incisive comments.

I extend heartiest thanks to all the excellent people of St. Martin's Press, especially Andrew Martin, David Rotstein, Hector DeJean, and Hannah Pierdolla.

Thanks, too, to Crary Pullen, Gary Nadeau, and Noah Shulman for telling the story in pictures. And to Jonathan Liss for making it sing online. Michael Weschler, you as well.

I tip my hat to those who facilitate the critical job of research: the cheerful staff of the Vartan Gregorian Center for Research in the Humanities at the New York Public Library, which put me up in the greatest of workspaces, and MuckRock, an unsung group devoted to helping the uninitiated navigate the FOIA process. I wish to extend my thanks, as well, to T. McElwee, who cast a light in the shadows on my behalf.

A number of retired detectives and agents kindly shared recollections. Thank you to Elaine Banar, Tony Casullo, Patrick Colgan, Eileen Dinnan, Bill Flack, Mike Foldesi, Phil Grimaldi, Bobby Intartaglio, Jim Kossler, Pat Lanigan, Kenny Luzak, Robert Marston, Joe Piraino, Frank Pergola, Kevin Sheehan, Lewis Schiliro, and Chuck Siriano, among others.

I would like to thank, as well, former prosecutors and defense lawyers who took the trouble to explain this story's legal entanglements: Tim Bakken, Judd Burstein, Robert Henoch, Mitra Hormozi, Rae Koshetz, Hugh Mo, Greg O'Connell, Vanessa Potkin (and her sister Zoe), Mike Vecchione, and Andrew Weissmann.

Lastly, a parting word of appreciation to my late father, Peter Cannell, who urged me to write about gangsters.

NOTES

1. A HOMECOMING

6 *I'd get smacked for looking*: Louis Eppolito, *Mafia Cop* (New York: Simon & Schuster, 1992), 41.

7 *I guess my father despised them*: Ibid., 102.

7 *You better head inside fast*: Ibid., 119.

8 *They all told me I'm crazy*: "Mafia Cops Interview," *Sally Jessy Raphael*, May 2, 1992.

8 *Hey, Louie*: Eppolito, *Mafia Cop*, 129.

8 *We broke their hands*: Ibid., 172.

9 *a reputation for quick thinking*: Cass Vanzi, "Decoy Cops Dress the Part to Protect Aged & Infirm," *New York Daily News*, February 21, 1977.

9 *I wasn't ignorant of the fact*: Eppolito, *Mafia Cop*, 180.

9 *In my mind I was being promoted*: Ibid.

9 *He was always telling crazy stories*: Author interview with Phil Grimaldi, December 8, 1992.

9 *The public will never understand the mentality*: Eppolito, *Mafia Cop*, 191.

10 *He was a tall guy, muscular*: Author interview with Frank Pergola, March 27, 2023.

10 *He was sort of bragging about it*: Author interview with Phil Grimaldi, December 8, 1992.

10 *It was known in the neighborhood*: Author interview with Phil Grimaldi, December 8, 1992.

10 *Oh? What does he look like*: Author interview with Frank Pergola, March 27, 2023.

11 *I figured who was it going to hurt*: Eppolito, *Mafia Cop*, 134.

11 *Suddenly this warm feeling kind of*: Ibid., 197.

12 *Take the kids on vacation*: Ibid.

12 *I almost drove off the highway*: Ibid.

14 *It's going to be very bad for us*: Ibid., 25.

16 *a collective derangement*: "Brooklyn Butchers," *New York Daily News*, September 20, 1992.

18 *I was somewhat overwhelmed knowing*: Eppolito, *Mafia Cop*, 15.

18 *I knew in Louie's mind*: Ibid., 17.

19 *Eppolito was wailing*: Author interview with Joe Piraino, August 10, 2022.

19 *It was nothing I hadn't seen before*: Eppolito, *Mafia Cop*, 28.

19 *Uncle Jimmy's face was just absolutely*: Ibid., 29.

19 *From that moment, I knew*: Ibid., 30.

21 *I felt like I was home*: Ibid., 214.

2. THE SIDEKICK

23 *They looked like Mutt and Jeff*: Author interview with Frank Pergola, March 27, 2023.

24 *He never asked me for anything*: Ibid.

25 *You know I can help your husband*: Patrick Gallahue, "Mafia Cop Raped Me, Gal Says—Drug-Bust Wife's Shocking Claim," *New York Post*, April 17, 2006.

25 *He put me on the bed and took my pants off*: Ibid.

25 *if you say anything*: Ibid.

3. THE GAMBINO FILE

27 *They'd shoot them in his district*: Eppolito, *Mafia Cop*, 237.

27 *Of course, it didn't help*: Ibid., 239.

27 *Only simple fear will deter*: "A New John Guido for the Police," *New York Times*, June 20, 1992.

28 *They'd hauled out the big guns*: Eppolito, *Mafia Cop*, 240.

30 *I just want to get this clear*: Ibid., 243.

30 *Alright, Detective . . . how do you explain*: Ibid., 244.

31 *He says it like we're all supposed to*: Ibid., 249.

31 *Okay, did you make copies of that material?*: Ibid.

31 *Detective, I have one more question*: Ibid., 244.

32 *Let me tell you something*: Ibid., 246.

33 *At that time I lost my stomach*: *Anger,* directed by Maxi Cohen (Maxi Cohen Studio, 1986), https://www.maxicohenstudio.com/anger.

33 *I knew that my life as I had known it*: Eppolito, *Mafia Cop*, 284.

34 *I figured by the time I got back*: Ibid., 264.

34 *I never asked them for a favor*: Greg B. Smith, "Secret Mob Cop Tapes," *New York Daily News,* July 17, 2005.

34 *When the take came in I had to laugh*: Eppolito, *Mafia Cop*, 284.

35 *Once in a while police officers came*: Author interview with Hugh Mo, April 26, 2022.

35 *I was astonished to see what information*: Author interview with William Flack, January 21, 2023.

35 *As the hearing unfolded it became*: Author interview with Hugh Mo, April 26, 2022.

36 *failed to substantiate those charges*: Eppolito, *Mafia Cop*, 307.

36 *I have read newspaper articles*: Ibid., 308.

36 *cannot speculate as to how those documents*: William K. Rashbaum, "Officer in Murder Case Got Benefit of Doubt in '85," *New York Times*, March 23, 2005.

37 *was no evidence before me other than that*: "Detective Cleared of Leaking Secrets," *New York Daily News,* April 21, 1985.

37 *As if I had anything to do with it*: Author interview with Hugh Mo, April 26, 2022.

38 *Who knows?*: Author interview with Mike Vecchione, December 14, 2020.

39 *I've been in seven gun battles*: Cohen, *Anger.*

39 *I lost my guts*: Ibid.

4. FRAMED

40 *I had great rapport with*: "Barry Gibbs," *The Leonard Lopate Show*, NPR, December 29, 2005.

41 *big nose, baggy face*: United States v. Louis Eppolito and Stephen Caracappa, 436 F. Supp. 2d 532 (EDNY, 2006).

41 *She was looking straight out at Jamaica Bay*: Ibid.

41 *I was transfixed*: Ibid.

41 *He got up and ran around the car*: Ibid.

42 *The teller said*: Ibid.

42 *I could have gone home*: Murray Weiss, "Marine Tells How 'Mafia' Cop Forced Him to Frame an Innocent Man for Slay," *New York Post*, October 4, 2005.

42 *just ignored everything I said*: Ibid.

43 *He started talking like a mob guy*: Ibid.

44 *I got thrown against the car*: Barry Gibbs, "The Moth Presents Barry Gibbs: Exonerated," *The Moth*, July 5, 2010, https://themoth.org/stories/exonerated.

44 *He says, 'You know who that is'*: Ibid.

44 *An innocent man has nothing to hide*: Ibid.

44 *But on the fourth or fifth question*: Author interview with Tim Bakken, March 3, 2023.

45 *He asked me if I heard what they said*: Gibbs, "The Moth Presents Barry Gibbs: Exonerated."

45 *We walk through the entranceway*: Ibid.

45 *New York is a particularly problematic*: Author interview with Vanessa Potkin, February 22, 2023.

46 *They called police departments*: Author interview with Vanessa Potkin, February 22, 2023.

46 *He kept calling us*: Author interview with Vanessa Potkin, February 22, 2023.

46 *Ultimately we just couldn't find*: Author interview with Vanessa Potkin, February 22, 2023.

5. A SILENT PARTNER

47 *I drove by myself*: United States v. Eppolito and Caracappa.

48 *He asked if I would go with him*: Ibid.

49 *We bought sweatshirts from China*: Ibid.

51 *Nobody could touch him*: Author interview with an anonymous source, June 28, 2023.

51 *I would just stop and knock*: Author interview with Patrick Colgan, August 2, 2023.

51 *We laughed and had a few jokes*: Author interview with Patrick Colgan, August 2, 2023.

52 *so she could get him out of jail*: Susan Edelman, "The Mafia Princess Who Became a NYC Judge," *New York Post*, May 22, 2005.

53 *I'm a doer*: United States v. Eppolito and Caracappa.

53 *We made some Quaalude moves*: Ibid.

54 *business on the side if the price was right*: Jerry Capeci, "Why the 'Mafia Cop' Was Sweating Bullets," *New York Sun*, March 17, 2005.

54 *Frankie approached me and said that*: United States v. Eppolito and Caracappa.

54 *had any serious problem*: Ibid.

54 *that they were good stand-up guys*: Ibid.

54 *didn't want to do business with any cops*: Ibid.

55 *At the time of my daughter's wedding*: Zach Haberman, "Judge-Daughter Sings Blues over Dad's Wedded Diss," *New York Post,* March 17, 2006.

56 *or he would be sorry*: United States v. Eppolito and Caracappa.

56 *I was not certain whether to believe him*: Ibid.

56 *We let the whole situation cool down*: Ibid.

58 *I turned the light on*: Ibid.

58 *Frankie told me that I got to help*: Ibid.

58 *I was afraid that*: Ibid.

59 *no one would believe me*: Ibid.

59 *Whatever I knew*: Ibid.

60 *We didn't know quite what*: Ibid.

60 *He was a very good man*: William K. Rashbaum, "Identity of Skeleton Is Linked to Mob Case," *New York Times,* April 15, 2005.

60 *As a child, I never felt normal*: Anthony M. Destefano, "A Lingering Loss," *Newsday,* June 4, 2006.

60 *They came home from school*: Ibid.

6. RICO RISING

62 *That's why so many of us Vietnam*: Howard Blum, *Gangland: How the FBI Broke the Mob* (New York: Simon & Schuster, 1993), 32.

62 *Here was the real problem with the Hoover system*: Ibid., 31.

62 *It was a week of spending time*: *Fear City: New York vs The Mafia,* Episode 1, dir. Sam Hobkinson, Netflix.

63 *Instead of going after*: Jules Bonavolonta and Brian Duffy, *The Good Guys: How We Turned the FBI 'Round—and Finally Broke the Mob* (New York: Simon & Schuster, 1996), 80.

64 *What about Big Boy?*: Gregory J. Wallance, "Outgunning the Mob," *ABA Journal,* March 1994.

64 *To me, it was an epiphany*: Author interview with Jim Kossler, September 28, 2023.

66 *I'm a professional*: Steve Wick, "Used and Left Unprotected," *Newsday,* December 23, 2001.

69 *We had RICO for almost ten years*: Selwyn Raab, "Curbing Mob Chiefs," *New York Times,* February 27, 1985

70 *It's about time law enforcement*: Wayne Barrett and Adam Fifield, *Rudy! An Investigative Biography of Rudolph Giuliani* (New York: Basic Books, 2000), 146.

70 *This is a great day for law enforcement*: Raab, "Curbing Mob Chiefs."

70 *Our aim is to try to destroy*: Ibid.

70 *a sort of Waterloo for the New York mob*: Alan Feuer, "Anthony Corallo, Mob Boss, Dies in Federal Prison at 87," *New York Times,* September 1, 2000.

7. THE BOTCHED HIT

72 *All of the families are in a state*: Selwyn Raab, "One of Mafia's Brutal Leaders Continues to Elude Police," *Scranton Times-Tribune,* November 29, 1992.

73 *They have a ceremony with the boss*: US Congress, Senate, Hearing Before the Permanent Subcommittee on Investigations, May 15, 1996.

74 *Gaspipe was the brains*: Selwyn Raab, "Most Ruthless Mafia Leader Left," *New York Times,* November 28, 1992.

76 *The shots rang out in the night*: Sammy Gravano, "Killing Paul," *Our Thing* (podcast), August 2021, http://tinyurl.com/mr3n4mar.

77 *They hated each other*: Author interview with Sammy Gravano, September 18, 2023.

78 *was a sweetheart*: Author interview with Lizzie Hydell, July 16, 2022.

78 *He gave her whatever she wanted*: Author interview with Lizzie Hydell, July 16, 2022.

78 *She liked to go out with a lot of guys*: Author interview with Lizzie Hydell, July 16, 2022.

81 *Jesus H. Christ, what happened?*: Philip Carlo, *Gaspipe: Confessions of a Mafia Boss* (New York: William Morrow, 2008), 161.

81 *He's not cooperating*: Franklin Fisher, "Hit Try Suspected in B'klyn Shooting," *New York Daily News*, September 15, 1986.

81 *I told Casso that my friend*: United States v. Eppolito and Caracappa.

82 *had done something for [Kaplan]*: Ibid.

82 *I opened [the envelope] and looked inside*: Ibid.

82 *a gift from my cousin and his partner*: Ibid.

83 *asked me to call my friends to see if they can arrest*: Ibid.

83 *They tried to grab me*: Tommy Dades, Mike Vecchione, and David Fisher, *Friends of the Family: The Inside Story of the Mafia Cops Case* (New York: William Morrow, 2009), 33.

83 *We just thought Jimmy did something*: Author interview with Lizzie Hydell, July 16, 2022.

83 *I pulled up right next to them*: Dades et al., *Friends of the Family*, 33.

84 *I asked who they were*: Ibid.

84 *Jimmy knew something was up*: Author interview with Lizzie Hydell, July 16, 2022.

86 *The kid saw me and he knew*: 60 Minutes, aired April 11, 2005.

86 *I was in somebody's house*: Ibid.

86 *I wanted to know why I was shot*: Ibid.

87 *We thought maybe he was just*: Author interview with Lizzie Hydell, July 16, 2022.

87 *He never did that before*: Author interview with Lizzie Hydell, July 16, 2022.

87 *I just assumed they were undercover*: United States v. Eppolito and Caracappa.

8. A TIME OF DISORDER

89 *This has been the Mafia's worst*: Robert D. McFadden, "The Mafia of the 1980s: Divided and Under Siege," *New York Times*, March 11, 1987.

89 *This is the twilight of the mob*: Bob Drogin, "8 Mob Leaders Guilty; Hailed as Blow to Mafia," *Los Angeles Times*, November 20, 1986.

90 *He was going through a nasty*: Author interview with Chuck Siriano, August 9, 2022.

90 *We arranged for Steve to meet*: Author interview with Chuck Siriano, August 9, 2022.

91 *Caracappa was very well-connected*: Author interview with Chuck Siriano, August 9, 2022.

91 *If I came in early*: Author interview with Joe Piraino, July 20, 2022.

92 *Even though he wasn't the boss*: Author interview with Joe Piraino, July 20, 2022.

92 *She sounded cute*: Author interview with Chuck Siriano, August 9, 2022.

92 *How could you let [Casso] live?*: Jerry Capeci, "Move Backfires on Anti-Mob Force," *New York Daily News*, November 14, 1989.

93 *I would have drove the car*: Ibid.

94 *a beautiful, hardworking kid*: Denis Hamill, "A Victim's Ghost Haunts 2 Accused," *New York Daily News*, March 19, 2006.

94 *He was sitting at the wheel*: United States v. Eppolito and Caracappa.

95 *They tell me that there is no word*: Pauline Pipitone, "She Lost Innocent Son in Botched-Rubout Tragedy," *New York Daily News*, July 3, 2006.

95 *There was always gossip*: John Marzulli, "Make 'Em Pay for It," *New York Daily News*, March 12, 2005.

95 *She used to say*: Ibid.

95 *Hey, it's a mistake*: Selwyn Raab, *Five Families: The Rise, Decline, and Resurgence of America's Most Powerful Mafia Empires* (New York: Thomas Dunne Books, 2005), 484.

96 *It was like hitting the lotto*: Author interview with Marvin Tolly, May 3, 2023.

97 *We told Bering*: Author interview with Marvin Tolly, May 3, 2023.

97 *Gaspipe will put me on a table*: "Mafioso: Cops In on Mob Hit," *New York Daily News*, May 2, 1995.

97 *Sure enough, he shows up*: Author interview with Larry Holland, August 24, 2023.

98 *looked like he'd seen a ghost*: Author interview with Larry Holland, August 24, 2023.

98 *It wasn't a home run*: Author interview with Larry Holland, August 24, 2023.

98 *They followed Gravano*: United States v. Eppolito and Caracappa.

98 *came up to them in a car*: Ibid.

100 *They were sitting in the first booth*: Ibid.

100 *Louie says, 'I'm pretty sure'*: Ibid.

100 *give you everything that we get*: Ibid.

100 *I didn't know his name*: Ibid.

101 *I would come down the block*: Ibid.

101 *one of the goals of the relationship*: Ibid.

103 *I was in regular contact with him*: Author interview with Patrick Colgan, April 27, 2002.

103 *The next day, law enforcement*: United States v. Eppolito and Caracappa.

104 *They arrived with enough food*: Guy Lawson and William Oldham, *The Brotherhoods: The True Story of Two Cops Who Murdered for the Mafia* (New York: Scribner, 2006), 88.

104 *He brought me information*: Author interview with Patrick Colgan, April 27, 2002.

104 *By FBI policy, he absolutely had*: Author interview with Patrick Colgan, April 27, 2022.

105 *I think you're a stool pigeon*: Lawson and Oldham, *The Brotherhoods*.

105 *I told him exactly what happened*: United States v. Eppolito and Caracappa.

106 *No matter what time of day I went*: Ibid.

106 *This will prove that I was right*: Ibid.

106 *I would sit around in a three-piece suit*: Author interview with Chuck Siriano, September 6, 2022.

107 *I worked alone*: Author interview with Chuck Siriano, September 6, 2022.

107 *I had friends all over the city*: Author interview with Chuck Siriano, September 6, 2022.

107 *So he knew he was going away*: Author interview with Chuck Siriano, September 6, 2022.

107 *I never met a safe I couldn't crack*: Larry Oakes, "A Mobster Turned Informer Exposed on the Iron Range," *Minneapolis Star-Tribune*, August 15, 1993.

108 *He was working under the impression*: Author interview with Chuck Siriano, September 6, 2022.

108 *We decided to let the burglary go down*: Author interview with Chuck Siriano, September 6, 2022.

108 *Al asked if I knew a guy*: Author interview with Chuck Siriano, September 6, 2022.

109 *They broke my skull in half*: Author interview with Chuck Siriano, September 6, 2022.

109 *When Dominick got shot*: Author interview with Chuck Siriano, September 6, 2022.

109 *His body was like soup*: Author interview with Chuck Siriano, September 6, 2022.

109 *I said there's a leak someplace*: Author interview with Chuck Siriano, September 6, 2022.

109 *One night I was sitting there*: Author interview with Chuck Siriano, September 6, 2022.

110 *I wanted nothing to go*: Author interview with Chuck Siriano, September 6, 2022.

110 *It really pissed Steve off*: Author interview with Chuck Siriano, September 6, 2022.

111 *The banks are just on their*: Jerry Capeci, "Once & Always, a Real Good Yegg," *New York Daily News,* September 29, 1993.

112 *go get that fat bastard*: Ibid.

112 *I took [Chiodo] down in the back*: United States v. Eppolito and Caracappa.

112 *He stood there and he was looking*: Ibid.

112 *For the most part the investigation*: Ibid.

113 *We can't let these guys walk around*: Ibid.

114 *I've been shot*: Ibid.

114 *I'm going to pass out*: Ibid.

115 *helping the FBI. So, you know*: Thom L. Jones, "The Evil That Men Do: The Killing of Robert Kubecka & Donald Barstow," Gangsters Inc., December 2, 2010, https://gangstersinc.org/profiles/blogs/the-evil-that-men-do-the.

117 *I started mowing weeds*: Author interview with Frank Pontillo, January 8, 2023.

117 *I drove slowly, really slowly*: Author interview with Frank Pontillo, January 8, 2023.

118 *In the corner of my eye I see him*: Author interview with Frank Pontillo, January 8, 2023.

118 *I looked like I was escaping*: Author interview with Frank Pontillo, January 8, 2023.

119 *I'm saying to myself*: Author interview with Frank Pontillo, January 8, 2023.

120 *extraordinarily accurate*: Tom Robbins, "Paint Removal," *New York Daily News,* September 6, 1992.

120 *It appears the killers knew he had a routine*: Jack Newfield and Kevin McCoy, "Ex-Union Big Was Stalked, Say Probers," *New York Daily News,* May 23, 1990.

121 *You couldn't help but feel*: John Connolly and Howard Blum, "Hit Men in Blue?," *Vanity Fair,* September 13, 2005.

121 *When we started throwing pictures*: Author interview with Frank Pergola, December 5, 2022.

122 *a safe place that nobody would know about*: Author interview with Frank Pergola, December 5, 2022.

122 *They said get out of there*: Author interview with Frank Pergola, December 5, 2022.

123 *He must have called somebody*: Author interview with Frank Pergola, December 5, 2022.

124 *three floors of mob chic*: Tom Robbins, "Absentee Owner," *New York Daily News,* July 19, 1992.

125 *always around my neighborhood*: Tom Robbins and Jerry Capeci, "Mob Boss Who Inspired Other Infamous Turncoats Dies in Witness Protection," *New York Post,* March 28, 2019.

126 *He told me, 'I'll see you'*: Selwyn Raab, "'Most Ruthless Mafia Leader Left'; Leader on the Lam Runs the Lucchese Family, Agents Say," *New York Times,* November 28, 1992.

126 *I feel terrific*: Dave Von Drehle, "15 Arrested in Alleged Plot to Rig Window-Repair Prices," *Miami Herald,* May 31, 1990.

127 *The mafia is not the entrenched*: Ruben Rosario and Jerry Capeci, "Mob Takes a Big Hit over City Contracts," *New York Daily News,* May 31, 1990.

9. GASPIPE IN EXILE

129 *Most all men in my life*: Carlo, *Gaspipe*, 185.

130 *I used to accumulate the money*: Frances McMorris, "Canary Tells of Amuso's 'Flight' Pay," *New York Daily News*, May 29, 1992.

130 *I'll be able to come home*: Gene Mustain Jerry Capeci, "For Gaspipe, No Silence on the Lam," *New York Daily News*, January 21, 1993.

130 *begged to be able to see his daughter*: Dan Mangan, "Gruesome Tale of Mob 'Canary' Killer," *New York Post*, January 13, 2004.

132 *I've got good news*: United States v. Eppolito and Caracappa.

132 *I was talking to Steve and I said*: Author interview with Chuck Siriano, September 7, 2023.

133 *He showed up alone*: Murray Weiss, "Mob Cops' Role in Hit on Gotti's Chauffeur," *New York Post*, June 13, 2006.

133 *next to the car, all full of blood*: Ibid.

134 *care for our brother Bobby*: Associated Press, "Funeral for Gotti's Chauffeur Revives Image of Past Era," *Elmira Star-Gazette*, April 19, 1991.

134 *You talk, you die*: Ibid.

134 *the fattest guy in world mafia history*: Jimmy Breslin, "Fattest Guy in the Mafia Sings His Song," *San Francisco Examiner*, September 22, 1991.

135 *You should feel the breeze*: Ibid.

135 *I happened to see the man*: Tom Wrobleski, "Mobster 'Fat Pete' Chiodo Is Shot 12 times but Lives as Mafia Assassination Goes Awry on Staten Island in 1991," *Staten Island Advance*, May 10, 2023.

135 *While I lay in a hospital bed*: Andrea Kanapell and Jay Maeder, "I Squealed to Spare My Wife," *New York Daily News*, September 17, 1991.

136 *I could go for a slice*: Ernest Volkman, *Gangbusters: The Destruction of America's Last Great Mafia Dynasty* (Boston: Faber and Faber, 1998), 260.

136 *I'm really dizzy, your honor*: Arnold H. Lubasch, "Mafia Captain Is Prosecution Witness," *New York Times*, September 12, 1991.

137 *last desperate acts*: James Bennet, "Sister of a Mob Informant Is Shot, Apparently as Mafia Vengeance," *New York Times*, March 11, 1992.

138 *I knew something was wrong*: United States v. Amuso, 21 F.3d 1251 (2d Cir. 1994).

138 *I'm leaving*: Ibid.

139 *That's it*: Associated Press, "From Mob Boss to Ruinous Informant," (Sioux Falls) *Argus-Leader*, May 28, 2006.

139 *I'm an hour away*: Author interview with Robert Marston, April 13, 2023.

139 *I tried just to be a good listener*: Author interview with Robert Marston, April 13, 2023.

140 *I didn't look in their bags*: Author interview with Robert Marston, April 13, 2023.

141 *I'm going to tell you what I know*: Volkman, *Gangbusters*, 3.

141 *Usually the answer was*: Author interview with Robert Marston, April 13, 2023.

141 *When guys from our crew*: Author interview with Robert Marston, April 13, 2023.

143 *Yes, I am*: Associated Press, "Final Arguments Scheduled in Murder Trial," *Akron Beacon-Journal*, June 11, 1992.

143 *There's been an injustice done*: Frances McMorris, "Quiet Goes Don, Not Kin," *New York Daily News*, October 10, 1992.

144 *We're getting closer*: Jerry Capeci, "Amuso Gave Mob Bad Name," *New York Daily News*, June 16, 1992.

10. OPERATION GANGPLANK

146 *Freddy was a nobody selling nickel*: Author interview with a DEA agent, April 22, 2023.

149 *Take what you need*: Frank Drew, Memo, "Puglisi Narrative in Chronological Order 1988–2020."

149 *Not that one*: Author interview with a DEA agent, April 22, 2023.

150 *You're sitting on a slight incline*: Author interview with Frank Drew, April 22, 2023.

151 *Frank had surveillance expertise*: Author interview with Mike Foldesi, May 17, 2023.

151 *We knew their regimens*: Author interview with Frank Drew, April 26, 2023.

152 *Silvestri stood on a little landing*: Author interview with Frank Drew, April 26, 2023.

152 *I hated those windows*: Author interview with Frank Drew, April 26, 2023.

152 *I knew he was into softball*: Author interview with Frank Drew, April 22, 2023.

153 *I wish you had*: Author interview with Frank Drew, April 22, 2023.

153 *Whatever they got they relayed*: Author interview with Frank Drew, April 22, 2023.

155 *Agents quickly realized*: Drew, "Puglisi Narrative in Chronological Order 1988–2020."

155 *We had no idea who this guy was*: Author interview with Frank Drew, July 8, 2022.

156 *The old man was Burt Kaplan*: Author interview with Frank Drew, July 8, 2022.

156 *Don't use that cell phone anymore*: Drew, "Puglisi Narrative in Chronological Order 1988–2020."

156 *Did you get rid of that cell phone?*: Ibid.

157 *We knew you were coming*: Ibid.

159 *The [Puglisi] case was major news*: Author interview with Frank Drew, May 24, 2023.

159 *smelled like a combination of antifreeze*: Andrea Giovino, *Divorced from the Mob: My Journey from Organized Crime to Independent Woman* (New York: Carroll & Graf, 2004), 1.

159 *addicted to the kind of high*: Ibid., 70.

159 *The bigger the criminals*: Andrea Giovino, "The Real Mob Wife—Andrea Giovino," *GlamMir*, August 18, 2017 (podcast), https://omny.fm/shows/glammir/the-real-mob-wife-andrea-giovino.

159 *He had the chiseled features*: Giovino, *Divorced from the Mob*, 127.

160 *He was the kind of guy*: Jemima Hunt, "Married to the Mob," *The Guardian*, March 9, 2002.

161 *He knew enough to know*: Giovino, *Divorced from the Mob*, 180.

161 *I thought my neighborhood*: Ibid., 215.

161 *There was no question that she*: Author interview with Frank Drew, April 26, 2023.

161 *You've got the wrong people*: Drew, "Puglisi Narrative in Chronological Order 1988–2020."

162 *Scotty was a kickboxer*: Author interview with Frank Drew, April 22, 2023.

162 *knew you were coming*: Drew, "Puglisi Narrative in Chronological Order 1988–2020."

162 *Nobody wants to talk in prison*: Ibid.

163 *That girl ain't ever heard anyone*: Ibid.

163 *Wild animals, people with no teeth*: Ibid.

163 *I don't know what kind of games*: Ibid.

164 *They knew you were coming*: Ibid.

164 *My god, I've never heard anything*: Ibid.

11. DESERT RETIREMENT

165 *gave me a guy who used to be*: Ray Liotta interview, *Jimmy Kimmel Live!*, ABC, May 21, 2015.

165 *All of a sudden, boom*: Ibid.

166 *Because he's a douche*: Ibid.

166 *This moron moves to Vegas*: Brad Hunter, "Mafia Cops: NYPD Legend, Sammy the Bull Talk Dirty Detectives," *Toronto Sun*, November 7, 2020.

168 *I was taken aback*: Author interview with Hugh Mo, January 20, 2023.

168 *Out of nowhere, here comes*: Ibid.

169 *We come out to Vegas*: John Marzulli, "Mob Cops Dots Connected," *New York Daily News*, March 12, 2006.

12. GRABBING GASPIPE

171 *He is the most dangerous*: Raab, "'Most Ruthless Mafia Leader Left.'"

172 *Another day, another don*: Selwyn Raab, "F.B.I. Arrests a Mafia Boss in New Jersey," *New York Times*, January 20, 1993.

174 *We were eating great*: Author interview with Frank Pontillo, January 23, 2023.

175 *That was the end of plan one*: Carlo, *Gaspipe*, 256.

176 *Was it something I said*: Volkman, *Gangbusters*, 273.

177 *I want to jump from our government*: John Gleeson, *The Gotti Wars: Taking Down America's Most Notorious Mobster* (New York: Scribner, 2022), 238.

178 *If you guys make*: Carlo, *Gaspipe*, 264.

179 *Don't knock yourself out*: Jerry Capeci, "Casso Girdles for End & Tells Wife to Scram," *New York Daily News*, March 8, 1994.

180 *complete, truthful and accurate*: United States v. Casso, 9 F. Supp. 2d 199 (EDNY 1998).

180 *extremely forthcoming*: Jerry Capeci, "Two City Detectives Gaspiped," *New York Daily News*, March 3, 1994.

181 *It was only talk at that point*: Robert E. Kessler, "U.S. Judge Steps Aside in Murder Sentencing," *Newsday*, September 11, 1997.

181 *When the kid showed up*: Raab, *Five Families*, 516.

181 *It had to be done*: Ibid.

182 *He's told us who they are*: "Mafia Plotted to Whack a Federal Judge," *New York Daily News*, September 10, 1997.

13. A FENCE IN HIDING

183 *A celebrated hero detective*: Jerry Capeci, "Hero Cops or Hitmen?," *New York Daily News*, March 26, 1994.

183 *I don't know anyone*: Ibid.

184 *I looked at [the newspaper] and said*: Author interview with Joe Piraino, August 10, 2022.

184 *Eppolito didn't surprise me at all*: Ibid.

184 *You have no idea how big a problem*: United States v. Eppolito and Caracappa.

184 *He was upset*: Ibid.

185 *take a guy like Casso*: Ibid.

185 *There was nothing illegal*: Author interview with Judd Burstein, September 7, 2023.

185 *that we've got a real problem*: United States v. Eppolito and Caracappa.

185 *I always felt Louie was a little flamboyant*: Ibid.

186 *were much like tarantulas*: Ibid.

186 *We started walking in the fruit*: Ibid.

187 *I will personally kill you*: Alan Feuer, "Finish This Job or Die, Ex-Detective Says in Filing," *New York Times*, July 6, 2005.

14. A MAN WITHOUT A COUNTRY

189 *Since this was not a very efficient*: "Mob Canary Hears Birds Singing," *New York Daily News*, January 20, 1997.

189 *I forgive you*: Raab, *Five Families*, 516.

190 *Charles [Rose] and I didn't want to*: Author interview with Greg O'Connell, August 28, 2023.

191 *stiff, formal and unfriendly*: Carlo, *Gaspipe*, 284.

192 *Simply put, criminal behavior*: United States v. Casso, 9 F. Supp. 2d 199 (EDNY 1998).

192 *I help them and I get life*: Raab, *Five Families*, 205.

15. THE LAST TRUE BELIEVER

193 *We began to see that*: Author interview with Frank Drew, April 26, 2023.

193 *We suspected something*: Author interview with Mike Foldesi, May 18, 2023.

194 *If you want to get Burt*: Frank Drew, Memo, "Puglisi Narrative in Chronological Order 1988–2020."

194 *He couldn't have been happier*: Ibid.

195 *drive like a total maniac*: Ibid.

196 *Are you kidding*: Ibid.

196 *nearly good-looking but not*: Lawson and Oldham, *Brotherhoods*, 406.

197 *Burt's got connections*: Ibid.

197 *That's one of our cops*: Ibid., 408.

197 *It was Monica who sunk us*: United States v. Eppolito and Caracappa.

198 *No disrespect*: Ibid.

198 *incapable of telling the truth*: Edelman, "The Mafia Princess Who Became a NYC Judge."

198 *My wife and daughter had been*: United States v. Eppolito and Caracappa.

199 *We're both men*: Ibid.

199 *He is probably the last true*: David L. Ulin, "Ratting Out the Mafia," *Los Angeles Times*, February 9, 2008.

16. A CASE REVIVED

205 *You know that everybody hates*: Dades et al., *Friends of the Family*, 13.

205 *I guess when Frankie saw that*: Author interview with Tommy Dades, August 11, 2021.

206 *He was just a stone-cold killer*: Author interview with Tommy Dades, August 11, 2021.

206 *He's in a cell and I start talking*: Author interview with Tommy Dades, August 11, 2021.

206 *Frankie Hydell and another*: Author interview with Tommy Dades, September 9, 2022.

206 *It was a little too personal*: Author interview with Tommy Dades, September 9, 2022.

206 *We had a hunch*: Jimmy Calandra, "Story of Mobsters Jerry Pappa & John Pappa," YouTube, March 7, 2022, https://www.youtube.com/watch?v=XFac1Y3dAfw.

207 *We both jump out of the car*: Author interview with Tommy Dades, September 9, 2022.

207 *I might [have been] seven feet*: Author interview with Tommy Dades, September 9, 2022.

208 *He never got his hands on the door*: Author interview with Tommy Dades, September 9, 2022.

208 *They're saying, 'We want to know'*: Author interview with Tommy Dades, September 9, 2022.

208 *He looked at me and pointed*: Author interview with Tommy Dades, September 9, 2022.

209 *Frankie gave us what we wanted*: Author interview with Tommy Dades, October 7, 2022.

209 *We begged him to come off*: Author interview with Tommy Dades, October 7, 2022.

209 *We spoke around dinner*: Carl Campanile, "Gotti Rat Hit After We Talked: Fed," *New York Post*, November 30, 2004.

210 *I said, 'You mean the night before?'*: Author interview with Tommy Dades, October 7, 2022.

210 *That was tough*: Author interview with Tommy Dades, October 7, 2022.

210 *I'm not going to say we*: Author interview with Tommy Dades, October 7, 2022.

211 *We were lucky if we*: Bill Cannon, "Real Crime Stories with Retired 1st Grade Detective Tommy Dades," *Police Off the Cuff*, March 9, 2021 (podcast), https://open.spotify.com /episode/4asu5t2GbosOlhFBbCgYwP.

211 *I felt like I didn't know*: Author interview with Tommy Dades, November 10, 2022.

211 *I was basically on my own*: Author interview with Tommy Dades, November 10, 2022.

211 *I was a good kid growing up*: Author interview with Tommy Dades, November 10, 2022.

212 *He still had pecs*: Author interview with Tommy Dades, November 10, 2022.

212 *I guess the scales*: Author interview with Tommy Dades, November 10, 2022.

212 *When you have confidence*: Author interview with Tommy Dades, November 10, 2022.

212 *If you tried to use*: Author interview with Tommy Dades, November 10, 2022.

213 *We hated the wise guys*: Author interview with Tommy Dades, November 10, 2022.

213 *If I applied myself*: Author interview with Tommy Dades, November 10, 2022.

213 *She was afraid I'd turn out*: Author interview with Tommy Dades, November 10, 2022.

213 *We were too young to get*: Author interview with Tommy Dades, November 10, 2022.

214 *He just said, 'Tommy, there's better'*: Author interview with Tommy Dades, November 10, 2022.

214 *You'd have thought I graduated*: Author interview with Tommy Dades, November 10, 2022.

214 *Being a cop was the best thing*: Author interview with Tommy Dades, November 10, 2022.

214 *You're standing on West 34th*: Author interview with Tommy Dades, November 10, 2022.

214 *In the morning, you're out there*: Author interview with Tommy Dades, November 10, 2022.

215 *Tommy was the kind of detective*: Author interview with Joe Piraino, August 10, 2022.

215 *We'd watch for anyone*: Author interview with Joe Piraino, August 10, 2022.

215 *Tommy knew the players*: Author interview with Joe Piraino, August 10, 2022.

215 *I would stop at Thirteenth Avenue*: Author interview with Tommy Dades, November 10, 2022.

215 *I had a good chin*: Author interview with Tommy Dades, November 10, 2022.

215 *I stopped counting*: Cannon, "Real Crime Stories with Retired 1st Grade Detectives Tommy Dades."

215 *he looks like Frankenstein*: Ibid.

216 *The worst part of being a detective*: Author interview with Tommy Dades, October 24, 2022.

216 *She was my best friend*: Author interview with Tommy Dades, October 24, 2022.

216 *When I got down there*: Author interview with Tommy Dades, October 24, 2022.

216 *She said, 'You be careful'*: Author interview with Tommy Dades, October 24, 2022.

217 *I didn't have a clue why*: Author interview with Tommy Dades, October 24, 2022.

217 *She was dying*: Author interview with Tommy Dades, October 24, 2022.

218 *only concern was terrorism*: Dades et al., *Friends of the Family*, 9.

218 *She would call me out of frustration*: Author interview with Tommy Dades, August 19, 2021.

218 *Whether you're a good guy*: Author interview with Tommy Dades, October 24, 2022.

218 *Tommy was a man of his word*: Author interview with Joe Piraino, August 10, 2022.

219 *She figured Eppolito was beyond*: Author interview with Tommy Dades, October 24, 2022.

220 *There were whispers around*: Author interview with Tommy Dades, October 24, 2022.

220 *I found it very far-fetched*: Author interview with Tommy Dades, October 24, 2022.

220 *I haven't forgotten*: Rashbaum, "Officer in Murder Case Got Benefit of Doubt in '85."

220 *You make your decision*: Ibid.

220 *a small gold nugget of information*: Denis Hamill, "'These Two Bums Who Disgraced the Badge Will Die in Jail.' Emotional Vow of Ex-Cop Whose Tireless Work Busted Notorious Mafia Killers," *New York Daily News*, April 3, 2005.

221 *I told her I'd try*: Hunter, "Mafia Cops: NYPD Legend, Sammy the Bull Talk Dirty Detectives."

221 *I used to say I was Tommy's DA*: Author interview with Mike Vecchione, August 23, 2023.

221 *And then Tommy walks in*: Author's interview with Mike Vecchione, August 23, 2023.

221 *Are you kidding me?*: Dades et al., *Friends of the Family*, 41.

221 *The word around the police*: Author interview with Mike Vecchione, August 23, 2023.

221 *that he'd gotten a new piece*: Jennifer Yoon, "The Inside Story of the Mafia Cops Case," *NY Law*, December 21, 2012, https://www.youtube.com/watch?v=4C1DA2G0qi0.

222 *I told him we were thinking*: Author interview with Mike Vecchione, August 23, 2023.

222 *It was overwhelming*: Author interview with Tommy Dades, October 24, 2022.

223 *[Eppolito] fooled a lot of people*: Author interview with Mike Vecchione, August 23, 2023.

223 *When I approached certain people*: Author interview with Tommy Dades, October 24, 2022.

223 *were respected by a lot of guys*: Cannon, "Real Crime Stories with Retired 1st Grade Detectives Tommy Dades."

223 *It was horrendous*: Author interview with Mike Vecchione, August 23, 2023.

224 *We were never able*: Author interview with Tommy Dades, October 24, 2022.

224 *If you don't have a father*: Author interview with Tommy Dades, October 24, 2022.

225 *I hope you're calling to say*: Author interview with Tommy Dades, October 24, 2022.

225 *I went over as much information*: Author interview with Tommy Dades, October 24, 2022.

225 *always believed Casso's information*: Author interview with Tommy Dades, October 24, 2022.

226 *It was something we had to do*: Author interview with Tommy Dades, October 24, 2022.

226 *No matter when you use the code*: Hamill, "'These Two Bums Who Disgraced the Badge Will Die in Jail.'"

226 *when I knew I was on the right track*: Rebecca Leung, "Ex-Mob Boss Points a Finger," CBS News, April 7, 2005.

226 *I'm just sitting there waiting*: Author interview with Tommy Dades, October 24, 2022.

227 *That was the first thing I saw*: Author interview with Tommy Dades, October 24, 2022.

227 *Caracappa would type in his code*: Hamill, "'These Two Bums Who Disgraced the Badge Will Die in Jail.'"

227 *Now we knew that we had something*: Author interview with Mike Vecchione, January 31, 2022.

227 *I said to the guys*: Author interview with Mike Vecchione, January 31, 2022.

227 *could almost hear*: Connolly and Blum, "Hit Men in Blue?"

227 *We needed somebody on the inside*: Author interview with Mike Vecchione, January 31, 2022.

17. THE RELUCTANT WITNESS

229 *part of what prison life is all about*: United States v. Eppolito and Caracappa.

229 *The old man is in Brooklyn*: Dades et al., *Friends of the Family*, 160.

230 *Ponzi had a silver tongue*: Author interview with Bobby Intartaglio, June 1, 2023.

230 *Mr. Oldham, I told you we*: Dades et al., *Friends of the Family*, 163.

230 *Ponzi could develop a good*: Author interview with Mike Vecchione, August 23, 2023.

231 *With all due respect*: Dades et al., *Friends of the Family*, 165.

231 *No disrespect to you*: Ibid.

231 *Young man, don't do that*: Ibid.

232 *Mr. Kaplan, I don't purport to know*: Ibid.

232 *I told them I wanted some time*: United States v. Eppolito and Caracappa.

232 *Law enforcement is a dirty business*: Robert Mladinich, "The Passions of Tommy Dades," *Sweet Science*, March 29, 2005.

233 *to put the finishing touches*: Ibid.

233 *I thought it was insane*: Author interview with Robert Henoch, November 11, 2021.

233 *get some teeth*: Dades et al., *Friends of the Family*, 176.

234 *If Italian inmates saw him*: Author interview with Bobby Intartaglia, June 1, 2023.

234 *I wanted someday to*: United States v. Eppolito and Caracappa.

235 *[Kaplan] had an incredible amount*: Author interview with Robert Henoch, November 11, 2021.

235 *My witness?*: Dades et al., *Friends of the Family*, 182.

235 *At that point the case is done*: Author interview with Robert Henoch, November 11, 2021.

18. THE UNDERCOVER ACCOUNTANT

237 *girlfriends, jewelry and going out*: United States v. Eppolito and Caracappa.

238 *We came across anything*: Author interview with Kevin Sheehan, October 13, 2023.

239 *Mike Frate said that he understood*: United States v. Eppolito and Caracappa.

239 *He said to me hang tight*: Ibid.

239 *They really weren't on my*: Author interview with Kevin Sheehan, October 13, 2023.

239 *We wanted eyes on what*: Author interview with Mike Vecchione, October 22, 2022.

239 *Friends and friends of friends*: Author interview with Mike Vecchione, October 22, 2022.

240 *Typical Vegas house*: Author interview with Timmy Moran, July 16, 2022.
240 *My first thought was, Louie*: Author interview with Timmy Moran, July 16, 2022.
240 *I don't know why they didn't burn*: Author interview Kenny Luzak, August 18, 2023.
241 *was like looking in the eyes*: Author interview with Kenny Luzak, August 18, 2023.
242 *I haven't trusted a man*: Ellen Barry, "Theatrics Open N.Y. Mafia Trial," *Los Angeles Times,* March 14, 2006.
243 *We need to talk*: Author interview with Kevin Sheehan, July 16, 2022.
243 *explained to me that they had*: Author interview with Kevin Sheehan, July 16, 2022.
243 *It was divine intervention*: "Associated Press, Accountant Played Key Role to Convict Mafia Cops," *San Diego Union-Tribune,* February 8, 2009.
243 *Did I ever feel bad?*: Greg B. Smith, "Secret Mob Cop Tapes," *New York Daily News,* July 17, 2005.
245 *This is drug money*: "Drugs Funded Mafia Cops' High Life: Feds," *New York Post,* April 11, 2005.
245 *It's like anything else*: Smith, "Secret Mob Cop Tapes."
245 *They're Hollywood punks*: Ibid.
246 *Because you're my dad's friend*: United States v. Eppolito and Caracappa.
246 *I got a panicky call*: Ibid.

19. A CASE DIVIDED
247 *What are you talking about*: Dades et al., *Friends of the Family,* 189.
247 *Don't you know?*: Ibid.
247 *They never said a word*: Author interview with Mike Vecchione, January 31, 2022.
248 *I can't believe you're doing*: Dades et al., *Friends of the Family,* 190.
248 *That's not really the way*: Ibid.
248 *Yeah, you* did *say that*: Ibid.
248 *No, but I think maybe*: Ibid.
248 *C'mon, what are you*: Ibid.
249 *As I thought about the case*: Ibid.
250 *Didn't I tell you right*: Dades et al., *Friends of the Family,* 196.
250 *It was never going to Brooklyn*: Author interview with Robert Henoch, October 25, 2023.

20. CUFFED AT PIERO'S
251 *I gave her the good news*: Author interview with Tommy Dades, November 21, 2022.
252 *Eppolito flexed hard*: Author interview with Kenny Luzak, August 18, 2023.
252 *It's been a long time coming*: Author interview with Kenny Luzak, August 18, 2023.
252 *Louie was trying to be brave*: John Marzulli, "2 Cops Who Killed for Mafia: Feds Say Retired Detective Pals Are Linked to at Least 8 Murders," *New York Daily News,* March 11, 2005.
252 *Well, I guess* they *won't*: Author interview with Kenny Luzak, August 18, 2023.
252 *She was yelling at us*: Author interview with Kenny Luzak, August 18, 2023.
252 *I said for the most part*: Author interview with Timmy Moran, August 24, 2022.
253 *Here's a guy who just got*: Author interview with Timmy Moran, August 24, 2022.
253 *These corrupt former detectives*: Kati Cornell Smith, "Feds:) Badges Shielded Mob— Ex-NYPD Detectives Charged with Killing for the Lucheses," *New York Post,* March 11, 2005.

253 *From a law-enforcement point of view*: Miriam Hill, "2 Ex-Officers Say Not Guilty in Mob Case," *Philadelphia Inquirer*, April 22, 2005.

254 *My father loved being a cop*: Ibid.

254 *If my brother had died*: Hamill, "A Victim's Ghost Haunts 2 Accused."

255 *We never thought eighteen years*: Anthony M. Destefano and Steve Freiss, "Victim's Kin Shocked Cops May Be to Blame," *Newsday*, March 12, 2005.

255 *There is a god*: Gibbs, "The Moth Presents Barry Gibbs: Exonerated."

255 *They took everything from me*: Ibid.

255 *Whatever you learn out here*: Ibid.

255 *I thought I was going to die*: John Marzulli, "Barry Gibbs, Wrongly Jailed for 19 Years, Will Never Forget the Crooked Cop Who Put Him in Prison," *New York Daily News*, June 6, 2010.

255 *I started to make plans*: Gibbs, "The Moth Presents Barry Gibbs: Exonerated."

256 *We reached out to say that*: Author interview with Vanessa Potkin, February 24, 2023.

256 *He broke down as soon they came*: Author interview with Vanessa Potkin, February 24, 2023.

256 *I'm scrubbing, and I'm crying*: "17 Years in Prison: War Veteran Falsely Accused of Murder," *Real Stories*, May 15, 2021, https://www.youtube.com/watch?v=PIw8AOwcaBQ.

256 *I was looking at Barney*: "An Exonerated Prisoner Shares What Freedom Is Like After 19 Years Behind Bars," *Huffington Post*, October 9, 2017.

258 *I was afraid*: United States v. Eppolito and Caracappa.

259 *I lived there for two years*: Robert D. McFadden, "Shock, but Some Praise, After Legal Ruling," *New York Times*, July 1, 2006.

260 *He's not an outlaw*: United States v. Eppolito and Caracappa.

260 *Words are important*: Ibid.

260 *Killing is imbedded*: Ibid.

261 *The charges seem to me*: Ibid.

261 *Which is how I envisioned*: Author interview with Tommy Dades, September 9, 2022.

261 *This is the first step of my trip*: Anthony M. Destefano, "Back on the Street—For Now," *Newsday*, July 22, 2005.

262 *I did none of these crimes*: Ibid.

262 *I knocked on the door*: Author interview with Lizzie Hydell, November 10, 2023.

262 *This case has to be tried*: Lawson and Oldham, *Brotherhoods*, 597.

21. JUDGE WEINSTEIN'S COURTROOM

264 *He would run red lights and speed*: Author interview with Lou Eppolito, Jr., June 10, 2023.

264 *Something as simple as looking*: Author interview with Lou Eppolito, Jr., June 10, 2023.

264 *He has a son who walks around*: John Marzulli, "Gay Son's Lonely Tale of Betrayal," *New York Daily News*, June 7, 2006.

264 *They wouldn't look at me*: Author interview with Lou Eppolito, Jr., June 10, 2023.

264 *I need to be there*: Zack Haberman, "Son Fears 'Mob' Cop Is 'Family' Man," *New York Post*, March 6, 2006.

264 *I just came down here*: Barry, "Theatrics Open N.Y. Mafia Trial."

265 *Everything went sour*: Author interview with Tommy Dades, September 22, 2022.

265 *The whole thing exploded*: Author interview with Tommy Dades, September 22, 2022.

265 *Anybody who knows me*: 60 Minutes, aired January 8, 2006.

266 *benevolent despot*: Laura Mansnerus, "Jack B. Weinstein, U.S. Judge with an Activist Streak, Is Dead at 99," *New York Times*, June 15, 2021.

266 *Sitting in the Brooklyn federal courthouse*: Jimmy Breslin, *The Good Rat* (New York: Harper, 2008), 38.

267 *Cutler talks like a guy*: Edward Hayes, *Mouthpiece: A Life in—and Sometimes Just Outside—the Law* (New York: Broadway Books, 2006), 93.

267 *I can get you out of anything*: Charles McGrath, "Fixer," *New York Times*, February 19, 2006.

267 *like a guy holding Shea Stadium*: Joyce Wadler, "The Runyonesque Voice atop the Savile Row Suits," *New York Times*, March 6, 2002.

267 *I think there will be some*: Associated Press, "Trial of Mafia Cops Starts Today," *Poughkeepsie Journal*, March 13, 2006.

267 *The defendants went into business*: United States v. Eppolito and Caracappa.

268 *They called each other tough guys*: Ibid.

268 *kill, kill, steal, sell drugs*: Ibid.

268 *at least ten murders, and maybe twenty*: Ibid.

268 *He had the courage to say*: Ibid.

269 *Steve Caracappa has spent*: Ibid.

269 *They used the power of their position*: Ibid.

269 *Until now, they've gotten away*: Ibid.

269 *I really wasn't going to court*: Ibid.

270 *His heart was bleeding*: Ibid.

270 *I don't want witnesses*: Ibid.

270 *looked more grandfatherly*: Associated Press, "From Mob Boss to Ruinous Informant," (Sioux Falls) *Argus Leader*, May 28, 2006.

270 *I said, 'What are you doing'*: Gibbs, "The Moth Presents Barry Gibbs: Exonerated."

271 *Keep your voice down*: United States v. Eppolito and Caracappa.

271 *Do you want an answer*: Ibid.

271 *Would you agree with me*: Ibid.

271 *I wouldn't agree with you*: Ibid.

271 *I don't know what the hell*: Ibid.

271 *Why should I be upset?*: Ibid.

272 *Five in the head*: Zach Haberman, "I Paid Murder $ to Cops—Go-Between Mobster Tells Jury of Chilling Contracts," *New York Post*, March 15, 2006.

272 *Whatever I would say*: Ibid.

272 *like a man that one might*: Alan Feuer, "Witness Says Ex-Detectives Served the Mob, and Killed for It," *New York Times*, March 15, 2006.

273 *Frankie approached me*: United States v. Eppolito and Caracappa.

273 *I felt it was something that could*: Ibid.

273 *the convict canary*: Zach Haberman, "Rat Squeals: 'Mafia Cops' Delivered Wiseguy to Executioner," *New York Post*, March 16, 2006.

273 *An unknown name steals*: Breslin, *The Good Rat*, 45.

273 *dreary and charmless*: Ibid., 47.

274 *I didn't think that*: Ibid.

274 *I would be at the defense table*: Ibid.

274 *Casso didn't do it*: Ibid.

274 *I always liked Steve*: Ibid.

275 *I think she loves me*: Ibid.

275 *You failed her, didn't you?*: Ibid.

275 *very offended that my father thought*: John Marzulli, "Cops Done In by Tell-All Tome," *New York Daily News*, March 17, 2006.

276 *If you continue your rambling*: United States v. Eppolito and Caracappa.

276 *I'm being honest*: Ibid.

276 *Believe me, that was on my mind*: Ibid.

276 *I walked up to him*: Author interview with Lizzie Hydell, November 10, 2023.

276 *He was five feet away*: "Cops Done In by Tell-All Tome."

276 *to please just stay with me*: United States v. Eppolito and Caracappa.

277 *Judge, can we have a*: Ibid.

277 *The reason you signed the cooperation*: Ibid.

277 *Anybody that's in jail*: Ibid.

277 *I have no money hidden away*: Ibid.

277 *Judge Weinstein knows better*: John Marzulli, "Time Tickin' on Mob Cop Case," *New York Daily News*, March 21, 2006.

278 *You would have to be a falling*: United States v. Eppolito and Caracappa.

278 *If a middle-aged man*: Ibid.

278 *He was civil as about it*: Author interview with Joe Piraino, August 10, 2022.

279 *There are several million*: United States v. Eppolito and Caracappa.

279 *This is a big problem*: Ibid.

279 *Then my stepmother decides*: Ibid.

280 *one of the most repulsive*: Author interview with Stephen Corso, June 10, 2023.

280 *He didn't care abou the source*: United States v. Eppolito and Caracappa.

280 *The FBI did not tell me to inject*: Ibid.

281 *There's no better way*: Ibid.

281 *You dishonored yourself*: Ibid.

282 *Aren't you interested*: Ibid.

282 *The impression that I received*: Ibid.

282 *You're saying that Eppolito*: Ibid.

282 *I'm just stating to you*: Ibid.

282 *We're keeping the daughter out*: Ibid.

282 *Louis was unfaithful to me*: Ibid.

283 *I wanted to see if they would*: Ibid.

283 *One was the big one*: Ibid.

284 *my paramour, my mistress*: Ibid.

284 *I was in the habit of*: Ibid.

284 *Burt [Kaplan] was getting*: Ibid.

285 *a thief, a liar*: Ibid.

285 *I was scared, because who*: Ibid.

285 *After the morning of February 10*: Ibid.

286 *It is not the prosecutor's province*: Ibid.

287 *I wish you luck*: Zach Haberman, "Feds Decided Early That Dopey Gaspipe Was Full of Hot Air," *New York Post*, April 8, 2006.

287 *I'd rather be doing this*: Connolly and Blum, "Hit Men in Blue?," *Vanity Fair*, September 13, 2005.

287 *The greatest lunches I had*: Ibid.

287 *It began in 1980*: Ibid.

287 *The concept of the US*: Ibid.

288 *Mr. Casso gives a completely*: United States v. Eppolito and Caracappa.

288 *of no significance*: Ibid.

288 *because, in effect, he was*: Ibid.

289 *He sort of wanted*: John Marzulli, "'Mob Cop' Attorney Tells Client to Zip It," *New York Daily News*, March 30, 2006.

289 *had a very important meeting*: United States v. Eppolito and Caracappa.

289 *I don't care what he had*: Ibid.

289 *be available over the next six*: Ibid.

290 *We rest*: Ibid.

290 *Ex-Detective's Defense Rests*: Alan Feuer, "Ex-Detective's Defense Rests Without Working Up Sweat," *New York Times,* April 1, 2006.

290 *It is one of the bloodiest*: United States v. Eppolito and Caracappa.

291 *Don't be fooled into*: Ibid.

291 *He knew he was finally caught*: Ibid.

291 *The fact of the matter is*: Ibid.

292 *Why bother having a jury*: Ibid.

292 *stir into a conspiracy casserole*: Ibid.

292 *Was there any way to revive*: Ibid.

293 *a Johnny-come-lately artificially*: Ibid.

293 *Some, like myself, thought his closing*: Steve Dunleavy, "Cutler Gnomes at the Mouth," *New York Post,* April 5, 2006.

293 *sweetheart pacts given to cretins*: United States v. Eppolito and Caracappa.

293 *a double life, triple life*: Ibid.

293 *a subhuman gnome*: Ibid.

293 *I've tried as best I can*: Ibid.

294 *The FBI has an arrogance*: Ibid.

294 *educated, sophisticated professionals*: Ibid.

294 *I know you have been after me*: Ibid.

294 *He is in your hands*: Ibid.

294 *When you make a speech*: Ibid.

294 *it's not a Washington case*: Ibid.

294 *big voice, big words*: Ibid.

295 *The fact that Mr. Caracappa*: Ibid.

295 *You're the best lawyer*: Ibid.

295 *You know when that psalm*: Ibid.

295 *You were amazing*: Anthony M. Destefano, "Convict Them, Says Prosecutor," *Newsday,* April 4, 2006.

296 *ticking time bomb*: John Marzulli, "Statute 'Bomb' Explodes in Front of Prosecutors," *New York Daily News,* July 1, 2006.

22. JUSTICE FORESTALLED

297 *Through count after count*: Jimmy Breslin, "Convicted by the Darkness of Their Pasts," *Newsday*, April 7, 2006.

298 *Bail is revoked*: Ibid.

298 *Dad, this is not over*: Anthony M. Destephano, "Married to the Mob," *Newsday*, April 7, 2006.

298 *It's only the first round*: Alan Feuer, "2 Ex-Detectives Guilty in Killings," *New York Times*, April 7, 2006.

298 *perverting the shield of good*: "Jury Decides They're Badfellas."

299 *I remember him standing up*: Author interview with Rae Koshetz, September 15, 2023.

299 *It's the* appearance *of justice*: John Marzulli, "Mob Cops Guilty, Face Life in Jail," *New York Daily News*, April 7, 2006.

299 *They put up no defense*: John Marzulli, "It's Splitsville!," *New York Daily News*, April 24, 2006.

299 *I wanted to take the stand*: Ibid.

300 *I don't want a defendant coming*: John Marzulli, "Married to Mob: Eppolito Hires 2nd Gotti Lawyer," *New York Daily News*, April 25, 2006.

300 *I apologize, your honor*: Ibid.

300 *a guttersnipe lawyer*: David Segal, "Crossly Examined: A Hit Man Says It's a Crime the Way Bruce Cutler Handled His Case. The Attorney Objects," *Washington Post*, June 24, 2006.

300 *not here to analyze*: Ibid.

301 *You took away our daddy*: Zach Haberman, "Mob Cops Face a Life in Hell—Judge Says He'll Throw Book at Duo After Kin Lash Out at Killers," *New York Post*, June 6, 2006.

301 *My family and I have kept*: Segal, "Crossly Examined."

301 *I know the feelings of every family*: John Marzulli, "Mafia Cops Will Die Behind Bars," *New York Daily News*, June 6, 2006.

302 *I can hold my head*: Ellen Barry, "'Mafia Cops' to Get Life in Prison," *Los Angeles Times*, June 6, 2006.

302 *do you remember me*: Marzulli, "Mafia Cops Will Die Behind Bars,"

302 *I'm the guy you put away*: Ibid.

302 *You don't remember what you*: Ibid.

302 *There has been no doubt*: Ibid.

302 *Every day in jail*: Ibid.

303 *To accuse a fighter*: Segal, "Crossly Examined."

303 *Tell him he's annoying me*: Alan Feuer, "Mafia Cop Trial Defense Was 'Excellent,' Judge Says," *New York Times*, June 26, 2006.

303 *put up his hand*: "Mafia Cops Trial Takes Turn," *Los Angeles Times*, June 24, 2006.

304 *You'll tell a lie if it will*: John Marzulli, "Mafia Cop Testifies It's True He's a Liar," *New York Daily News*, June 24, 2006.

304 *to hurt their feelings*: Ibid.

304 *his face mutated into a giant*: Eppolito, *Mafia Cop*, 188.

304 *this wonderful heady urge*: Ibid., 218.

304 *You're fighting for your life*: Alan Feuer, "In 'Mafia Cops' Case, the Prosecution Comes to the Defense of the Defense," *New York Times*, June 24, 2006.

304 *I didn't want to tick off*: Anthony M. Destefano, "Finally on the Stand," *Newsday*, June 24, 2006.

305 *My father was raised on*: John Marzulli and Michelle Caruso, "Mob Cop Kayoed: Judge Drops Gavel on Eppolito Retrial Hope," *New York Daily News*, June 27, 2006.

305 *It's just another attempt*: Ellen Barry, "'Mafia Cops' Claim Lawyers Botched Case," *Los Angeles Times*, June 24, 2006.

305 *Did I make any mistakes?*: Ibid.

305 *I'm delighted that you filled*: Marzulli and Caruso, "Mob Cop Kayoed."

306 *Getting Away With Murder*: Greg B. Smith, "Getting Away with Murder," *New York Daily News*, July 1, 2006.

307 *kidnapped, murdered and assisted*: Zach Haberman, "Judge: Killer Mob Cop Duo Guilty As Sin—& I Have to Let Them Walk," *New York Post*, July 1, 2006.

307 *conspiracy that began in the 1980s*: Ibid.

307 *A retired contractor who opens*: Ibid.

307 *It will undoubtedly appear peculiar*: Alan Feuer, "Judge Throws Out Mafia Cops Convictions," *New York Times*, June 30, 2006.

308 *I was afraid that I was*: John Marzulli, "Judge Rubs Out Mob Cop Verdict: Overturns Convictions Due to Time Technicality," *New York Daily News*, July 1, 2006.

308 *I know my husband will be unhappy*: Ibid.

308 *it was like the world stopped*: Ibid.

308 *I thought the government overreaching*: Ellen Barry, "Judge Tosses Mafia Cops Convictions," *Los Angeles Times*, July 1, 2006.

308 *We thought this was over*: Marzulli, "Judge Rubs Out Mob Cop Verdict."

308 *It was like a slap in the face*: Ibid.

308 *I had the sense that he did*: Author interview with Robert Henoch, October 25, 2023.

309 *I dare say most marriages would flounder*: Alan Feuer, "Bail Denied for 'Mafia Cops' Facing Trial in Drug Case," *New York Times*, July 26, 2006.

23. JUSTICE FULFILLED

310 *Mr. Eppolito and Mr. Caracappa now*: Alan Feuer, "Ex-Detectives May Go Free in Mob Case," *New York Times*, July 25, 2006.

311 *I remember [Brooklyn District Attorney Charles Hynes] calling*: Author interview with Mike Vecchione, August 23, 2023.

312 *I will be praying for my husband*: "Court of Appeals to Hear Mafia Ex-Cops Legal Arguments," *New York Daily News*, October 18, 2007.

312 *I don't see the relationship*: Associated Press, "Appeals Court Seems Receptive to Arguments of Alleged 'Mafia Cops,'" *Staten Island Advance*, October 18, 2007.

312 *received money for each crime*: Anthony M. Destafano, "Convictions Stand," *Newsday*, September 18, 2008.

313 *These Two Mafia Cops Will Rot in Jail*: John Marzulli, "These Two Mafia Cops Will Rot in Jail," *New York Daily News*, September 18, 2008.

313 *This isn't over*: Ibid.

313 *Thank God a small measure of justice*: Ibid.

313 *My father and Steve made a choice*: Author interview with Lou Eppolito, Jr., June 10, 2023.

313 *They looked as if*: Jim Dwyer, "'Mafia Cops' Will Continue to Draw Pensions," *New York Times*, March 6, 2009.

313 *Twenty years ago these*: Marzulli, "These Two Mafia Cops Will Rot in Jail."

314 *Daddy, I cannot even bring*: Ibid.

314 *You are going to die every day*: Denis Hamill, "Rejoicing at Mafia Cops' Hell," *New York Daily News*, March 16, 2009.

314 *We don't need any pats*: Jerry Capeci, "RIP for Joe Ponzi, One of the Best There Ever Was at Nabbing the Bad Guys," *Gang Land News*, April 21, 2022.

EPILOGUE

315 *I've been in a lot of*: John Marzulli, "Mafia Cop Rat Close to Get-Out-of-Jail Deal," *New York Daily News*, September 8, 2006.

316 *Who says he's dead?*: Tom Robbin, "Breslin on Death of Mob Canary: You Sure He's Dead?," *Village Voice*, July 22, 2009.

316 *deliberately fabricated witness statements*: A. G. Sulzberger, "City to Pay $9.9 Million over Man's Imprisonment," *New York Times*, June 3, 2010.

316 *I had my freedom taken away*: Associated Press, "NY Man Framed by Mafia Cop Gets $9.9M," (Appleton, Wisconsin) *Post-Crescent*, June 4, 2010.

316 *I've got a lady in her eighties*: John Mazulli and Larry McShane, "Rot, Mob Cop Scum!," *New York Daily News*, March 7, 2009.

316 *How could anyone believe*: Pauline Pipitone, "Mother's Letter to Bloomberg," *New York Daily News*, July 3, 2006.

317 *witnesses crying*: "Ma Opens Up for 1st Time Since Son Was Slain 22 Years Ago in Mob-Cop Fiasco," *New York Daily News*, January 4, 2009.

317 *So he didn't make any sounds*: Ibid.

317 *What do you mean by 'sound'?*: Ibid.

317 *It is un-American as far as*: John Marzulli, "Ex-NYPD Honcho Won't Discuss Ruling on Mafia Cop Louis Eppolito," *New York Daily News*, October 14, 2011.

317 *inexplicable failure*: Pipitone v. City of N.Y., 06-CV-3101 (EDNY September 30, 2014).

318 *systematic failure*: Ibid.

318 *powerful evidence*: Ibid.

318 *This tragic matter involves*: Ibid.

318 *Please know I have been*: Mira Wassef, "Staten Island 'Mob Cop' Begged for His Freedom Before Dying in Jail," *Staten Island Advance*, April 12, 2017.

318 *There is nothing I can do*: Ibid.

AFTERWORD

319 *You're teaching them how to jump rope*: Author interview with Tommy Dades, June 28, 2023.

319 *After that I said, I can't do*: Author interview with Tommy Dades, June 28, 2023.

320 *My whole life I went to work*: Author interview with Tommy Dades, June 28, 2023.

320 *Joe broke a thousand hearts*: Author interview with Tommy Dades, June 28, 2023.

321 *If you hold things in for a long*: Author interview with Tommy Dades, June 28, 2023.

321 *I said, 'Wait, wait, Tommy'*: Author interview with Phil Grimaldi, December 8, 2022.

321 *If we were still on the job*: Author interview with Frank Drew, April 22, 2022.

INDEX

A

Abramson, Alan, 258
Adams, Brad, 258
America's Most Wanted, 142
Amuso, Vittorio ("Vic"), 74
  on *America's Most Wanted,* 142
  arrest of, 142, 170
  conviction of, 143
  in hiding, 123–24
  Rose on, 142
Anastasia, Albert, 123, 128
Avellino, Sal ("The Golfer"), 67–68, 112–15

B

Bakken, Tim, 44
Banar, Elaine, 176
Barstow, Donald
  Casso ordering murder of, 113–15
  secret recordings, 66–67
Bartzer, Beverly, 55–56
Bergen Beach, 79–80
Bergin Hunt and Fish Club, 76
Bering, Bob, 78–80, 96
  law enforcement cooperation of, 97–98
Billotti, Rosemarie, 129, 170
Bilotti, Tommy, 1, 23, 75–76
Bishop, Jimmy, 119–21
Blake, Edward T., 45
Blakey, G. Robert, 63–64, 69, 248
Block, Frederick, 192

Bonavolonta, Jules, 61–62, 127
Bondy, Joseph, 300
Borriello, Bobby, 132–34
Bradley, Ed, 265
Bravatti, Guido, 245–46, 252
Brennan, Scotty, 160, 162
Breslin, Jimmy, 264
  on Chiodo, 134
  on Kaplan, 273–74, 316
Brief, Matthew, 179
Brigante, Steven, 42
The Brotherhoods (Oldham & Lawson), 310
Buchalter, Lepke, 89
Burkle, Ron, 289
Burstein, Jerry, 184–85, 279
  on Kaplan, 199
Bypass Gang, 102–4
  Casso escape attempts and, 175
  Siriano on, 107–11

C

Cama, Cabrini, 101, 282–83
Campanella, Joe, 230, 257
Canderozzi, Richard, 42
Capeci, Jerry, 182–83, 224
Capozzalo, Patricia, 137
Caproni, Valerie, 190–91
Caracappa, Stephen, 22, 32
  acquittal of, 306–9
  arrest of, 252

Caracappa, Stephen (*continued*)
  bail hearing, 260–62
  Casso naming, 181–84, 220, 225
  Casso warned by, 123–24
  daily reports from, 92
  death of, 318
  on drug dealing, 245
  Gravano tailed by, 98–99
  Guido, N., computer search by, 226
  Hayes on, 291–92
  Hydell, J., kidnapped by, 84–85
  indictment of, 253
  information supply chain from, 93
  joining police, 23–24
  at Metropolitan Detention Center, 259–60
  Moran, T., on, 253
  moving to Las Vegas, 168–69
  pension of, 165
  Pergola's suspicions of, 123
  Piraino on, 91–92, 184
  police records used by, 278
  retirement of, 165
  sentencing of, 313–14
  Siriano on, 90–91, 184
  60 Minutes interview, 265
  undercover narcotics work, 24–25
  watch photograph of, 278–79
Carola, Maryanne, 43
Casso, Anthony ("Gaspipe"), 50
  on *America's Most Wanted*, 142
  arrest of, 171–72
  background of, 72–73
  Barstow murder and, 113–15
  Bradley interview, 265
  Caproni meeting, 191
  Caracappa named by, 181–84, 220, 225
  Caracappa warning, 123–24
  Castellano warned by, 77
  confession of, 181–85, 192
  cooperation agreement violated by, 191
  credibility gap of, 189–90
  death of, 318
  debriefing of, 180–81
  Eppolito, Louie, named by, 181–84,
    220, 225
  escape attempts of, 174–75
  first murder of, 72–73
  girlfriend of, 129
  on Gravano, 190
  handwriting sample of, 178
  hearing of, 179–80
  in hiding, 126, 128, 170
  home of, 124
  hospital visit of, 81
  Hydell, J., and, 80–83, 86–87
  indictment in absentia, 171
  induction ceremony of, 73
  innocent plea of, 173
  jailhouse routine of, 173–74
  Kaplan alliance with, 51
  Kubecka, R., murder, and, 113–15
  law enforcement cooperation of, 178–80
  leadership of, 74–75
  letter from, 286–88
  loyalty demands on, 177–78
  Maloney on, 171
  messenger system, 129–30
  murders ordered from hiding, 130–31
  O'Connell and, 74, 175–76, 189–90
  prison smuggling, 174, 188–89
  revenue forms of, 74
  rise of, 71–72
  Rose and, 175–76, 189–90
  sentence of, 192
Castellano, Paul, 1, 12
  Casso warning, 77
  Eppolito, J., meeting with, 13
  murder of, 75–76
Cerny, Howard, 27, 31
Chiodo, Peter ("Fat Pete"), 111
  Bishop murdered by, 119–21
  Breslin on, 134
  law enforcement cooperation of,
    135–36, 171
  Rose meeting with, 135–36
  shooting of, 134–35
  testimony of, 136
  threatening, 135
  wiretapping, 112
Coffey, Joe, 253
Cohen, David, 217–18
Cohen, Gangi, 128

Cohen, Maxi, 38–39
Cohen, Michael, 104
Colangelo, Robert, 91
Colgan, Patrick, 51, 102–3
Colon, Clarissa, 194
Commission Case, 68–70
  Barstow and, 113
  Kubecka, R., and, 113
  sentencing, 88–89
conspiracy, 63
Conti, John, 238
Corallo, Antonio ("Tony Ducks"), 50,
  66–67, 71
Corrao, Joseph ("Joe Butch"), 86–87
Corso, Stephen
  cross-examination of, 280–82
  Eppolito, Louie, meeting with, 241–46
  raid on, 237–38
  sentencing of, 315
  undercover work of, 238–39
  at *United States v. Eppolito and
    Caracappa*, 280–82
Costa, Dominick, 107
  arrest of, 111
  law enforcement cooperation of, 108–9
  recovery of, 110
  shooting of, 108–9
  in Witness Protection Program, 110–11
Criminal Records Division, 277–78
Cutler, Bruce, 260
  closing statements, 293–94
  D'Arco, A., and, 271–72
  defending himself, 303–6
  Dunleavy on, 293
  on government witnesses, 268
  interviews with, 287–88
  opening statement, 268
  reputation of, 266–67

D

Dades, Tommy, 203, 310
  boxing and, 212, 215
  on Cohen, D., 218
  detective promotion of, 214
  early life of, 210–14
  Gallo's home searched by, 225–26

  Grimaldi on, 215
  Hydell, B., and, 218–19, 221
  Hydell, F., meeting with, 205
  on Hydell, F., 209
  mother's death, 217
  Nicastro meeting with, 224–25
  Pappa surveillance of, 206
  Park Hill Boxing Gym coaching, 232
  Piraino on, 215, 218
  Ponzi, J., meeting with, 224
  on Ponzi, J., 320
  retirement of, 232–33, 320
  return to police department, 319–20
  September 11 and, 216–17
  undercover work, 214–15
  Vecchione meeting with, 221–22
Daidone, Louis ("Louie Bagels"), 130
Daley, Wes, 48
D'Arco, Alphonse ("Little Al"), 111
  on blood tests, 141–42
  as boss in absence, 124–26
  clean break of, 138–39
  Cutler and, 271–72
  FBI phone call, 139–40
  law enforcement cooperation of,
    139–42, 170–71
  replacing, 138
  testimony of, 143
  *United States v. Eppolito and
    Caracappa* and, 270–72
  in Witness Protection Program, 142
D'Arco, Joseph ("Little Joe"), 116
DeAntone Productions, 242
Dearie, Raymond J., 317–18
DeCarlo, Lenny, 204
Defendis, Angelo, 82–83
Dellacroce, Aniello, 68
DeMeo, Roy, 15–16
DeSantis, Mike ("Big Mike"), 138
DiBari, Michael, 238
DiBiasi, Annette
  Hydell, J., abducting, 78
  murder of, 79, 96–97
DiLapi, Anthony, 115–16, 272
DiLapi, Mary Ann, 272
Dinnan, Eileen, 153, 196–97

double jeopardy, 308–9
Drew, Frank, 150, 152
  on Brennan, 162
  on Fogarty, 162
  Fogarty meeting, 161–64
  Foldesi on, 151
  on Kaplan, 193
  Kaplan pulled over by, 156
  on Sly, 194
Drury, Bob, 166
Dwyer, Jim, 313

E

Ehrlich, Susan, 156
Ellsworth, John, 13, 14
Eppolito, Andrea, 254
Eppolito, Jim-Jim, 13–14
  murder of, 16–19
Eppolito, Jimmy ("Jimmy the Clam")
  Castellano meeting with, 13
  funeral of, 5–6
  murder of, 16–19
Eppolito, Lou, Jr., 279–80
Eppolito, Louie, 5
  acquittal of, 306–9
  arrest of, 252
  bail hearing, 260–62
  book promotion of, 167–68, 219
  case dismissed against, 36
  Casso naming, 181–84, 220, 225
  Corso meeting with, 241–46
  Daily News report on, 33
  death of, 318
  defense fund, 34
  detective promotion of, 9
  enrollment into police academy, 7–8
  evidence against, 35–36
  family at trial, 263–64
  Gambino, R., confronting, 33
  General Order 15 interview, 27–32
  Gibbs targeted by, 42–43
  Gravano on, 166–67
  Gravano tailed by, 98–99
  Hydell, J., kidnapped by, 84–85
  indictment of, 253
  information supply chain from, 93
  Internal Affairs charge, 33–34
  Kaplan meeting, 100–101, 186–87
  memoir of, 166–67
  at Metropolitan Detention Center, 259–60
  Mo on, 38
  Moran, T., surveillance of, 239–43
  movie career of, 165–66, 241
  moving to Las Vegas, 168
  Nicastro on, 220
  pension of, 165
  promotion of, 37–38
  reassignment of, 21, 37
  retirement of, 165
  retirement party of, 116–17
  screenplays of, 241–42
  sentencing of, 313–14
  Siriano on, 184
  street justice tactics of, 8–11
  trial of, 34–35
  Vecchione on, 223
Eppolito, Ralph ("Fat the Gangster"), 6–7
Eppolito, Tony, 245–46
  arrest of, 252
Evidence, Cases and Materials
  (Weinstein), 266

F

Facciolo, Bruno, 130–31, 269
Farenga, Bobby, 92–93
Father and Son Pizza, 26
Fava, Anthony, 124, 143–44
Feldman, Mark, 184, 222, 240
  Vecchione meeting with, 248–49
Feuer, Alan, 70, 272
Filocamo, Victor, 109
Flack, William, 35
Flannery's, 212
Fogarty, John ("Big John")
  arrest of, 160
  Drew meeting, 161–64
  Drew on, 162
  Giovino on, 159–60
  on Kaplan, 164
  law enforcement cooperation of, 163–64
  on Puglisi, 162
  in rehab, 160

Foldesi, Mike, 151–52
Forlenza, Joe, 150
Fox, James M., 172
Franzone, Peter, 57–59, 257
  at *United States v. Eppolito and Caracappa*, 285
  in Witness Protection Program, 258
Frate, Mike, 239
Friends of the Family (Dades & Vecchione), 310
Furnari, Christopher ("Christie Tick"), 50, 71

G
Gaggi, Nino, 13, 17–18
Gallo, Jimmy, 85–86
  Dades searching, 225–26
Galpine, Monica, 196–98
Galpine, Tommy, 52–53, 103, 148–49
  affair of, 194–95
  arrest of, 198
  cross-examination of, 285
  at *United States v. Eppolito and Caracappa*, 284–85
Gambino, Carlo, 12
Gambino, Rosario
  arrest of, 26
  Eppolito, Louie, confronting, 33
  police file of, 28–32
Gardell, Stephen, 27, 36
Garson, Gerald, 221
Gemini Lounge, 15–17, 94
Gibbs, Barry, 40
  arrest of, 44
  conviction of, 45
  death of, 316
  Eppolito, Louie, targeting, 42–43
  Innocence Project and, 45–46
  lost police file of, 45–46
  Mitchell, P., testifying against, 44–45
  release of, 255–57
  settlement to, 316
  at *United States v. Eppolito v. Caracappa*, 302
Gigante, Vincent ("The Chin"), 126
Giordano, Jack ("Good Looking"), 86–87

Giovino, Andrea
  arrest of, 159, 161
  on Fogarty, 159–60
Giuliani, Rudy, 68
  background of, 69–70
Glasser, Leo, 163
Gleason, Bobby, 212
Goldstock, Ronald, 72
The Good Rat (Breslin), 273
Goodfellas (film), 165
Gotti, John, 1, 75–76
  bodyguard of, 132
  conviction of, 143
  on Gravano, 177
  rumors spread by, 76
  style of, 77
Grand Mark Tavern, 7
Gravano, Sammy ("The Bull"), 75
  Caracappa tailing, 98–99
  Casso on, 190
  Eppolito, Louie, tailing, 98–99
  on Eppolito, Louie, 166–67
  Gotti on, 177
  law enforcement cooperation of, 177
  Santora tailing, 98–99
  testimony of, 177
  Witness Protection Program enrollment of, 177
Graziano, Jean Marie, 178
Greenwald, Israel, 55
  burial of, 259
  digging up, 258–59
  Hormozi on, 269
  law enforcement cooperation of, 56
  as missing person, 59–60
  murder of, 58–59, 225, 257–59
  settlement to family of, 318
  as test case, 61
Greenwald, Leah, 259
Grimaldi, Phil, 9, 215
Guarneri, Al, 7, 84, 108–9
Guglielmo, Joey ("Dracula"), 15–16
Guido, John, 27–28
Guido, Nicky, 80, 92–93, 254–55
  Caracappa computer search for, 226

Guido, Nicky (*continued*)
  Hormozi on, 269–70
  murder of wrong, 94–95

H
Hart, Geraldine, 259
Hart, Jack, 90–91
Hayes, Edward, 266
  on Caracappa, 291–92
  defending himself, 306
  interviews with, 287–88
  leaving for Los Angeles, 289
  New York Times on, 267
  opening statement, 269
  reputation of, 267
Heidel, John ("Otto"), 101
  arrest of, 104
  law enforcement cooperation of, 102–4
  murder of, 105–6
  tapes of, 106
Heim, David, 147–48
Henoch, Robert, 233
  Kaplan debriefed by, 235–36
  at *United States v. Eppolito and Caracappa*, 294–96
Holland, Larry, 96–98
Hoover, J. Edgar, 62
Hormozi, Mitra
  on Facciolo, 269
  on Greenwald, I., 269
  on Guido, N., 269–70
  on Lino, E., 269
  opening statements, 267–68
  United States v. Eppolito and Caracappa and, 269–70
Howard, Charles, 116
Hydell, Betty
  Dades and, 218–19, 221
  at *United States v. Eppolito and Caracappa*, 283
Hydell, Frankie, 203
  Dades and, 205, 209
  law enforcement cooperation of, 205
  murder of, 210
  protection shakedowns of, 204–5
  Tormey meeting with, 205

Hydell, Jimmy, 77
  Casso and, 80–83, 86–87
  DiBiasi abducted by, 78
  Kaplan on, 274
  kidnapping of, 84–85
  murder of, 86–87, 225
Hynes, Charles, 253

I
Innocence Project, 45–46
Intartaglio, Robert, 121, 225–26
International Year of the Child charity, 14

K
Kallstrom, Jim, 62, 64–65
Kaplan, Burt
  alias of, 186
  arrest of, 51, 197–98
  background of, 48–49
  Breslin on, 273–74, 316
  Burstein on, 199
  Casso alliance with, 51
  Casso's confession and, 184–85
  Colgan on, 51
  conviction of, 198–99
  corpse transported by, 47–48
  cross-examination of, 276–77
  on daughter, 275
  death of, 316
  debts of, 48
  disappearance of, 185–86
  Drew and, 156, 193
  Eppolito, Louie, meeting, 100–101, 186–87
  Feuer on, 272
  Fogarty on, 164
  Galpine, M., on, 197–98
  gambling addiction of, 48–50, 228–29
  hearing, 198
  Henoch debriefing, 235–36
  on Hydell, J., 274
  Las Vegas garment business of, 186
  law enforcement cooperation of, 233–34
  marijuana smuggling, 52
  at Metropolitan Detention Center, 229
  Oldham meeting with, 229–30

Ponzi, J., meeting with, 230–32
Puglisi meeting, 148
quaalude arrest of, 53
on Santora, 273
stolen clothes and, 49
surveillance of, 193–94
at *United States v. Eppolito and Caracappa,* 272–77
Vecchione on, 227
in Witness Protection Program, 234, 315–16
Kearse, Amalya L., 312–13
Kennedy, Robert, 63
Kimmel, Jimmy, 165
Kincaid, Barry, 162
Kojak (film), 165
Koshetz, Ray, 282
Kubecka, Jerry, 65
Kubecka, Robert
Casso ordering murder of, 113–15
secret recordings, 66–67

L
LaRossa, James, 75
Lastorino, Frank ("Big Frank"), 94, 133
Lawson, Andrew, 229
Lawson, Guy, 310
Lieb, Judith, 198
Lino, Eddie, 1–2, 131–32, 269
Lino, Frank, 148
Liotta, Ray, 165–66
Little Caesar (film), 64
Longo, Mark, 316
Louis Eppolito Defense Fund, 34
Lucchese, Rob, 146
Luhrs, Bernice, 98
Lundy, Frederick, 53
Luzak, Kenny, 240–41, 252

M
Mafia Cop (Eppolito, Louie, & Drury), 166, 219
Major Case Squad, 91
Maloney, Andrew J., 171
A Man of Honor (Bonanno), 69
Mancini, Ray ("Boom Boom"), 242

Mandylor, Costas, 241–42
Marino, Toddo, 11
Marston, Robert, 139
Massino, Joseph, 267
Mauskopf, Roslynn, 249, 253
McCormack, Robert, 28, 31, 32
McCormick, Jane, 242, 264
Miciotta, Salvatore ("Big Sal"), 188–89
Minkoff, Edith, 146
Mitchell, John, 63
Mitchell, Peter, 40–43
testifying against Gibbs, 44–45
Mo, Hugh, 35–38
deposition of, 317
Molini, Bobby, 154, 173
arrest of, 157
testimony of, 198
wiretap on, 156–57
Molini, Marie, 146
Montiglio, Dominick, 121–23
Moore, Thomas, 174
Moran, Neil, 96
Moran, Tommy, 239–43, 253
Mouthpiece (Hayes), 287

N
New York fiscal crisis, 20–21
New York State Organized Task Force, 66
Nicastro, Richard, 37
Dades meeting with, 224–25
on Eppolito, Louie, 220
Nickerson, Eugene H., 173, 192
19th Hole Bar, 50
Nobel, Daniel, 300
North, Don, 144

O
O'Connell, Greg
Casso and, 74, 175–76, 189–90
retirement into private practice, 190
Oldham, William, 310
Galpine, M., meeting, 196–97
Kaplan meeting with, 229–30
Operation Gangplank, 150–52, 193
arrests from, 156–59
wiretaps, 153

P

Pagliarulo, Richard ("Richie the Toupee"), 135
Pappa, John, 205
  arrest of, 207–8
  conviction of, 208–9
  surveillance of Dades by, 206
  trial of, 208
Paradiso, Michael ("Mickey Boy"), 77, 84
Parasole, Frankie, 204
Pearlson, Ross, 163
Penny, Herman, 29–30
Penny, Patrick, 17–18
Pergola, Frank, 10–11, 23
  Montiglio and, 121–23
  suspicious of Caracappa, 123
Pesci, Joe, 166
Peterson, Loren, 160
Pete's Towing, 257
Piacenti, Peter ("Petey 17"), 16–18
Pipitone, Pauline, 269–70
  deposition of, 317
  settlement, 318
Piraino, Joe, 19
  on Caracappa, 91–92, 184
  on Dades, 215, 218
Pitera, Tommy, 104–5
Pontillo, Frank ("Frankie Steel"), 117–18
Ponzi, Emilio, 22
Ponzi, Joe
  Capeci on, 224
  Dades and, 224, 320
  funeral of, 320
  Kaplan meeting with, 230–32
  Vecchione on, 230–31
Potkin, Vanessa, 45–46
Private Sanitation Industry Association, 65
proffer, 163
Puglisi, Freddy, 145
  arrest of, 157, 193
  Fogarty on, 162
  Kaplan meeting, 148
  marijuana operation of, 146–50
  profits of, 148
  stash houses of, 147
  wiretapping, 153–54, 156

R

Racketeer Influenced and Corrupt Organizations Act (RICO), 63–65
  Mitchell, J., on, 63
  time limit of, 248, 292–93
  Weinstein on, 261
Rastelli, Philip, 68
RICO. *See* Racketeer Influenced and Corrupt Organizations Act
Robertson, Virginia, 42, 44
Roder, Paul, 17
Rodriguez, Steven, 277–79
Romano, Sal, 147–48
Rose, Charles
  on Amuso, 142
  Casso and, 175–76, 189–90
  Chiodo meeting with, 135–36
  retirement into private practice, 190
Rosen, Mike, 177–79
Rudolph, Richard, 178
Ruggiero, Angelo ("Quack Quack"), 77
Russo, Frank, 107, 118

S

Sally Jessy Raphael, 167–68, 219
Salmon, Phillip, 105–6
Santora, Frank, 20, 53
  Gravano tailed by, 98–99
  Kaplan on, 273
  murder of, 99, 257
Santoro, Salvatore ("Tom Mix"), 71
Scarpa, Gregory, Sr. ("The Grim Reaper"), 173
Schultz, Dutch, 123
Schwartz, Edward ("Blackie"), 211–12
Senate Subcommittee on Criminal Laws and Procedures, 63
September 11, 216–17
Shargel, Gerald, 51, 275
Shea, Jimmy, 28
Sheehan, Kevin, 238–39
Signorino, Frank, 137
Silvestri, John ("Bubblegum"), 152–53
Singleton, Monica, 92

Siriano, Chuck
  on Bypass Gang, 107–11
  on Caracappa, 90–91, 184
  on Eppolito, Louie, 184
  new processing methods of, 110
Sly, Rich, 194
Sparacino, Sal, 206–7
Spatafora, Frank, 104
Spero, Anthony ("The Greek"), 173
Spinelli, Mike ("Baldy Mike"), 147,
  160–61, 173
Spinelli, Rob, 147, 160–61
Stamboulidis, George, 190–91
stand-up guy, 54
Sun Luck Club, 61–62, 64–65
Sutter, Mickey, 148
Sweeney, Bill, 29, 32

T
Tabak, Herman, 55, 56
Taylor, Larry, 131
Tennien, Richard, 66
Testa, Joseph, 94
Tiger Management, 111–12
Tolly, Marvin, 96
Tormey, Matt, 205

U
United States v. Eppolito and Caracappa
  acquittal in, 306–9
  appeal hearings, 311–13
  Breslin at, 264
  Burstein at, 279
  Cama at, 282–83
  convictions reinstated, 312–13
  Corso at, 280–82
  D'Arco, A., at, 270–72
  defense witnesses, 289–90
  Eppolito family at, 263–64
  Franzone at, 285
  Galpine, T., at, 284–85
  Gibbs at, 302
  Henoch at, 294–96
  Hormozi at, 269–70
  Hydell, B., at, 283
  Kaplan at, 272–77

  McCormick at, 264
  media attention on, 264–65
  opening statements, 267–69
  replacement lawyers, 299–300
  Rodriguez at, 277–79
  sentencing, 313–14
  summation, 290–91
  verdict, 297–98
  victim testimonials, 300–302
  Wenner at, 290–91

V
Valachi, Joe, 180
Varriale, Carmine, 99
Vecchione, Mike, 38, 310
  Dades meeting with, 221–22
  on Eppolito, Louie, 223
  Feldman meeting with, 248–49
  harassment of, 223–24
  on Kaplan, 227
  on Ponzi, J., 230–31
Veriale, Albert, 28
Visconti, Al ("Flounderhead"), 131

W
Walsh, John, 32
Ward, Ben, 36–37, 220
Warme, Richard, 24–25
Webster, William, 64, 69
Weinstein, Jack B., 52, 260, 266
  on RICO, 261
  on statute of limitations, 296
Weiss, Murray, 33
Wenner, Daniel, 290–91
Witness Protection Program, 89, 134
  Costa in, 110–11
  D'Arco, A., in, 142
  Franzone in, 258
  Gravano enrolled into, 177
  Kaplan enrolled into, 234
Wright, Edward, 137
Wright, Thomas J., 163

Z
Zappola, George ("Georgie Neck"),
  93–94, 176

ABOUT THE AUTHOR

Michael Weschler

MICHAEL CANNELL is the author of *A Brotherhood Betrayed: The Man Behind the Rise and Fall of Murder, Inc.* and three other works of nonfiction. He has worked as an editor at *The New York Times* and has contributed to *The New Yorker* and many other publications. He lives in New York City. A more complete catalog of his work may be found at michaelcannell.com.